THE FONTANA
HISTORY OF E

General Editor: Carlo M. Cipolla

There is at present no satisfactory economic history
of Europe – covering Europe both as a whole and
with particular relation to the individual
countries – that is both concise enough for convenient
use and yet full enough to include the results of
individual and detailed scholarship. This series is
designed to fill that gap.

Unlike most current works in this field the
Fontana Economic History of Europe does not end at the
outbreak of the First World War. More than half
a century has elapsed since 1914, a half-century that
has transformed the economic background of
Europe. In recognition of this the present work has
set its terminal date at 1970.

The source material available for Europe in the
last half-century is immensely greater than that
for the whole world from the remotest origins of
economic life. The scale of these concluding
volumes reflects this fact.

The Fontana Economic History of Europe

The Twentieth Century

Part One

Editor Carlo M. Cipolla

Collins/Fontana Books

First published in this edition 1976

© Carlo M. Cipolla 1976
© Miloš Macura 1974
© A. S. Deaton 1975
© Walter Galenson 1975
© Giorgio Pellicelli 1976
© Georges Brondel 1975
© Roy and Kay MacLeod 1976
© Robert Campbell 1975

Made and Printed in Great Britain by
William Collins Sons & Co Ltd. Glasgow

Contents

Introduction

Carlo M. Cipolla

The half century that followed the First World War is the theme of this and the succeeding volume. The period 1920-1970 is not rigidly or pedantically defined in the contributions that follow but its choice has purpose and meaning. It reflects the decision to leave out from our inquiry the story of the economic conduct of the First World War. Not that that story is uninteresting or irrelevant but its inclusion would have made an already uncomfortably large mass of material intractable. More important than that, the choice of 1920 as an approximate starting date indicates that in some subtle way these two volumes are not the pure and simple continuation of the preceding volumes. The war which to Asian eyes looked like 'the great European Civil War' created a dramatic discontinuity in European history. A new trend clearly emerged. We are ourselves too much part of this trend which is still unfolding to be able to assess it critically. Significantly, while all the contributors to the previous volumes were historians, a large proportion of the contributors to the present two volumes are not. The inclusion of economists and statisticians among the contributors to these volumes has deepened and extended the technical analysis of the abundant statistical and economic material available. As economists well know, however, choices imply costs and what is gained in one direction is lost in another. If the previous volumes suffer from lack of homogeneity and cohesiveness (a defect almost unavoidable in collective works), the present two volumes are even more open to the same objection. Not only are there many more contributors but in addition they come from different fields, and there is a limit imposed by courtesy and by respect for alternative approaches and ideas on how far an editor can go in the distasteful responsibility of exercising cultural dictatorship.

As a reaction to the position of those economists who traditionally regarded capital formation as a condition both

necessary and efficient for economic development, a number
of other economists have recently spent much time, energy
and ingenuity in reappraising the role of capital and em-
phasizing instead the role of other factors. According to
some calculations (whose validity, however, is in need of
closer scrutiny), the contribution of capital, labour and
total factor productivity to the rate of growth in selected
European countries over the period 1950-62 has been as
follows (in percentages):

country	capital	labour	productivity	total
France	17	11	72	100
Germany	20	26	54	100
Italy	12	19	69	100
UK	21	32	47	100

The conclusion drawn by those who produce such figures is
that capital has a limited importance and the holy ghost of
productivity is in fact the most powerful person of the
economic trinity. Although I find that most of the calculations behind the theory suffer (as do most calculations
by social scientists) from a cavalier handling of the basic
data which would horrify a scientist of the non-social
sciences, I do not find the theory objectionable provided it
isn't carried too far. After all, it is simply a matter of common
sense to admit that capital formation is a necessary but not
sufficient condition for economic growth. If in the present
volume the reader does not find a chapter on capital,
however, the reason is not to be found in the iconoclasm of
the general editor but rather in the more prosaic, less
edifying, fact that the scholar who had undertaken the
chapter regrettably failed to turn in his contribution. Both
the publisher and the general editor hope to make up for
the deficiency in the next edition and in the meantime they
console themselves with the thought that after all the gap is
already partly filled, though in an unsystematic way, by
what the contributors both to volume 5 and to volume 6
have to say about capital formation in connection with their
own topics.

TABLE 1:   Selected European geo-economic regions rated :
level of per capita income in 1961

Rank	Geo-economic region	Yearly per capita income ('000 $)
1	Paris region	1·79
2	Switzerland	1·66
3	London region	1·47
4	Rhine-Ruhr basin	1·42
5	East-Central England	1·35
6	Westphalia	1·35
7	Central England	1·26
8	Southern France	1·23
9	Elbe-Weser basin	1·20
10	South-Western England	1·15
11	Rhine-Main Basin	1·15
12	North Western England	1·14
13	Ems basin	1·12
14	Southern Saxony	1·12
15	Western Rhineland	1·11
16	South Eastern France	1·11
17	North Western England	1·09
18	South Eastern Bavaria	1·09
19	South Western France	0·98
20	Northern France	0·98
21	South-Central France	0·97
22	Wales	0·97
23	Scotland	0·96
24	Lombardy (Italy)	0·94
25	Eastern France	0·91
26	Piedmont and Liguria (Italy)	0·90
27	Western France	0·82
28	Lazio and Abruzzi (Italy)	0·65
29	Emilia and Marche (Italy)	0·64
30	Ireland	0·61
31	Tuscany and Umbria (Italy)	0·60

Following the practice adopted for the period 1700-1914,
the economic history of the period 1920-70 has been dealt
with from two different points of view. In volume 5 it is
analysed topically with chapters on demand, labour,
organisation, technology, etc. In volume 6 the story is
retold from the point of view of the individual national
states. States however are not homogeneous entities and an

analysis focused on regional developments would possibly be more accurate and meaningful (see Table 1). Some pioneer studies are now being undertaken in this direction but they are still inadequate for a work of synthesis.

It is in the very nature of the statistician's, econometrician's and economist's work to measure variables such as saving, investment, capital, output, etc. and to investigate their relationships. However, if a society is capable of saving and investing a given share of a given income, if that particular society is able to reach a certain level of productivity, if it produces and consumes certain things rather than others, if it distributes its income and its wealth in a given way rather than in another, if its administrators take certain decisions of economic policy rather than others, all this derives from historically specific cultural patterns whose analysis lies outside the narrow domain of economics.

Contrary to received opinions, the really difficult task is not that of programming a computer to calculate some new regressions among economic variables. The real challenge is to uncover the subtle, often intangible and unquantifiable relationships between economic change and 'all the rest'.

As I wrote in the general introduction to this series 'Economic History in itself is a partition and a most arbitrary one. It has been adopted for convenience of analysis and academic training. But life has no such compartment; there is only History'.

The dominating theme in the history of this century has been Europe's loss of her world pre-eminence. Toward the end of the nineteenth century keen observers could see the challenge emerging overseas, but as a French writer recently put it 'au début du siècle, on comptait six puissances mondiales. Elles se trouvaient toutes en Europe. Si l'on citait aussi le Japon et les Etats-Unis c'était presque par politesse et par souci de faire preuve de connaissances géographiques étendues'. By 1970 the situation had totally changed. European leadership was unquestioned in 1900; it had vanished by 1970 and one wonders where the new leadership is – in fact one wonders whether there is any leadership at all. Paradoxically Europe is economically much better off, much richer in the 1970s than it was seventy years earlier. But Europe's life looks uncomfortably precarious. Europe is now divided into two halves, each one under the protective umbrella of a more powerful ally. For both food and energy Europe is largely dependant on overseas supplies.

TABLE 2: The Patterns of World Grain and Oil Trade, 1974

	Grain (million metric tons)	Oil (million metric tons)
Western Europe	−23	−712
Eastern Europe	− 6	+52
USSR	+ 1	
North America	+70	−294
Latin America	+ 5	+ 74
Africa	− 7	+242
Asia	−47	+672
Australia & New Zealand	+ 7	− 14

Plus sign indicates net exports, minus sign net imports

Internally both her cultural heritage and her social and political structures show dangerous signs of stress. Europe is richer and at the same time poorer. It is more developed and yet more insecure. It has advanced and yet slipped backwards. All this cannot be explained without reference to economic factors and changes. On the other hand, the economic history of the period cannot be understood solely in economic terms without reference to the developments which took place at all levels of human activity – from the spiritual to the biological, from the individual to the social.

It is with this profound awareness of its limitations that this work is offered to the reader.

1.   Population in Europe 1920 – 1970
Miloś Macura

One of the most manifest signs of progress during the eighteenth and nineteenth century was a demographic transition in the western and northern regions of Europe. Thanks to a gradual but steady decline in mortality followed by a somewhat slower decline in natality, the rate of population growth and population numbers increased markedly. This demographic transition supported as it was by such factors as improved sanitation and health conditions, agricultural and industrial progress, and scientific and intellectual development had lasting effects. It was a challenge to economic and social organisation, which required substantial adjustments to be made.

Throughout the twentieth century demographic transition was in progress in virtually all European countries. While mortality and fertility continued to decline in the western and the northern regions of the continent, this new pattern of population growth spread gradually to the eastern and the southern regions. In the 1920s there were still economic and demographic differences between European countries in Europe; in the late 1960s there was virtually no difference in fertility and mortality levels between them.

There were no natural disasters and calamities recorded in the twentieth century, like those that in earlier ages used to decimate European population. However, the two World Wars (1914 to 1918 and 1939 to 1945), the first of which was followed by an epidemic influenza, and the Great Depression of the 1930s had definite adverse demographic effects. During the two wars several nations experienced substantial population losses due either to the war or postponed marriages and births. The sex and age structure of these nations was therefore heavily damaged. After the two wars there were also significant changes in the political map of Europe associated with large-scale migration. Eight sovereign nations were founded during the period and eight established themselves as socialist states. I do not intend to discuss this tremendous and intricate change in the present paper. For the purpose of the discussion of population change in Europe during the twentieth century, the present boundaries of individual states will be used as the geographical framework, irrespective of modifications that have taken place in the past decades.

The question of what constitutes Europe is neither a new one nor is it irrelevant. Different definitions have been put forward and used by individual authors, national governments and the international organisations. In the following discussion a wide concept has been adopted, that of Europe including the USSR, but excluding the European territory of Turkey. For the sake of convenience and whenever necessary, two sets of data for Europe are given: including the USSR population, and excluding it.[1]

IMPROVEMENT IN DEMOGRAPHIC KNOWLEDGE

In contrast to medieval history, the twentieth-century history of European population enjoys the privilege of reliable and abundant source material. In Europe there are fairly good statistical data and other pertinent information as well as a rich literature on population. In addition to the relevant legislation and parliamentary debates, the policies relating to population are well recorded, at least for some critical periods, and are accessible to the researcher. Demographic research is advanced and some of its findings are crucial for an understanding of population change in Europe, as well as for speculation on the complex processes of adjustment imposed by economic, demographic and social realities. However, it should be pointed out that the availability and quality of historical sources differs widely. While we have fairly good information for most of Europe

[1] The total population of Europe as defined was slightly over 702 million in 1970. Without the Soviet Union it was 459 million. Population of the USSR was 242 million, out of which 183 million were in the European regions, and 59 million in Asia.

on the demographic situation since the mid-twentieth century, evidence is not available for all countries in the earlier period. Information is particularly scarce for the regions which were under Turkish rule.

Population censuses were already regularly taken in Europe in the nineteenth century. During the period under consideration, most of European countries took decennial population censuses, though in different years. Vital statistics registration which was rather poor in many countries in the 1920s, has undergone significant improvement after the Second World War. Since the mid-1950s the quality of census data and of vital statistics seems to be adequate. Considerable international standardisation of methods and techniques was achieved between the wars thanks to the combined efforts made by national governments and the League of Nations. The action taken by the United Nations in this field has been supported since the mid-1950s by virtually all European governments. Statistical progress, as far as population statistics are concerned, was slow but steady.

Considerable statistical problems are encountered when an attempt is made to consider the fifty-year period as a whole. As the data has been improved in many countries during this period, we do not know to what extent a change in data means a real change or reflects a previous error. Many countries have taken no census in individual periods, or have developed their vital statistics system only at a late date. Another serious problem is the lack of a national time series because of wars and many changes in national boundaries. Finally at the time of completion of the present analysis there were still some ten countries for which final 1970 population census data was not available.

The intensification of the use of statistical sources for purposes of population research, as well as the growth of scientific curiosity and criticism, had a tremendous impact on quality and comparability of population statistics. In the early 1930s, the International Statistical Institute and the League of Nations were already giving serious consideration to the problem of accuracy and international comparability.

Impressive work was undertaken by individual scholars, governmental agencies and international bodies with a view to establishing reliable statistical series. In 1936 Carr-Saunders published his 'revised estimate of the population of the world, 1650-1933' in which he evaluated national data and amended the original Willcox estimate. Bunle has compiled population census data as well as vital statistics for all European countries for which such data was available for the period 1906 to 1936. Since the mid-1940s the United Nations has undertaken the task of standardising demographic data for all countries of the world. Standardisation has been made with regard to time, territory and subject-matter. For those countries and periods for which data was lacking, estimates were made to complete statistical series. Most of the past and current demographic information has been published in the United Nations *Demographic Yearbook* (since 1948), and in other technical publications and papers.

Another source of our knowledge of population came from demographic research. Since Graunt and Petty, the study of population has been an attractive area of intellectual exercise and speculation, particularly in England, France, Germany and Sweden. After a stagnation during the nineteenth century, there was a renewal of interest in the science on population. It was marked by Landry's famous treatise on *révolution démographique* which was published originally in 1909. Landry undertook to explain the mechanics of population change in France and laid the foundation of what was later termed a theory of demographic transition.

During the first four decades of the century, population study was a matter of scientific curiosity and personal involvement for individual scholars. Landry, Carr-Saunders, Kuczinsky, Gini, Ptukha, Winkler, Hersh and the next generation of demographers represented by Sauvy, Glass and others were scholars who made a significant contribution to European demography. International conferences have been sponsored since the late nineteenth century, first by the International Statistical Institute, and later, in the twentieth century, by the International Union for the

Scientific Study of Population. These have provided opportunities for scientific debate, although they have done little to encourage organised research.

During the 1930s sharp falls of fertility were experienced in a number of European countries. Governments became concerned by this new situation and a revival of interest in optimum population theory and in national policies were one among the consequences. In Sweden, France and elsewhere there was a great deal of research and debate on the social implications of demographic stagnation which resulted in new concepts of, and approaches to, population policies. Another consequence of the demographic situation in the 1930s was the initiation of international action. In 1939 after a series of negotiations, the League of Nations decided to study problems related to rapid population growth and declining population, as well as those relating to low population density. The war, however, prevented this taking place in Europe. It was thanks to the University of Princeton (USA), whose Office of Population Research already had an experience in demographic research, that four studies of European population were undertaken to implement the League of Nations programme.

This was the first large scale, international and institutionalised research programme on European population. The war-time conditions make it difficult to ascertain the extent of influence of this important work. In the mid-1940s Europe was concerned with the aftermath of war: reconstruction and political re-structuring, which left little time for population research. Two nations however were interested in their demographic future, France and England. The organisations they set up; the Population Investigation Committee (London) and *l'Institut National d'Etudes Demographique* (Paris) were followed in the late 1950s and early 1960s by other specialised population research institutes in Hungary, Italy, Sweden, Czechoslovakia, Yugoslavia, The Netherlands, Belgium, the USSR and in other countries.

The institutionalisation of demographic research and of teaching of demography proved to be technically very productive. Demographic information and research findings became regularly available to governments and the general public. A new variable – that of population – was gradually introduced to public and private calculations. Interest in national demography exploded into an international interest. In the 1950s, a research programme on Western Europe was launched by Sauvy. This was followed in the 1960s by a growing collaboration in population research within the Council of Europe in Western and the Council of Mutual Economic Cooperation in Eastern Europe. The United Nations agencies have also extended international programmes into such vital areas as population census, fertility research, manpower and migration analysis, demographic projections and the like.

The state of ignorance which had prevailed pre-war was replaced in the early 1950s by a fierce controversy concerning one of the world's most critical issues, that of fertility control. Great differences in opinion influenced by ideological factors dominated the 1954 World Population Conference, and to a less extent the 1965 Conference. In the 1950s and the early 1960s no inter-governmental debates concerning population policies took place in Europe. But many European nations were active in United Nations bodies and until 1966 expressed marked differences with regard to population policies. At the national levels, population policy issues attracted wide interest, particularly in the late 1960s. Concerns about the scarcity of manpower or the excessive supply of it, population decline, high population pressure, migration, urban congestion and particularly environment, were voiced in different quarters. The population problem became a matter of both naïve popular curiosity and thorough scientific investigation of a multidisciplinary nature. By the 1970s, population was recognised as a central national and international issue which deserved governmental attention and action. Europe faced new trends in policy making, in scientific development and in national and international attitudes to the subject.

POPULATION TRENDS IN EUROPE: AN OVERVIEW

By the turn of the century, Europe including the USSR, had a population of 430 million, by mid-century 570 million, by the end of the century Europe may have over 850 million people. The net increase in population during the past fifty years, including births, deaths and migration balance was about 224 million, during the last fifty years of the nineteenth century it was 146 million, or one third less. This occurred in spite of a rapid decline in fertility (the effects of which were offset by rapid declines in mortality) and massive emigration to overseas territories in the 1920s and the 1950s.

REGIONAL VARIATIONS

The decennial growth rate of European population in the 1920s was 10·9 per cent despite massive overseas migration. In the 1930s emigration was smaller, but the rate fell to 7·6 per cent, perhaps as a consequence of the Great Depression in Europe, and agricultural reorganisation in the Soviet Union. The 1940s witnessed a net loss of population caused by the war. The demographic recovery of the 1950s produced the highest decennial growth rate of the last fifty years (11·5 per cent) which in the 1960s declined to 10·1 per cent.

National and regional population growth as result of the interaction of mortality, fertility and migration rates was neither stable nor uniform. Wars and post-war conditions, the Great Depression, the social reorganisation of Russia and eastern European countries, industrialisation throughout Europe and political tensions in the 1930s and during the Cold War, must have affected peoples' behaviour in different ways. Demographic adjustment to those conditions can be observed as can the progress of demographic transition.[2]

[2] There are a few excellent contributions made for the pre-war period, notably by Landry, Glass, Notestein, Sauvy, Moore, Lorimer

The varied conditions prevailing in Europe during the last fifty years are reflected in the sharp variations of population growth in individual periods and in marked differences among the regions.[3] When the implications of the changing population rates are considered, the demographic situation of Europe appears to be both dynamic and complicated. They were the immediate cause of many economic and social problems, including those of manpower and employment, schooling, urban development, migration, protection of the aged and the like. Northern Europe was

TABLE I : Decennial per cent change of regional population was as follows

	1920s	1930s	1940s	1950s	1960s
Europe and the USSR	10·9	7·6	−0·4	11·5	10·1
Europe without USSR	8·9	7·1	3·4	8·1	8·5
Western Europe	7·1	4·2	8·1	9·9	10·2
Southern Europe	11·8	10·7	5·7	8·3	9·0
Eastern Europe	11·4	8·1	−6·8	8·1	7·3
Northern Europe	4·8	5·2	6·1	4·5	6·2
USSR	15·3	8·9	−7·7	19·1	13·2

the only region with stable decennial population growth, although hereto there were visible annual fluctuations. The fifty year trend was less stable in western and southern Europe; it was very disturbed – with marked high points and depression in eastern Europe and the Soviet Union.

Changes in regional population growth can be explained only partially by the working of demographic transition. Natality and mortality trends and the resulting rates of

and others, but no thorough analysis of post-war conditions has been made so far.

[3] Individual regions consist of the following countries and territories: *western Europe:* Federal Republic of Germany, France, Netherlands, Belgium, Austria, Switzerland, West Berlin, Luxemburg, Monaco and Liechtenstein; *southern Europe:* Italy, Spain, Yugoslavia, Portugal, Greece, Albania, Malta, Gibraltar, San Marino, Andorra and Holy See; *eastern Europe:* Poland, Romania, German Democratic Republic, Czechoslovakia, Hungary and Bulgaria; *northern Europe:* United Kingdom, Sweden, Denmark, Finland, Norway, Ireland, Iceland, Channel Islands, Isle of Man and Faroe Islands; *USSR:* whole of the territory, Asian republic inclusive.

natural increase in population had definite effects on the growth and size of population in individual regions. But if these had been the only component of population growth, the regional demographic map of Europe would have been quite different. In fact, two additional components had a significant influence: the excess of deaths over normal mortality caused by the war, and international migration.

WAR LOSSES 1939–45

War-related population problems in the belligerent countries of Europe were manifold. Forced migration, deportation, displaced persons, broken families, postponed marriages and births were some of the factors which indirectly affected population growth in the late 1930s and the 1940s. War losses, both military and civilian directly affected the growth, and in addition the sex and age structure of the population. There are no reliable statistics on war losses for obvious reasons, but there are many estimates made by national authorities and individual scholars. Urlanis estimated both military and civilian World War II losses at 30 million, over three times as much as the losses during World War I.[4] American sources' estimates of military losses are in the area of 15 million, and British and Vatican estimates of both kinds of losses were 22 million. An International Committee's summary suggested that European military and civilian losses did not exceed 19 million.[5] Frumkin's estimates based on the balance-sheet method were produced in great detail for Europe excluding the USSR. After a thorough analysis he concluded that 'the

[4] War losses affecting the European population during the twentieth century were cited by Urlanis as follows: Russian-Japanese War 139 thousand, Balkan Wars 224 thousand, World War I 9,442 thousand, Civil War in Soviet Union 800 thousand, Spanish War 450 thousand.

[5] Kirk seems to support these estimates, although with some reservations. The respective estimates of losses are as follows: USSR 7 million, France 820 thousand, Poland 4·6 million, Yugoslavia 1,680 thousand, Czechoslovakia 190 thousand, Holland 204 thousand, Belgium 125 thousand, Greece 490 thousand, Norway 11 thousand, Great Britain 398 thousand, Germany 3·6 million.

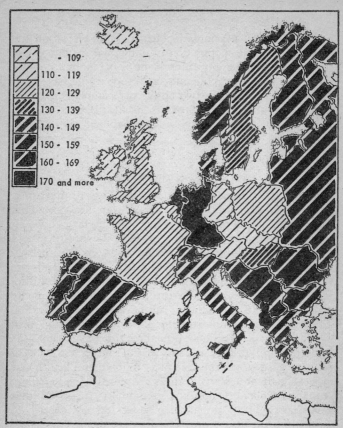

Fig. 1: Fifty year increase in Population: 1920-70
Index Numbers 1920=100

toll of the war and the genocide which accompanied it
accounted ... for the death of 15 million persons, about 6
million being military deaths, and over 9 million deaths
among civilians'. Out of the civilian losses 4·9 million were
non-Jewish and 4·4 million were Jewish. Soviet war losses
alone were estimated between 7, 17 and 25 million, quite a

wide margin of disagreement. Estimates of German losses vary between 3·9 and 4·2 million, and those of Yugoslavia between 1·5 and 1·7 million. The only bright spot in this dark era in Europe was that neither epidemics nor famines followed the war, as they did after World War I and the earlier wars.

Thanks to Frumkin's estimates, we have a rough picture of the demographic consequences of World War II in individual European regions. In western Europe there were 982 thousand military personnel and civilians killed, over 1·5 per cent of the 1940 population of France, Netherlands, Belgium and Austria. In Germany as a whole there were between 3·9 and 4·2 million war losses (between 6·5 and 7 per cent) perhaps two-thirds of which were in western Germany. In southern Europe losses were about 2·1 and 2·3 million (3·1 and 3·4 per cent of combined population of Yugoslavia, Italy and Greece), and in northern Europe 483 thousand, or 0·8 per cent of 1940 population of the United Kingdom, Denmark, Finland and Norway. Eastern Europe's war toll was near to 7 million deaths (8·9 per cent), due to very high losses in Poland (5·8 million or over 18 per cent of her total population). The population of the Soviet Union was also affected by very high losses (8·7 or 12·8 per cent according to the two most commonly used estimates). War losses were the obvious factor of negative growth rate of the USSR and eastern Europe. It took individual nations some two to eight years to reach the pre-war population size and in some cases even longer because of war-related migration.

MIGRATION BALANCE

During the period under consideration, the growth of European population was strongly affected by inter-continental migration. Regional differentials were affected by both the inter-continental and intra-continental migration, the later gradually having gained in importance. While migration to and from the continent and migration between European countries had direct effects on population growth in individual countries, internal migration within individual countries which did not have this effect was nevertheless important.

Over the centuries, Europe has been a continent of emigration and an important source for the colonisation of the Americas and Oceania. The flow of emigrants was significant for both the sending and the receiving continents. Return migration, which always existed, was negligible and immigration to Europe never was of any importance. An excess of emigrants over immigrants was consequently a traditional pattern of the European migration balance.

This pattern continued until the last decade when the migration pattern of Europe was radically changed. For reasons to be discussed at a later stage, there was in the 1960s an excess of immigrants and repatriates over the number of emigrants. In addition, intra-continental migration seemed to be of higher demographic and economic importance than previously. It is difficult to predict whether this change indicates a new trend of European migration in the future.

We are fortunate to have two migration balances of European countries; Kirk's (for 1920 to 1939) and Adams' (for 1950 to 1966). These balances cover a period of almost fifty years. Migration statistics for the period 1901–15 indicate that this was a period of intensive emigration from Europe, in which both the regions of 'old migration' and the regions of 'new migration' participated.[6] The migration balance for all European regions must have been negative before World War I, for there was no massive immigration to Europe or significant repatriation to offset the emigration effects. For the subsequent periods a rearrangement of Kirk's and Adams' data, which is not fully comparable and must be used therefore with great

[6] Kirk has compiled statistics from various sources from 1846 to 1939, which make it clear that the largest emigration from Europe was recorded in 1901–5 (an annual average of 1·0 million), 1906–10 (1·4 million) and 1911–15 (1·3 million). Emigration from regions of 'new migration' consisting of Italy, Austria, Hungary, Czechoslovakia, Russia Balkan areas, Spain and Portugal amounted to 785 thousand, 1·1 million and 1·0 million in the respective periods.

caution, suggests that the regional deficit and surplus due
to international migration was as follows:

TABLE 2: Decennial percentage deficit or surplus due to migration

	1920–30	1930–39	1950–60	1960–66
Western Europe	−1·7	+0·2	+3·0	+3·0
Southern Europe	−1·0	−0·7	−3·1	−1·5
Eastern Europe	−1·8	−0·1	−2·8	−0·9
Northern Europe	−1·9	+0·4	−0·6	+0·3

The economic, political and other conditions under which
migration took place, as well as the possible motivation of
individuals and the policies of governments will be discussed
at a later stage. At this stage we should remember that the
south and east were, and continued to be, regions of
emigration, the north was a region which was both sending
and receiving migrants, and the west, which earlier was an
emigration area, was able to attract an impressive number
of foreign emigrants. Of course, this is a part of the explanation of the differential regional population rates we considered earlier.

As far as the Soviet Union is concerned, the change in
the patterns of migration was quite different. Before World
War I Russia, like the rest of Europe, was an emigration
area, and a significant number of people emigrated from
Russia during and after the Revolution and the Civil War.
However, in addition to westward emigration, eastward
emigration was also characteristic of Russia for several
decades. The latter gained an increasing importance with
Soviet economic expansion to the Asian republics, to Siberia
and the Soviet Far-East. Although it had nothing to do
with the size and the growth of population of the USSR, it
is nevertheless of great interest as it involved European
territories. From 1940 to the early 1970s the Ukrainian,
Bielorussian and the European economic regions of the
Russian Federation increased by some 10 million (or 8 per
cent) to a population of 122 million in 1940. Middle-Asian
and Khazakhstan economic regions, known for high
fertility, doubled their population during the same period.

The Ural, Siberian and Far-eastern economic regions gained a total of 13 million (or 47 per cent) to an initial population of 28 million. It is obvious that in addition to differential rates of natural increase in population, the differences in migration flows and balances had a significant bearing on differential demographic changes in the Soviet Union.

SPREADING DEMOGRAPHIC TRANSITION

Initiated in France and the north-western regions as a phenomenon associated with the modernisation of Europe, modern demographic transition has taken a double course during the last seventy years: that of intensification in the west and north, and that of expansion to the south and east. The intensification course brought down death rates from about 16 to 19 per thousand to 9 to 11, and the birth rates from between 21 (France) and 30 per thousand (Netherlands and Finland) to between 14 (all Scandinavian countries and Belgium) and around 16 per thousand (France, England and Wales, Switzerland and others). The expansion of the transition was fast and drastic, for crude death rates were reduced from over 20 to less than 9 per thousand. Birth rates declined from between over 40 per thousand (the Balkans, Poland, Romania, Russia) and over 30 (Italy, Spain, Czechoslovakia, Hungary) to 14–17 per thousand. The only exceptions in Europe were Ireland and Albania, both of which experienced so far significant declines in mortality, but very stable fertility: Albania at a level of over 35 births per thousand, and Ireland at a level between 20 and 22.

Neither of the two courses was flat and uniform. But following the general declining trend, the vital rates also demonstrated marked fluctuations. These were caused either by the excessive mortality during the wars and war-associated conditions, or by restriction of reproduction during social crises and conflicts, followed by sharp but temporary recovery. The onset and the rate of the downward trends in national vital rates demonstrate a complete lack of uniformity. While the western and northern regions as well as parts of Italy, Hungary and Spain entered the twentieth century with a heritage of a fairly advanced demographic transition, most of the nations in the south and east had to make initial steps towards this end. According to Coale, Bulgaria, Romania, Poland and Russia had already experienced before World War I a downturn in marital fertility. But even at the beginning of World War II marital fertility was still not reduced to 50 per cent of its original level in parts of Italy, Spain, Portugal, most of the Balkan regions and of Soviet Russia. However, by the late 1960s, 'there has developed in essentially all of Europe a control of fertility within marriage effective enough to reduce marital fertility by at least 50 per cent. The few exceptions are in Ireland, some provinces in Spain and Portugal, Albania and one or two areas in Yugoslavia.'

Progress in health standards and the fall in mortality can be explained by improvement in sanitation and medicine, amelioration of living conditions and the development of public health facilities which have taken place throughout Europe. Differences in crude death rates recorded in the late 1960s were mainly a consequence of differences in the age structure of individual populations.

On the other hand the explanation of decline in fertility, which was affected by combinations of various factors is more difficult. The association of the spread of birth control and fertility decline with industrialisation, economic progress, improvement in standards of living, better education, urbanisation, and the change in social norms and attitudes was proposed by many authors as an explanation of the phenomenon. Availability of birth control methods and the respective facilities provided by public schemes might have had in the last decades also important effects. However, how the process was initiated and under what kind of circumstances it worked is difficult to ascertain. At the end of the 1960s scholars were still not satisfied with the hypotheses and theories made till then, and were looking for additional, more subtle, explanations.

When we consider the final result of the interplay of vital

rates in Europe, we observe that there was also a significant change in levels of natural increase in population. But this change was less regular than that of its components, owing to the different time schedules of declines of natality and mortality.

In the early 1920s there were several nations with rates of natural increase exceeding 15 per thousand and only one, France, with a very low rate. This was perhaps the reason for Landry's analysis of *dépopulation* in his 1909 and 1934 papers, and a strong motive in his policy recommendations aimed at counteracting the economic disadvantages of procreation in a modern society.

In the late 1930s there were differences in the rates of natural increase: north-west at the low and south-east at the high level with only few exceptions. Moore's generalisation of the situation was typical of the contemporary explanations of this: 'If one were to draw a circle on a map of Europe, with a centre in the North Sea off the English Coast and with a radius of some 800 miles, the arc dividing the European Continent would approximate the boundary between the relatively prosperous industrial economics of the north and west and the relatively underdeveloped and predominantly agrarian economics of south and east. Within the area of the circle lie most of the major commercial and industrial centres of Europe, and the regions with virtually stationary populations; beyond its border lie countries of meagre wealth and growing population.' Notestein and his colleagues saw Europe of the mid-1940s 'approaching demographic stability in the world which is rapidly developing'. He envisaged the north-west experiencing a cessation of population growth, and the south-east a much slower growth than in the 1930s. Among the possible consequences of such trends, Notestein pointed to the movement of people from east to the west, and reverse movement of capital, as well as a readaptation of Europe in which a higher importance would be given to the east, particularly in economic and political affairs.

In the late 1960s there were still differences in the rates of natural increase in population, but less significant and at a lower level. In spite of economic progress throughout the continent, south and east were still regions of moderate opportunity, quite rapid demographic expansion, and a source of population transfers. In the north and west national economies reached an unprecedented high level, which owing to moderate growth in the domestic labour force was accompanied with large demand for additional foreign labour. Further industrial concentration and immigration did not encourage a rapid reduction of economic differences between the two parts of the continent. But they have aggravated the already existing difficult problems of the north-west relating to high population density, urban congestion, industrial pollution and the human environment.

CHANGING AGE STRUCTURE

An appreciable change in the sex and age structure of population which took place during the last decades was another aspect of demographic transition. Virtually all countries of Europe have experienced the ageing of their populations in which the older age-groups acquired a higher percentage share in total population. The sex and age structure of those populations which were exposed to wars were affected by war losses and the deficiency of births. Several countries suffered significant deformation of the population structure during World War I, especially France, Belgium, Russia, Serbia, Germany, Bulgaria and Austria. During World War II the most affected were the populations of Poland, the USSR, Yugoslavia, Germany, Austria and others. A shortage of men and manpower, as well as female reproductive stock were among the consequences of the war for these countries.

The long-term modification in age composition was associated with the downward trend of natality. The process of ageing was initiated by a relative reduction in the child population and the simultaneous increase in proportion of adults and the aged. It was influenced in some countries by migration and war losses. But in all countries the influence of vital forces was dominant. The number and percentage of population of over 65 years continued to rise, while the percentage share of population between 15–64 demonstrated first an increase and then a slight decline.

The long-term change in age structure may be exemplified by data for Sweden and Yugoslavia, which represents examples of the older and the more recent demographic transition. Of course, modifications in the age structure of

TABLE 3: The age structure of the populations of Sweden and Yugoslavia (per cent of total population)

Age groups	Sweden				Yugoslavia			
	1910	*1930*	*1950*	*1969*	*1921*	*1931*	*1953*	*1971*
0–14	31·7	24·8	23·5	20·9	34·8	34·6	30·5	26·8
15–64	59·8	66·0	66·3	65·6	59·9	60·1	63·5	65·2
65 and over	8·5	9·0	10·2	13·5	5·3	5·3	6·0	8·0

individual countries did not follow a uniform pattern. In the early 1950s, when fertility reached a low level in all European countries except Albania and parts of Yugoslavia, the range of percentage of population of 65 years of age and over was between 11·8 in France and 6·0 in Yugoslavia. France was followed in the increase of the age of the population by England and Wales, Austria, Belgium, Sweden and Denmark, while the USSR, Poland, Hungary, Netherlands, Italy and Spain had a lower proportion of old people in the population. The rest of the age structure also was not uniform: the highest proportion of adult population was in Hungary, England and Wales (over 67 per cent), and the lowest was in the Netherlands (61 per cent). The Netherlands and Yugoslavia had the highest proportion of children (31·4 and 30·5 per cent respectively) and France and England and Wales had the lowest (21·7 and 22 per cent respectively). Throughout the period under consideration, Albania and the Kosovo province of Yugoslavia had the most youthful population (42 per cent of the population were children and 5 per cent old people).

Although they had all been affected by demographic change, European populations in the 1970s still had quite different age structures. Proportions of individual age groups varied widely as did the shapes of the sex and age pyramids. A selection of pyramids is given in Fig. 2 which illustrates the various sex and age compositions existing in Europe.

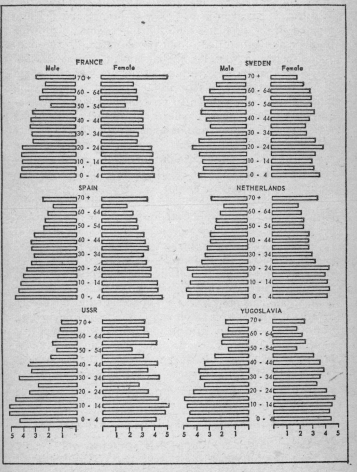

Fig. 2: Age-sex pyramids: around 1970

The social and economic implications of a changing age structure were numerous, particularly in the post-war period. In the 1950s some countries experienced heavy pressure on education and related services, while the ageing of the population was a matter of concern in other countries. Inquiries undertaken in the 1960s in France and Belgium pointed to the problems and difficulties which a growing number and proportion of old people faced. In the mid-1960s there was speculation that student unrest was not only a consequence of institutional rigidity, but also a sign of the inability of society to accommodate increasing numbers of young people. In view of the changing demographic situations, social policies introduced in the 1950s were further developed and/or amended after World War II and new ones were devised. Of particular interest were those concerning public health, education, social security and the schemes for the elderly, which had to provide services to individual age groups.

Correlated with the change in age structure was also the formation and growth of the labour force. The economically active population did not grow at the same rate as the total population because of changing age composition and social factors. Nearly all countries experienced a relative expansion and contraction of the labour forces at different times associated with the changing age structure of their population. This process was not appreciated in the earlier decades, for there were ample supplies of labour emanating from both population growth and under-employment in agriculture. However, in the late 1950s and 1960s the process of demographic ageing affected the growth of labour force in several countries, and these became a matter of governmental and international concern.

FIFTY YEARS OF NATIONAL GROWTH

The long history of Europe has witnessed very many changes in national territories reflecting political, ethical, and social realities and the last fifty years is no exception. During the last decades Europe has been organised in a varying number of some thirty sovereign countries in addition to some six territories with a different status.

DEMOGRAPHIC SIZE OF EUROPEAN COUNTRIES

By 1910, in addition to Russia, which had a population of 130 million, there were five large countries each with a population of over 25 million, *viz.* Germany, France, United Kingdom, Italy and Austro-Hungary. Their combined population was 210 million, or 63 per cent of population of Europe without Russia. In 1920 four countries, namely Germany, United Kingdom, France and Italy, each with over 30 million of people, had a combined population of almost 170 million, or 52 per cent of Europe's population.

In 1970 the situation was as follows. Soviet Union had a population of 243 million; six countries each with a population of over 30 million, *viz.* Federal Republic of Germany, United Kingdom, Italy, France, Spain and Poland had a combined population of 285 million. This was 62 per cent of the populations of Europe without the USSR. Six countries each had a population of between 10 and 20 million. The combined population was 92 million or 20 per cent of the population of Europe. Twenty-two countries and territories with less than 10 million had a combined population of 80 million, which was 18 per cent of population of Europe. Out of these, there were seven countries with more than 5 million people. (See Table 4.)

The large disparities between the population sizes of European countries have attracted the attention of academics, policy makers and the general public. In the past population numbers were considered an important component of size, power and economic strength. What constituted a 'large' or a 'small' country was indeed a matter of opinion depending on various factors, and subject to change. Landry considered, for example, that population size and growth was essential to national power, defence capacity, and the political, economic, intellectual and

TABLE 4: Population of Europe: 1920–70
(midyear estimates in millions)

	1920	1930	1940	1950	1960	1970
Europe and the USSR	480·1	532·8	573·8	571·7	637·8	704·1
Europe without USSR	324·8	353·8	378·8	391·7	432·4	462·4
Western Europe[a]	101·4	108·6	113·2	122·1	134·5	149·3
Federal Republic of Germany	35·0	37·5	40·6	47·8	53·2	59·4
France	38·8	41·2	41·3	41·7	45·7	50·8
Netherlands	6·8	7·9	8·8	10·1	11·5	13·0
Belgium	7·6	8·1	8·3	8·6	9·1	9·6
Austria	6·5	6·6	6·7	6·9	7·1	7·4
Switzerland	3·9	4·1	4·2	4·7	5·4	6·3
West Berlin	2·6	2·9	2·9	2·1	2·1	2·1
Luxemburg	0·2	0·3	0·3	0·3	0·3	0·3
Southern Europe[b]	82·8	92·6	102·5	108·4	117·5	129·5
Italy	37·0	40·3	43·8	46·6	49·6	53·6
Spain	21·2	23·4	25·8	27·9	30·3	33·8
Yugoslavia	12·4	14·4	16·4	16·3	18·4	20·4
Portugal	6·0	6·8	7·7	8·4	8·8	9·6
Greece	5·1	6·4	7·4	7·6	8·3	8·9
Albania	0·8	1·0	1·1	1·2	1·6	2·2
Malta	0·2	0·2	0·3	0·3	0·3	0·3
Eastern Europe	78·7	87·7	94·8	88·4	95·6	103·2
Poland	26·0	29·5	31·5	24·9	29·7	32·5
Romania	12·4	14·2	15·9	16·1	18·4	20·2
German Democratic Republic	14·3	15·4	16·8	18·9	17·9	17·2
Czechoslovakia	12·9	13·9	14·7	12·4	13·6	14·5
Hungary	7·9	8·6	9·3	9·3	9·9	10·3
Bulgaria	5·1	6·0	6·7	7·3	7·8	8·5
Northern Europe[c]	61·9	64·9	68·3	72·5	75·8	80·4
United Kingdom	43·7	45·8	48·2	50·6	52·5	55·7
Sweden	5·9	6·1	6·4	7·0	7·5	8·0
Denmark	3·2	3·5	3·8	4·3	4·6	4·9
Finland	3·1	3·4	3·7	4·0	4·3	4·6
Norway	2·6	2·8	2·9	3·2	3·6	3·8
Ireland	3·1	2·9	2·9	2·9	2·8	2·9
Iceland	0·1	0·1	0·1	0·1	0·2	0·2
USSR	155·3	179·0	195·0	180·0	214·4	242·7

[a] Including: Monaco and Liechtenstein.
[b] Including: Gibraltar, San Marino, Andorra and Holy See.
[c] Including: Channel Islands, Isle of Man and Faeroe Islands.

Source: *World Population Prospects as Assessed in 1963, Demographic Yearbook 1970* and *Population and Vital Statistics Report* (data available as of 1 April 1972) – all United Nations publications.

artistic potential of a nation. In the 1930s nationalists in some countries argued that population was the basis of national strength and territorial expansion. In the post-war times concern was shown for human well-being and economic advancement, rather than for the factors associated with grandeur. Among the smaller nations, the idea of regional economic integration was advanced as a means of counteracting the disadvantages of small national markets. Economic integration became acceptable to most European countries, but its geographic extension never could overcome the frontier between East and West.

DIFFERENTIAL POPULATION GROWTH

National statistics for 1920 to 1970 indicate a variety of population growth patterns. These reflect both the long range demographic change and the short range variation in all growth components. A number of countries in the north and west had relatively stable but low annual growth rates. In the south and east there was a declining trend in the originally high population rates due to a decline in fertility and emigration. In some countries, i.e. the USSR, the rate of increase of population followed first an upward then a downward course. A negative annual growth was experienced by many countries which took part in the war. In some other countries, such as Ireland and East Germany, emigration was greater than the natural increase in population. Negative growth also affected some countries during the depression years, and others during severe political or social crises.

The cumulative effect of fifty-years' population growth also showed marked differences. The range of percentage increase of population of individual countries from 1920 to 1970 was between —4 for Ireland and 175 for Albania. The percentage increases recorded for the whole of period under consideration were as follows:

10–20 per cent: Austria, Czechoslovakia and German Democratic Republic; however, Czechoslovakia and German Democratic Republic experienced decennial declines in population numbers; the former in the 1940s, the latter from 1950 to 1970;

20–30 per cent: Belgium, France, Poland and United Kingdom; Poland had about 7 million people less in 1950 than in 1940;

30–40 per cent: Greece, Hungary and Sweden; Hungary had in 1950 approximately the same number of population as in 1940;

40–60 per cent: Italy, Denmark, Finland, Norway, Portugal, Spain and Yugoslavia. The Yugoslavian population was a little smaller in 1950 than it was in 1940;

60 per cent and over: Bulgaria, Federal Republic of Germany, Romania and Switzerland.

Albania and the Netherlands had an extremely high percentage increase in population, over 90 per cent from 1920 to 1970. Luxemburg, Malta, Iceland and other countries also had a larger population in 1970 than in 1920.

POPULATION DENSITY

The population density increased accordingly: in Europe from 66 in 1920 to 94 persons per square kilometre (henceforth abbreviated to km²) in 1970, and in the USSR from 7 to 11. The European continental pattern of population distribution established in the nineteenth century and recorded for the period around 1930 in the Sydow-Wagner's *Methodischer Schulatlas* had changed little by 1970. The change that had occurred was more in the direction of the intensifying of traditional population densities than a creation of new centres of dense settlements, e.g. the Danube area and south-western Soviet Union.

The highest national density of population in 1970 was found in the Netherlands (319 persons per km²), Belgium (317), Federal Republic of Germany (240) and United Kingdom (228). These were followed by Italy, Switzerland, German Democratic Republic and Luxemburg (178 to 131 persons per km²), and then by France, Poland, Czechoslovakia and other neighbouring countries. These countries, or parts of them, belonged to the high-population-

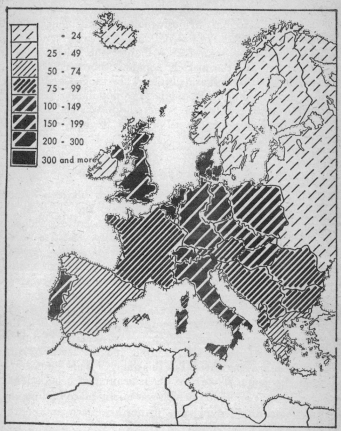

Fig. 3: Density of population: 1970
Population per km²

density belt extending from the United Kingdom through the Low Countries, Rhine valley, Saxony and Bohemia to Silesia and the Russian south-west.

Another traditional aspect of population distribution in Europe which has not changed much is the low population density of Iceland (2 persons per km²), Norway (12),

Finland (14), Sweden (18) and northern regions of Russia. The cold climate has obviously inhibited settlement in those regions, and affect the low national averages given above. Between the two extremes – that of the thickly settled central belt and the sparsely populated northern regions – were areas of moderate densities. They ranged between 44 in Ireland and 85 in Romania. The population density of the European parts of the Soviet Union was 99 Moldavia, 78 Ukraine, 57 the central Russian Regions, 48 in the Russian Black Lands.

DEMOGRAPHIC AND ECONOMIC GROWTH

Owing to the complex interrelationships between demographic, economic and social factors, the increase in numbers and population density which were experienced by European nations during the last fifty years are much more complex than they appear at first glance. For reasons which go beyond the scope of present discussion, industrialisation and the diversification of economic activity were quite advanced in the west and north, while lagging behind in the east and south. Colin Clark's analysis of differential productivity on the three sectors of economy may help the understanding of the large differences between the European countries as far as national output and the levels of consumption are concerned. But this analysis is also important from the point of view of diversification of occupational structure of population, which was taking place in different times and at different rates in north-western and south-eastern regions of Europe.

In the eighteenth and nineteenth century there has been a significant redistribution of population and manpower at the sub-national levels in northern and western regions, which brought people from the countryside to the urban and industrial areas. According to Bairoch's historical statistics on manpower, there was already high industrial concentration in those regions at the turn of century. Examples of such concentration were the United Kingdom with over

6 million workers in manufacturing, Germany with nearly 6 million, France with over 5 million, Belgium with over 1 million, as well as the Netherlands, Northern Italy, Denmark, Switzerland, Austria and Bohemia with smaller numbers but a high proportion of industrial labour. Banking, commerce, transportation and other modern sector services were concentrated in the same regions. The share of agriculture in the total labour force was as low as 9 per cent in United Kingdom, 27 per cent in Belgium, 31 per cent in the Netherlands, etc. On the other side there were countries with the predominant agrarian characteristics: Russia had only 3·8 million employed in manufacturing and 17 million, or 59 per cent, in agriculture. Countries with a high proportion of agricultural workers were Portugal (65 per cent), Spain (68 per cent), Hungary (over 69 per cent), Romania and Balkans (over 80 per cent). The situation remained almost the same during the 1920–40 period, with, however, slow and hesitant improvements in the south-east which were outpaced in the north-west and the Soviet Union.

After World War II the restructuring of economy and regions took place in Italy, Spain and Greece as well as in the socialist countries. In the later group the process differed widely, as Mihailovic has pointed out depending on the stage of economic advancement, industrial growth and regional development schemes. In general, the development of manufacturing industries, of agriculture, trade and commerce and of transportation made it possible to support a larger population at higher levels of living. This was directly related to the shifts of population from agriculture to non-agricultural industries and the growth of productivity, which were also taking place in the north and west of Europe.

The situation can be partly explained by further change in the distribution of manpower. Around 1960 all except four countries of western and northern Europe had 80 per cent and more of their labour force employed in secondary and tertiary industries.[7] Important exporters of agricultural

[7] Primary industries include agriculture, forestry and fishing. The

commodities such as France had only 20 per cent employed in the primary sector, while Denmark had 17·5 per cent and the Netherlands 10·6 per cent.

The growth of non-agricultural employment and the relative decrease in agricultural labour was visible in the south and east, but was much slower.

TABLE 5: Agricultural labour force as a percentage of the total labour force southern and eastern Europe: around 1940 and 1960

	1940	1960
Italy	42·2	25·2
Spain	57·9	34·6
Yugoslavia	77·8	58·4
Portugal	48·8	43·0
Greece	48·2	55·3
Poland	57·2	47·7
Romania	78·7	69·6
German Democratic Republic	29·2	17·4
Czechoslovakia	37·7	23·6
Hungary	52·9	32·7
Bulgaria	75·5	64·2

Note: for Italy, Greece, Yugoslavia, Poland, Romania and Bulgaria closest census year
Source: Bairoch, *The Working Population and Its Structure.*

In the 1960s all southern and eastern European countries as well as the USSR still had more than 20 per cent of their labour force employed in agriculture. Out of twelve countries in this group eight had more than one third of their labour force in agriculture.

When the national per capita income and the industrial composition of labour force are considered one can understand why southern and eastern Europe lagged behind the rest of the continent. It seems that during the last fifty years the process of demographic homogenisation of Europe has been faster than that of economic homogenisation. For reasons which we do not fully understand, the working of demographic transition was more effective than that of

four countries with primary manpower exceeding 20 per cent were: Austria (22·8 per cent), Iceland (24·3 per cent), Ireland (35·2 per cent) and Finland (35·5 per cent).

economic development irrespective of differences in social and political systems.

NATALITY AND MORTALITY

During the period under consideration additional techniques for controlling the natural forces which govern vital processes have been developed. Fertility regulation and the postponement of death gradually spread over Europe and became a common though not yet a universal asset. The effects of these improvements during the last five decades led to a variety of demographic transitions occurring in individual countries and regions. Both mortality and natality rates reached low levels eventually with few exceptions.

The spread of control over death was both rapid and far-reaching. At the beginning of the twentieth century about 60 per cent of European population, Russia included, lived in countries with a crude rate of mortality of over 20 per thousand of the population. In the mid-1930s the same percentage of European people lived in countries with a mortality rate below 17 per thousand. In 1970, however, 67 per cent lived in countries with mortality rates of less than 10 per thousand.

Expansion of birth control during the same period was faster and even more radical. The birth rate exceeded 30 per thousand in countries with a combined population of over 73 per cent of the total European population. By the mid-thirties, 63 per cent of population lived in countries with a birth rate below 30 per thousand. In 1970 75 per cent of population of Europe, the USSR included, had a national birth rate between 16 and 20 per thousand, and 24 per cent had a rate lower than 16. Variations in natural increase of population were very marked and followed an appreciable downward trend.

TOWARDS LOW FERTILITY

Within this general trend, the birth rates of individual countries took paths which varied according to the onset

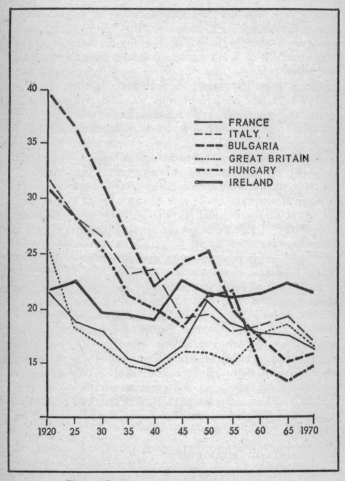

Fig. 4: Births per 1000 population: 1920-70

Legend:
- FRANCE
- ITALY
- BULGARIA
- GREAT BRITAIN
- HUNGARY
- IRELAND

TABLE 6: Birth rates of European countries: 1920–70 (per 1000 of population)

	1920	1930	1950	1960	1970
Western Europe					
Federal Republic of Germany	25·9[a]	17·6[a]	16·5	17·8	13·3
France	21·4	18·0	20·7	17·9	16·7
Netherlands	28·3	23·1	22·3	20·8	18·4
Belgium	22·1	18·8	16·9	16·9	14·7
Austria	21·3	16·8	15·6	17·9	15·1
Switzerland	20·9	17·2	18·1	17·6	15·9
Luxemburg	21·6	21·3	13·9	16·0	13·0
Southern Europe					
Italy	31·8	26·7	19·5	18·3	16·8
Spain	29·5[b]	28·3	20·2	21·8	19·8
Yugoslavia	36·7[b]	35·5	30·2	23·5	17·6
Portugal	33·7	29·9	24·4	24·2	18·0[b]
Greece	...	31·4	20·0	18·9	17·4[b]
Albania	...	...	...	43·4	35·6[b]
Malta	...	...	...	26·1	16·3
Eastern Europe					
Poland	32·2	32·5	30·7	22·3	16·7
Romania	34·7	35·0	26·2	19·1	21·1
German Democratic Republic	25·9[a]	17·6[a]	16·9	17·2	13·9
Czechoslovakia	26·8	22·7	23·3	15·9	15·8
Hungary	31·4	25·4	20·9	14·7	14·7
Bulgaria	39·9	31·4	25·2	17·8	16·3
Northern Europe					
United Kingdom	25·5	16·3	15·9	17·2	16·0
Sweden	23·6	15·4	15·6	13·7	13·6
Denmark	25·4	18·7	18·7	16·6	14·4
Finland	25·3	20·6	24·5	18·5	13·7
Norway	26·1	17·0	19·1	17·3	16·2
Ireland	21·6	19·9	21·3	21·4	21·8
Iceland	26·5	26·3	28·2	28·0	20·7[b]
USSR	...	44·3[b]	26·7	24·9	17·4

[a] For Germany in pre-war boundaries.
[b] Closest available year.
... Not available.
Source: *United Nations Demographic Yearbook* and national publications.

and the rate of the decline. Annual birth rates of individual countries for the period 1920–70 are given in the table below.

All countries except Albania and Ireland had reached by the end of the 1960s, a rather low natality level. However, the times taken to do so differed widely. To reduce the birth rate from about 33 to about 16 per thousand (disregarding exceptional and irregular situations) it took Italy, for example, 64 years (from 1906 to 1970). Spain had the same birth rate as Italy in 1906, but in 1970 it still was near to 20 per thousand. The time-span in Germany was 43 years, from 1906 to 1949; in Hungary 45 years, from 1913 to 1958. Both Bulgaria and Yugoslavia had a birth rate of about 33 in 1927/28 but the former has reached 16·7 in 1962 while the latter's 1970 record was 17·6 per thousand. The shortest time-span was found in Romania – 28 years, from 1931 to 1962, and in the Soviet Union – 28 years, from 1938 to 1967.

The birth rate is quite adequate measure of natality as a component of population growth but it cannot alone explain variations in a complex phenomenon like human reproduction and more refined measurements have been developed by demographers during the period under consideration.

The marriage pattern was to a large extent responsible for the differences in fertility in Europe, which existed prior to the widespread use of birth control within marriage. Hajnal pointed out that west of a line drawn from Trieste to Leningrad the proportion of married women was significantly lower (45 or 50 per cent of women of ages 15 to 50) than the east of that line (60 to 70 per cent). Hajnal's line was confirmed by Coale and his team 'as the division between European and non-European marriage pattern'. Social institutions must have been pretty strong, for this dual pattern persisted till World War II. However, in the post-war period, Glass noted: 'marriage patterns have changed and in general most sharply in those countries in which fairly late marriage was customary ... and in which the proportion of women in the age group 45 to 49

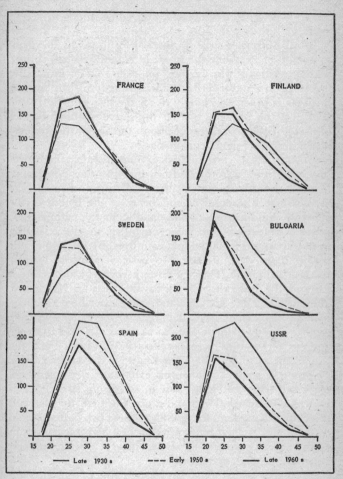

Fig. 5: *Live-birth rates specific for age of mother*

years ever married tended to be not much above 85 per cent.' This in part explains the striking difference in fertility levels before birth control was widespread and also shows why greater uniformity has come about in recent years.

In all European societies marital fertility was the main source of births, while the resort to voluntary birth control within marriages was the most important factor in natality levels. Birth control did not affect equally all the parties, nor was it practised equally in all the age groups. In the course of the fifty-year period the shape of the curves in Graph 5 (live birth rates specific to the age of the mother) has undergone a significant change.

Older women were the first to demonstrate a high propensity to refrain from child-bearing. In other age groups birth control also spread gradually. Differences in the age at marriage, the onset of childbearing, the length of the effective childbearing period, and changes within these factors, have each and all contributed to the changing fertility patterns in individual countries. By the end of our period there were at least two basic varieties of fertility pattern in Europe. The first pattern was typical of eastern Europe. In Bulgaria, Czechoslovakia, eastern Germany, Hungary, Poland, Romania and Yugoslavia the highest age specific birth rates were found in a single five-year age group – among mothers of 20 to 24 years of age. In Greece and the Netherlands there was also a 'fertility peak' but in the age group 25 to 29. The second pattern was characteristic of western Europe. Childbearing extending over a period of ten years, with the highest rate in age group 20 to 29, was typical of Denmark, Finland, France, Portugal, Sweden and the United Kingdom. Exceptions to these two patterns were Albania and Ireland both of which had high birth rates in all the ages of mothers. The latter, however, at an appreciably lower level than the former.

Another measure of natality change, that of reproduction of female population was advanced in the late twenties. The gross reproduction rate (average number of daughters that would be born per woman during her reproductive period in accordance with the prevailing age-specific fertility rates) and the net reproductive rate, which makes allowances for death rate, were for long considered adequate for the measurement of change in natality. Thanks to their simplicity, reproduction rates became a popular tool of demographic analyses.

Both rates have shown a significant decline over the last fifty years, and there has also been a visible reduction in the discrepancy between them due to increased life expectation. In the 1920s all nations had a net reproduction rate over unity, with the exception for one or two years of France, England, Germany and Austria. During the depression years there were at least five countries with a net reproduction rate below unity, and some twelve with a gross reproduction rate below that level. All these except Czechoslovakia and Hungary were northern and western countries. In 1937 Czechoslovakia and Austria again had a reproduction rate below unity, which can be explained partly by the unfavourable political and national situation. During the war years most of the belligerent countries must have had a rate of reproduction below unity, but statistics are only available to show this in England and Wales, Norway, France, Finland and Belgium. Although not involved directly in the war, Switzerland and Sweden had also reproduction rates below unity in 1939/1940, and in 1940/1941.

The post-war demographic recovery extending to the early 1950s brought reproduction rates up to higher levels. For this period reproduction rates are not available for all countries, but the increase is obvious. Among the few exceptions were Germany and Austria with a net reproduction rate below unity. However, this was only for a short period. Since the mid-1950s, in most of the eastern European countries reproduction rates have taken a downward trend. From 1963 to 1965 Romania had a gross reproduction rate below unity, which was increased by radical intervention from the state. In the late 1960s, Bulgaria and Hungary both had a gross reproduction rate below unity, and Czechoslovakia and Greece a net reproduction rate below 1. On the other hand net reproduction rates higher than in the preceeding periods were recorded in France, the United Kingdom, Norway and Ireland. The final result of this

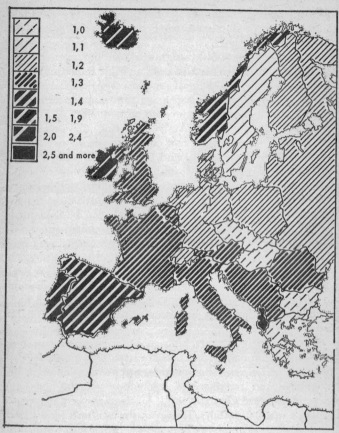

Fig. 6: Gross reproduction rates: 1965-70

Legend:
- 1,0
- 1,1
- 1,2
- 1,3
- 1,4
- 1,5 1,9
- 2,0 2,4
- 2,5 and more

complex process was a rather uniform situation with regard to reproduction in the late sixties, as shown in Fig. 6.

Traditional sub-national variations of fertility, such as regional, ethnic, urban–rural ones and those relating to socio-economic status of families were significantly reduced during the period under consideration. Appreciable regional fertility differentials still persisted in the 1960s only in Yugoslavia, Spain, Portugal, Albania and USSR. In some countries, such as the USSR and Yugoslavia, high-fertility areas were correlated with ethnic composition of population and the cultural traditions of Muslim origin.

TABLE 7: Regional birth rate differentials USSR and Yugoslavia

USSR (1970)		*Yugoslavia (1971)*	
The highest regional birth rates			
Tadzikskaya SSR	36·8	Kosovo	37·2
Turkmenskaya SSR	34·7	Macedonia	23·2
The lowest regional birth rates			
RSFSR	15·1	Croatia	14·7
Latviskaya SSR	14·7	Voivodina	12·9

In general, both urban and rural families followed the small-size pattern, and differences, to the extent they still existed, were small and irregular. Factors which led to the use of birth control techniques being used less frequently by the poorer classes had virtually disappeared by the end of the period. A moderate fertility pattern became common to all socio-economic groups and on all levels of educational attainment, with minor exceptions in some eastern European countries. In other countries, however, such as England and Wales, Western Germany and Norway there was in the 1960s a reshuffling of natality, in which higher social or education groups demonstrated higher fertility. This phenomenon described as the 'U-shaped curve' attracted a great deal of attention from scholars, but no final interpretation of it has been accepted.

GOVERNMENTAL POLICIES AND ACCESS TO BIRTH CONTROL METHODS

Matters related to marriage, fertility and birth control were not left purely to the discretion of the individual and family. In addition to religious norms and beliefs, legislation provided a framework for individual behaviour. Laws concerning marriage, family, health, drug administration and the like, most of which were developed in the nineteenth century, have been changed on many occasions and supplemented since the 1930s with provision for social insurance and security. In those regions which were under the Turkish rule until the Balkan wars, modern legislation was introduced in the 1920s. In Soviet Russia, along with changes in many social institutions, abortion was legalised in conformity with the new doctrine, which considered that abortion was a matter of democratic freedom. This doctrine was later, after World War II, adopted by most of the eastern European socialist countries.

France and Belgium were known before World War II for their pro-natalist policies, the main characteristic of which was family allowances. Introduced first by individual industries and then by the state as a measure intended to counteract the rising cost of living, the family allowance system was made obligatory in France in 1932, and in Belgium in 1929. Influential pro-natalist groups have subsequently encouraged governments towards reducing the economic disadvantages of large families. In 1939 France adopted *le Code de la Famille*, which was praised by Sauvy as 'a true revolution in French institutions and a profound innovation'. Positive measures were supported by repressive legislation concerning birth control. *Le Code Pénal* (1810) declared abortion illegal; it was amended in 1923 and later, and made more strict. Both French and Belgian legislation prohibited birth control publicity and the advertising of contraceptives. Nevertheless, birth control was widely practised; abstention, *coitus interruptus* and the 'safe period' were legal, and abortion was the illegal method.

The population policies of the Scandinavian countries were gradually developed in the 1930s, as an outcome of growing concern over low fertility experienced during the depression. According to Glass, a book by Alva and Gunnar Myrdal, two distinguished social-democrats strongly influenced public opinion in Sweden. In 1935 a Royal Commission on Population was first appointed in Sweden, then in Denmark, and later in Finland; it seems, however, that Sweden's population policy may be considered typical of Scandinavia. Glass pointed to two characteristics of the

Scandinavian approach: 'investigation of the various aspects of population problem' which preceded the passing of legislation, and 'the initial assumption that parenthood shall be voluntary'. The latter was supported by measures encouraging fertility and by those which provided for information on birth control methods. Penalties for abortion have been reduced by subsequent reform of the Penal Codes, and the networks of birth control clinics have been expanded. Provision was made to encourage marriage, to reduce extra costs incurred by families with children, and to increase facilities for helping mothers in the rearing of children. All this was part of a conscious effort to secure equal status for women, a concept which included a range of measures, from employment to the protection of unmarried mothers and their children. The four main aspects of the Scandinavian approach, namely its scientific foundation, appreciation of the social character of population questions, voluntary parenthood, and the overriding humanitarian orientation have made a significant impact on the post-war debates regarding population policy and its development.

Comprehensive pro-natalist policies were initiated and developed in Italy by the Fascist regime from 1926 and in Germany by the National Socialist Government from 1933. Both policies were evolved in view of 'demographic power'; the latter was also strongly influenced by the racial and eugenic considerations. Throughout the 1930s a system of governmental measures based on ideological inducement was consistently promoted in both countries. However, by the end of the war the pro-natalist policies and the supportive system of measures had collapsed, and only the commonly accepted measure remained operative.

Alarming projections of population trends for England and Wales, preoccupation with the falling birth rate, a comprehensive pro-natalist policy in Germany as well as the policies of France, Belgium and other countries raised an interest in population policy in Great Britain too. In 1937 a revision of the vital statistics system was undertaken resulting in The Population (Statistics) Act (1938). Suggestions were also made to set up a Royal Commission to investigate the population problem. But, because of the war the Royal Commission was appointed only in 1943. After having studied the economic, statistical, biological and medical problems, the Commission issued its report in 1949. The report was widely praised but never considered by Parliament. Grebenik suggested that 'there were a number of reasons for this: enthusiasm for social reconstruction was distinctly smaller in 1949 than in 1944, and the recovery of birth rate which had taken place from 1943 onward seemed to many to have made the population problem a considerably less urgent one'.

After World War II a number of social policy measures, some of them with an explicit or implicit demographic objective, were launched or extended throughout Europe. A United Nations study states that high family allowances were granted in the early 1960s at least in seven European countries, low in some six others, in the rest of the countries family allowances at moderate levels prevailed. Reduction in income tax payments were granted to persons with family responsibilities in many countries, while in some others the imposition of taxes for bachelorhood were introduced. Aids to maternity, rewards to mothers, grants or loans to newly married, various facilities for children and the like were gradually developed in most of Europe. In principle, all these measures are of pro-natalist character, for they reduce family expenditure with regard to rearing children by the measure of 'external costs' borne by society. Most of the measures have their own social merits, and they have gradually come to be taken for granted with no direct relation to fertility and size of family.

Among the countries which had a policy between the two wars, France was one to proclaim in the 1945 *Ordonnance* her 'determination to halt declining fertility', notably by means of a new family allowance scheme. However, later in 1967 the sale and distribution of contraceptives was legalised, while abortion as well as birth control propaganda and advertising remained illegal. Scandinavian countries pursued the policy of voluntary parenthood by facilitating access to birth control information and services including,

TABLE 8: Crude death rates in European countries: 1920–70 (per 100 of population)

	1920	1930	1950	1960	1970
Western Europe					
Federal Republic of Germany	15·1[a]	11·0[a]	10·5	11·1	11·6
France	17·2	15·6	12·8	11·4	10·6
Netherlands	12·0	9·1	7·5	7·7	8·4
Belgium	13·8	13·4	12·5	12·4	12·4
Austria	18·1	13·5	12·4	12·7	13·2
Switzerland	14·4	11·6	10·1	9·7	9·0
Luxemburg	13·1	12·9	11·6	11·8	12·2
Southern Europe					
Italy	18·7	14·1	9·8	9·8	9·7
Spain	23·4	16·9	10·9	8·8	8·6
Yugoslavia	20·9[b]	19·0	13·0	9·9	8·9
Portugal	23·7	17·2	12·2	10·8	9·7
Greece	...	16·4	7·1	7·3	8·1[b]
Albania	...	...	14·0	9·3	8·0[b]
Malta	...	...	10·3	8·3	9·4
Eastern Europe					
Poland	26·9	15·5	11·6	7·5	8·1
Romania	26·7	19·4	...	8·7	9·6
German Democratic Republic	15·1[a]	11·0[a]	11·8	13·3	14·1
Czechoslovakia	19·0	14·2	11·5	9·2	11·4
Hungary	21·4	15·5	11·5	10·2	11·6
Bulgaria	21·4	16·2	10·2	8·1	9·1
Northern Europe					
United Kingdom	12·4	11·4	11·7	11·5	11·7
Sweden	13·3	11·7	10·0	10·0	9·9
Denmark	12·9	10·8	9·2	9·5	9·8
Finland	15·9	31·2	10·1	9·0	9·5
Norway	12·8	10·6	9·1	9·1	9·8
Ireland	14·7	14·3	12·7	11·5	11·5
Iceland	...	11·6	7·9	7·9	7·1[b]
USSR	...	23·3[b]	9·7	7·1	8·2

[a] For Germany in pre-war boundaries.
[b] Closest available year.
... Not available.
Source: *United Nations Demographic Yearbook* and national publications.

abortion. In the United Kingdom family planning was made available in 1967, and the Abortion Act (1967) allowed greater latitude to doctors in deciding on induced abortions.

The USSR was the first country in Europe to legalise abortion (1920) but revoked the law in 1936. Abortion was again made legal in 1956, and became the main method of fertility control leading to a sharp decline of natality. In the mid-1960s Soviet policy emphasised contraception and 'related instructional and health-educational material'. Permissive legislation with regard to abortion was passed in 1956 in Poland, Bulgaria, Hungary and Romania, in 1957 in Czechoslovakia, and in 1960 in Yugoslavia. Contraceptive methods became available in these countries only in the early 1960s with a consequence that abortion was up to that point the most important method of birth control.

A steep decline of fertility in eastern Europe gave rise to concerns of future population growth and particularly the labour supply. In 1966, the government of Romania practically forbade abortion and adopted a series of pro-natalist measures. Birth rate, which was as low as 14·3 per thousand of population jumped to 27·4 in 1967 and reached 21·1 per thousand in 1970. Czechoslovakia also introduced measures favouring higher fertility. Bulgaria amended her abortion act in 1968 and extended benefits to large families, as did Hungary in the same year which, in addition, provided facilities to employed mothers. In the USSR no drastic change was introduced until the end of the 1960s but the need for an average family of three children was emphasised on demographic grounds. The response to falling fertility was rapid in eastern Europe, indeed; it relied on both restrictive and positive policy measures, the effects of which still remain to be evaluated.

DECLINES OF MORTALITY

In the early 1920s, the incidence of mortality was high (20 and more deaths per thousand population) in most of southern and eastern Europe and the USSR; it was low (less than 13 per thousand) in the Netherlands, the United Kingdom, Denmark and Norway; whilst in the rest of the continent it lay between the two extremes. Decline in mortality was faster in those countries in which it began later: to reduce the crude death rate from 18 to 10 per thousand it took e.g. Hungary 30 years (from 1925 to 1955) while Romania only took 11 years (from 1946 to 1955). The process was slower in those countries in which a downward trend in mortality was recorded in the nineteenth century or the early twentieth century. The recent rapid declines in mortality were achieved thanks to the accumulated medical and sanitary knowledge and experience in this group of countries, which was easily transferred elsewhere. Antibiotics and disinfectants played in this regard an important role. As Hansluwka and Smith suggested, 'in the countries where mortality began to fall quite early, the contribution of specific health and medical measures must have been negligible for the first hundred years and the early decline must be attributed mainly to general improvements in the standard of living. In the countries with more recent, sharper declines in mortality, the causes must be much more substantially related to specific public health activities and medical care.'

In the late 1960s the crude death rate was low in the whole of Europe, and lower in the south-east and the Soviet Union than in the north-west. In addition, countries having a long experience of declining mortality have recently recorded a slowing down of that decline, and some of them even a slight increase in the death rate. Both of these aspects were associated with the marked differences in age structure of individual populations and the changes therein. The age-specific death rates were in general lower in the north-west than in the south-east, but a higher proportion of the aged, and the process of demographic ageing in the former group provided for differences reflected in crude death rates.

The most spectacular improvement in mortality conditions was in the infant mortality rate. During the period

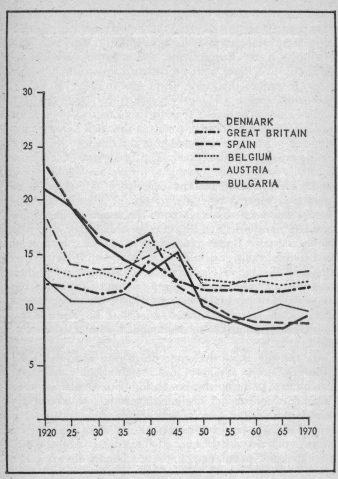

Fig. 7: Deaths per 1000 population: 1920-70

under consideration it was drastically reduced: in countries with originally excessive mortality by 5·5 to over 7 times, and in countries with moderately high mortality by 4 to 6 times. Examples of this impressive change are given in the table below.

TABLE 9: Infant mortality rate selected countries: 1920–70 (deaths of infants under 1 year of age per 1000 live births)

Country	1920/24	1930	1950	1970
Bulgaria	156·8	138·3	...	27·3
Czechoslovakia	160·0	134·5	77·6	22·1
Spain	148·2	118·0	69·8	27·8
Austria	141·6	99·5	66·1	25·9
United Kingdom	79·2	63·1	31·4	18·6
Netherlands	74·4	50·9	25·2	12·7
Norway	53·3	45·6	28·2	13·7

A low infant mortality rate was a characteristic of Europe in the late 1960s, with a few exceptions only, e.g. Yugoslavia and Albania. The percentage share of infants in total mortality was drastically reduced too. While, for example, in Bulgaria in the early 1920s over one-quarter of all deaths were those of infants, in the Netherlands in the late 1960s infant deaths accounted for less than one-twentieth of all the deaths.

Analytic methods for the study of infant mortality were developed further during the period under consideration. Considering pre-, intra-, and early post-natal mortality as 'three phases forming one pathogenic unit', Peller suggested that 'perinatal mortality' really belonged to the study of infant mortality. Bourgeois-Pichat made a distinction between endogenous and exogenous causes of infant death. A widely accepted classification distinguished between the neonatal and post-neonatal mortality. It was observed that, in all the societies that have experienced a mortality decline, the post-neonatal component has fallen much faster than the neonatal one.[8] It was suggested that in countries in which infant mortality is very low, prenatal and intra-natal factors were the ones which predominantly determined the incidence of infant deaths.

Since it was originally high and it affected the youngest age group, the fall in infant mortality produced significant

[8] According to Peller, infant mortality per 1000 born alive has declined in Vienna from 1910–14 to 1959–62 as follows: during the first week from 29 to 22, during second to fourth week from 24 to 2·5, during first year without first month from 92 to 8.

effects on the expectation of life at birth. By the turn of the century, life expectancy at birth for males was around 39 years in Austria, Bulgaria and Czechoslovakia, and that of females around 41 years. In England and Wales, the Netherlands, Norway and Sweden it ranged from 51 to 55 years and from 53 to 57 years, respectively. Progress was impressive after World War I, and particularly after World War II. However, the extension of life expectance of males was slower than that of females, resulting in marked and increasing differences between the sexes. This process was obviously affected by recent trends in which sex differentials have increased, particularly after the age of 45 years.

TABLE 10: Expectation of life at birth selected countries: early 1930s and late 1960s

Country	Early 1930s		Late 1960s	
	male	female	male	female
Bulgaria	45·9	46·6	68·8	72·7
Czechoslovakia	51·9	55·2	67·3	73·6
Spain	48·7	51·9	67·3	71·9
Austria	54·5	58·5	66·5	73·3
England and Wales	58·7	62·9	68·7	74·9

It is obvious that countries with a lower initial life expectation had a better chance to extend it. During the thirty-year period, the average annual gain in expectation of life for males was in Spain, 0·6 years; in Bulgaria, 0·59; in Czechoslovakia, 0·4; in Austria, 0·32 and in England and Wales, 0·3 years. That for females was 0·67 years in Bulgaria and Spain; 0·5 in Czechoslovakia; and 0·3 years in England and Wales and Austria. Women had a 0·7 year higher life expectancy than men in the 1930s (Bulgaria) and 4·2 years (England and Wales), while in the 1960s it ranged between 3·9 years (Bulgaria) and 6·8 years (Austria).

In Europe of the late 1960s there were no large differences in the expectation of life at birth (see fig. 8). Virtually all the countries have reached a high life expectancy – over 66 years for men and over 70 years for women. There were only a few exceptions with male life expectancy at birth of less than 65 years, and that of females less than 69 years, namely Albania, Portugal and Yugoslavia.

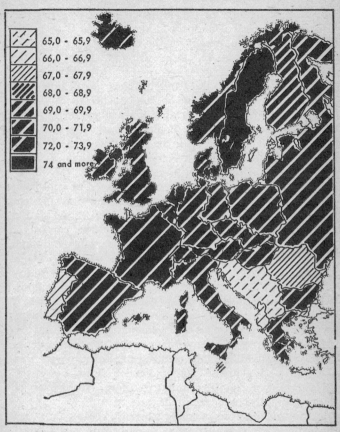

| 65,0 - 65,9 |
| 66,0 - 66,9 |
| 67,0 - 67,9 |
| 68,0 - 68,9 |
| 69,0 - 69,9 |
| 70,0 - 71,9 |
| 72,0 - 73,9 |
| 74 and more |

*Fig. 8: Expectation of life at birth: 1965-70
in years for both sexes*

The underlying factors of the improved health and mortality conditions were manifold. The control of environment, a higher standard of living and better nutrition, medical progress and public health measures, and the consequent change in causes of death have all contributed

to the prolongation of life, although in varying degrees.
During the period under consideration there were no
famines in Europe, except for the mass famine during the
Civil War in Russia. The last epidemic in Europe, known
as 'Spanish influenza', was recorded in 1918. The severity
of the disease and the complications (bronchitis and
pneumonia) were great and in consequence there was an
extremely high rate of mortality, particularly in Portugal
(40·8 per thousand), Italy, Spain, Bulgaria (35 to 32 per
thousand) and Serbia. With the exception of the Spanish
Civil War and World War II there were no violent man-
made conditions for massive mortality.

Among the specific health measures aimed at improving
health and preventing disease those intended to prevent
infectious diseases are of particular interest. A United
Nations study has found in 1963 that 'the control of
infectious diseases has played a leading part in the decline
in mortality. Scarlet fever, diphtheria, measles and whoop-
ing cough, diseases which formerly caused high mortality
in childhood, have declined considerably . . . Tuberculosis,
which a few decades ago ranked first as a cause of death, is
now of slight numerical importance in advanced countries,
owing to the effectiveness of vaccination and new drugs . . .
Measures employed in accordance with the International
Sanitary Regulations have confined small-pox, plague and
cholera to a few areas.' The eradication of malaria in the
Mediterranean countries initiated before World War II
was successfully completed in the early 1950s.

Aetiological aspects of falling mortality became thus very
important, although difficult to study because of statistical
problems and deficiencies. The international classification
of causes of disease and death produced by Bartillon in 1893
has been revised several times during the last fifty years,
and health statistics have been compiled by the World
Health Organisation. The 1963 United Nations study
grouped all diseases according to 'their resistance to medical
progress and public health measures' into five categories:
I. infectious and parasitic diseases and respiratory diseases,
II. cancer, III. diseases of the circulatory system, IV.

accidents and violence, and V. other diseases. The findings of the study were later broadly confirmed by Pirc and Milat (1970) and Hansluwka and Smith (1971) and others.

It was agreed that mortality varied considerably by age, sex and nation, and that the importance of individual causes of death (in terms of rates and proportions) has significantly changed during the last fifty years. Mortality from infectious and parasitic diseases has been reduced to small proportions in all of Europe. While it is difficult to establish precisely the long-range trends in mortality caused by cancer, its increasing importance was often emphasised. Lung cancer was considered 'the only important form of cancer from which mortality is increasing'. There is statistical evidence, however, that cancer is the first or second important cause of death in many European countries. Cardiovascular and lung diseases have also increased their proportions in total mortality. Their long-range trend was summarised by Hansluwka and Smith as follows: 'a marked fall during the past fifty years at ages up to 44 years, largely stable rates in the age range 45–64 years and slightly rising rates at ages over 65 years.' Peace-time violence in the form of accidents, more particularly automobile accidents, is between the 4th and 6th most important killer in most of Europe. Automobile accidents increased particularly during the first thirty years of the century, then relatively slowly. However, in the countries of recent automobile boom, this cause of death has recorded growing importance. It should be added that all these changes in mortality pattern were associated with a general decline in other causes of death, control of which became more effective over the decades.

PUBLIC HEALTH MEASURES

Governmental interference in health matters and disease control has a long history, but the modern concept of public health mainly belongs to the twentieth century. The application of medicine and hygiene by state agencies with the objective of preventing disease and promoting health has experienced a two-fold expansion during the last 50 years: first with regard to its scope, and second in view of the number of states which have declared it a national policy. Health legislation gradually became an important tool of health policy[9] as it regulated fundamental aspects of life and death. There was no country in Europe of the late 1960s which did not have an elaborated system of health measures and agencies to implement them.

Owing to the increasing mobility of people, and to the growing international exchange of goods and services national measures did not seem sufficient. Already in the inter-war period the League of Nations had been active in various fields of medicine and public health. In 1948 the World Health Organisation was set up and all the European states became members. The Organisation was active and successful in checking some critical diseases (polio, cholera, malaria, tuberculosis, etc.), in international prevention of the spread of communicable diseases, in developing international conventions concerning sanitary and quarantine requirements and the like. In the mid-1960s, it extended the activities of its maternal and child health programme to family planning and contraception.

Prevention and control of disease and the postponement of death was universally considered a matter of governmental responsibility and national policy. Opinions regarding the extent of state involvement might have differed, but the responsibility of the state in principle was hardly questioned. Mortality was the only component of population growth enjoying such a privileged status. Neither fertility nor migration were considered by all the European nations

[9] Examples of areas where legislation has been passed are: standards of public health, inspection of persons and goods entering the country, vaccination and inoculation, quarantine, control of communicable diseases, supervision of purity of water and food supply, sanitary regulations, licensing persons who dispense health services, regulations concerning hospitals and clinics, the maintenance of hospitals for mental disease and tuberculosis and some other health institutions, protection at work, health insurance, registration of vital events, legal acts concerning international health conventions, etc.

an appropriate domain of state interference. Consequently, there were no internationally adopted standards, measures and conventions with regard to fertility and migration. The consequences of this are difficult to discuss, for no thorough evaluation has been made of this apparent inconsistency.

The relative importance of health measures cannot be overstated, particularly in conditions in which low mortality prevails. It is true that, in order to achieve low mortality, the combination of a satisfactory standard of living, control of environment, universal education and adequate public health measures are needed. But, besides the improvements of economic and social conditions in most of Europe during the last fifty years, health measures were indispensable to bring infant mortality down to 15 per thousand live births or to prolong life expectancy to over 70 years.[10]

The concept of 'satisfactory health services' encompassing a variety of activities aimed at the promotion of health has developed during the last thirty or forty years. In the postwar period most European countries have adopted a systematic approach to health problems through central administration and health planning. An indication of the progress of health services is the increase in the supply of physicians: in France the number of inhabitants per physician decreased from 1500 in 1938 to 1100 in 1954 and to 854 in 1967; the corresponding numbers for Sweden were 2200, 1300 and 840 respectively. The 1967 population-physician ratio was 933 in the United Kingdom, in Yugoslavia 922 and in Bulgaria and the USSR as low as 568 and 391 respectively. Health centres and services of various kinds became more available and easier to reach, because of decentralised schemes and/or better transportation. Hospital facilities were improved in both qualitative and quantitative terms. By the end of the 1960s there were 175 inhabitants per hospital bed in Yugoslavia, 140 in

[10] There have been a number of papers published on the subject. A concise evaluation of the development of health measures relative to mortality decline was published in the United Nations study on recent trends of mortality in the world (1963).

Bulgaria, 126 in France and 112 in England; the ratio was as low as 89 in the USSR and 69 in Sweden.

Health insurance systems which were gradually developed in European countries 'have made medical services accessible to ever larger proportions of the population'. In addition to private schemes, both commercial or non-profit-making, a compulsory system concerning accidents and sickness was established first in Germany in 1883–4. After World War I similar compulsory systems were established in France, England, the USSR and Scandinavia. The British National Health Insurance Act of 1946, which came into effect in 1948, introduced the most comprehensive compulsory medical care plan in the west. Compulsory health insurance of lesser scope was introduced, or extended to new groups of population in other countries of the west. Eastern European socialist states have since developed national health insurance programmes, most of which cover the whole of the population. The availability of health services was thus supplemented with a fuller accessibility to these services. Benefits of these developments were enjoyed by those segments of the population which otherwise could not have been provided with satisfactory medical care.

Among the specific health measures which have contributed to the decline in mortality, the control of infectious disease has already been mentioned. Another important factor was the progressive development of maternal and child health services, thanks to which maternal and infant mortality had been reduced to low levels in almost all the European countries. Improvements in environmental sanitation in general, and water supply and sewage disposal in particular, were also important factors in health improvement. But, while traditional aspects of environment protection were well under control, increasing water and air pollution had become a matter of growing concern since the 1960s. Vaccination and other large-scale disease-control campaigns were instituted as a part of public health routine. Thanks to health education of the public, which became widespread during recent decades, the cooperation of individuals and families in health activities was promoted and brought to satisfactory levels. The progress in curative medicine and the availability of new drugs was 'responsible for the saving of a great number of lives'. While praising the progress made during the last decades, the 1963 United Nations study also established that the modern sanitary and medical techniques do not rely any longer on general economic development to the extent that they did in the nineteenth century.

INTERNATIONAL MIGRATION

The Great Migration, which since the seventeenth century has taken some 60 million Europeans to other continents, is perhaps the most significant single migration stream in the world's history. It has produced lasting economic social and political effects in both Europe and the rest of the globe, and has facilitated the diffusion of European civilisation throughout the world. Mass emigration from Europe saw its climax in the early twentieth century, a steep decline during World War I, and its halt during the Depression years. But this was by no means the end of mass movements of European people. 'As a means of adaptation to varying local needs and opportunities', a United Nations study pointed out, 'the importance of migration is probably as great as it ever has been, but its predominant character has undergone much change.'

The vital forces of Europe, which populated three continents and provided for a significant population growth at home were of continuous interest to researchers. In the mid-1930s Carr-Saunders spoke of 'the population situation in those countries which collectively constitute Europe overseas'. In the United States and Australia the study of European emigration also attracted a great deal of time and attention from historians, economists and demographers.

In addition to international migration, internal migration and urbanisation also became an important area of demography and statistics. Methods were gradually developed which facilitated better analyses of what happened in the past and improved the knowledge of current migration and urban growth. More recently, after a slight decline in migration study, students of migration are inclined to interpret migration as a single process in which the peoples and the societies of both the sending and the receiving areas are involved. Overseas, intra-continental and the internal migrations, were looked upon as specific types of movements with, however, a good deal of interdependence. But, owing to statistical problems and the complexity of the subject, it was rather difficult to assess the overall migration process and its changing pattern in twentieth-century Europe. This problem affects the present discussion too. Instead of approaching migration as a single though varied process, international migration will be considered first in this section, and the questions relative to rural–urban movements will be discussed in the next section.

AN OVERVIEW

Notwithstanding statistical deficiencies, there is a great deal of agreement among the scholars with regard to the change in European migration during the twentieth century. Maselli summarised the changes in both the extent and character as follows. 'Large spontaneous movements took place up to 1914 (perhaps 20 million); sizeable migration continued from 1920 to 1929 (5 million); movements dropped between 1930 and 1939 due to the world economic depression and the political regimes prevailing in some parts of Europe (only 1 million); millions of people were displaced or forced to migrate during World War II; several international organisations (UNRRA, IRO, etc.) helped many displaced persons to repatriate or resettle between 1944 and 1951 (8 million); both migrants and refugees were resettled by ICEM[11] from 1952 to the present time (1,800,000); many persons moved especially from Africa and from Indonesia, as a consequence of decolonialisation; many millions of migrants moved within Europe or to Europe from 1958 (9 million).'

The major change in migration has occurred during

[11] The Intergovernmental Committee for European Migration.

the last twenty years, a very short period indeed. According to Maselli, a formidable development of internal and intra-continental migration in Europe was a new trend, which was accompanied by the growing interdependence of internal, intra-continental and overseas migration. In addition, there was an increasing recognition that a better distribution of human resources was an indispensable factor of development. This had an important policy implication, namely 'the establishment and functioning of internationally organised and assisted migration' which never before existed in such proportions.

Indeed, the change in European migration was both profound and rapid. Over three centuries Europe had been known as an emigration continent. During the period under consideration inflows and outflows were in balance at several points in time: Europe apparently became self-sufficient and developed an impressive intra-continental migration. More recently Europe even became an immigration continent in spite of sizeable movements of Europeans to Northern America and Oceania.

With the exception of the war and post-war periods, both the overseas and the intra-continental migration affecting Europe were basically determined by economic factors. Promising economic prospects and employment opportunities in the receiving countries coincided in the sending countries with poverty and/or aspirations for better living. Complementarity between demand for, and the supply of labour was the chief factor in migration. Whenever such complementarity existed, policies favoured international movements; whenever it was broken, policies became restrictive. The policies of the receiving countries had a decisive effect in both cases.

Ethnic, national, political and ideological factors played an important role in international movements particularly after World War I, the civil wars in Russia and Spain, and on the eve of and after World War II. Changes in national boundaries, the emergence of new nations, the deliberate policy of the Nazi Government in Germany, and the revolutionary change affecting political and social structures in the east were the immediate causes of massive population transfers in the last fifty years. Non-economic factors – national feelings and political or ideological affiliation must have been strong motives for people to move at these three critical points of the period.

OVERSEAS EMIGRATION

Europe entered the twentieth century by sending to other continents more people than ever before mainly from what was termed the regions of 'new migration'.[12]

TABLE 11 : Average annual overseas gross emigration (in thousands)

Date	Total	Regions of 'old' migration	Regions of 'new' migration
1901–1915	1280·3	300·3	979·9
1916–1920	405·5	123·9	281·8
1921–1930	592·5	274·3	318·3
1931–1939	139·1	55·2	84·1
1946–1963	585·0	353·0	232·0

Source:1901–39: Dudley Kirk, *Europe's Population in the Interwar Years.* 1946–63: W. D. Borry, *The Growth and Control of World Population.*

In the early twentieth century, the Americas and Oceania offered attractive opportunities and needed additional population and manpower to develop abundant resources. This in combination with poverty and agrarian over-population particularly of southern and eastern Europe was the main factor which led to the unprecedentedly large migration. Development in overseas transportation and in communication made migration an acceptable proposition, and an easier undertaking than before. In general, there were no governmental measures to prevent emigration from the sending countries of Europe. On the other side, overseas governments favoured immigration, and imposed only

[12] Regions of 'new migration' include Italy, Austria, Hungary, Czechoslovakia, Russia, Poland, Finland, Baltic countries, Spain, Portugal and Balkans. Regions of 'old migration' consist of the British Isles, Germany, Norway, Sweden, Denmark, France, Switzerland and the Low Countries.

limited control on grounds of health and legal considerations. This was a *laissez faire* situation in which immigrants, including those emigrating for only a limited period of time, took all the risks with the hope that they would pay off through better opportunities.

War conditions from 1915 to 1918 practically blocked emigration from Central Europe, Germany, Russia and Balkans, and reduced the number of immigrants from the rest of Europe to a half and even a third the pre-war level. In the post-war period the factors which led to emigration in Europe were affected by war losses, the Russian Revolution, and the hopes for improvements prevalent in some newly established national states. But, in general there was no major change in the economy and demography of Europe which affected the propensity to migrate overseas. The main factor of the migration shrinkage in the 1920s was a restrictive policy of the United States first introduced by the 1921 Quota Law. This temporary legislation was replaced by the 1924 Immigration Restriction Act which drastically reduced the immigration quota and discriminated against migrants from south-eastern Europe.

The collapse of the economy and mass unemployment were factors which reduced migration to a minimum during the Depression years. The United States, which was the single largest country of immigration virtually ceased to receive European migrants. In Europe too, unemployment was large and France and Belgium were not able to provide immigrants with jobs. The prospects in their native land, although poor, must have seemed better to many emigrants than the urban unemployment abroad. Many moved back to their countries of origin during this period. The economic recovery of the mid-1930s was neither sufficient nor long-lasting enough to stimulate new migration. Immigration policies were still restrictive in the receiving countries and new policies discouraging emigration were introduced in Italy and Germany.

World War II imposed on most of Europe new policies which arose because of the expansionist objectives of the National-Socialist regime in Germany. The emigration of

Jews, the transfer of German minorities from Central Europe to Germany, prisoners of war, political prisoners and the forced labour were the various aspects of forced migration caused by the war. However, by the end of war and immediately after new factors intervened. The collapse of Germany gave rise to a large westward migration of Germans and those who had supported German occupation. Political change in eastern Europe was another factor which significantly affected migration. Finally, the change in the political map of eastern Europe caused additional migration in Poland, East Germany, the Soviet Union, Czechoslovakia and Hungary, and to a lesser extent Italy and Yugoslavia. Characteristic of most of the war-related migration was a total confusion, a lack of the absorbative capacity needed to accommodate migrants, high political tension, and an unprecedented number of displaced persons and refugees.

In his penetrating analysis of European migration Borrie proposed that 'by the 1930s the complementarity of the *emigration* needs of European countries and the *immigration* needs of the New World had been broken'. After the war there was a coincidence of several factors which, according to Borrie, gave impulses to a new wave of migration. 'The demographic profile' of Europe was not such as to encourage overseas movements, and the overseas opinion was rather cautious. 'The one area in which these overseas countries felt morally bound to act concerned the resettlement of displaced persons' who were not able to find a home in western Europe. This factor 'had an unexpected result of reopening channels of international migration', said Borrie. Since millions of people were involved, overseas migration from Europe to other continents occurred again in large numbers. An additional aspect of the immediate post-war migration was that most of it was assisted and organised by international efforts.

Reconstruction of western economies in the early 1950s was followed by an impressive economic expansion in the late 1950s and early 1960s. The high demand for labour needed for further expansion was initially met by inflows of emigrants from eastern Europe, particularly eastern

Germany. It was evident that the economic growth of western countries depended to a large extent on imported labour and particularly on those skills which were not locally available. In 1957 the European Economic Community established by six western European nations, proclaimed, *inter alia*, the free movement of capital and labour. The establishment of an international labour market was, at least as a principle, far-reaching, but had at that time limited migration effects. Another important factor was, according to Livi Bacci, 'the increasing supply of manpower from the mediterranean countries' which 'has found new outlets heading northwards to the more developed European countries'. This complementarity and the crucial reorientation of European migration will be discussed at a later stage.

When we consider the source of European emigration during the last fifty years two distinct features can be observed: there were continuously high proportions of emigrants from the British Isles, and declining proportions of those who were emigrating from the regions of 'new migration'.

The percentage share of the latter group was in 1910–14 80 per cent, in the 1920s 54 per cent, in the 1930s 60 per cent, and in 1946–63 40 per cent. The 1924 Emigration Act of the United States allocated to the 'new migration' group of countries only 16 per cent of the annual immigration quota. This was an important factor in the decline of emigration from this group and consequently of total emigration. Another factor was that in the 1920s the Soviet Union ceased to send emigrants abroad which, with a similar policy adopted in the 1950s by Poland, Czechoslovakia and other socialist countries, drastically reduced the area of emigration.

With a share in total emigration of 22 to 30 per cent at varying periods, the British Isles was the most important single emigration region throughout the last fifty years. Next was Italy with a share of 16 to 21 per cent, and then the Iberian Peninsula with about 12 per cent. German emigration was half as large as the Italian, except in the post-war years. Emigration from Russia was the third or fourth largest in the past, but almost stopped during World War I and never appeared again. Taken together the four largest emigration regions, *viz.* the British Isles, Italy, Iberian Peninsula and Germany had the lion's share in overseas emigration: 77 per cent in the 1920s, 70 per cent in the 1930s and 75 per cent in the post-war period. Smaller countries where emigration was common, such as the Netherlands and Sweden, never had a large share in European emigration in spite of the fact that it was important in relation to the size of their population.

Among all the people who left Europe about three-quarters went to the United States, over one-fifth to Latin America, one-tenth to Canada, and the rest to Oceania, Africa and Asia. In the post-war period the attraction of Australia has significantly increased, as a consequence of demand for labour and deliberate policy. Cultural and linguistic affiliation, the early settlement of individual ethnic groups overseas, and the working of 'chain migration' played a definite role in the decisions made by individuals with regard to the choice of country of destination.

EUROPEAN INTER-CONTINENTAL
MIGRATION BALANCE

There is no reliable data on reverse migration, and statistics on immigration to Europe are lacking or suffer from serious deficiencies. There were at all points of time emigrants who decided to return to their homeland, and those who have gone overseas for a limited period of time only. Reasons for return migration and repatriation must have been very many and must have differed at various points of the overseas migration cycle. Kirk has found statistically significant return migration during the 1930s, most probably as a consequence of the reduced economic opportunity overseas and the Great Depression. 'Considerable backwash from overseas' was recorded in Portugal, 'large return balance' in Spain, as well as in Sweden, the United Kingdom and elsewhere.

In her summary of migration statistics for 1960–6 Adams suggested that return migration from North America to United Kingdom and Germany was high, but return to Italy was slight. Return movements from Latin America amounted to over half of the immigration figure. She concluded that 'with employment opportunities beckoning from the nearby countries of Western Europe, Latin America seems to have lost much of its power of attraction for prospective emigrants from Southern Europe.' Adams also estimated a net immigration to Europe of 2 million, consisting mainly of people coming from Asia, Africa and West Indies. Half of it was 'repatriation of nationals of European countries following the gaining of independence by former colonies'. About 900 thousand French citizens moved from North Africa and settled in France. The other half was economically motivated immigration, out of which 500 thousand emigrants came from India, Pakistan and West Indies to the United Kingdom. The rest of this intercontinental migration was at close range from northern Africa to France, and from Turkey to West Germany and some other countries.

The final results of overall inter-continental migration affecting Europe's population in individual periods are rather difficult to describe. Kirk's and Adams' migration balances referred to earlier, give an indication of its magnitude, but their figures must be considered with due caution for reasons given in their valuable papers. Through emigration Europe might have lost in the 1920s some 5 million people. For the 1930s the estimates suggest some one-quarter of a million as a net loss, which however appears to be pretty low. For the 1950s net emigration was estimated by Adams at 2·6 million. Considering that most of the resettlement of displaced persons took place between 1944 and 1950, this seems a plausible figure. Net immigration to Europe from other continents in 1960–6 amounted to 1·7 million.

The preceding analysis gives an insight into the changing pattern of European overseas migration and an explanation of how Europe became in 1960–6 a continent of immigration. Whether this situation is likely to last is difficult to say, but two facts must be kept in mind while speculating about the future. Repatriation of European citizens was a once only occurrence, which could hardly be repeated for obvious reasons. As far as economically motivated immigration was concerned, two different trends have occurred. In the United Kingdom a Commonwealth Immigration Act came into effect in 1962 aiming at the restriction of immigration from the countries of the Commonwealth. This policy, if pursued, would have marked effects on migration into the United Kingdom and consequently into Europe. On the other hand, Germany, France and some other countries have kept doors open to immigrants from North Africa and the Middle East. Effects of these policies can hardly be evaluated in view of the short time and limited experience, and a possible change in factors which determine governmental policies. But, whatever policies and practices may develop in the future, the fact is that Europe was faced with a new source immigration, which was somehow, more economically than socially, accommodated.

INTRA-EUROPEAN MIGRATION IN THE 1960s

The diverse pattern of European economic growth and demography was already affecting intercontinental migration in the inter-war period. If it had not exerted its full influence, it was mainly because of factors related to overseas migration in the 1920s and the economic and political event of the 1930s discussed earlier. The west-bound migration of Germans after World War II was very significant for the economic growth of the Federal Republic, but this was not wholly the result of economic supply and demand in the labour force. The provision made in 1957 and later to stimulate movements of workers within the Common Market was also not pertinent, since only one country among the six had a surplus of labour. Real complementarity of interests and needs existed in principle between the north-west and most of south-east of Europe. Here again eastern Europe was excluded from the intra-continental migration process, since it belonged to another economic integration scheme, in which the USSR took part as well. Characteristic of this later integration was, *inter alia*, that it practically never promoted inter-country migration of population and the labour force. Consequently only the north-west and the south of Europe were involved with the exception of Albania.

The growth of intra-continental migration was primarily due to an increase in demand. In the north-western countries there was not a sufficient supply of labour to meet the requirements of the rapidly growing industries. Declining rates of natural increase in the past, the changing age structure and a number of social factors had all affected the supply by the 1950s. Among the social factors that were particularly important were the expansion of schooling, earlier retirement, the extension of paid holidays and reduction of hours at work, as well as less underemployment in agriculture which used to be a source for low-skill and low-paid jobs. On the other hand, in the south, economic growth was fast also, but not fast enough to absorb high annual increments in manpower and the backlog of underemployment in agriculture. Differences in standards of living and wage levels were great, and made it possible for north-western countries to attract workers from the south.

There were a variety of secondary factors to support massive migration. Short distances between the sending and receiving countries, cheap transportation, liberal passports control, the possibility of supporting families from abroad, and the internationalisation of the labour market have all contributed to intra-continental mobility. Those were also among the reasons for which the migration of the 1960s had developed specific features constituting within most of Europe a new migration pattern.

Neither current statistics nor population census data give complete and accurate information on these movements. In the mid-1960s some international organisations, particularly the ECE and OECD have drawn the attention of the European public to the international significance of the new migration trend. Later in the decade Livi Bacci prepared a paper for a population conference organised by the Council of Europe in 1971. He proposed that the entire immigrant population in eight European countries[13] 'can be estimated at between 8·50 and 9 million, and active population at between 5·50 and 6 million. Of these figures, more than half come from the Mediterranean countries of emigration,[14] while perhaps one-third concentrated in France and Great Britain, come from extra-European countries.' Austria, Belgium, the Federal Republic of Germany, France, the Netherlands and Switzerland each had over 50 per cent of foreigners coming from the Mediterranean countries. Livi Bacci further estimated that as much as 500 to 900 thousand Mediterranean workers leave their country every year, and that most of them return home after a shorter or a longer period of work abroad. Italy showed an uninterrupted decreasing trend throughout the 1960s; Greece and the Iberian Peninsula followed an increasing trend which reached its peak in the mid-1960s; emigration from Turkey and Yugoslavia began only in the early 1960s and increased rapidly. Livi Bacci also observed that 'emigrant workers make up about 50 per cent on the average of the potential increase of the labour force in their countries', however with higher proportions in Yugoslavia, Italy and Spain, and very low in Turkey.

The migration of Mediterranean workers to the north-west became thus the most important component of international migration in the 1960s. This was a short to medium distance migration often accompanied by the rural–urban shifts. Most of it was of limited duration, or at least so intended. Few migrants took their families to the country of destination. Unskilled and semi-skilled manpower was the major component. There was a very high proportion of young people among the migrants and among migrants from such countries as Turkey, Greece and Yugoslavia there was also a high proportion of males.

[13] Austria, Belgium, the Federal Republic of Germany, France, Great Britain, Netherlands, Sweden and Switzerland.

[14] Greece, Italy, Portugal, Spain, Turkey and Yugoslavia.

It seems that this migration pattern used to suit economically both the sending and the receiving countries. As the migration became larger, governments had to take policy positions. There was apparently little opposition to migration, mainly on the ground of economic consideration. But the economic advantages of temporary migration were accompanied by social disadvantages. Integration of migrants was difficult under such conditions; isolated enclaves and ethnic ghettos were a well known aspect of it. The urgent desire to save in order to send more money home had ill-effects among the migrants such as poor housing, malnutrition, and social isolation. Isolation was further stimulated by the lack of receptivity: the local community often considered migrants a menace who abused the social infrastructure and locally provided facilities. Back at home many problems came to be considered migration-associated problems such as unsolved questions relating to social insurance of those who worked abroad and the health insurance for their families, broken families, education of children and the like. It was, therefore, not surprising that in the mid-1960s the trade unions of both sending and receiving countries voiced concern over the social aspects of temporary migration. These were shared by several governments, by the International Labour Organisation and some other inter-governmental organisations. The consequence was that by the end of the 1960s there was a great deal of study, projection, and search for new solutions to regulate inter-European migration in the coming decades.

NATIONAL MIGRATION BALANCES

The story of external migration of individual European nations was one of demographic change and economic effort, and in many cases one of response to important political events. If we think, however, of the individual we must realise the variety of pressures to which he was exposed before making a decision to move from his native country. There were of course exceptions, but for the majority of migrants moves were imposed by hardship and the necessity and desire to improve their life and fortunes. Times were hard for migrants particularly during the wars and immediately after and during the Depression. In general, it seems that conditions relating to peaceful migration were better in the 1960s than in earlier decades, both from the point of view of facilities and of treatment. But even in the last decade the conditions offered were far from satisfactory to all those who moved. In spite of humanitarian consideration and the governmental intervention movement from one country to another was not easy to make because of the economic, social and bureaucratic obstacles interposed.

The inter-war migration balance of all the European countries except France and to some extent Belgium was affected by the factors relating to recovery and the shrinkage of overseas movements. The post-war migration balance of individual countries seems to be more complex, because of the change in migration pattern which was discussed earlier.

In the 1920s all the countries listed in the table below used to send more people than they received, with only four exceptions. According to Kirk's data, France was the largest receiver of immigrants who came either from Poland, Italy, Spain, Portugal and North Africa to seek jobs, or from Russia and Turkey to seek asylum. The sources of migration to Belgium were mainly Poland, Italy and Central Europe; it was basically directed to the mining regions of the country. The Netherlands had acquired some population from Germany and Central Europe. After the end of the war in 1922 there were about one million Greek refugees who came from Asia Minor to Greece, and several hundred thousands of Turks who went from Greece to Asia Minor. This was the largest war-related population transfer in the 1920s through which Greece gained half a million people. Transfers related to World War I and to some extent to the Balkan Wars have also taken place between Bulgaria, Romania, Greece, Yugoslavia and Turkey. There were smaller moves of German minority from Central Europe to Germany too.

TABLE 12: Migration balances of European countries: 1920 to 1960–6
(in thousands of population)

	1920s	1930s	1950–60	1960–6
Federal Republic of Germany	−20[a]	+65[a]	+273	+396
France	+195	−21	−108	+318
Netherlands	+2	−1	−14	+12
Belgium	+14	+4	+5	+30
Austria	−3	−21	−14	−1
Switzerland	−6	−0·5	+30	+65
Luxemburg	...	...	+6	+2
Italy	−104	−60	−117	−94
Spain	−30	−	−82	−160
Yugoslavia	−20	−4	−58	−18
Portugal	−1	+6	−66	−39
Greece	+69	−7	−19	−45
Malta	...	...	−4	−7
Poland	−95	−13	−19	−26
Romania	−15	−8	−13	−19
German Democratic Republic	−9[a]	+20[a]	−187	−113
Czechoslovakia	−20	−4	−	−1
Hungary	−7	+7	−16	−
Bulgaria	−1	−14	−16	−1
United Kingdom	−65	+24	−4	+46
Sweden	−9	+6	+9	+21
Denmark	−4	+6	−5	+2
Finland	−1	+2	−7	−5
Norway	−8	−0·4	−1	−1
Ireland	−34	−11	−40	−24

[a] Rough estimates based on Kirk's data for pre-war Germany.

Source: 1920s and 1930s: Kirk, Dudley, *Europe's Population in the Interwar Years*; 1950–60 and 1960–6: Edith Adams, *International Migration Trends Affecting Europe in the 1960s*.

Out of 23 countries for which data is available 17 have sent large or significant numbers of emigrants overseas. Cross-ocean emigration was still the most important component of economically motivated migration. Some countries with a negative migration balance, such as the United Kingdom, used to send migrants to other countries while receiving immigrants from the neighbouring countries.

The migration flows in the 1930s are difficult to trace because of the complex and diverse conditions, which occurred in a short time-span due to such different factors as economic depression, revival of militant nationalism, racial and political persecution and the upheavals of war. Out of 23 countries eight had a positive migration balance and fifteen had experienced losses. In spite of the expulsion of the Jews and politically motivated emigration, Germany had the largest net gain attributable to migration. Gains were caused chiefly by the planned movements from Austria, the Sudetenland and some Danubian states. The United Kingdom's migration surplus consisted of return migration from overseas, immigration from Ireland, and later also from immigration of refugees. Excess of immigrants over emigrants in Sweden, Denmark, Finland and Portugal can be attributed mainly to return migration in the early 1930s associated with the Great Depression. Migration to Hungary from territories incorporated in 1940 and 1941 was large enough to offset moderate emigration.

Between 1931 and 1936, France, which had in the past been a country whose attraction for immigrants had been the strongest in Europe, experienced a net loss of some 100 thousand people. Poles returning to Poland were the largest group in the return-migration stream, followed by Spaniards and Portuguese. Belgium, another country of long immigration experience, also became less attractive as far as economic migrants were concerned. The surplus which was recorded between 1931 to 1938 included immigration between 1931 and 1932 and the entry of refugees from 1936. The migration of refugees from 'Germany after 1933 and from Spain after the Civil War, as well as those from Austria and other European countries occupied by Germany was difficult to follow and to evaluate.

After the war, more specifically in 1945–7, some 30 million people were repatriated by the United Nations Relief and Rehabilitation Administration. Between 1947 and 1951 the International Refugee Organisation resettled over a million of 'non-repatriable displaced persons'. About 700 thousand of these persons were from Germany and over

300 thousand from Poland. This migration is only in part
reflected in the above table.

In the 1950s migration was still over-shadowed by the
post-war situation, but also included new components of
peaceful development. During the decade there were only
six countries which have had a surplus of immigrants. The
Federal Republic of Germany became the country with the
largest net immigration, which was over 2·5 times as large
as net immigration into France. Switzerland's economy
depended a great deal on foreign labour as did the economy
of Luxemburg. Sweden also became an importer of foreign
labour, while immigration to Belgium was still moderate.

Migration motivated by factors other than economic
ones still persisted. The largest single stream was the west-
bound migration of Germans. The Democratic Republic of
Germany had experienced the largest loss due to migration
in both the 1950s and the 1960s, but many Germans moved
from other Central European countries too. Jewish emigrants
from a number of European countries went in appreciable
numbers to Israel and the USA. The Turkish minorities
from Yugoslavia, Bulgaria and perhaps from some other
countries again emigrated to settle in Turkey. In the mid-
1950s there was an outflow from Hungary to Austria and
some other western countries, most of which eventually
reached the USA. But, emigration motivated by non-
economic factors was already in the 1950s far less important
than that which took place on economic grounds. The
redistribution of manpower within Europe already in the
late 1950s contributed to the growth of the European
economy and has since gained a new and promising
significance.

Characteristic of the 1960–6 period was that nine north-
western countries had a migration surplus; that southern
Europe established itself as a region of temporary emigration
with, however, significant losses; that a few western
countries experienced only negligible change relating to
migration; and that three countries of eastern Europe had
losses of minor economic significance. We have seen already
how this change occurred, how it was affected by immi-

gration from other continents, and how it established new relations between the south and the north-west.

Of course, it is not appropriate to generalise on observations made over so short a period of time, but nevertheless a few comments seem necessary. There were in the 1960s some nine countries in Europe whose demographic profile and economic activity required additional labour from abroad. All of these were highly industrialised countries, many of them with a high density of population. There were some eight countries that had a labour surplus which could not possibly be productively engaged because of insufficient productive capacity. Some of these countries have provided an increasing supply of labour to foreign markets, while in other countries local demand for labour was such as to cut into the labour surplus which used to emigrate. Complementarity between these two groups was obvious, and the labour–capital relation issue was mainly solved through the mobility of labour. This was how intra-European migration became an acceptable proposition, at least in northern, southern and western European countries. Demographic–economic relations in eastern Europe and the Soviet Union had also demonstrated a certain degree of complementarity. However, there was no international migration of labour force within these regions, with the exception of experiments of negligible economic significance. Migration of labour was not considered at all until only recently, when Professor Minkov of Bulgaria spoke of 'manpower migration among socialist countries as an objective necessity'.

The issue of intra-continental migration appeared to be surrounded by a series of questions. The economic benefits and social cost relating to migration, mobility of labour versus mobility of capital, migration as a factor of integration of Europe, environmental problems in high density countries, and the most fundamental questions of human well-being and the mobility of modern man were among those that urgently required an answer. Some of the questions have been raised in political and academic circles, but no innovatory theory and policy nor even a major contribution to it was produced before the end of the sixties.

URBAN POPULATION GROWTH AND CONCENTRATION

During the twentieth century there has been an impressive growth of cities and urban population throughout Europe and the USSR. The older conglomerates of heavily urbanised regions in south-east England, the Low Countries, the western portion of Germany and the northern part of France were supplemented with the recent large concentrations of industries and population in Czechoslovakia, Romania, Poland, the south of Moscow, the Dnieper region and elsewhere. But, in spite of this there still has been a great deal of diversity in Europe with regard to the settlement pattern and the urban–rural distribution of population. The difference was particularly visible in the countryside; it was less in the urban zones. A countryside inhabited by a small number of farmers and a great deal of non-agricultural workers prevailing in some north-western countries coexisted with the villages of traditional type and occupation in most of the Balkans, Spain and Portugal as well as in the Alps. Differences in the countryside with regard to physical aspects of settlement, employment pattern of population, and the spread of urbanism as mode of life were still persistent and marked. These were accompanied by the differences between urban and rural areas. There is no doubt that the sharp differences in the 1920s became smaller in the late 1960s. In some countries the distinction between the urban and the rural almost lost its meaning, while in other countries it was still essential for the understanding of human conditions.

When considering the national variations and the change during the period, one can appreciate the difficulty of compiling internationally and historically comparable statistics. Urban–rural population statistics must be read with a great deal of caution, and with an awareness of the bias built in. Thanks to the pioneering work of the United

Nations, carried out by Kingsley Davis and others, it is possible to trace with a certain confidence the change in urban–rural population. There are two concepts of urban population applied in international studies of urbanisation. The 'agglomerated population' concept refers to population living in localities with 20 thousand inhabitants and more. 'Nationally defined' urban population relies on the national definition used in individual countries. The latter concept does not ensure comparability, but seems to reflect national conditions better.[15]

THE OVERALL CHANGE

The reputation of Europe as a continent of older urbanisation derives to a great extent from the urban tradition of her north-western regions. Already by 1920 there were 27 big cities with a population exceeding 500 thousand in these regions; in 1960 there were 35 such cities. In 1920 London had 7 million inhabitants, Paris almost 5 million, Berlin over 4 million, Manchester 2·3 million, and Vienna, Brussels, Birmingham, Glasgow, Hamburg, Leeds and Liverpool had each more than 1 million. The south and east were much less urbanised: in 1920 there were only 12 big cities, and Budapest was the only one that had over 1 million. In 1960 there were 22 cities above the 500 thousand limit, out of which 11 had more than 1 million inhabitants. The change was still faster in the USSR: Moscow with 950 thousand and Leningrad with 720 thousand inhabitants were the only two big cities in 1920. In 1940 there were 12 big cities, in 1960 as many as 27, and in 1970, 30, according to Soviet statistics. Out of these there were 10 cities with a population of over 1 million.

The level of urbanisation was also affected by the growth of cities of a medium size and of smaller towns. The systems

[15] The figure for urban population of the United Kingdom was in 1950 according to the 'agglomerated' concept 34·8 million, according to 'national' definition 39·2 million. In West Germany it was 21·9 and 33·9 million respectively; in Italy 19·2 and 19·5 million; in the USSR 50 and 71·2 million. For technical discussion see: United Nations, *Growth of the World's Urban and Rural Population, 1920–2000.*

of towns and cities widely differed. Hungary, France and Austria were known by the importance of their capital cities which have attracted a large proportion of the economic activity and national population. In the United Kingdom, Italy, the Soviet Union, Belgium and the Netherlands strong regional centres, in addition to the capital cities, have absorbed much of the national population and economic activity. Switzerland and Yugoslavia followed a decentralised pattern of urbanisation, which was perhaps related to the decentralised organisation of the state. But, irrespective of national peculiarities urban concentration was a dominant feature of Europe in the late 1960s.

Immigration was the chief source of supply of population to urban areas. Modern urban growth was associated with the centralising power of manufacturing, trade and banking, and the expansion of public administration. There is no full agreement on the cause-and-effect relationship between concentration of people and industrialisation. Indeed, the process was neither uniform nor continuous, and the operating 'pull' factors must have been diversely supported by the 'push' factors. But, if association between economic and urban growth existed, it does not necessarily mean that industrial advancement and population concentration have both kept in step and reached the same levels.

THE URBAN–RURAL POPULATION GROWTH

Between 1920 and 1970, the rural population of Europe virtually remained at the same level, while urban population almost doubled. In the Soviet Union the rural population slightly declined from 1920 to 1970 (over 7 per cent), but urban population increased more than six times. This was a very rapid growth, which, taking place in a predominantly rural milieu, was basically caused by rapid industrialisation.

The process of urban–rural redistribution of population was correlated with growing mobility, both occupational and spatial. Kirk's analyses of migration occurring in Europe between the two wars points to the complexity of internal, intra-continental and overseas migration, and the variety of demographic, economic, social and political factors involved. The post-war redistribution was even more complex, because of the larger number of people taking part in migration and because of a change in the underlying factors. A summary of growth and redistribution of urban and rural population in Europe and the USSR is given by the following statistics.[16]

TABLE 13: The growth and distribution of urban and rural population (population in millions)

| | Europe | | | | Soviet Union | | | |
	1920	1940	1960	1970	1922	1940	1960	1970
Urban	150	200	245	292	22	63	104	136
Rural	175	178	178	170	114	131	109	106
Percentage of urban	46	53	58	63	16	33	49	56

Between the wars urban population grew at an average annual rate of 1·5 per cent in Europe, and in the USSR at a rate of 6 per cent. Rural population was stagnant in Europe and grew at a rate of 0·8 per cent per annum in the Soviet Union. In the 1960s, the average annual rate of growth of urban population was in Europe 1·8 per cent and in the Soviet Union 2·7 per cent, and the rate of decline of rural population —0·5 per cent in the former and —0·3 per cent in the latter. In 1920, both Europe and the Soviet Union had an excess of rural over urban population, 25 million and 92 million respectively. However, in 1970 there was an excess of urban population over rural of 122 million in Europe and 30 million in the Soviet Union. In the final analysis the whole population growth in the course of some fifty years was absorbed in towns and cities in both Europe and the USSR.

Within Europe itself the highest concentration of population coincided with the longest period of modern urban growth experienced in the north. In 1970 this region had as much as 62 million people in urban areas (76·3 per cent)

[16] For Europe: United Nations estimates of urban population 'as nationally defined'; for the USSR: Soviet official estimates.

and only 19 million in rural ones. With a high level of urbanisation, the rate of urban growth was moderate, between 0·8 and 1·1 per cent per annum in the post-war decades. Western Europe was in 1970 the second most urbanised region with 70·6 per cent of the population urbanised (108 million living in urban and 41 million in rural areas). The average rate of growth of urban population was in 1950–70 fairly high, 1·7 per cent per year. In eastern Europe 57 million people lived in towns and cities (55 per cent) and 47 million in the countryside. The annual rate of urban growth in the two post-war decades was 2·2 and 2 per cent respectively. With 65 million urban population (50·9 per cent), southern Europe was the least urbanised region. However, its rate of urban growth was the highest in Europe, on the average 2·2 per cent per annum.

NATIONAL VARIATIONS

There are abundant sources for the study of urban history in Europe. Most of these deal with individual cities as centres of political and economic power, and with their contribution to the advancement of culture, science and art. Some sources refer to population change too, and make it possible to understand how urban growth responded to changing economic opportunities. But, for the study of redistribution of population at a national level, the sources are surprisingly scarce. There are only a dozen countries in Europe for which statistics on urban and rural population are available for 1900. Such statistics were more regularly compiled only after World War I, but even then the series were neither comparable nor satisfactory.

At the turn of the century most of the population of Europe lived in rural areas, perhaps as much as 70 per cent.[17]

[17] The United Kingdom was, with 77 per cent of urban population, the only highly urbanised country. In Germany 56 per cent of population was urban, while all other countries for which statistics are available had less than 50 per cent including France (41·0 per cent), Denmark (38·2 per cent) and perhaps Belgium. Sweden had only 22 per cent of population living in urban areas, Bulgaria 19·8 per cent, Russia 15 per cent and Finland 10·9 per cent.

With agriculture as the main source of livelihood and the single largest employer,[18] and with expensive transportation and poor communication, rural modes of life prevailed in most of the countries. Exceptions were the United Kingdom and Germany, and to some extent France and the Low Countries. It is true that western rural societies had already undergone significant progress arising from the radical improvements in agricultural methods made in the eighteenth and nineteenth century. But the profound change, initiated earliest in England, occurred in Europe only during the twentieth century. This was a radical change in the structure of economy and manpower, an impressive growth of the national product, and a rapid increase in productivity which induced massive migration from the countryside to towns and cities. The spatial distribution of the population was no longer determined by the low productivity in agriculture, which required a high proportion of manpower simply to produce sufficient food for the nation. On the contrary, regional and urban–rural distribution followed the impulses of the diversification of the economy, which by its very nature called for large concentrations of people.

The spread of urbanisation from the early industrialised regions to the rest of Europe followed the southward and eastward direction, but with many exceptions. In 1900 Spain had a larger proportion of urban population than Sweden, and Hungary than Finland, but in 1970 the situation was reversed. Switzerland, Austria and Czechoslovakia remained only moderately urbanised in spite of their economic advancement. Italy was known for her urban tradition throughout her history, but in 1970 she had a smaller proportion of urban population than the USSR which 70 years previously had been virtually entirely rural. The urban spread was less marked than the demographic

[18] In 1900 the percentage share of agriculture in national manpower was as high as 69·7 per cent in Hungary, 68·1 per cent in Spain, 53·5 per cent in Sweden and 51·9 per cent in Finland (however, with 24·2 per cent ill-defined). France, Germany and Norway had about 40 per cent of their labour force employed in agriculture. Only the United Kingdom had less than 10 per cent in primary industries.

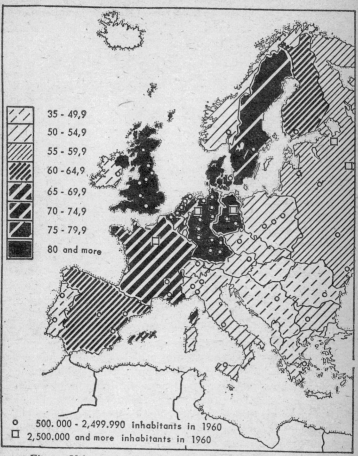

	35 - 49,9
	50 - 54,9
	55 - 59,9
	60 - 64,9
	65 - 69,9
	70 - 74,9
	75 - 79,9
	80 and more

o   500.000 - 2,499.990 inhabitants in 1960
□   2,500.000 and more inhabitants in 1960

Fig. 9: Urbanisation levels and cities with over 500 thousand
Per cent of urban population

transition: by 1970 the proportion of urban population in highly urbanised north-western countries (the United Kingdom, the Germanies, Denmark and Sweden) was twice as high as the proportion in the fringe-countries (Ireland, Portugal, Albania, Yugoslavia and Romania).

TABLE 14: Urbanisation levels and rates of European countries: 1920–1970

Country	A	B	U	Country	A	B	U
Federal Republic of Germany	1·1	1·7	81·1	Italy	1·7	1·9	53·0
France	1·3	2·2	67·1	Spain	2·6	1·7	60·9
Netherlands	2·0	1·8	70·8	Yugoslavia	2·9	5·0	36·8
Belgium	0·6	1·0	69·3	Portugal	2·0	1·5	36·5
Austria	0·4	0·7	57·8	Greece	3·5	2·2	48·5
Switzerland	0·9	2·9	54·8	Albania	...	7·2	37·5
United Kingdom	0·9	0·7	80·7	Poland	2·3	3·2	52·9
Sweden	1·8	1·7	79·6	Romania	3·5	3·1	41·7
Denmark	2·4	1·5	80·0	German D.R.	1·2	0·4	81·2
Finland	3·0	3·0	61·0	Czechoslovakia	1·7	1·8	52·1
Norway	1·4	2·1	53·0	Hungary	1·4	1·3	43·4
Ireland	0·8	0·8	47·0	Bulgaria	4·7	4·3	51·5

A=Average annual rate of growth of urban population from 1920 to 1940; B=from 1950 to 1970; *U*=Urban population as per cent of total population.

Looking at the levels of urbanisation in 1970, three distinct groups of countries could be distinguished: those highly urbanised, with four-fifths of population residing in urban areas; those with more than half of population living in rural areas; and an intermediate group with a half to four-fifths of urban population.[19]

The highest concentration of urban population in 1970 was recorded in the United Kingdom, the Federal Republic of Germany, the German Democratic Republic, Sweden and Denmark. Their combined population was 145 million in 1970, representing 31·7 per cent of population of Europe. The United Kingdom and Germany had already reached a high urban concentration early in the twentieth century, whilst Denmark and Sweden have attained high levels of urbanisation only after World War II. All five countries had been losing their rural population for several decades. Urban growth was slower in the United Kingdom and the German Democratic Republic than in the rest of the group. Urban population grew in East Germany at a low rate of

[19] Countries and territories with a small population are not discussed in the following analyses for obvious reasons.

0·4 per cent per annum in 1950–70, and in West Germany at a rate of 1·7 per cent.

A characteristic of the high concentration of population in the United Kingdom and Federal Republic of Germany was several large cities with a population of over 1 million. These cities were responsible for a large portion of urban population growth. Yet the growth of individual cities was quite different. According to the United Nations estimates, the six largest cities of the United Kingdom had between 1920 and 1960 an increase in population of 2·3 million, those of the Federal Republic 3·6 million. The growth of these cities is shown in Table 15.

TABLE 15: Population of selected cities 1920 and 1960

	1920	1960		1920	1960
London	7·236	8·190	Ruhrgebiet	3·730	4·960
Manchester	2·306	2·427	Hamburg	1·545	2·030
Birmingham	1·694	2·333	Stuttgart	615	1·300
Glasgow	1·630	1·782	Cologne	1·065	1·283
Leeds	1·445	1·702	Munich	670	1·240
Liverpool	1·201	1·386	Frankfurt-Offenbach	810	1·213

The growth of cities was a complex process consisting of natural increase in population, immigration, extension of city territory, transformation of smaller localities into larger ones, merging of cities, and suburbanisation. Conurbations, metropolitan areas, urban clusters, urban agglomerations and zones, and twin-cities were examples of recent urban development. The Ruhrgebiet exemplified a type of sustained non-planned growth of a large urban zone in which human settlement, an industrial complex and a large transportation system intermingled. London was an interesting example of a planning effort. The United Nations compiled statistics indicative of the gradual redistribution of population within the London metropolitan region, given in the table on page 80.

Regional and city planning was adopted in all the countries concerned, particularly from the early 1950s, as a means of regulating human settlement and economic activity.

TABLE 16: Distribution of London population 1938, 1951 and 1961

	1938	1951	1961
County of London	4·063	3·358	3·180
Inner urban ring	1·911	1·779	1·620
Total, Inner London	5·974	5·137	4·800
Suburban ring	2·366	2·684	2·698
Total, built-up area	8·340	7·821	7·498
Green belt ring	977	1·322	1·661
Outer country ring	833	1·008	1·400
Total, Greater London planning region	10·150	10·157	10·559
Surrounding ring	1·263	1·502	1·907
Total, London metropolitan region	11·413	11·653	12·466

While institutional and organisational aspects and underlying ideologies differed, the objectives of planning were
similar.

The intermediate group France, Belgium, the Netherlands and Finland, with a combined population of 78
million in 1970 (17 per cent of Europe's population), were
at a higher level in the urbanisation scale. Northern
France, Belgium and the Netherlands belonged to the same
group of older urbanisation, while urban growth in Finland
was recent. Since World War II France and Finland have
demonstrated a rapid decline in rural population, Belgium
a slow one, while rural population in the Netherlands
remained in 1970 at the level of 1950. Urban growth was
very fast in Finland during the last fifty years and in
Belgium was moderate. The Netherlands had a faster rate
of urban growth between the two wars (2 per cent per
annum) than after World War II (18 per cent); in France
urban growth was slower in the first period (1·3 per cent)
than in the second (2·2 per cent).

The largest city, Helsinki (584 thousand population in
1960), absorbed about one-quarter of Finland's urban
population. In the Netherlands, Amsterdam and Rotterdam
already had over 500 thousand population each before
1920; by 1960 The Hague was the third city in this size
group. Brussels (1425 thousand), Antwerp (865 thousand)
and Liege (600 thousand), all had a long urban tradition.

They were principal centres with a number of smaller cities and towns spread over the mining and industrial area of Belgium. Urban population growth in France was highly centralised in Paris, as indicated below (in thousands):

	1920	1940	1960
Paris	4,965	6,050	7,140
Lyons	665	710	855
Marseilles	600	650	780

Neither a large port, such as Le Havre, or industrial and commercial centres, such as Bordeaux, Lille or Strasbourg, nor a centre of a *départment* had reached the 500 thousand mark in 1960.

The other intermediate group, with a combined population of 78 million in 1970 (35 per cent of population of Europe), consisted of Italy, Spain, Poland, Czechoslovakia, Bulgaria, Austria, Switzerland and Norway. This was a rather heterogeneous group with regard to length of urban history and the pace of urban growth. Austria's urban population grew slowly in both these aspects between the wars and the post-war period; urban growth accelerated in the second period in Switzerland and Norway and decelerated in Spain. Italy and Czechoslovakia had moderately high rates of urban growth, Poland very high and Bulgaria extremely high. During the last twenty years the rural population has remained virtually static in Austria, Switzerland, Norway, Czechoslovakia and Poland, but has fallen appreciably in Italy and Bulgaria.

Big cities were characteristic of urban growth in Italy, and to some extent in Spain and Poland, but on a smaller scale than in the most urbanised group of countries. Cities over 500 thousand population have increased from 1920 to 1960 as shown in Table 17.

In most of the countries concerned there was a network of smaller cities and towns. The former ranged between 100 and 400 thousand, and many of them were significant regional economic centres, such as Bratislava, Padua, Plovdiv, Katowicz, or ports such as Trieste, Danzig, and

TABLE 17: Population of selected cities 1920 and 1960 (in thousands)

	1920	1960		1920	1960
Rome	629	2,020	Warsaw	920	1,120
Milan	666	1,491	Lodz	...	700
Naples	762	1,160	Wroclaw	...	650
Turin	...	963	Cracow	...	505
Genoa	...	764	Prague	665	1,000
Palermo	...	596	Sofia	...	700
Madrid	742	2,223	Vienna	1,845	1,625
Barcelona	698	1,543	Zurich	...	535
Valencia	...	505	Oslo	...	577

others. In Switzerland, the distribution of urban population favoured smaller towns; in addition to Zurich, there were only six cities of medium size, between 100 and 350 thousand of inhabitants. In Austria, Vienna was three times bigger than any other city.

The seven least urbanised countries were in 1970: Yugoslavia, Romania, Hungary, Portugal, Greece, Ireland and Albania. Their combined population was 74·9 million, or 16·4 per cent. With the exception of Ireland which had a low, and for Hungary which had a moderate rate of urban growth, the rest of this group experienced rapid growth of urban population although in different ways. Romania had high growth rates of urban population in both periods 1920–40 and 1950–70; in Greece the rate declined and in Yugoslavia jumped up in the later period. In Albania urbanisation took place only after World War II, but was very fast. The rural population was at the same level in 1970 as in 1950 in Hungary and Romania; it declined slightly in Ireland, Greece and Yugoslavia; and was larger in 1970 than in 1950 in Portugal and Albania.

There were few big cities in 1920 in these countries. Only Budapest had over one million and Lisbon more than 500 thousand population in 1920. The population growth of the seven cities is shown in Table 18.

The Yugoslav urban network is very decentralised, and consists of eight capitals of six states and two provinces in addition to several subregional centres. Hungary and Greece both have large capital cities absorbing the bulk of

TABLE 18: Population of selected cities 1920 and 1960 (in thousands)

	1920	1960		1920	1960
Belgrade	...	575	Lisbon	640	1,320
Bucharest	...	1,325	Porto	...	740
Budapest	1,225	1,825	Athens	...	1,815
Dublin	...	586			

their urban population. Romania and Portugal lie between these two patterns of urban distribution.

POLICIES AFFECTING URBAN GROWTH

Few examples of policies aimed at direct restriction of growth of large cities. More common were policies stimulating emigration from over-crowded cities, by such methods as licensing industries, developing suburban housing schemes, erecting satellite cities, and the like. All these were rather recent, post-war policies. While some of these, such as that of London or Prague, have often been praised, it still remains to be seen to what extent they have been effective.

There were a variety of policies in Europe which have directly or indirectly affected the growth and composition of population in urban and rural areas. Reconstruction of slum areas and low income housing was typical policy of many national and/or municipal governments between the two World Wars. Vienna was famous in the early 1920s for its experiment in workers' housing development, while many cities in Switzerland, England and the Scandinavian countries subsidised the building of dwellings at moderate price. A few countries provided public assistance for rural housing, among them was Sweden and Poland. In most socialist countries the state undertook responsibility for housing construction and management, while in the western countries most schemes relied on cheap loans and taxation rebates.

Town planning, which was an older concept, was gradually supplemented by the more recent concept of regional planning. Regional planning which comprised urban development, suburban transportation, distribution of industries and employment opportunity became an important instrument of social policy in many countries such as the United Kingdom, the Netherlands, Sweden, France and Italy. In France regional development was aimed at encouraging economic and demographic growth in less advanced areas; it included several schemes including the *amenagement du territoire*. In post-war Italy, regional development attracted a great deal of public interest, particularly the plans and activities promoted by the *Cassa per il Mezzogiorno*, *Vanoni Plan* and other schemes. Uvalić rightly pointed out that regional planning in the West gradually focused on regions in which underdevelopment prevailed and became in one way or another a part of broader national schemes and programmes.

In eastern European countries regional planning was conceived of as a part of national planning and followed different directions. In the Soviet Union 28 economic regions were established for the purpose of planning and development, some of them covering large territories (Far-Eastern region 6 million sq. km., East Siberia 4 million sq. km., etc.), while others were smaller (Southern region in the Ukraine 113 thousand sq. km., Baltic region 189 thousand sq. km.). According to Mihailović regional policy in eastern Europe was held 'to be an integral part of socio-economic development. This point of view is based both on the fact that territorial and sectorial mobility of capital formation, an attribute of the collective economy, makes it possible to integrate regional in overall development and on the opinion that social and economic phenomena form an indivisible whole.'

BIBLIOGRAPHY

ADAMS, EDITH. 'International migration trends affecting Europe in the 1960s' in: *International Population Conference*, London (1969) International Union for the Scientific Study of Population.

BAIROCH, PAUL, *et al. The Working Population and Its Structure.* Bruxelles, Editions de l'Institut de Sociologie (1968) 236 pp.

BERENT, JERZY. 'Causes of fertility decline in eastern Europe and the Soviet Union, II: Economic and social factors.' *Population Studies* (London) 24(2), (1970) 247–292 pp.

BORRIE, WILFRED DAVID. *The Growth and Control of World Population.* London, Weidenfeld and Nicolson (1970) 340 pp.

BUNLE, HENRI. *Le mouvement naturel de la population dans le monde de 1906 à 1936.* Paris, L'Institute national des études démographiques (1954) 541 pp.

CARR-SAUNDERS, ALEXANDER. *World Population: Past Growth and Present Trends.* Oxford, Clarendon Press (1936) 336 pp., 60 tables.

COALE, ANSLEY J. 'The decline of fertility in Europe from the French Revolution to World War II.' *In Fertility and Family Planning: A World View.* University of Michigan Press, Ann Arbor (1969) 503 pp.

FRUMKIN, GRZEGORZ. *Population Changes in Europe Since 1939; a Study of Population Changes in Europe During and Since World War II as Shown by the Balance Sheets of Twenty-four European Countries.* New York, Kelley (1951) 191 pp.

GLASS, DAVID V. *Population Policies and Movements in Europe.* Oxford, Clarendon Press (1940), (1967), 490 pp.

GREBENIK, E. in: *The Study of Population*, P. M. Hauser and O. D. Duncan (eds.). The University of Chicago Press, Chicago (1959) 863 pp.

HANSLUWKA, H. and SMITH, A. *Report on the Demographic Aspects of Mortality, II European Population Conference, Council of Europe* (1971).

KIRK, DUDLEY. *Europe's Population in the Interwar Years.* Princeton University Press, Princeton, N.J. (1946) 303 pp.

KOSINSKI, LESZEK A., *The Population of Europe.* Longman, London (1970), 161 pp.

LANDRY, ADOLPHE. *La révolution démographique; études et essais sur les problèmes de la population.* Paris, Sirey (1934) 227 pp.

LIVI BACCI, MASSIMO (ed.). *The Demographic and Social Pattern of Migration from the Southern European Countries.* Firenze, (1972), 261 pp.

LORIMER, FRANK. *The Population of the Soviet Union: History and Prospects.* Geneva, League of Nations (1946) 289 pp.

MASELLI, G. 'World population movements,' *II European Population Conference, Council of Europe* (1970).

MIHAILOVIĆ, KOSTA. *Regional Development: Experiences and Prospects in Eastern Europe.* Mouton, Paris (1972) 225 pp.

MINKOV, MINKO. *Migratziya na Naselenieto.* Partizdat, Sofia (1972), 212 pp.

MOORE, W. E. *Economic Demography of Eastern and Southern Europe.* Geneva, League of Nations (1945), 299 pp.

NOTESTEIN, FRANK W., *et al. The Future Population of Europe and the Soviet Union: Population Projections, 1940–1970.* Geneva, League of Nations (1944) 315 pp.

PELLER, SIGISMUND. *Quantitative Research in Human Biology,* Wright, John (1967) 422 pp.

PIRC, B. and MILAT, D. *Osnove istraživanja u zdravstvu.* Informator, Zagreb (1970) 435 pp.

SAUVY, A. in: *The Study of Population, op. cit.,* 180-189 pp.

UNITED NATIONS. *Demographic Yearbook, 1970* and other years.

UNITED NATIONS. *Measures, Policies and Programmes Affecting Fertility, with Particular Reference to National Family Planning Programmes* (1972) 168 pp.

UNITED NATIONS. *Population Bulletin of the United Nations, No. 6, 1962; with Special Reference to the Situation and Recent Trends of Mortality in the World* (1963) 210 pp.

UNITED NATIONS. *Population Bulletin of the United Nations, No. 7, 1963; with Special Reference to Conditions and Trends of Fertility in the World* (1965) 151 pp.

UNITED NATIONS. *Population and Vital Statistics Reports.*

UNITED NATIONS. *World Population Prospects as Assessed in 1963* (1966) 149 pp.

UNITED NATIONS. *The World Population Situation in 1970* (1971) 78 pp.

URLANIS, B. T. *Voiny i narodonaselenie Evropy.* Moskva, Izdatelstvo sotsialno-ekonomischeskoi literatury (1960) 566 pp.

USSR. *Narodnoe hazyaistvo USSR 1922–1972* (1972). [in Russian]

UVALIĆ, R. *Underdeveloped Regions in Developed Western Countries.* Serbian Academy of Sciences and Arts, Beograd (1972) 244 pp. [in Serbo-Croat]

2. The Structure of Demand in Europe 1920–1970

A. S. Deaton

In the half-century before 1970, the level and quality of consumption standards in Europe rose dramatically. Much of this advance was the direct counterpart of increases in output and real income, but much was also due to the diffusion of new technology into household living and transport patterns, and to the increasing responsibility assumed by the state for the provision and distribution of greatly improved community services, particularly in the fields of health, education and housing. Progress was nevertheless uneven; improvements in living standards were interrupted, first, by the great depression of the 1930s and then, almost immediately afterwards, by the Second World War. In many countries, increases in living standards were sacrificed, either temporarily or as a matter of long-term policy, in order to meet some overriding aim of economic management, such as rapid industrialisation or a satisfactory balance of international trade. But even in the postwar period, after sustained expansion nearly everywhere, there still existed great discrepancies in living standards, within individual countries, as well as between the richer and poorer areas of Europe.

Average European consumption levels rose more than threefold in real terms over the period, and this change in scale was accompanied by changes in structure. At the broad level of resource allocation, a larger proportion of output was accounted for by capital investment and by the current expenditures on goods and services of central and local government, so that the share of household consumption in total demand decreased. However, part of this decrease is due to the increased share of collective consumption and part to the much higher proportions of output devoted to capital investment, without which the rapid upward movement in living standards which has taken place in most European countries since the Second World War could not have been sustained.

Within the total of private expenditures there have been systematic changes in the pattern of demand in response to a number of factors general enough to have operated in most European countries. Prime amongst these are increases in real income and changes in the technology of household consumption, i.e. in the way in which goods and services are used to satisfy the underlying wants and desires of consumers. But these are by no means the only causes of structural change. Relative prices have varied both secularly and cyclically, governments have acted so as to influence the distribution of income and to encourage or discourage the consumption and supply of particular goods, and, as an accompaniment to economic growth, the economic and social environment has been subject to a whole complex of changes exerting influences which have often been independent of those due to the increase in real income itself. In many cases, all these factors have operated simultaneously. For example, the fall in the share of food expenditures can partly be ascribed to the rise in real income and partly to decreases in the relative prices of food, yet much of this movement has been offset by increases in packaging and processing as well as by the increasing costs of transport and distribution associated with greater urbanisation. Increased general prosperity can be credited with the spread in the consumption of services such as private transport, foreign travel, and many types of recreation and entertainment which, before the First World War, were regarded as the prerogative of the very rich. Yet the rise in the share of durable goods, which is partly a similar phenomenon, primarily reflects technical change in the provision of household services, and the durable goods themselves, by their mode of operation, have enforced important modifications elsewhere in the budget.

TOTAL CONSUMPTION AND NATIONAL INCOME

In the long run, total resources available for consumption are determined by total domestic production plus disinvestment in inventories plus whatever other countries are prepared to provide through imports over and above what is demanded in return as exports. This constraint must be sharply distinguished from that in the short-run Keynesian situation where supply is determined by the level of demand. The growth of total output in Europe since 1920 is described and analysed in Chapter 10 of this volume; in this section we shall examine how this growth affected the structure of the various components of gross national product and how the competing claims of government, capital investment and private consumption were reconciled within the total available.

Government and investment expenditures are more nearly exogenous to the economic system than is consumption, since the latter is fairly closely constrained by the total disposable income available to consumers. Even so, the allocative mechanism varies from country to country. In centrally planned economies, the planners have tended to give first priority to state expenditure and to the investment necessary to sustain given targets of economic growth. This procedure is not without constraints; consumption must attain a certain minimum, and high investment levels cause great difficulties for the production and procurement of sufficient food for industrial workers. In mixed economies, the mechanism of prices and incomes is used to limit private purchases to those goods available once other demands have been met, and this is done partly automatically and partly by government interference. Direct taxes are used to increase or decrease disposable income, indirect taxes to alter prices, and the level of interest rates to divert capital expenditures. Again, the government is subject to constraints; it cannot raise the level of taxation indefinitely and attempts to do so may lead to its removal from office or to individual groups attempting to avoid the sacrifices imposed on them. In periods of rapid structural change or after major external shocks, for example after both wars in many European countries, or in Germany after the French occupation of the Ruhr in 1922, attempts by governments to maintain their real level of expenditure out of sharply diminished available resources will lead to rapid price inflation with its arbitrary allocation of resources away from those dependent upon fixed money incomes or those foolhardy enough to hold more than the minimum amount of money for the minimum possible time.

Changes in the scale of total resources available and in private and public consumption are shown in Table 1.

TABLE 1: Annual average percentage growth rates of real GDP, consumption, and government expenditure

Country	GDP			Private consumption		Public consumption	
	1920 -38	1950 -60	1960 -70	1950 -60	1960 -70	1950 -60	1960 -70
Austria	2.3	5.7	5.8	5.7	4.8	3.2	3.0
Belgium	1.7	3.0[d]	5.0	3.0[d]	4.1	2.8[d]	5.5
Denmark	3.0	3.3	4.9	2.5	4.7	4.1	6.8
Finland	4.6	5.0	5.2	4.2	4.9	4.1	5.7
France	2.2	4.6	5.8	4.3	5.6	3.7	3.5
Germany	4.2	7.8	4.9	7.4	5.0	5.5	4.3
Greece	2.8[a]	5.9	7.6	5.1	7.1	2.2	5.7
Ireland	1.0[a]	1.7	4.2	1.1	3.8	1.6	4.1
Italy	2.2	5.6[e]	5.6	4.7[e]	6.1	3.5[e]	3.9
Netherlands	2.1	4.7	5.4	3.6	6.2	3.6	3.5
Norway	3.1	3.2[e]	5.0	3.3[e]	4.1	4.3[e]	6.3
Portugal	—	4.0	6.3	—	6.2	—	9.5
Spain	1.0[b]	5.2	7.5	—	7.1	—	5.8
Sweden	2.6	3.4	4.5	2.6	3.8	4.6	5.4
Switzerland	2.2[c]	4.4	4.4[f]	3.2	4.6[f]	2.4	4.9[f]
United Kingdom	1.9	2.7	2.8	2.4	2.4	1.6	2.1
OECD European average	—	4.8	4.9	4.2	4.8	3.7	3.9

Notes: a 1920–37, b 1920–35, c 1924–38, d 1953–60, e 1951–60, f 1960–69.

Sources: Maddison (1973), OECD (1970), OECD (1973).

Growth rates in Eastern European countries, not shown in the table, were of comparable magnitude, and in some cases very much above the average. These figures imply that, on average, per capita available resources expanded some threefold between 1920 and 1970; in the most rapidly growing countries by much more, four-and-a-half times in Sweden and West Germany, and perhaps eight or nine times in the USSR. Much of this increase has taken place since the Second World War; all the countries shown grew more rapidly after 1950 than in the interwar years, and since 1950, with the exceptions of Austria and West Germany, the rate of increase in output and living standards has itself tended to rise so that growth in the 1960s has been even more rapid than that of the 1950s.

There is a long-run tendency for consumption to expand less rapidly than total output; this is shown for a number of countries for which data are available in Table 2 and for a

TABLE 2: Percentage distribution of national product
(based on current price totals)

	PCE	GCE	GNCF
Austria			
1924–30	76.1	9.5	14.4
1931–37	81.9	12.9	5.2
1951–60	63.0	13.2	23.8
1961–70	58.6	13.9	27.6
Denmark			
1920–30*	87.8		12.2
1931–39*	85.1		15.0
1948–52*	83.0		17.1
1950–59	68.6	12.5	18.9
1961–70	62.9	16.7	20.4

Notes: PCE = private consumption expenditure, GCE = government current expenditure. GNCF = gross national capital formation. Items marked * relate to gross *domestic* rather than *national* product.

Germany

1928	76.1	7.2	16.7
1929–38	73.2	12.8	14.0
1950–59	58.7	14.4	26.8
1961–70	55.9	15.4	28.7

Italy

1921–30	78.5	5.6	15.9
1931–40	73.5	9.4	17.1
1946–55	74.0	7.9	18.1
1950–59	68.2	12.0	19.8
1961–70	64.0	13.3	22.7

Norway

1915–24	78.1	8.5	13.4
1925–34	77.5	8.7	13.8
1930–39	72.7	8.4	18.8
1947–56	61.3	11.0	27.7
1950–59	60.0	12.5	27.5
1961–70	54.6	16.5	28.9

Sweden

1921–30*	76.7	8.0	15.3
1931–40*	73.3	9.2	17.6
1941–50*	67.5	12.0	20.5
1950–59	61.9	16.8	21.4
1961–70	57.5	18.9	23.5

United Kingdom

1921–29	82.0	8.9	9.1
1930–39	79.7	11.4	8.9
1945–54	68.2	19.2	12.6
1950–58	66.9	16.9	16.2
1961–70	60.9	18.9	20.2

Sources: Kuznets (1962), OECD (1973), Österreichischen Institutes für Wirtschaftsforschung (1965).

wider range over the postwar years by the comparative growth rates in Table 1. In the six countries in Table 2 where all components are distinguished, the shares of both government current expenditure and capital formation roughly doubled between the 1920s and the 1960s, so that there was a corresponding drop in the share of private consumption in gross national product from 75–80% in the 1920s to 55–65% forty years later. However, these statistics are misleading in a number of respects. It can be seen from Table 1 that for many countries in the postwar period, government expenditure has not been growing as fast in real terms as has gross domestic product, so that the postwar increase in the government share shown in Table 2 represents an increase in the relative cost of providing government services rather than an increase in the government's share of real resources. This relative price change has been universal throughout postwar Europe; in OECD European countries as a whole, the price index of government expenditure rose at an average annual rate of 5.1% from 1950–70 compared to a rate of 3% for the price of consumption goods. This differential is caused by the very high wage element in the cost of government services compared to that in consumer goods' industries so that the relative price of the latter falls with productivity growth. Consequently, although there is no doubt of the increase in the government real share from the interwar to the postwar years, the increase in the money share since 1950 has not been matched by any real increase. In some countries government expenditure has grown faster than real output, but on average since 1950 it has grown slightly less rapidly than either real output or real consumption.

The second correction that should be made is for that part of the increase in government expenditure which relates to collective consumption, some of which, in the early years, would have been provided by private expenditures. Long-run data on the breakdown of government expenditure do not exist in sufficient quantities to make this correction, but it is still possible to give some idea of its magnitude. For those countries where recent data is available, some 40–45% of government expenditure in 1970 was accounted for by expenditure on health and education; in 1920, taking the UK experience as indicative, the figure was probably closer to 25%. If a correction is made in line with this very rough estimate, much of the increase in the government share is removed, and the main structural change which remains is a fall in the *total* (i.e. private plus collective) consumption share matched by a corresponding increase in the share of investment. This is exactly the type of structural change that might be expected to be necessary for the transition from a period when the rate of growth of output was very low to an era of much more rapid progress.

Cross-section data also show an inverse association between gross national product and the share of private consumption. Taking 1960 as illustrative, we find consumption to gross domestic product ratios of 76.3% in Portugal, 75.5% in Greece, 75.2% in Ireland, and 69.3% in Spain, with per capita incomes in US dollars ranging from $280 to $650, while at the other end of the distribution, a number of countries, namely Austria, Finland, Germany, the Netherlands, Norway and Sweden, have ratios below 60%, though here the association with income is much less sharply defined. The range of incomes across these countries in 1960 is not very different from the range within the richer countries from 1920 to 1970, and the fall in the consumption ratios is very similar; however, the share of government expenditure devoted to collective consumption in the poorer countries, though lower than in the richer nations, is unlikely to be as low as the figures for the advanced countries in the 1920s. In consequence the ratio of total consumption to national product falls rather more sharply across countries than it does over time. This is a phenomenon which appears even more sharply if longer historical perspectives are taken and has been discussed at length by Kuznets (1962). He suggests that the cross-section represents more truly the effect of income, with total consumption having an income elasticity considerably less than unity, whereas, over time, this effect is offset by pressures for higher consumption, associated with changes in urbanisation and transport patterns and in the range of new goods and services available. Since at least some of these changes may be transmitted to poorer countries without necessarily accompanying or engendering any rise in per capita income, we should expect these influences to have less impact on cross-country comparisons than on comparisons over time. This argument is given further credence by the fact that in studies where these dynamic technological and sociological factors are completely absent, i.e. in cross-sections of families in the same country at the same time, or in studies of the short-run impact of changes in income, the negative association between the consumption ratio and income is at its most marked, and is even sharper than in the cross-country comparisons.

The rise in state provision of collective services since the interwar period can partly be ascribed to rising demand for these services and partly to a weakening of the financial constraints binding governments. The demand for many government services, such as health, education and roads, can be expected to grow rapidly with rising real income, and it may well be that on a large scale many of these are provided more efficiently by a central authority than by autonomous local units. With better communications, consumers rapidly become aware of developments and improvements elsewhere so that there is a demand for uniformity of services at the level of the best currently available. A similar effect was caused by the high mobility of workers and members of the forces during the war and, in many cases, the experience of 'temporary' services provided by the state in wartime induced a permanent postwar continuation, for example, the National Health Service in Britain. Meeting these demands, even if universally thought to be desirable, depends upon the state's ability to transfer additional resources from the private sector through increased levels of taxation. It was only very shortly before 1920 in some European countries (1910 in Sweden, 1914 in France, 1920 in Germany) that income tax was accepted as a permanent impost, but since then there has been a steady increase in norms of taxation. This has been helped by increases in real income and the price level which, under a system of progressive taxation, cause government revenue to rise more rapidly than total income although, as we have seen above, this is partially offset by the increasing relative cost of government services. During wartime, taxes were necessarily raised to extremely high levels, in many cases using new methods of taxation and collection, and once these levels had been experienced it was found politically unnecessary after the war to reduce them to the original level. These factors permitted much of the increased demand to be met.

The increases in the shares of government expenditure and of capital formation have implied a relative decline in household consumption. This result has been accomplished primarily by a corresponding fall in the share of total resources available to consumers, since real disposable income has grown less rapidly than total output. It is only to a minor extent that households have made voluntary sacrifices by saving a higher proportion of their incomes. The hypothesis that the saving to disposable income ratio is constant in the long term, based originally on American data, has now become a centrepiece of much writing on the consumption function. However, it is not clear to what extent the European evidence, given in Table 3, is consistent with this; household saving ratios were higher in the late 1960s than in the early 1950s, and in the United Kingdom, where longer-run evidence is available, the saving ratio has been higher postwar than prewar. These changes may not be attributable to higher income. If there exists wide-scale unemployment, as there was in Britain for many of the interwar years, many households will dissave in an attempt to protect their living standards, even temporarily, so that an abnormally low saving ratio is to be expected. Similarly, immediately after the war, when many goods had become obtainable again after a long period of un-availability, and when, in many countries, consumers had accumulated previously unspendable income, a temporary spending boom occurred. Finally, as real income rises, consumption can be expected temporarily to lag behind, and the more quickly real income is rising, the larger the shortfall. Consequently, we should expect to observe a positive relationship between the rate of growth of real disposable income and the saving ratio. These three factors

TABLE 3: Household saving ratios in postwar Europe
(Annual average percentages of disposable income)

	1950–4	1955–9	1960–4	1965–8
Austria	2.2	8.1	8.9	9.2
Belgium	—	9.6	11.1	14.1
Denmark	9.0	8.9	11.6	9.5
Finland	6.3	8.3	11.5	12.0
France	4.5	7.4	10.3	11.2
Germany	9.3	13.7	13.1	13.1[a]
Greece	—	—	11.1	13.3[a]
Ireland	7.8	6.8	8.8	10.9[a]
Italy	—	—	15.2[b]	15.1
Netherlands	1.2	11.8	13.1	14.3
Spain	—	—	9.5	9.8
Sweden	7.4	10.2	10.9	9.6
Switzerland	4.4	6.8	10.2	13.4
United Kingdom	−0.5	2.0	5.5	5 8

Notes: a 1965–7, b 1961–4 Continuation of the series beyond 1968
has been sacrificed in order to give full comparability over
time.
Source: OECD (1970), Pt. V.

can explain a good deal of the variation shown in Table 3,
even on the assumption that the ratio is normally constant.
Out of the ten countries showing both 1950–4 and 1955–9,
eight show an increase from the former to the latter, and
in some cases the increase is very large. Taking 1950 alone
(not shown in the table), household saving was negative
not only in the United Kingdom but also in the Netherlands, while in Austria and Switzerland it was less than
one per cent of disposable income. Examining the other
saving ratios over time and over countries, and comparing
with Table 1, we can see that there is a tendency for the
ratio to be highest when and where growth is most rapid,
so that, for example, the United Kingdom shows very low
saving ratios throughout; there is a general increase towards
the end of the period as growth rates accelerated; and in
Germany where growth rates in the 1960s were markedly
less than in the 1950s, the ratio shows a corresponding
decline. If this explanation is accepted, we can see that

households have released some additional resources voluntarily through higher saving as the growth rate of income has increased, but that most of the increase in government expenditure and capital formation has been financed through decreases in the share of personal disposable income to national income, either through increased taxation by government, or through increased retention of profits by companies.

THE STRUCTURE OF PRIVATE CONSUMPTION EXPENDITURES

A broad classification of consumers' expenditures for fifteen European countries in the postwar period is presented in Table 4. A comparable and fully consistent set of information for the interwar years does not exist, but for five countries some data are available and a selection is presented in Table 5.

By the late 1960s, on average over the countries listed, some 30% of the budget was devoted to food, 11% to clothing, 10% to rent, 10% to purchases of durable goods, and 39% to other goods and services. The share of food has been falling throughout the period in virtually all countries, while those of durable goods and other goods and services have been rising. The share of clothing has shown some tendency to fall, especially in the richer countries, whereas that of rent has risen as a consequence of the rising price of rentals relative to other items of expenditure. The relative prices of food, clothing and durable goods have tended to fall, with corresponding rises in the relative prices of rents and other goods and services.

These trends describe Western Europe only and a basis does not exist for similar statements about Eastern Europe. National accounts for the socialist economies are not drawn up on a comparable basis, so that, for example, services are excluded, nor are time series of budget allocations available. Instead, we must rely on estimates for isolated years. For the USSR in 1964–5, Hanson (1968) has estimated that 43% of the budget was devoted to expenditure on food and that prices of foodstuffs are high compared with Western Europe. This is compensated by very low relative prices for rent and household utilities so that the budget share for this item is only 5%. Clothing, like food, is very expensive and accounts for a very high 18% of expenditure; durables make up 7%, leaving 27% for other goods and services. This pattern, which corresponds to that expected for a very poor country by European standards, may partly be explained by the very low proportion of production which is devoted to consumption in Russia, for example Kuznets (1962) estimates the postwar ratio as low as 67%, so that living standards are low relative to gross national product. Hanson also argues that there have been systematic distortions in Soviet planning in favour of the production of manufactures, especially investment goods, and these have militated against the efficient expansion of agriculture. Consequently, food and clothing, which depend on agricultural production, have remained relatively expensive, although in recent years consumers have benefited from an increased availability and cheapness of consumer manufactures produced by the more efficient industrialised sector.

The use of current price budget shares to describe demand patterns is useful in that such quantities do not depend on national units of measurement nor on exchange rates and so are comparable across countries. However, they are inadequate in a number of respects. First, they do not measure adequately the expenditure pattern of the 'average' consumer. The value share is computed by dividing aggregate expenditure on each good by the total of aggregate expenditures, so that a greater weight is given to the expenditure patterns of rich consumers who spend a great deal than to those of the poor who spend little. Consequently, luxury goods are over-represented and necessities under-represented so that the calculated expenditure pattern is likely to be representative of consumers whose income is well above the average. This may be illustrated by an example which, although rather extreme, is nevertheless suggestive. Consider a country where 70% of the population is ex-

TABLE 4: The Structure of Consumption in Postwar Europe
(Percentages of Current Price Totals)

	GDP ($)	(1)	(2)	(3)	(4)	(5)
Austria						
1950-4	645	48.6	15.5	4.9		31.0
1955-9	890	38.2	14.3	4.6		42.9
1960-4	1,084	32.3	13.9	5.2	9.9	38.8
1965-8	1,273	28.9	13.5	5.8	10.8	41.0
Belgium						
1955-9	1,221	28.9	9.8	13.1	9.6	38.6
1960-4	1,434	26.9	9.9	11.5	11.4	40.3
1965-8	1,694	25.0	9.1	10.5	12.0	43.4
Denmark						
1950-4	1,207	27.8	12.3	6.7	10.9	42.3
1955-9	1,343	26.2	9.7	7.8	13.4	42.9
1960-4	1,670	22.4	8.6	8.2	17.2	43.6
1965-8	1,976	21.7	7.7	8.8	16.7	45.1
Finland						
1950-4	941	35.7	17.8	5.1	5.3	36.3
1955-9	1,102	34.4	12.7	9.5	6.5	37.0
1960-4	1,382	31.2	10.6	11.0	8.4	38.8
1965-8	1,618	29.2	8.9	11.1	8.5	42.5
Ireland						
1960-4	761	34.0	10.3	5.9	8.3	41.5
1965-7	873	31.7	10.0	6.3	8.9	43.1
Italy						
1951-4	575	41.6	12.3	7.7	7.3	31.1
1955-9	711	40.3	10.3	9.5	7.3	32.6
1960-4	919	38.7	9.8	10.2	8.8	32.5
1965-8	1,110	37.8	9.3	9.9	8.4	34.6
Netherlands						
1950-4	859	35.1	18.1	6.3	8.0	32.5
1955-9	1,028	32.9	16.3	7.0	10.1	33.7
1960-4	1,194	29.8	15.7	7.8	12.1	34.6
1965-8	1,417	26.5	14.4	7.9	13.1	38.1
Norway						
1951-4	1,193	31.5	18.0	5.5	8.4	36.6
1955-9	1,310	31.9	15.5	7.4	8.7	36.5
1960-4	1,517	30.1	14.4	7.9	11.0	36.6
1965-8	1,836	29.2	13.3	8.0	11.1	38.4
Spain						
1960-4	475	47.7	13.1	6.3	7.6	25.3
1965-8	621	42.7	13.4	7.2	9.1	27.6

	GDP	(1)	(2)	(3)	(4)	(5)
France						
1950–4	1,147	37.2	14.1	3.6	6.0	39.1
1955–9	1,377	33.5	12.5	5.0	7.8	41.2
1960–4	1,678	30.8	11.9	7.1	9.7	40.5
1965–8	2,037	28.5	10.9	9.1	9.5	42.0
Germany						
1950–4	945	41.6	14.4	6.4		37.6
1955–9	1,307	39.7	12.9	6.5		40.9
1960–4	1,641	36.3	12.1	8.2		43.4
1965–7	1,872	33.6	11.8	10.0		44.6
Greece						
1950–4	305	46.4	10.2	12.9		30.5
1955–9	397	44.4	11.2	13.0	4.5	26.9
1960–4	515	40.9	12.1	12.9	4.4	29.7
1965–8	694	38.5	12.8	12.2	4.3	32.2
Sweden						
1950–4	1,613	31.0	14.2	8.0	9.2	37.6
1955–9	1,859	29.7	12.5	8.7	10.1	39.0
1960–4	2,247	28.1	11.6	9.0	11.5	39.8
1965–8	2,621	26.6	10.2	9.8	11.1	42.3
Switzerland						
1950–4	1,449	28.2	9.3	12.4		50.1
1955–9	1,684	26.5	9.0	12.1		52.4
1960–4	1,944	24.7	8.9	11.2		55.2
1965–8	2,158	24.2	8.0	11.8		56.0
United Kingdom						
1950–4	1,228	29.7	12.0	8.8	6.9	42.6
1955–9	1,371	30.2	11.3	9.1	8.5	40.9
1960–4	1,559	27.0	10.8	10.4	9.2	42.6
1965–8	1,739	24.5	10.0	11.9	8.9	44.7

Key: GDP is per capita gross domestic product at 1963 prices and 1963 exchange rates. (1) Food, except for Germany where figures include drink and tobacco. (2) Clothing. (3) Rent. (4) Durable goods. (5) Other goods and services.

Source: OECD (1970), OECD (1973).

TABLE 5: The Structure of Consumption in the Interwar Period
(Percentages of Current Price Totals)

Italy	Food, drink and tobacco	Other non-durable goods	Durables	Services
1921–25	65.9	16.9	1.4	15.8
1926–30	63.2	16.4	1.7	18.7
1931–35	58.9	14.0	1.8	25.3
1936–40	55.6	16.9	2.3	25.2

Netherlands	Food	Drink and tobacco	Clothing	Durables	Other
1922–25	32.5	9.3	14.6	9.0	34.6
1926–30	30.8	9.4	14.4	9.1	36.3
1931–35	28.0	8.9	13.0	8.5	41.6
1936–39	28.9	8.7	12.9	8.1	41.4

Norway	Food	Drink and tobacco	Rent and fuel	Clothing	Household goods	Other
1930	32.0	6.8	16.8	13.7	5.4	25.3
1935	32.5	6.4	17.5	13.2	6.0	24.4
1939	32.1	6.6	15.6	13.6	7.7	24.4

Sweden	Food	Clothing	Housing	Other
1926	32.1	10.6	13.1	43.2
1938	26.5	11.1	12.3	50.1

United Kingdom	Food	Clothing	Housing	Non-durable goods	Durables	Services
1921–25	32.1	11.2	8.3	22.8	6.1	19.5
1926–30	30.6	10.9	9.1	22.4	6.6	20.4
1931–35	27.6	10.0	10.5	23.0	7.0	21.9
1936–38	26.5	9.9	10.4	23.7	7.6	21.9

Sources: Italy, based on data from Barberi (1961); Netherlands from Barten (1962); Norway from Norwegian Central Bureau of Statistics (1969); Sweden from Kuznets (1962); United Kingdom from Feinstein (1972).

tremely poor and spends all of its income on food, whereas the other 30%, who, we shall assume, receive 70% of total income, spend 20% on food and 80% on luxury goods. The budget shares for the economy as a whole would then be 44% on food and 56% on luxuries, even though the majority of households spend nothing whatever on the latter. A more useful statistic, but one on which we usually have no information, might be the average of the budget shares of the individual households themselves; in this case such a calculation would imply budget shares of 76% and 24% for food and luxuries respectively. Second, budget share calculations do not separate the quantities of goods bought from their prices so that if shares were recalculated on a common price basis, a different picture would emerge. Thus, if food is relatively cheap in the poorer countries, such as Spain and Greece, recalculation of the budget shares using average European prices would much increase the expenditure shares on food in those countries. However, relative cheapness maintained over a long period may well lead to higher purchases than in a more expensive country, and if the response to prices is elastic, will lead to a higher budget share. Disentangling these two effects is often difficult, and in any case, there is very little information on cross-country variation in the structure of relative prices with which to make the correction.

FOOD

Figure 1 illustrates for the postwar data the most famous of empirical propositions in demand analysis. This is Engel's Law, which states that the budget share on food declines with rising income. Income in this diagram is taken to be per capita gross domestic product taken at constant 1963 prices and converted to United States dollars at constant 1963 exchange rates; the data are given in the first column of Table 4. This is a very crude measure with which to compare living standards between countries, but it is sufficient to illustrate the major trends. Although Engel's Law was postulated for cross-sections of family budgets for

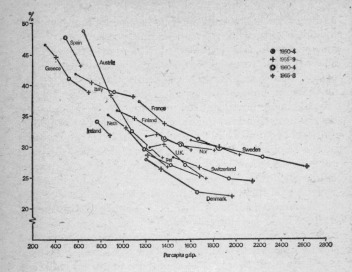

Fig. 1: Proportions of expenditure devoted to food; W. Europe, 1950–68

a single country, Figure 1 shows that it holds equally well for time series data and for cross-country comparisons. And, in spite of a good deal of dispersion, there is a remarkable degree of consistency between the change as a country grows richer and the change as we move from poorer to richer countries. For example, countries which consume a high proportion of food, i.e. Spain, Italy, France and Sweden, lie along a continuous curve in order of increasing income. Similarly, there is a continuity between the experiences of Greece, the Netherlands, Belgium and Denmark, who spend consistently less on food in relation to their incomes. The differences between these groups can partly be ascribed to cultural factors influencing preferences, though, as we shall see below, there are differences both in the relative price of food between countries and in the way demand responds to these differences. The case of Ireland, which has a very low value share for food, is rather special and it seems that a considerable part of the sustenance of its inhabitants is taken in more liquid form; in 1970, over 12% of the budget was spent on alcoholic drink, and this figure is twice as much as the next highest in Europe. (Finland and the UK each spend 6–7% of the budget on alcoholic beverages.)

Looking again at the diagram as a whole and ignoring price differences for the moment, we can calculate a rough estimate of the income elasticity for food at around 0.7%; i.e. a one per cent increase in real income will generate only a 0.7% increase in the quantity of food bought and thus a 0.3% decrease in the budget share.

Some of this fall is removed if allowance is made for relative price changes. Due to the generally observed phenomenon that economic growth is associated with larger increases in productivity in agriculture than elsewhere and due to some worsening in the terms of trade of primary producers, the relative price of food has tended to fall over time. However, since food comprises a large share of the total budget, there is limited scope for changes in the price relative to the price of total expenditure, and, on average, this has only fallen some 2% from the early 1950s to the late 1960s. Consequently, while the current price value share has fallen from 36.5% to 30.9% there has only been a slightly smaller fall, from 36% to 31.3%, in the constant price share. It is thus unlikely that Figure 1 gives a misleading impression of the relation between income and food consumption, or that the average elasticity need be modified very much. For individual countries, income and price elasticities are available from a study by Goldberger and Gamaletsos (1970) using data similar to that in Table 4. There appears to be some variation in income elasticities between different European countries ranging from 0.4 in Denmark and Sweden, 0.5 in Belgium and France, 0.6 for the UK and the Netherlands, 0.7 for Greece, Ireland and Norway, and 0.8 for Italy. (Austria, Finland, Spain and Switzerland were not covered.) These figures are roughly consistent with the diagram and seem to imply a possible negative relationship between income and the elasticity.

This suggests the existence of some 'saturation' level of food consumption at which the income elasticity becomes zero. However, such a conclusion should be treated with caution, since there are countries such as Norway which appear to be exceptions to the rule, and it is clear that with changes in quality, packaging and processing, the limits of food consumption are not determined by anything so prosaic as the capacity of the human stomach. Relative prices seem to have relatively little effect within each country; in only Belgium, Italy and Norway could significant price elasticities be found, and even in these cases, variations in prices explained very little relative to changes in real income. This is not very surprising since, as we have seen, there has been little change in the relative price of food in the postwar years. Further, it is to be expected that, in contrast to its composition, the total of food purchases will not be very sensitive to price changes; consumers cannot give up food, but they can substitute one food for another.

Some of these effects are revealed in a cross-country study for the single year 1950 by Gilbert and associates (1958). This work is particularly important because the authors undertook the complex task of measuring quantities and prices in comparable terms for nine different countries, the United States, Belgium, Denmark, France, Germany, Italy, the Netherlands, Norway and the United Kingdom. The price of food as a whole showed relatively little variation across these countries; taking the US relative price of food as 100, the UK was cheapest at 74, with Italy (87) and Belgium (88) the most expensive. However, the prices of the individual items showed much greater variation; meat was almost twice as expensive in Belgium as in the UK, while fish was very cheap in Norway, Denmark and Germany compared with the UK or Italy. Other notable features were the high price of vegetables in Norway, the high price of sugar products in France and Italy, and the low price of non-alcoholic beverages in the UK. Differences of this sort for a single year are of limited interest, but many of these are clearly the result of geographical factors or of deliberate government policy and can be expected to persist for long periods of time. They are given further interest by the fact that, in spite of undoubted international differences in tastes, variation in relative prices, along with income, can explain much of the cross-country variations in the pattern of food consumption. For the total, the result is much the same as within countries, an income elasticity of 0.5 with no detectable price responsiveness, i.e. countries will spend a low proportion on food if they are rich and if the price of food is low. Individual foodstuffs also have low income elasticities, the only exception being non-alcoholic beverages, with an income elasticity of 1.1. However, the consumption of these commodities appears to be extremely sensitive to international price differentials so that, for example, the price elasticities of vegetables and of fruit are each greater than 2, while those for fish and for sugar products are greater than 1. These numbers are much larger than are usually found within countries over time; this suggests that consumers' responses to price difference are large in the long term when these differences are allowed to persist, but are much less marked over shorter time spans.

When we turn to the available long-run data the simple explanations with which we have been working no longer fit the facts. The majority of the interwar data, and indeed of the data from before the First World War, shows that the food share falls very little, if at all. In Norway the 1930 figure of 32% is identical with the 1955-9 average. In the United Kingdom, the current price share does fall, and although the 1955-9 ratio is admittedly only fractionally below the 1926-30 figure, the late 1950s in the UK were the first years of complete de-rationing after the war and may have seen exceptionally high food consumption. In constant prices, the value share fell in the postwar period, but not at all between the wars. It rose to a peak during the depression, but by the late 1930s it was no lower than in 1920 or in 1900; hence, for the first sixty years of the century, the constant price value share of food showed no downward trend. In Sweden, although the current price share fell from 37.3% in 1913 to 26.5% in 1930, the constant price share fell by much less, from 37.3% to 32.1%.

Similarly, in Holland, the constant price share fell only marginally, from 31% to 30% from the early 1920s to the end of the 1930s. Only in Italy, where there is only data for the aggregate of food, drink and tobacco, is there a marked fall in both constant and current price shares during the interwar period. Thus, apart from this single case, the long-run evidence seems to contradict not only the postwar experience, both across countries and over time, but also the evidence from cross-sections of family budgets. Certainly, real income grew very slowly in many of these countries between the wars, but in none did total consumption fall in real terms for more than one or two years during the worst of the depression. Nor can changes in prices explain the stability of the share; commodity prices fell rapidly in the early 1930s, causing a relative cheapening of foods, but, as we have seen, there are no grounds for believing that this would have led to any marked increase in food consumption. Even if the price elasticity had been higher then than in the postwar years, neither this nor the pattern of income growth would appear to be able to explain a secular stability before 1950 coupled with a decline thereafter.

Kuznets (1962 and 1966) has proposed a number of possible explanations for this phenomenon. He identifies a number of factors accompanying economic growth which operate so as to modify the effects of Engel's Law. Increasing urbanisation is one of the most important of these; not only does this induce changes in the social environment which free consumers from traditional constraints but, from a purely technical point of view, requires increases in distribution and retailing services as consumers move away from sources of supply. Consequently, food, as defined in 1970, contains a much larger content of incidental services than it did in 1920 and a correspondingly lower share of commodities. This tendency is further reinforced by other types of 'repackaging'; with increasing real income, consumers are prepared to pay for a higher degree of pre-processing so as to save on cooking or preparation time. A further effect of urbanisation is that, since less food is consumed by original producers, the coverage of the statistics tends to improve. However, these factors do not obviously explain why the food share has not continued to be relatively stable since the 1950s. It may be that the much more rapid rise in real income since the war has been enough to offset these forces and it is true that many, although not all, of the changes in retailing and distribution had been accomplished before 1939. Urbanisation itself has slowed down in some countries since the war, but in others, notably in Scandinavia, it has been much more rapid, while in the UK there has been very little increase even since the 1920s. A firm answer to these questions cannot be given without a good deal more research, but it should not be assumed that the postwar experience will necessarily continue. It may be that it is not the long-run data which are anomalous, but rather those of the last fifteen or twenty years, and if growth rates slow down in the 1970s, as is quite possible, the secular stability in the food ratio may well reassert itself.

No description of patterns of food demand would be complete without some discussion of the means employed for allocating food during and immediately after the Second World War. The disruption and diversion of supplies during wartime would lead, under normal market conditions, to enormous rises in price and to extremely in-egalitarian distribution. To combat this, and so as to restrict demand to allow maximum production of war-related goods, there was near universal rationing of necessary foods throughout Western Europe. Rationing cannot be successful alone. It must be accompanied by price control, so that consumers may always purchase their allotted quotas, and by state control over supply and distribution so that rations are effectively guaranteed. These conditions were not always met in Europe during the war, especially in occupied territories where there was no strong indigenous government. The severity of the situation varied considerably from country to country. In Germany, Italy and those areas of Europe occupied by German forces, virtually all foodstuffs, including bread, were rationed by specific per capita allowances. Since these areas had not been fully self-sufficient in food even before the war, and since much of the high protein food, particularly meat, was requisitioned for transportation to Germany, there were severe shortages. In Germany, Denmark and Bulgaria the daily calorie intake fell little compared with prewar levels, although more protein was consumed through milk and less through meat. At the other end of the scale, in the Baltic States, Slovakia, parts of Italy and France, Poland, Greece, Yugoslavia, and the occupied areas of the USSR, daily rations provided only 1,000–1,500 calories – barely sufficient to sustain life. Worst of all was the treatment of Jews in Poland who were accorded only the equivalent of 700 calories per day. In all these countries the quality of food declined as the consumption of cereals rose relative to that of animal foods, and in many of the occupied countries as well as in Italy, price rises meant that many could not even afford these basic rations. In the neutral countries and in Britain, experience was much more favourable. Ireland and Portugal were barely affected, and conditions were bad in Spain only as a consequence of the upheavals of the civil war. Switzerland had specific rations on the German pattern but these were considerably more generous. But it was Sweden and Britain which ran the most successful systems. Sweden had an enormously complex system of rationing based on need and the more egalitarian distribution of some commodities improved nutritional standards in spite of the curtailment of available resources. In Britain, supplies from North America ensured that during the war bread was never rationed, and a flexible 'points' rationing scheme allowed consumers to choose among limited supplies of semi-luxuries such as canned foodstuffs. This flexibility was enormously popular among consumers and although the points scheme removed the need to guarantee all supplies, it was less popular among administrators who had to fix and alter points prices. In Britain and in Sweden, as the allocation mechanism became more effective and its administrators more self-confident, the opportunity was seized not merely to maintain but to improve nutritional standards, and many of the advances in dietary theory of the 1920s and '30s could be applied on a national scale. Schemes for the distribution of milk and vitamin foods were only the beginning; as Hammond (1951) remarks, 'The restrictive, anti-inflationary, public-safety machine of food control was to be converted, through the application of dietary standards, into an instrument for doing in wartime what no modern government had attempted even in peace. The initiative that had begun with the National Milk Scheme was to run through the whole of subsequent food policy.' The success of these measures, in a time of great austerity, was to exert an important influence on the direction and scale of postwar welfare provision.

CLOTHING

Compared to food, there is a wide dispersion of the shares of the budget devoted to footwear and clothing, from less than 8% to more than 18% in the postwar data alone, and only a small part of this variation can be explained by systematic differences in prices and income. Estimates of income elasticities for clothing using time series data tend to be close to unity so that we should not expect any trend relationship between the value share and income. Consequently, the dispersion must be explained by other factors. This is in contrast to family budget data where a close relationship is usually found between clothing expenditure and income implying an income elasticity of between one and two; there is no evidence in Table 4 to suggest that this is consistent with either the cross-section or time series postwar evidence. For comparisons over time *within* countries, and with the exception of Greece and Spain, the two poorest countries, there is a general tendency for the value share to fall. However, most of this can be accounted for by the fall in the relative price of clothing – due to increased use of synthetic materials combined with some cheapening of primary commodities – so that the *constant* price value shares within countries tend to remain stable. The time series data both pre- and postwar are thus broadly consistent with a unitary income elasticity. Relative price changes seem to be even less important over time than for food; in the Gold-berger and Gamaletsos study, no significant price elasticities of the right sign could be found for any of the countries examined. The cross-country analysis of Gilbert is of doubt-ful relevance here since it refers to 1950, which in many countries saw abnormally high prices and expenditures. In any case, although a detectable cross-country price elasticity was found, it was less than unity, and even with the effects of income, a good deal of variation was left unexplained. Some of this is undoubtedly due to geographical influences, and although, for example, Norway and Sweden spend a high proportion on clothing relative to their incomes and *vice versa* for Greece, Spain and Italy, there are exceptions such as Denmark where the proportion is low even though clothing is relatively expensive. One possibility for recon-ciling the family budget with time series data would be to explain the high income elasticity of the former in terms of differences in relative rather than absolute income, in the way first proposed by Duesenberry (1949). Thus, richer consumers spend more on clothing not simply because they are rich, but because it is expected of them given their social position and place in the income distribution. Over time, each income group continues to spend the same proportion on clothing irrespective of changes in their absolute income and, in consequence, the average share will be stable over time.

RENT AND HOUSING

Table 4 shows even less systematic variation in the share of rent in the budget than it does for clothing. There is con-siderable variation across countries, from as low as 4% to as high as 13%, with many observations clustering around the postwar average of 8%. There is some tendency for the share to rise through time within countries, and this can be accounted for by an increase in rents relative to the price of other commodities. The average Western European price relative rises from 79 in 1950–4, through 89 in 1955–9, 98 in 1960–4, to 111 in 1965–8, so that the average constant price share has tended to fall. In Eastern European countries, rents are much lower, a figure of 2% has not been atypical.

Although, like other commodities, building materials are traded between countries, the housing stock itself is im-mobile and so there is little basis for cross-country comparisons of price and income elasticities in the way that is possible for many of the other items of the budget. While the demand for more and higher quality housing increases with higher incomes, the supply depends on the history of construction dating back decades, if not centuries. Prices are subject to a great deal of government interference through rent control, incentives to building and state construction programmes so that there is great variation in conditions and in rents from country to country. A full account of housing in Europe since 1920 and of the development of rent policies and other state intervention would have to be done on a country by country basis and is obviously beyond the scope of this chapter. Instead, we may only attempt to summarise some of the main developments.

There has been an almost universal shortage of housing in Europe throughout the twentieth century. Its roots can be traced back to the industrial revolution and to the large scale urbanisation which accompanied it. By 1900, the quantity of houses was in many places still extremely in-adequate and the quality was very low, particularly of working-class homes. The situation was made still worse by the virtual cessation of housing construction during World War I so that by 1920 the provision of homes had become a major political issue. By then, the belief that private enterprise would provide housing as successfully as it had provided other commodities had been eroded by the evidence to the contrary, and governments, which had first been forced to interfere in the interests of public health, were ready to adopt a much more interventionist position. The nature of this varied from country to country; in most instances governments offered financial incentives or raised special taxes to finance construction of certain specified types of houses, and in a few cases, most notably in the

UK, a great deal of construction was directly carried out by the state. On the other hand, to protect existing tenants from the effects of shortages, many governments resorted to rent control particularly of working-class dwellings. Such policies are frequently necessary and have been frequently used but always carry the danger of reducing the incentive to private construction.

From 1920 to 1929, rising incomes in most European countries produced a situation favourable to private house-building and there were housing booms in France, Germany, the Netherlands, Switzerland, Denmark, Sweden and Finland, and these gathered momentum through the decade, see Table 6. In the UK, income growth was very

TABLE 6: New dwellings per 1,000 inhabitants: 1920–38
(annual averages)

	Den.	Fin.	Fr.	Ger.	It.	Neth.	Swe.	Swit.	UK
1920–4	1.9	4.1	0.9	1.6	0.4	5.7	2.4	2.1	2.1
1925–9	2.5	6.6	2.1	4.0	0.7	6.3	4.1	3.6	4.8
1930–4	3.9	3.8	3.8	3.0	1.3	5.9	4.7	4.9	5.5
1935–8	4.2	5.9	2.1	3.9	1.6	4.2	7.7	2.5	7.6

Key: Countries are Denmark, Finland, France, Germany, Italy, Netherlands, Sweden, Switzerland, and the United Kingdom.

Source: Svennilson (1954).

slow and there was widespread unemployment so that the increase in house-building which took place depended on considerable government support, indeed, two-thirds of the 1.5 million houses built in the 1920s were state-aided. Paradoxically, in the 1930s, while the rate of building declined rapidly in Germany and France as the general level of activity fell, housebuilding continued to rise in the UK, almost all construction being carried out by private enterprise. A number of special factors made this possible. Construction became cheaper as a consequence of the depression; raw materials cost less, money wages were lower, and there was a considerable increase in productivity in construction, so that a new working-class house fell in price by some 15% between 1931 and 1933. But it was the supply of finance and its efficient channelling through an expanding building society movement which was of prime importance. The unprofitability of other types of investment meant that interest rates were lower, funds were diverted to housebuilding, and building societies encouraged borrowing by lengthening maximum repayment periods and relaxing deposit requirements. In consequence, mortgage repayment and interest charges combined fell to levels comparable with rents in municipal housing, and a whole class of better-off workers, artisans and clerical staff could become home-owners for the first time.

In some European countries, notably Denmark and Sweden, the depression was less severe, and building activity continued to rise; in others, the rearmament boom at the end of the 1930s stimulated demand. Throughout Western Europe the quality of housing also improved in the interwar period; electricity was made widely available by the construction of national power networks, and water and sanitary provision were greatly improved. However, by 1939 there remained shortages in many countries, and the great destruction of houses during the war as well as the six-year halt in construction left a severe postwar problem. It was estimated by the UN in 1949 that 9% of the European housing stock had been totally or partially destroyed in the war, and in some countries, e.g. Greece and Poland, the proportion was as high as 20%. Much has been done in the postwar years to remedy the situation; some of the most important available indicators are given in Table 7. In nearly all countries there has been a steady improvement in the number of houses and in the facilities available. Building rates have been generally high compared with the prewar experience with annual rates of 10 per thousand population not uncommon, and in many countries between 6 and 7% of gross domestic product has been devoted to house construction. Only in Britain has progress

T.C.   E

TABLE 7: European Housing Standards

	Houses (%)	Persons/Room	Water (%)	Electricity (%)
Austria				
1939	29.7	1.9	—	—
1970	36.1	0.9	85.3	—
Belgium				
1939	30.1	0.9	—	—
1947	33.7	0.8	48.4	95.4
1961	34.4	0.6	76.9	99.6
Bulgaria				
1956	22.6	1.8	—	64.2
1965	25.0	1.2	28.2	94.8
Czechoslovakia				
1930	22.4	—	—	—
1950	29.3	1.5	29.9	82.8
1961	27.9	1.3	49.1	97.3
Denmark				
1950	30.2	—	—	—
1965	33.9	0.8	96.7	99.5

	Houses (%)	Persons/Room	Water (%)	Electricity (%)
Ireland				
1939	22.1	1.1	—	—
1966	23.8	0.9	—	—
Italy				
1936	24.1	1.3	—	—
1961	28.1	1.1	62.3	95.9
Netherlands				
1939	23.8	1.3	—	—
1956	22.5	0.8	89.6	98.1
Norway				
1939	25.0	1.1	—	—
1960	30.6	0.8	92.8	—
Poland				
1939	19.9	2.1	—	—
1970	25.5	1.5	46.8	85.0
Portugal				
1960	27.7	1.1	28.9	40.5

	Houses		Water	Electricity
(country name not visible — top of page)				
1960	27.2	1.3	47.1	88.6
1966	28.2	1.4	—	48.6
France				
1936	31.4	1.1	—	—
1946	28.9	1.3	37.0	—
1968	36.5	0.8	90.8	98.8
W. Germany				
1950	19.8	1.2	77.9	98.4
1968	32.3	0.7	99.0	99.0
E. Germany				
1961	34.6	1.1	65.7	—
1971	38.0	1.0	82.1	100.0
Greece				
1939	26.0	1.9	—	14.2
1971	35.2	0.9	65.0	88.3
Hungary				
1939	26.0	2.6	36.4	—
1970	30.5	1.2	—	92.1

	Houses		Water	Electricity
Spain				
1960	25.4	0.9	45.0	89.3
Sweden				
1939	30.5	1.5	—	—
1945	31.6	—	67.0	94.0
1970	39.4	0.7	97.0	—
Switzerland				
1939	26.4	1.0	—	—
1960	29.1	0.7	96.1	99.0
USSR				
1954	19.5	1.7	—	—
1965	25.5	1.3	—	—
UK				
1939	27.4	0.7	—	—
1961	31.5	0.7	98.7	—
Yugoslavia				
1961	22.0	1.6	—	54.5

Key: Houses are expressed as a % of the total population: Water and Electricity are the % of houses with inside running water and with electric lighting, respectively.

Sources: UN (1949) and UN Statistical Yearbooks.

been slower than in the prewar years. Table 7 also shows how much remains to be done. Taking the latest available figures and judging on the basis of persons per room, the situation seems to be worst in the Eastern European countries, with Yugoslavia and Poland at the bottom of the league, closely followed by Romania, Russia, Czechoslovakia, Bulgaria and Hungary. Some of these countries were among those worst affected by World War II, and in many of them priority has been given to industrial investment rather than to housebuilding. Rapid urbanisation, partly as a consequence of this, and encouraged by low rent policies, has contributed to the problem. In Western Europe, Italy and Portugal appear to be worst off, and although the ratio of houses to population is less than 30% in Ireland, the Netherlands, Spain and Switzerland, this is offset by the large average size of houses in those countries. Nevertheless, as the upward trend in rents shows, the problem of shortage is still present even in the richer countries.

DURABLE GOODS

Consumer durables are often thought of as one of the most income elastic categories of the budget, and Table 4 shows a strong positive relationship between the budget shares and income. However, this positive association is stronger within countries than it is across countries, and even in the former, the rate of increase falls towards the end of the period. In all of the countries shown, the rise between the last two observations is less than the preceding increase, and in five countries, Denmark, France, Italy, Britain and Sweden, the share actually falls between the early and late 1960s. Even so, Goldberger and Gamaletsos in the study already referred to, estimated income elasticities greater than unity for all the countries they examined, although there was considerable inter-country variation with estimates as low as 1.16 (UK) and as high as 3.58 (Denmark). Across countries Gilbert and associates found an income elasticity of over 2 for household goods but of less than unity for purchases of motor cars. Relative prices of durable goods have fallen considerably in Western Europe, but the average fall of some 12% is insufficient to explain more than a small proportion of the observed increases in the budget share, even on the basis of the highest price elasticities found by Goldberger and Gamaletsos.

It is fairly clear, however, that although incomes play an important part in determining how much is spent on durable goods, a more complex explanation is required which can account for the rise of new durable goods, the replacement of old ones, and the speed with which these changes take place. One such explanation draws an analogy between the diffusion of ownership of a new good and the spread of a contagious disease. In the first instance, only a few consumers possess the good; these play the role of 'carriers' and 'demonstrate' their acquisitions to friends or neighbours, some of whom also purchase. The growth of demand is thus very slow at first, but gathers momentum as the number of purchasers increases. Eventually, the process slows down as the number still to be 'infected' decreases and finally demand stabilises at some saturation level; thus, over time the ownership level increases along an S-shaped or sigmoid curve. This explanation is suggestive and works well for small inexpensive items of expenditure, for example, the spread of ice-cream consumption in the United Kingdom in the 1920s. An alternative explanation pays more attention to economic factors and is particularly useful for analysing expensive durable goods such as cars, refrigerators and televisions. It is assumed that for each consumer there is a price relative to his income at which he can afford to purchase the good. Consequently, as incomes rise, or as relative price falls, perhaps because of economies of scale in the production of the good, the price of the item falls relative to income and a greater number of consumers can afford to buy. Once again, as incomes increase, the ownership level will follow a sigmoid path since the good is bought first by few relatively wealthy consumers, and later by the much larger number of those with median or below median incomes. Using this explanation, it is possible to see why the income elasticity is so variable and why the cross-country relationship is less strong than that over time. An increase in income will have a large effect if it brings the good within the range of a large number of extra consumers, i.e. if it is cheap enough to be widely consumed but still too expensive for a substantial proportion of consumers; it will have a small effect if very few people are wealthy enough to afford the good or if nearly everyone who wants the good has already purchased. Across countries, the relation with income is loose because with different distributions of income, different prices, and different dates of introduction, each country will be at a different point on its diffusion curve.

Many of the most important new commodities introduced in Europe since 1920 have been durable goods, although many items included in this category were well established before then. Furniture, carpets, floor coverings and household textiles, as well as heating and cooking equipment, made up an important part of the budget before the First World War, and although more modern versions have been substituted, so that, for example, advantage may be taken of oil, gas and electricity as sources of heat and power, these items do not appear to have been the major source of the growth in durable goods. Other goods in the group were in declining or stable demand by 1970. Radios, which were a new good in the 1920s, had reached an apparent saturation point in the richer countries by 1970, although in poorer countries, ownership still rose rapidly with income. The highest figures for radio ownership in Europe are around 300 per thousand, which at more than one per family might seem a reasonable upper limit. However, the concept of saturation is a flexible one and in America, where radios are extensively installed in cars, the corresponding ownership ratio in 1970 was over 1,400. Bicycle and motor cycle ownership follow a similar pattern, with demand rising with income in poorer countries and falling off in the richer ones. Here there are considerable geographical influences, with bicycle ownership very high in the Netherlands, Denmark and Sweden, and motor bicycles still very popular in Italy. For refrigerators and washing machines, there is again a positive cross-country relationship between ownership and income, and these goods are also presumably still in the process of diffusing through the population although the comparative time-series data do not exist in order to confirm this.

Two of the most important new goods of the twentieth century, cars and televisions, are well documented and the data for selected years are presented in Tables 8 and 9. Motor cars existed in Europe prior to the First World War, but the diffusion process was in its early stages and demand was confined to the very rich. In the interwar years, the infant European motor industry in Britain, France, Germany and Italy was protected from American competition by tariffs, and during the 1920s as incomes rose, demand expanded rapidly and ownership grew four-fold between 1922 and 1930. Growth was less rapid during the depression, but even without general economic expansion, the diffusion process kept demand for motor cars rising, and there was a further 70% increase in the average ownership level by 1938. However, much of this expansion was in the better off Western European countries – which also had relatively good road systems – and by 1938 only Denmark, France, Germany, Sweden and the United Kingdom had ownership rates over 2%. The real expansion came after the Second World War when American techniques of mass production, first developed thirty years before, were applied on a large scale in Europe. This allowed the relative price of cars to fall, and along with rapid post-war increases in incomes, set off a new and much more rapid growth in ownership. Although for the richer countries it seems that by 1970 the point of fastest growth on the S-shaped curve had been passed, demand still seems to expand roughly proportionately with income, so that there is no saturation level within sight. For the poorer countries and for Eastern Europe the process has hardly begun and it seems that the period of most rapid growth in the numbers of private cars is yet to come.

Television is one of the few goods for which dates of introduction are precisely known; in the United Kingdom,

TABLE 8: Passenger Cars per 1,000 population

	1922	1926	1930	1935	1938	1948	1950	1955	1960	1965	1970
Western Europe											
Austria	—	—	—	—	4.8[c]	4.9	7.4	21	57	109	162
Belgium	3.8	6.5	13	13	17	21	32	55[d]	82	142	213
Denmark	5.4	18	22	25	29	26	28	50	89	156	218
Finland	—	6.5[b]	—	—	7.6	4.8	6.7	20	41	99	152
France	5.1	14	26	38	48	37	—	69	121	196	252
Germany[a]	1.3	3.4	7.8	13	21	6.3	13	30	81	158	227
Greece	—	—	—	—	1.2	0.8	1	2.6[d]	5.2	12	26
Ireland	—	11[b]	—	—	18	23	31	46	62	99	134
Italy	0.7	2.7	5.2	6.6	7.9	4.8	7.4	18	40	106	192
Netherlands	2.8	5.8	9.1	10	11	8.8	14	25	45	104	192
Norway	—	8[b]	—	—	19	19	20	36	63	125	193
Portugal	1.6	2	3.7	3.9	4.7	6	7.1	11	18	35	60
Spain	—	—	—	—	—	3	3.2	4.5	9.3	26	70
Sweden	3.9	13	17	18	25	26	36	88	160	232	285
Switzerland	—	12[b]	—	—	18	23	31	54	95	155	221
UK	7.4	17	25	33	42	40	46	69	105	165	209
Eastern Europe											
Czechoslovakia	0.6	1.4	3.6	6.1	5.2	—	—	—	20	29	57
East Germany	—	—	—	—	—	—	—	—	18	41	73
Hungary	0.4	0.8	1.5	1.3	1.8	—	—	—	4[e]	10	24
Poland	0.1	0.5	0.9	0.6	0.8	1.5	—	1.5	3.9	7.8	15
Romania	0.3	0.7	1.5	0.9	1	—	—	—	1.3[f]	1.8	2.2
Yugoslavia	0.2	0.5	0.7	0.5	0.8	0.5	0.4	0.7	3	9.6	35

Notes: a from 1948, West Germany; before 1948, Germany: b 1928: c 1937: d estimated figure: e 1961: f 1962.
Sources: 1922, 1926, 1930, 1935 figures from Svennilson (1954); later figures from UN Statistical Yearbooks; population data for deflation from Svennilson and UN Demographic Yearbooks.

TABLE 9: Television Sets per 1,000 population

	1950	1955	1960	1965	1970
Western Europe					
Austria	—	0.2	27	98	192
Belgium	—	8	68	163	216
Denmark	—	2	119	228	266
Finland	—	.02	21	159	221
France	—	6	41	131	201[a]
Germany (W)	—	5	83	200	272
Greece	—	—	—	—	10[a]
Ireland	—	—	17	89	172
Italy	—	4	43	117	181
Netherlands	—	7	69	172	223[a]
Norway	—	—	13	131	220
Portugal	—	—	5	20	38
Spain	—	—	8	55	174
Sweden	—	1	156	270	312
Switzerland	—	2	24	104	203
UK	11	105	211	248	293
Eastern Europe					
Bulgaria	—	—	0.6	23	121
Czechoslovakia	—	2	58	149	214
Germany (E)	—	0.8	60	201	282
Hungary	—	.05	10	82	171
Poland	—	.01	14	66	129
Romania	—	.01	3	26	73
USSR	.08	4	22	68	143
Yugoslavia	—	—	1.4	30	88

Note: a 1969.

Source: UNESCO (1963), for 1950–60, UN Statistical and Demographic Yearbooks thereafter.

the first broadcasts were transmitted in 1936, but the service was discontinued during the war, and for practical purposes began in 1946. Other Western European countries followed from 1952. For reasons of space it is not possible to illustrate the expansion paths of television ownership for each country, but Figure 2 gives five examples covering most of the range of European experience. It is clear from the diagram and from Table 9 that diffusion is faster in the richer countries,

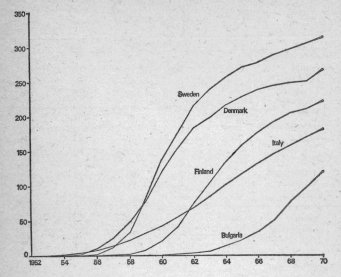

Fig. 2: Televison ownership per 1,000 population in selected countries

and in several of these, Sweden, Britain, East and West Germany, and Denmark, the process appears to be almost complete. Even so, the introduction of colour television has had a noticeable upward effect on the curve in several countries, and once again, looking to America, where ownership is over 400 per thousand, we see that much higher levels than those already observed are possible. In the poorer countries and some of Eastern Europe where television is much more expensive relative to income, diffusion has been much slower and there is clearly considerable expansion yet to come. Within countries, there are studies for England and Wales by Bain (1964), and for Sweden by Törnqvist (1967), which provide useful information on the factors governing the speed of diffusion. Between different groups of households, diffusion was faster for those in higher social groupings, for those with above average incomes, and for those households with children. Geographically, the spread of ownership was controlled primarily by the existence of transmission facilities, although once broadcasts were available, diffusion was more rapid in densely populated areas and in those where transmission began relatively late compared to the rest of the country. Extensions of the range of programmes and even especially good programmes had noticeable impacts on purchases. All of this makes good intuitive sense and fits well into explanations which emphasise the transmission of information as one of the key factors controlling diffusion.

OTHER GOODS AND SERVICES

The total of all other goods and services forms a rising share of the budget and, with a few exceptions, the cross-country experience is consistent with the time-series data, indicating an income elasticity of around 1.2. The most obvious exception is Ireland, where, as previously noted, expenditure on alcohol – included here – takes up an abnormally high proportion of the budget. Otherwise, consistency is good and the long-run and family budget data conform to the general pattern. This is perhaps surprising given the heterogeneity of the group and a full explanation of why this happens would require more disaggregation than is possible for international comparisons such as these.

The value shares of two sub-groups, drink and tobacco, and household fuels, certainly do not show any strong tendency to increase with rising incomes. The first of these probably has an income elasticity close to unity but is, and has been, subject to a wide range of special factors. Price varies widely over time and across countries as governments change the level of taxation; the composition of alcoholic drink between beer, wine and spirits varies greatly according to geography and local custom; while cigarette smoking is subject to major secular changes in tastes, from its spread among women in the interwar period, through a major upsurge in demand during the war, to the anti-smoking sentiments of the present day. The share of fuel, likewise, shows little tendency to increase with increases in income. Certainly, as household technology has changed, the demand for electricity has risen rapidly, but in general this has been compensated for by the decline in the demand for solid fuel.

A category, the share of which does grow through time, is transport and communication. The growth of this, although owing much to increases in income, has been an integral part of the whole process of economic growth and the changes which accompany it. The spread of public transport between the wars brought, through local bus services, a whole new system of communication to the countryside, and in the cities allowed new patterns of urbanisation and suburbanisation based on the existence of a flexible means of transport between workplace and residence. Public transport is still an income elastic good in the poorer European countries, and air transport is so universally; in the richer countries, private transport has replaced some rail and road services as the number of private motor vehicles has increased.

Many of the other goods and services in the group are either luxuries (many personal services, recreational goods, foreign travel, etc.) or semi-luxuries, i.e. items like insurance, health, or educational expenditures, which, once absolute necessities have been met, become almost essential. There is thus a direct causal link between rising incomes and the rising budget share of these items. However, there are important distortions in the general pattern of increase many of which can be associated with the presence and spread of durable goods. Purchases in petrol, oil, garage services, and insurance have risen very rapidly in line with increases in car ownership. Inside the home, domestic appliances have not only substituted for paid domestic help but have relieved housewives of much of the unpaid drudgery of housekeeping. Increased use of television has also meant a declining demand for entertainment outside the home, particularly in cinemas and theatres. Here, as in many areas of the budget, the interacting forces of income growth and technical progress have been the main factors leading to structural change.

BIBLIOGRAPHY

Many of the issues discussed in this chapter are dealt with in more detail and for a wider range of countries by Kuznets (1962); in his book, Kuznets (1966), which deals with wider aspects of economic growth, much of the material on consumption is repeated in abbreviated form. Clark (1957) presents a wide range of material on consumption patterns from many countries, much of it based on family budget surveys. At a more technical level, a number of econometric studies of cross-country consumption patterns exist; those of Goldberger and Gamaletsos (1970) and of Gilbert and associates (1958) have been referred to in the text, and there is a useful survey of family budget studies by Houthakker (1957). There is a vast econometric literature on the modelling of consumption behaviour; this is surveyed in Brown and Deaton (1972). The broader questions of the allocation of domestic product are dealt with in this volume by Maddison (1973), and there is much useful material for the prewar period in the books by Richardson (1967), Svennilson (1954) and Lewis (1949).

The main data sources have been listed with the tables in the text, and full references are given below. On particular topics, a number of specialist works should be mentioned. The material on food rationing comes from two reports of the League of Nations (1942) and (1944) and from the official British war histories, especially Hancock and Gowing (1949) and Hammond (1951); the economic theory of rationing is dealt with in a survey by Tobin (1952). For housing, the UN (1949) report gives valuable information on wartime destruction and links the pre- and postwar housing data, and a useful eye-witness report on the situation in Europe between the wars is given in Denby (1938). Richardson (1967) and Mowat (1956) discuss housing in Britain over the same period. The growth of government expenditure is studied in Peacock and Wiseman (1961). Ironmonger (1972) discusses the introduction and diffusion of new commodities, while for durables, in addition to the studies of television by Bain (1964) and Törnqvist (1967), there are more general surveys by Maizels (1959), Knox (1959), and Bonüs (1973).

Bain, A. D., *The Growth of Television Ownership in the United Kingdom*, Cambridge University Press, 1964.

Barberi, B., *I Consumi Nel Primo Secolo Dell'Unita D'Italia 1861–1960*, Dott. A. Giuffre, Milan, 1961.

Bartun, A. P. and J. I. Viorst, 'De consumptiere bestedingen van gezinshuishoudingen in Nederland, 1921–1939 en 1948–1958.' Report 6202 of the Econometric Institute of the Netherlands School of Economics, 1962.

Bonüs, H., 'Quasi-Engel Curves, Diffusion, and the Ownership of Major Consumer Durables', *Journal of Political Economy*, Vol. 81, 1973.

Brown, J. A. C. and A. S. Deaton, 'Models of Consumer Behaviour: A Survey', *Economic Journal*, Vol. 82, 1972.

Clark, C., *The Conditions of Economic Progress* (3rd edition), Macmillan, London, 1957.

Denby, E., *Europe Re-housed*, Allen and Unwin, London, 1938.

Feinstein, C. H., *National Income, Expenditure and Output of the United Kingdom 1855–1965*, Cambridge University Press, 1972.

Gilbert, M. and associates, *Comparative National Products and Price Levels*, OEEC, Paris, 1958.

Goldberger, A. S. and T. Gamaletsos, 'A Cross-country Comparison of Consumer Expenditure Patterns', *European Economic Review*, Vol. 1, 1970.

Hammond, R. J., *Food. Vol. I: The Growth of Policy*, Longmans, London 1951. (*History of the Second World War: United Kingdom Civil Series*, ed. W. K. Hancock.)

Hancock, W. K. and M. M. Gowing, *British War Economy*, H.M.S.O., London, 1949. (*History of the Second World War: United Kingdom Civil Series*, ed. W. K. Hancock.)

Hanson, P., *The Consumer in the Soviet Economy*, Macmillan, London, 1968.

Houthakker, H. S., 'An International Comparison of Household Expenditure Patterns Commemorating the Centenary of Engel's Law', *Econometrica*, Vol. 25, 1957.

Ironmonger, D., *New Commodities and Consumer Behaviour*, Cambridge University Press, 1972.

Knox, F., 'Some International Comparisons of Consumers' Durable Goods', *Bulletin of the Oxford Institute of Statistics*, Vol. 21, 1959.

Kuznets, S., 'Quantitative Aspects of the Economic Growth of Nations: VII. The Share and Structure of Consumption', *Economic Development and Cultural Change*, Vol. 10, 1962.

Kuznets, S., *Modern Economic Growth*, Yale University Press, New Haven, 1966.

League of Nations, *Wartime Rationing and Consumption*, Geneva, 1942.

League of Nations, *Food Rationing and Supply 1943/44*, Geneva, 1944.

Lewis, W. A., *Economic Survey 1919–1939*, Allen and Unwin, London, 1965.

Maddison, A., *Economic Policy and Performance in Europe 1913–1970*, Chapter 10 of this volume.

Maizels, A., 'Trends in World Trade in Durable Consumer Goods', *National Institute Economic Review*, No. 6, November 1959.

Mowat, C. L., *Britain Between the Wars 1918–1940*, Methuen, London, 1956.

OECD, *National Accounts of OECD Countries 1950–1968*, Paris, 1970.

OECD, *National Accounts of OECD Countries 1960–1971*, Paris, 1973.

Osterreichischen Institutes fur Wirtshaftsforschung, *Osterreichs Volkseinkommen 1913–63*, Vienna, August 1965.

Peacock, A. T. and J. Wiseman, *The Growth of Public Expenditure in the United Kingdom*, Princeton University Press, 1961.

Richardson, H. W., *Economic Recovery in Britain 1932–9*, Weidenfeld and Nicolson, London, 1967.

Stone, R. and D. A. Rowe, *The Measurement of Consumers' Expenditure and Behaviour in the United Kingdom 1920–1938*, Vol. II, Cambridge University Press, 1966.

Svennilson, I., *Growth and Stagnation of the European Economy*, UN Economic Commission for Europe, Geneva, 1954.

Tobin, J., 'A Survey of the Theory of Rationing', *Econometrica*, Vol. 20, 1952.

Törnqvist, G., *TV agandets utveckling: Sverige 1956–65*, Almqvist and Wiksell, Stockholm, 1967.

UN, *Demographic Yearbook*, New York, annually.

UN, *Yearbook of National Accounts Statistics*, New York, annually.

UN, *Statistical Yearbook*, New York, annually.

UN, *The European Housing Problem: A Preliminary Review*, Geneva, 1949.

UNESCO, *Statistics on Radio and Television 1950–1960*, Paris, 1963.

3. The Labour Force and Labour Problems in Europe 1920-1970

Walter Galenson

A history of European labour market developments since 1920 is divided logically into two periods hinging on World War II. The first twenty years, from the Treaty of Versailles to the outbreak of war, were characterised by little, if any, economic growth; chronic unemployment; and a pattern of industrial relations that may better be described as industrial warfare. With few exceptions, trade unions fared poorly in this environment. Their allied labour parties succumbed one by one to forces of fascism, leaving only Great Britain and the northern fringe of countries to hold the torch of democratic socialism aloft.

The end of the war witnessed a rapid revival of the idea of social democracy, and within a relatively short time the welfare state had spread from its Scandinavian stronghold to a good part of Europe. There were some conspicuous exceptions. For a variety of reasons, the Iberian Peninsula, the Balkans, and Eastern Europe were unable to free themselves from totalitarian rule. But the major industrial nations of Europe experienced an upsurge of trade union organisation and activity and the evolution of orderly systems of collective bargaining. The unprecedented rate of economic growth was a major contributor to these developments.

The first portion of this brief history of an eventful half-century will commence with the aftermath of World War I and carry forward to 1939. Little will be said about the 1940s, when trade unionism and industrial relations were overshadowed first by war, then by the exigencies of reconstruction. By 1950, or a few years thereafter, a normal economic life had been restored in most of Western Europe, and labour problems began once more to emerge. But they took on quite a different character. As time went on, inflation replaced unemployment as the paramount economic concern. Collective bargaining became firmly established as the method by which wages and other labour conditions were determined. Political parties of the left greatly increased their parliamentary representation, and in most countries attained political power, for shorter or longer periods.

It would be impossible, in a brief essay, to cover the labour developments of all Western European countries. To reduce the material to manageable proportions, the scope of the essay will be limited to the four major industrial powers – France, Germany, Italy, and the United Kingdom – plus Sweden as representative of Scandinavia and as an examplar of the social democratic welfare state. The interesting labour developments in Austria, Belgium, Denmark, the Netherlands, Norway and Switzerland will have to be excluded from the discussion. Even within the restricted sample it will be necessary to be highly selective of topics treated. As far as possible, the focus is on comparison, though a certain amount of reference to events in individual countries is unavoidable.

THE ECONOMIC BACKGROUND

The records of prewar and postwar European growth are so different that it is scarcely possible to believe the same continent is involved. For the prewar years there was at best low growth, followed by the Great Depression. This is not to say that economic fluctuations disappeared after the war, but in terms of amplitude, they have little resemblance to what had gone before.

The data in Tables 1 and 2 describe economic growth in the five European countries in terms of what happened to the national product. Interwar growth was neither smooth nor very substantial, due in large measure to the impact of the Great Depression. Sweden recovered most rapidly, accounting for its relatively good performance. The large jump in German output from 1935 to 1939 was a consequence of the command economy introduced by the Nazis in preparation for war.

The postwar data in Table 2 reveal a completely different

TABLE 1: Indexes of Total Volume of Output, 1920–1939
(1920 = 100)

Year	France	Germany	Italy	Sweden	United Kingdom
1920	100	100	100	100	100
1925	134	126	120	107	109
1930	149	147	124	131	117
1935	138	158	137	134	128
1939	154	232	159	168	141
Average annual rate of increase, 1920–1939	2.30	4.53	2.47	2.77	1.82

Source: Angus Maddison, *Economic Policy and Performance in Europe 1913–1970*, The Fontana Economic History of Europe, Table 22.

TABLE 2: Indexes of Total Volume of Output, 1950–1970
(1950 = 100)

Year	France	Germany	Italy	Sweden	United Kingdom
1950	100	100	100	100	100
1955	124	156	134	118	114
1960	156	212	175	140	130
1965	207	271	227	182	154
1970	275	340	304	220	172

| Average annual rate of increase, 1950–1970 | 5.19 | 6.31 | 5.72 | 4.02 | 2.75 |

Source: Angus Maddison, *Economic Policy and Performance in Europe, 1913–1970*, The Fontana Economic History of Europe, Table 22.

picture and help explain the great change in the atmosphere of the labour market. With national product growth rates far in excess of the prewar level, it was much easier to maintain social harmony, an essential ingredient for good industrial relations. When all incomes are rising faster, controversy among social groups over the distribution of income tends to be less intense.

A word of caution: it is not necessarily true that the mitigation of social strife is a direct function of the *level* of national income. The most militant workers are rarely to be found among the poverty stricken, who cannot sustain lengthy strikes. It is true that absolute living standards were higher after than before the war, but this was probably of less importance to the establishment of a good economic base for industrial relations than the fact that living standards were increasing at a steady and substantial rate. When this rate slackened, trouble developed.

The data in Tables 3 and 4 reflect the impact of the varying growth rates on real wages. For the prewar decades, only Sweden had a substantial increase in real wages, and that came largely before 1930. German and French workers had little improvement in two decades, and the British

TABLE 3: Indexes of Real Wages During the Interwar Period
(Prewar = 100)

Country	Series	Base year	1924	1930	1935	1938	Average annual per cent increase, base year to 1938
France	To 1929 – daily earnings[a]	1911	100	—	—	—	—
	1929–1938 – weekly earnings[b]	1911	—	111	123	119	0.70
Germany	Weekly earnings[b]	1913–14	87 (1925)	105	103	114	0.55
Sweden	Daily earnings[c]	1913	123	147	151	154	1.74
United Kingdom	Weekly earnings[d]	1914	111	122	132	128	1.03

(a) Small industry in Paris.
(b) Industry.
(c) Industry, handicraft, commerce, transport.
(d) Non-agricultural, excluding government.

Source: Ingvar Svennilson, *Growth and Stagnation in the European Economy*, Economic Commission for Europe, 1954, p. 235

TABLE 4: Indexes of Real Hourly Wage Rates in Manufacturing, 1950–1970
(1950 = 100)

	1950	1955	1960	1965	1970	*Average annual % increase, 1950–1970*
France	100	133	146	174	219	4.00
Germany	100	119	148	189	235	4.36
Italy	100	108	121	156	200	3.53
Sweden	100	124	140	175	217	3.95
United Kingdom	100	105	117	122	136	1.55

Source: 1950–1959: OEEC, *Europe and the World Economy*, 1960.
1960–1970: OECD, *Main Economic Indicators*, various issues.
Wage data for Sweden are hourly earnings. For all countries except Italy, money wages were deflated by the consumer price index. For Italy, the GNP price deflater was used for the period 1950–1959 and the consumer price index thereafter.

record can scarcely be termed brilliant. The postwar years were an entirely different matter. For four of the five countries, real wages more than doubled from 1950 to 1970. Moreover, the improvement was fairly steady, with little of the gross cyclical movement that characterised prewar Europe.

These comparisons, however brief, suggest that the entire quality of European economic life changed after World War II. It has been argued that the commitment of American trade unions to the method of collective bargaining owes a great deal to the steady rise of real wages in the United States for a century, interrupted only very briefly during the worst years of the Great Depression. This may help to explain why European unions tended to turn from political action to collective bargaining after the war.

THE LABOUR FORCE

Wages are only part of the story, and perhaps not the most important part. The insecurity of employment contributed greatly to interwar tensions. The remarkably high levels of employment in postwar Europe stand in marked contrast to the heavy unemployment that prevailed between the wars.

If one examines the population data for the years 1920–1940 (Table 5), two notable facts emerge. The first is the extraordinarily low growth of the population of working age in France. The second is the substantial increase in the labour supply for the rest of the countries. Apart from France, the availability of labour would certainly not have been a constraint on economic growth. The same conclusions emerge even more strongly from the data in Table 6. In addition to the natural growth of the labour force, people were leaving the farms to work in non-agricultural occupations, particularly in Italy and Sweden. The extent to which the services, rather than manufacturing, benefited from the increasing labour supply is evident from Table 7, which contains a sectoral breakdown of employment for twelve European countries. Manufacturing employment just maintained its relative position in the structure of the labour force, while the entire net decline in agriculture was reflected in increased employment in the services.

These labour force trends had some interesting implications for the institutions of the labour market. The trade unions had their main base in industry, and the absolute predominance of industrial sector employment nourished their power. Scandinavia in particular experienced a great upsurge in its industrial labour force from 1920 to 1940, some 43 per cent,[1] and this is certainly not unrelated to the rise of unionism and political socialism.

1. Ingvar Svennilson, *Growth and Stagnation in the European Economy* Geneva, 1954, p. 76.

TABLE 5: Population Aged 15 to 64 Years, 1920–1940
(thousands of persons)

Country	Population, 1920	Population, 1940	Per cent increase, 1920–1940	Per cent increase, of male population, 1920–1940
France	26,600	27,290	2.6	4.8
Germany	40,206	48,295	20.1	24.5
Italy	23,380	28,210	20.7	21.1
Sweden	3,660	4,459	21.8	24.1
United Kingdom	28,762	33,165	15.3	17.7

Source: Ingvar Svennilson, Growth and Stagnation in the European Economy, Geneva, 1954, pp. 238–239.

TABLE 6: Non-Agricultural Manpower, 1920–1940
(millions of persons)

Country	Manpower outside agriculture, 1920	Increase of total manpower, 1920–1940	Manpower outside agriculture, 1940	Per cent increase in manpower outside agriculture, 1920–1940
France	16.3	0.7	17.0	4.3
Germany	30.8	8.1	38.9	26.3
Italy	10.6	4.8	15.4	45.3
Sweden	2.0	0.8	2.8	40.0
United Kingdom	25.9	4.4	30.3	17.0

Source: Ingvar Svennilson, *Growth and Stagnation in the European Economy*, Geneva, 1954, p. 241.

TABLE 7: Distribution of the European Labour Force[a] by Major Economic Sector, 1920–1940

	Number occupied (millions)			Per cent change, 1920–1940	Per cent of total number occupied		
	1920	1930	1940		1920	1930	1940
Agriculture	16	15	14	−12.5	27	24	22
Industry	27	29	30	+11.1	44	44	44
Services	18	20	23	+27.8	29	32	34

(a) Includes United Kingdom, Ireland, Germany, France, Belgium, the Netherlands, Switzerland, Sweden, Norway, Denmark, Finland and Austria.

Source: Ingvar Svennilson, *Growth and Stagnation in the European Economy*, Geneva, 1954, p. 75.

Another fact that emerges from the data is the gradual establishment of the service industries as the type of employment distinctive to the postwar period. However, the political and social implications of this trend are not a simple matter. The service sector is a very heterogeneous one, consisting in part of highly productive and well-paid jobs, and in part of traditional, low-paid jobs. The many small retail shops that existed in France and Germany provide an example of the latter. The French situation is well known, but what is not as well appreciated is the fact that, in prewar Germany, the labour force (including proprietors) in small enterprises in retailing, handicraft production and catering was twice as large as the labour force in large-scale industry. The owners of large corporations may have supplied the Nazis with funds, but the votes came primarily from the lower middle class, working mainly in the service sector.

Coming, finally, to unemployment, it must first be noted that the data for the prewar period are anything but satisfactory. The unemployment rates shown in Table 8 differ in concept and coverage from those contained in the contributions to this volume by Angus Maddison and B. R. Mitchell. In particular, the Maddison rates, which are much lower, relate unemployment to the total labour force at a time when the European agricultural sector was still large. The data in Table 8 are generally limited to manufacturing, mining and construction, and cannot be compared directly with the postwar figures, which cover the entire labour force. Nevertheless, it is abundantly clear that except for France, for a good part of the postwar period the levels of unemployment would have been completely unacceptable in the countries with which we are dealing.

The French exception is an interesting one. Until the depression hit France, the country was importing workers, particularly for unpopular jobs in the coal mines. Foreigners constituted 10 per cent of all wage and salary earners in 1931. From 1931 to 1936, there was a net decline of 400,000 foreign workers. The French concentrated unemployment on these workers; the rate of unemployment could be kept

TABLE 8: Estimated Rates of Unemployment, 1920–1938
(Per cent)

	1920	1925	1930	1935	1938
France[a]	5.0 (1921)	3.0	2.0	14.5	7.8
Germany[a]	—	5.2	23.2	16.2	3.2
Sweden[b]	5.4	11.0	11.9	15.0	10.9
United Kingdom[c]	3.2	11.3	16.1	15.5	10.5

(a) Wage and salary earners in manufacturing, mining and construction.
(b) Based upon trade union reports in manufacturing, transportation, building and commerce.
(c) Employees covered by unemployment insurance.

Source: Walter Galenson and Arnold Zellner, 'International Comparison of Unemployment Rates', in National Bureau of Economic Research, *The Measurement and Behavior of Unemployment*, Princeton, N.J., 1957.

down by the simple expedient of withdrawing their working and residence permits. The initial need for these workers stemmed from the very low growth of the French labour force consequent on the devastating manpower losses sustained in World War I.

Turning to the postwar data, it is apparent from Table 9 that the rate of labour force increase from 1950 to 1970 was substantially lower than that of 1920 to 1940, except again for France. Since the 1970 figures include a substantial number of foreign workers, the discrepancy is even greater. There was thus a smaller pool of labour with which economic growth could be fuelled. The other side of the coin was that with fewer people of working age coming into the labour market the pressure to supply gainful employment was less severe.

A favourable factor on the supply side was the continuing shift of workers out of agriculture. In Germany, for example, farm employment dropped by more than 1.2 million from 1960 to 1970, while non-agricultural employment rose by 2 million. The corresponding figures for Italy were 2.9

TABLE 9: Population Aged 15 to 64 Years, 1950–1970
(thousands of persons)

Country	Population, 1950	Population, 1960	Per cent increase, 1950–1960	Population, 1970	Per cent increase, 1960–1970	Per cent increase, 1950–1970
France	27,577	28,319	2.7	31,659	11.8	14.8
Germany	—	37,596	—	38,599	2.7	—
Italy	30,862	33,097	7.2	35,515	7.3	15.1
Sweden	4,651	4,926	5.9	5,268	6.9	13.3
United Kingdom	33,881	34,195	0.9	35,268	3.1	4.1

Source: OECD, *Labour Force Statistics*, various issues.

million and 1.7 million, and for France, 1.3 million and 3.0 million. Only in the case of England, where agricultural employment had reached the low level of 4 per cent of total employment by 1960, was a further labour supply from agriculture unavailable.

The relatively rapid growth of the service sector, which had already begun during the interwar years, accelerated after 1960 (see Table 10). By 1970, Sweden had become a service-oriented nation, with more than half of all employment in that sector, and only in Germany and Italy did employment in industry still exceed that in services. If the sectoral distribution of employment in Table 10 is compared with that of gross domestic product in Table 11, it appears that, country for country, the two were roughly equal by 1970 (except for Italy, where service output substantially exceeded employment), suggesting that little remained in the way of the prewar traditional low-productivity service activity. This conclusion must be accepted with some reservation because of the well-known difficulties involved in estimating service output. Nevertheless, the conclusion is not surprising. Low income services are often an alternative for unemployment, and few needed this opportunity by 1970.

Some notion of the importance of women in the labour force can be secured from the data in Tables 12 and 13. The female labour force participation rate was quite high, except for Italy, which still had a substantial reserve of womanpower in 1970. Not that all of these women were idle; on the contrary, many of them were fully employed in households and on small farms, for want of more remunerative occupations, and were not included in the labour force.

As Table 13 shows, women were employed predominantly in the services (as well as in agriculture for which there are no data). The female-male employment ratios for German industry would have been higher if foreign workers, almost all male, were excluded from the count. Compared with the interwar years, women were more heavily represented in the services by 1970, except for Sweden, where the inter-

TABLE 10: Sectoral Distribution of the Labour Force, 1950–1970
(Per cent of total employment)

	1950 A	1950 I	1950 S	1955 A	1955 I	1955 S	1960 A	1960 I	1960 S	1965 A	1965 I	1965 S	1970 A	1970 I	1970 S
France	—	—	—	27.0	37.6	35.3	22.4	37.8	39.8	17.7	39.4	42.9	14.0	38.8	47.1
Germany	24.7	42.9	32.5	18.5	46.9	34.6	14.0	48.8	37.3	11.1	50.1	38.8	9.0	50.3	40.7
Italy	—	—	—	38.2	33.4	28.4	32.8	36.9	30.2	26.1	40.7	33.3	19.6	43.7	36.7
Sweden	—	—	—	—	—	—	—	—	—	—	—	—	8.1	38.4	53.5
United Kingdom	5.6	47.7	46.7	4.9	49.0	46.1	4.1	48.8	47.0	3.3	48.1	48.6	2.9	46.6	50.6

A — Agriculture
I — Industry
S — Services

Source: OECD, *Labour Force Statistics*, various issues.

TABLE 11: Gross Domestic Product, by Sector of Origin, 1969
(Per cent of total)

	Agriculture	Industry	Services
France	6	48	46
Germany	4	52	44
Italy	11	39	50
Sweden	4	41	55
United Kingdom	3	43	54

Source: B. R. Mitchell, *Statistical Appendix, 1920–1970*, in The Fontana
Economic History of Europe, Volume 6, pp. 130–134.

war representation was already very high. The combination of high levels of employment and the growth in demand for services in postwar Europe enabled women to play a significantly greater role in the labour market than had been possible before.

Although migratory labour was already of some consequence in interwar Europe, particularly in France, what occurred after the war dwarfed the earlier experience. Apart from Switzerland, France and Germany were the main host countries. Great Britain admitted 350,000 Irish from 1946 to 1959; 460,000 Europeans between 1946 and 1951; and over 650,000 Indians, Pakistanis and West Indians between 1955 and 1968, but these were in the main permanent settlers rather than temporary workers.[2] Italy was an exporter rather than an importer of labour. Sweden had 173,000 foreign workers in 1969, constituting 5 per cent of the labour force.

Almost 2.7 million foreign workers and their dependants entered France between 1946 and 1970. At first Italians, then Spanish and Portuguese were the principal foreign groups coming in. In addition, 600,000 Algerians were admitted on the basis of claims to French citizenship. The immigrant groups constituted 6.3 per cent of the labour force at the end of 1969; in construction, they provided 20 per cent of total manpower, and in manufacturing, 8

2. Stephen Castles and Godula Cosack, *Immigrant Workers and Class Structure in Western Europe*, Oxford, 1973, pp. 28–32.

TABLE 12: Labour Force Participation Rates for Women, 1950–1970
(Female civilian employment as a percentage of female population aged 15 to 64 years)

	1950	1955	1960	1965	1970
France	—	47.0	45.8	43[a]	—
Germany	—	—	49.3	49.0	48.6
Italy	—	27.4	36.7	31.0	29.1
Sweden	—	—	49.8	54.1	59.4
United Kingdom	42.3	45.9	48.6	51.0	52.1

(a) United Nations, *Investment in Human Resources and Manpower Planning*, New York, 1971, p. 10.

Source: OECD, *Labour Force Statistics*, various issues.

TABLE 13: Proportion of Women to Men in Civilian Employment, 1960–1970
(Per cent)

	1960	1965	1970
Industry			
Germany	35	34	33
Italy	33	26	26
Sweden	—	—	25
United Kingdom	35	34	35
Services			
Germany	86	91	89
Italy	51	50	49
Sweden	—	—	92
United Kingdom	81	87	94

Source: OECD, *Labour Force Statistics*, various issues.

per cent.[3] German reliance on immigrant labour was similarly heavy. In 1969, foreign labour constituted 7 per cent of the total labour force, 12.4 per cent in construction, and 8.8 per cent in manufacturing.[4] About 80 per cent of these entered Germany on fixed term contracts, usually for one year, although most had their contracts renewed.

In the earlier years of the migrant traffic, the problems of adjustment were not severe and the migrants were glad to have jobs at what seemed to them excellent rates of pay. But as their concentration in particular cities increased, and housing facilities lagged, difficult social problems arose, and contributed to industrial unrest at the end of the 1960s.

The increased use of women and migrants suggests that unemployment was at a low level, and this is borne out by the data in Table 14. For the decade of the 1960s, unemployment must have been near the irreducible frictional minimum. Apart from Italy, which still had a soft labour market in the South, unemployment had ceased to be a matter of social consequence in these countries. This, more than anything else, was the key to the development of trade unionism and orderly systems of industrial relations.

3. *ibid.*, p. 4.   4. *ibid.*, p. 73.

T.C.

F

TABLE 14: Rates of Unemployment, 1950–1970
(Unemployed as a percentage of the civilian labour force)

	1950	1955	1960	1965	1970
France	—	1.5	1.3	1.4	1.7
Germany	7.0	3.8	1.0	0.6	0.6
Italy	—	7.6	4.0	3.7	3.2
Sweden	—	—	1.5a	1.2	1.5
United Kingdom	1.2	0.8	1.3	1.2	2.2

(*a*) 1962.

Source: OECD, *Labour Force Statistics*, various issues.

TRADE UNIONISM

The years before World War II were not good ones for the European labour movement. Ground between totalitarianism of the left and the right, democratic unions were able to survive only on the northern fringes of the Continent. From 1940 to 1945, in only three nations of all Europe, embattled Britain and neutral Switzerland and Sweden, did trade unions continue to function. With the restoration of peace came a renascence of unionism wherever democracy was established. Since then, the union movement has grown in scope and power and in many countries has become the single most important economic institution.

Europe was shaken by a burst of revolutionary fervour when hostilities ended in 1918. Spurred on by the establishment of the Soviet Union, left-wing groups in other countries sought to create the conditions for similar social changes. These movements failed of their purpose, but there remained a residue of power in the form of communist-dominated political parties and trade union organisations that hindered subsequent efforts to create viable democratic labour groupings. Of the countries in our sample, only in Britain and Sweden did communism play an insignificant role.

The most short-lived of the interwar labour movements was the Italian. But from the vantage point of 1918, it would have been difficult to predict the fate that overtook Italian trade unionism just a few years later. The General Confederation of Labour, the main union body, increased its membership from 250,000 in 1918 to 2.2 million in 1920. However, the moderate leadership of the Federation found itself powerless to contain the turbulence consequent upon the revolutionary stance of the Socialist Party to which Italian workers looked for political leadership. Direct action in the form of strikes in which factories were taken over by the strikers became the order of the day, and led inevitably to strong employer reaction. Benito Mussolini, who had earlier been a leading Socialist and the editor of *Avanti*, the Socialist newspaper, was able to capitalise upon middle-class fears of revolution to rally support for his fascist strongarm squads. The Confederation of Labour tried desperately to bring about unity among the various left of centre political groups, each attempting to preserve its doctrinal purity, but to no avail. When Mussolini became Prime Minister in 1922, Confederation membership had fallen to 400,000 and, by 1924 the organisation had ceased to exist, to be replaced by government-controlled syndicates that persisted until the overthrow of fascism.[5]

Freedom lasted somewhat longer in Germany, but the end was even more grim. During the near-revolution that followed the abdication of the Kaiser in November 1918, the trade unions generally supported the moderate Social Democratic Party and were a major factor in forestalling attempted coups from both the left and, later, from the right. The unions grew very rapidly; membership of the free (non-confessional) trade unions rose from 2.6 million in 1913 to 5.5 million in 1919. The German Federation of Labour, by 1923, claimed 7 million members, and this plus a million more in two smaller federations constituted about 27 per cent of the entire non-agricultural labour force. But an employer counter-offensive, growing unemployment, and Communist opposition to the Social Democratic leadership of the Federation reduced its membership to 4.2 million in 1925.

Between the end of the hyper-inflation of 1923 and the onset of depression in 1929, the trade unions and the Social Democratic Party, despite the shortness of the time, managed to enact into law a good social welfare system and to establish a comprehensive framework for collective bargaining. But the collapse of the economy, accompanied by soaring unemployment, put labour on the defensive. When the Nazis came to power in 1933 they dissolved the unions and incarcerated the leaders. What many had

5. For an excellent account of the tragic events of this episode in Italian labour history, see Daniel L. Horowitz, *The Italian Labor Movement*, Cambridge, Mass., 1963.

believed to be the most solidly built labour movement in the world simply ceased to exist.

French trade unionism persisted until the nation's military defeat in 1940, but the history of the interwar period is nonetheless depressing. For several years after the termination of World War I, the fortunes of the General Confederation of Labour (CGT), the traditional centre of French unionism, were on the ascendant, but a disastrous general strike in 1920 led to a membership decline, from 2 million to 400,000. Recrimination among the various political parties followed, with the result that communists, anarchists and syndicalists were expelled and set up their own organisations. Although the CGT survived the split and managed to pick up new members, particularly among civil servants, the intransigence of French employers and their refusal to recognise the legitimacy of unions precluded any real progress. By 1933, only 7.5 per cent of the workers in industry and commerce were covered by collective agreements.

The impact of the Great Depression upon the French economy was not as severe as in most of the rest of Europe. Moreover, the worst of the burden of unemployment was placed upon foreign workers. France was nevertheless shaken, and seemed for a while to be moving into a new stage of labour development. The CGT and the Communist-led labour federation agreed to a merger in 1935. This was a consequence of the Moscow-initiated Popular Front phase, leading further to an electoral victory for the parties of the left in 1936. In the midst of a national epidemic of occupation strikes, Leon Blum, a Socialist, assumed the premiership and proceeded to negotiate with the CGT and the employers' federation the famous Matignon Agreement. Under its terms, the major employers of France agreed in principle, for the first time, to collective bargaining. Workers rushed into unions and, within a year, the CGT claimed 5.3 million members, by far the largest number in French history. The Communist Party, with a well-disciplined core of activists, threw itself into the work of organisation, and quickly gained control over some of the major unions, a policy that paid off handsomely after 1945.

Although the practice of collective bargaining spread, its success was short-lived. The Popular Front government proved unable to deal with the current economic crisis, let alone to bring about the major reforms to which it was committed. The governing coalition collapsed and, in 1938, when the Communists persuaded the CGT leadership to engage in a general strike against the Daladier government that had replaced it, the swift employer reaction badly hurt the unions. When the war broke out in 1939, CGT membership was down to 2 million. The CGT was dissolved by the Vichy government, and only the memories of the heady events of 1936 and 1937 remained to sustain those who were committed to a free labour movement.[6]

Moving north, this catalogue can be concluded on a somewhat happier note. The British trade unions proved to be very durable, despite two decades of high unemployment. They emerged from World War I with 8 million members, double the prewar level. They soon ran into trouble, however, in the form of a sharp recession in 1920, and for the next two years they lost 2½ million members in vain efforts to resist wage cuts. Ramsay MacDonald became the first Labour Prime Minister, in January 1924, but before the year was out his Government had fallen, not least because of friction with the trade unions, which saw this as an opportunity to advance claims for higher wages in the face of substantial unemployment.

The most dramatic event in the interwar history of British labour was the General Strike of 1926. It originated in a coal mine pay dispute, as has so much of British labour strife. The Trades Union Congress, which is the central federation of British labour, called for sympathy strikes to support the miners, and 1½ million men went out, in addition to a million miners, including most transport workers. The Conservative Government used troops and police to man essential services, and on the ninth day of

6. These events are treated in detail in Val R. Lorwin, *The French Labor Movement*, Cambridge, Mass., 1954.

the strike the TUC negotiated a settlement that was in fact a surrender, leaving the miners alone and bitter. An election in 1929 that was fought against the background of very heavy unemployment resulted in a large increase in Labour's parliamentary strength. MacDonald, with the support of the Liberal Party, formed a new government, but it was brought down in 1931 by worsening economic conditions. Against the advice of most of his Labour Party colleagues in Parliament, MacDonald agreed to form a new coalition government with the Conservatives and Liberals, which led to his expulsion from the Labour Party. This episode proved disastrous, and in elections held in October 1931, Labour's representation was reduced to a handful.

Despite this loss of political power and continued depression, the trade unions slowly recouped what they had lost after the 1926 General Strike. Union membership rose from 4.4 million in 1932, the lowest figure since 1915, to 6.3 million in 1939. Attempts by the Communist Party to gain influence were thwarted by the moderate Socialist leaders, with Ernest Bevin, the general secretary of the giant Transport and General Workers' Union, as their chief spokesman. The unions were also instrumental in preventing the intellectual wing of the Labour Party from committing the labour movement to a suicidal pacifist, anti-rearmament position in the face of growing fascist military power. This was critical in preserving the credibility of the Labour Party as a responsible alternative to the Conservatives. To summarise: the British labour movement emerged from the trauma of 1926 and the Great Depression in a surprisingly strong position, and proved to be an essential element in enabling Britain to resist the German onslaught. Clement Attlee, the leader of the Labour Party, and Ernest Bevin were key members of Churchill's wartime government.

In Sweden, finally, the trade unions and their closely allied Social Democratic Party continued on a growth path that had commenced in 1910, and the end of the 1930s saw labour firmly in power. Trade union membership grew from 280,000 in 1920 to 971,000 in 1940. Except for the years 1920–1924, when the unions were resisting wage cuts, the industrial relations scene was relatively peaceful. This was due in no small measure to the formation of a Socialist-led government in 1932, and to its adoption of a Keynesian policy of economic expansion involving a large public works programme financed by a budget deficit, at a time when the conventional wisdom dictated paring government expenditures to the bone. Thus began the long reign of Swedish socialism, the longest tenure of democratic socialist government thus far experienced.[7]

The end of the war in 1945 marked the inception of a new era in European labour history. Within a decade, trade unions were no longer suppliants seeking recognition from employers. The century-old quest for democratic socialist government, which appeared to have been finally frustrated by fascism, became a reality. The welfare state came into its full flowering, with the working class the chief beneficiary.

It would have been difficult to predict that trade unionism should have its outstanding success in Germany. Although pre-Nazi union membership was substantial, political divisions and an untidy structure reduced union effectiveness. The architects of the revived movement were not hampered by an established power system; this was a real advantage, because trade unions are extremely conservative institutions where structural change is involved. They were able to establish a new federation consisting of just 16 national industrial unions, which embraced all but a small portion of the nation's organised workers. The German Federation of Trade Unions (DGB) attained a total of 5 million members by 1949, a figure that had increased by 2 million twenty years later.[8] There was in addition an independent union of civil servants with about

7. For further details on the interwar labour movement in these and other countries, the interested reader should consult Adolf Sturmthal, *The Tragedy of European Labour*, New York, 1943.

8. Although the DGB 1970 membership of 7 million roughly equals the interwar peak of its predecessor federation, it should be recalled that the postwar figure covers only West Germany.

700,000 members. For most of the postwar years, the DGB has represented about one-third of the entire labour force, compared with less than 25 per cent for the powerful American labour movement.

To avoid the political fissions that had such tragic consequences before the war, the DGB, from the start, insisted upon political neutrality with no formal ties to any political party. In fact the DGB has maintained close informal ties to the Social Democratic Party. Most trade union officials are SPD members (90 per cent in a recent survey compared with 4.5 per cent who were members of the Christian Democratic Union). A large proportion of SPD Members of Parliament hold membership in a DGB union.

The general concord of views between the DGB and the Social Democrats does not mean that the trade unions have followed in the Marxist footsteps of their prewar ancestors, since the SPD itself has adopted a reformist position in the Scandinavian tradition. By 1970, a year after a Social Democratic government had assumed office, the trade union movement of Germany was more firmly established as a pillar of society than at any time in the past.

The British unions emerged from the war with their status confirmed by the stunning electoral victory of the Labour Party in 1945. Union membership exceeded prewar levels with 9.3 million in 1950, 84 per cent of them in unions affiliated with the Trades Union Congress. Membership reached 11 million by 1970, 43 per cent of the entire British labour force, a degree of organisation scarcely paralleled elsewhere.

With collective bargaining the almost universal method of determining labour conditions, and strikes subsidised by state welfare payments, whatever weaknesses the British labour unions had were internal. The authority exercised by the TUC over its affiliates was minimal. What was worse, many national unions had little control at the enterprise level. Because of overlapping jurisdictions, a consequence of failure to rationalise historical boundary lines (the German and Swedish unions were able to do this), as well as the failure to organise sound local unions, a great

deal of power devolved upon shop stewards, a disproportion-
ate number of whom belonged to the Communist Party.

Another problem was that there was no unionist of the
stature of Ernest Bevin, who could act as a link between
unions, political party and government, a function that is
essential if unions are to play a reasonable and constructive
role in the formation of public policy. An attempt by the
Labour Government in the late 1960s to deal with some
of these problems was defeated by the militant wing of the
unions, and it was left to a Conservative Government, in
1971, to force an Industrial Relations Act through Parliament over bitter trade union opposition. This Act has since
been repealed and the Conservatives have disavowed any
intention of renewing it.

Membership in the Swedish Federation of Labour (LO)
had risen to 1.3 million in 1950, and reached 1.7 million
in 1970. But a new and interesting development occurred
in Sweden. The white-collar and professional employees,
most of them in the rapidly growing service sector, refused
to join the traditional blue-collar labour federation and
instead formed federations of their own. The most important
of these are the Central Organisation of Salaried Employees
(TCO) with 720,000 members in 1970, and the Central
Organisation of Swedish Professional Workers (SACO)
with 120,000 members. Taking all these organisations
together, Swedish unionism embraced 65 per cent of the
labour force, which must have been a world's record.[9]

The multiplicity of union organisations has not been a
source of weakness, since each federation caters to a different
constituency. LO represents primarily blue-collar workers,
TCO the white-collar workers, in both private and public
enterprises. SACO represents employees with academic
training, including university professors, lawyers, physicians
and clergymen. (TCO, incidentally, numbers among its
affiliates unions of commissioned and non-commissioned
army officers and police.) The causes of the division are to
a large extent political in origin. Ever since the 1880s, LO

9. This statement excepts totalitarian states, where membership in
government controlled unions is often universal.

was closely tied to the Social Democratic Party, and provided the Party with a good portion of its finances through collective affiliation by local unions.[10] Since many white-collar and professional workers tended to support parties other than the Social Democrats, this proved a barrier to their affiliation with LO. TCO and SACO are politically neutral, although they do take positions on political issues when the economic interests of their members are involved, and they co-operate with LO on matters of mutual concern.

Sweden is the first democratic nation in which there is almost complete organisation of the working population on the basis of economic interests. Not only industrial workers, but farmers, employers, salaried employees, and professionals, all have associations that bargain for them collectively. Traditional concepts of labour-management relations begin to lose their relevance in this situation.

Trade union membership data are not of great value in assessing the extent and influence of French trade unionism. It has been said that the French worker is willing to die on the barricades but not pay union dues. There is general agreement that the largest labour federation in the country is the General Confederation of Labour (CGT) with something on the order of 1.5 million members. Next comes the Democratic Confederation of Labour (CFDT), with anywhere from 600,000 to one million members. Bringing up the rear is the Workers' Force (FO) with half a million. Although this represents one of the lowest levels of organisation in Western Europe, many more workers can be marshalled for strike action in times of crisis. The French unions have demonstrated time and again that they must be taken seriously.

There is no difficulty in characterising the orientation of the CGT: it is controlled by the Communist Party. Although the CGT was the traditional organisation of French labour, the Communists managed to gain complete control in 1946, and they have never relinquished it. The non-

10. Recently, the institution of a system of government subsidies for political campaigns has lessened Party dependence upon the unions.

Communists broke away to form FO, which tends to co-operate with the Socialist Party, although there are no formal ties. The CFDT is the descendant of a prewar federation, the French Confederation of Catholic Workers.

The general secretary of the CGT has generally been a member of the Politbureau of the French Communist Party, and a Communist cadre exists at every level of organisation. The CFDT, which adopted its present name in 1964, has undergone a rather remarkable metamorphosis. Originally linked with the Social Christian Party, it gradu-ally rid itself of confessional trappings and moved sharply to the left. By 1970 it had adopted a fairly strong socialist position, and was advocating direct action in the French syndicalist tradition. A sizeable minority opposed the new programme, and where the organisation will finally come to rest is not clear.

All three federations, through their constituent national unions, have members in most large enterprises. The CGT is relatively strong in heavy industry, the CFDT in light industry, particularly textiles, and FO among white-collar workers, the civil service above all else. All share a common structural deficiency: local organisation is weak, if it exists at all. The basic unit at the plant level is the enterprise committee, elected by proportional representation from lists nominated by the various unions. The individual worker, facing competing unions, and separated from the trade unions by representative bodies that are not part of any union, has no particular incentive to join. He demon-strates his adherence to one or another group by his vote for enterprise committee members and by obeying strike calls. This system is hardly designed to create a financially viable labour movement.

There are many parallels between Italy and France. Even before the end of World War II, representatives of the various pre-fascist labour factions met secretly in Rome and pledged that they would avoid the divisions that had enabled Mussolini to gain power. The man who would probably have headed the united movement, Bruno Buozzi, a socialist, was caught and executed by the

Germans, and the leadership devolved upon Giuseppe di Vittorio, a communist. The newly created organisation, the General Federation of Italian Labour (CGIL), grew rapidly after liberation. However, the Communist Party managed to gain effective control, and as East-West tensions increased, the inevitable fissions occurred. In 1949, Christian Democratic supporters withdrew from the CGIL to establish the Italian Federation of Trade Unions (CISL), while the socialists founded the Italian Union of Labour (UIL). There have been numerous efforts to bring about unity, without success. As in the case of France, firm membership data are difficult to come by, but the ordinal ranking appears to be CGIL in first place, followed by CISL, with UIL a poor third.

CISL has been moving away from its originally close alliance with the Christian Democrats, but it has not gone as far to the left as the CFDT. The CGIL has recently been demonstrating some independence from the policy lines of the Communist Party, and has been willing to work closely with CISL on economic matters of mutual interest.

Italian unions have the same structural weakness as the French. The local bodies to which workers look for representation in day-to-day matters are factory councils elected from union-nominated lists of candidates, rather than the local unions. The results of these elections in large plants, such as the Fiat plant in Turin, are regarded as perhaps the most important indication of relative union strength, and receive wide press coverage.

To summarise: by 1970, trade unions had attained an apparently unshakable position in Northern Europe. Not only were they recognised as the legitimate representatives of special worker economic interests, but in addition they exercised a good deal of political power through allied socialist parties. They still had their problems, but these were nothing compared with the political schisms that continued to divide the workers of France and Italy. British, German and Swedish employers were not faced with the dilemma of bargaining with labour organisations that were formally committed to their elimination through revolutionary means. How powerful Communist trade unions could continue to operate within the framework of liberal democratic economies remained high on the agenda of unsolved problems in 1970.

INDUSTRIAL RELATIONS

The history of prewar industrial relations parallels the development of the labour movement. Where trade unions were well established, as in Great Britain and Sweden, orderly systems of labour relations prevailed. The level of industrial strife was high at times, but collective bargaining was recognised as the appropriate means of setting wages. Where unions were weak, wages were fixed either by employers unilaterally, by the state, or by some combination of the two.

The data in Table 15, working days lost due to industrial disputes, show one facet of the outcome of industrial relations. They are given in absolute numbers, and it should be kept in mind that the countries involved varied considerably in size. At this time, the non-agricultural labour force of Great Britain was about 80 per cent that of Germany; France about half; and Sweden about 7 per cent of the German. Other bases could be used if one wanted to make inter-country comparisons, each with its own logic: total population, total labour force, the 'organisable' sector, trade union membership; the results would vary depending upon which was employed. However, the time series tell a good deal, and for rough comparisons, one would not be too far off by adjusting on the basis of the non-agricultural labour force.

Collective bargaining in Great Britain from 1920 to 1925, all years in which the number of man-days lost in strikes was very high, took place against a background of economic stagnation. Although a depression that began in the summer of 1920 tended to dampen labour militancy, wage cuts imposed upon the coal miners led to a long and bitter strike. But this was nothing compared with what happened six years later. The miners, again faced with a wage reduction, sought the co-operation of the Trades Union Congress (TUC), leading to the General Strike of 1926 that has already been described. Their defeat convinced the unions that direct action was not the best way to improve conditions for their members.

They now settled down in a new spirit of sober realism to build as best they could upon the solid foundations they had laid in other ways. The employers – at least the more enlightened among them – had also learned their lesson. The constant trials of strength between themselves and their workpeople were undeniably very bad business and were losing them their markets in the world. 'Peace in Industry' was the new slogan readily accepted by the government and by most of the leaders on both sides of industry.[11]

The data in Table 15 reflect this new attitude. The incidence of strikes declined dramatically, and remained relatively low throughout the next decade. The Great Depression emphasised the need for mutual accommodation, since work stoppages made little sense in the presence of 15 per cent unemployment. It is nevertheless worth emphasising that at a time when much of the rest of Europe was undergoing what almost amounted to class warfare, the employers and trade unions of Great Britain did manage to settle their differences in a more orderly fashion.

Much the same can be said of Sweden. Wages were forced down in 1921 and 1922, the first time since 1900. Union militancy rose as soon as the economy turned up, and Sweden had some very bad years, as in 1928, when its strike losses, in absolute man-days lost, exceeded the British level. In 1931, however, when the full impact of the depression hit Sweden, employers came to a decision not to attempt to repeat the earlier policy of wage reductions, but rather to work closely with the unions towards a more rational solution of their mutual difficulties. The famous Swedish collective bargaining system, with its interplay

11. Allan Flanders, 'Great Britain', in Walter Galenson, *Comparative Labor Movements*, New York, 1952, p. 10.

TABLE 15: Number of Working Days Lost Due to Industrial Disputes, 1920–1938
(Thousands)

	France	Germany	Sweden	United Kingdom
1920	23,112	16,756	8,943	26,568
1921	7,027	25,875	2,663	85,872
1922	3,936	27,733	2,675	19,850
1923	4,172	12,478	6,907	10,672
1924	3,863	36,198	1,205	8,424
1925	2,046	17,105	2,560	7,952
1926	4,072	1,399	1,711	147,233
1927	1,046	6,044	400	1,170
1928	6,377	20,288	4,835	1,390
1929	2,765	4,490	667	8,290
1930	7,209	3,936	1,021	4,400
1931	950	2,002	2,627	6,980
1932	2,244	1,112	3,095	6,490
1933	1,199	—	3,434	1,070
1934	2,394	—	760	960
1935	1,182	—	788	1,960
1936	n.a.	—	438	1,830
1937	n.a.	—	861	3,413
1938	n.a.	—	1,284	1,334

Source: Arthur M. Ross and Paul T. Hartman, *Changing Patterns of Industrial Conflict*, New York, 1960, pp. 198–199.

between central and local negotiation, came to maturity in the early 1930s. The year 1934 marked a sharp break with the older methods of economic warfare and a new spirit of collaboration that had a good deal to do with subsequent Swedish affluence.

The German story was altogether different. Scarcely had the fervour of the post-Armistice revolution died down when the hyper-inflation of 1923 once more shook the economy. It was several years before a recovery set in and economic activity began to pick up. Real wages rose and for a few years there seemed some hope for a stable pattern of industrial relations. But German employers reacted very differently from the Swedes to a further onset of rising prices. A severe deflationary policy was adopted, leading to wage cuts and rapidly mounting unemployment. Resistance by the Social Democrats and the trade unions proved ineffective, and unemployment rates running over 20 per cent created an electorate that proved receptive to the appeals of extremists of the left and right.

In contrast to Germany, France enjoyed relative prosperity throughout the 1920s. There was no postwar recession, unemployment remained low, real wages rose. But the weakness of the trade unions, divided along ideological lines, with Communists in a fairly prominent position, provided employers with a convenient reason for opposing collective bargaining.

The first real chance of a movement towards orderly industrial relations came with the Popular Front government and the Matignon Agreement cited earlier. The Agreement was reinforced by legislation making collective bargaining mandatory, establishing a basic 40-hour week, and providing for paid vacations. A substantial proportion of French employers signed union agreements, many for the first time. But this brief episode of labour-management cooperation came to an end with the general strike of 1938. What remained were the collective bargaining precedents and paid vacations, but little else. France had still not achieved a viable system of industrial relations when the Third Republic came to an end.

There was little doubt about the path European industrial relations would take after 1945. The increase in union power and the leftward trend in government afforded employers no alternative but to acquiesce in collective bargaining agreements. The periodic wage cuts that had done so much to embitter industrial relations before the war were no longer in order, if only because of favourable economic conditions. The problem became one of limiting the rate of wage increases in the face of price inflation. Constraints on collective bargaining were no longer employer resistance, but rather government efforts to curb wage-price spirals.

The pattern of money (not real) wage increases, by five-year intervals, is shown in Table 16. By prewar standards,

TABLE 16: Average Annual Increase in Manufacturing Wages, 1950–1970

	France[a]	Germany[b]	Italy[a]	Sweden[b]	United Kingdom
1950–1955	14.8	7.8	5.8	14.0	8.7[a]
1955–1960	9.7	9.8	4.7	6.8	5.2[b]
1960–1965	8.7	11.5	12.8	9.9	4.9[b]
1965–1970	11.0	8.6	9.6	10.7	7.7[b]

(a) Hourly rates.
(b) Hourly earnings.

Source: ILO, *Yearbook of Labour Statistics*, 1950–1955.
OECD, *Main Economic Indicators*, 1955–1970.

they were very substantial throughout the years 1950–1970. British wages failed to advance as rapidly as did those of the other countries; but correspondingly low increases in labour productivity led to constant pressure on prices nonetheless.

In Great Britain, there was no break with the pre-existing collective bargaining system. The great majority of blue-collar workers, and an increasing number of white-collar workers, were covered by collective agreements. But difficulties arose out of the propensity of the system to produce inflationary wage settlements. The task of curbing inflation devolved increasingly upon government. Every postwar government, Labour and Conservative alike, was faced with the problem in one form or another. Labour governments were reluctant to confront their trade union constituents with the need for moderation; after all, why were the workers paying a political levy, if not to improve their relative economic position when the party they supported came into office? The Conservatives were opposed ideologically to government intervention in both the labour and product markets. Yet both were obliged to react with an incomes policy at a number of critical junctures.

Whether these attempts to contain wages and prices were successful has been a matter of considerable dispute. There was usually an initial dampening effect, followed by a resumption of the previous trend. Although it is difficult to prove, these interventions probably had a long-run impact on wages and prices if only because they interrupted expectations of higher wages and prices. It is worth repeating, moreover, that British wage increases were relatively moderate by international standards.

For most of the period, the number of man-days lost to strikes was not unduly severe, as can be seen by reference to Table 17. Particularly in the second decade, however, most strikes were unofficial, called by militant shop-stewards rather than formal trade union bodies. These were costly in that they came without notice and interfered with production scheduling, but they were normally of short duration. Official strike activity began to pick up in 1968, however, and in 1970 it reached levels not experienced since the General Strike of 1926.

An exhaustive inquiry into industrial relations by a Royal Commission led to the issuance of a report in 1968 (the Donovan Report) that pointed to the increasing gap between the formal bargaining system, in which industry-wide agreements were negotiated at fairly regular intervals, and the informal system at the plant level. A consequence of this dichotomy is that actual earnings often differed from negotiated wage rates because of local determination of incentive schemes, hours of work, and other practices. The Industrial Relations Act of 1971 was aimed at correcting this and other problems reported by the Donovan Commission. The Act proved to be a dead letter when the unions refused to co-operate. It demonstrated, if nothing else, that the trade unions in Britain had become sufficiently powerful to challenge government.

It is too soon to assess the basic causes behind the apparent decline in the effectiveness of the British system of labour relations that developed at the end of the 1960s. Despite some shortcomings, it had functioned fairly well for almost half a century. The difficulties have been attributed to 'social changes which are world-wide in their significance – a general breakdown of established patterns of authority,

TABLE 17: Number of Working Days Lost Due to Labour Disputes,
1950–1970
(Thousands)

	France	Germany	Italy[a]	Sweden	United Kingdom
1950	11,729	—	7,761	41	1,389
1951	3,495	1,593	4,515	531	1,694
1952	1,733	443	3,531	79	1,792
1953	9,722	1,488	5,828	582	2,184
1954	1,440	1,587	5,377	25	2,457
1955	3,079	857	5,622	159	3,781
1956	1,423	1,580	4,137	4	2,083
1957	4,121	1,072	4,619	53	8,412
1958	1,138	782	4,172	15	3,462
1959	1,938	62	9,190	24	5,270
1960	1,070	37	5,786	19	3,024
1961	2,601	61	9,891	2	3,046
1962	1,901	451	22,717	5	5,798
1963	5,991	1,846	11,395	25	1,755
1964	2,497	17	13,089	34	2,277
1965	980	49	6,993	4	2,925
1966	2,523	27	14,473	352	2,398
1967	4,204	390	8,568	0.4	2,787
1968	n.a.	25	9,240	1	4,690
1969	2,224	249	37,825	112	6,846
1970	1,742	93	18,277	156	10,980

(a) Excludes political strikes.

Source: ILO, *Yearbook of Labour Statistics*, various years.

expectations of a continually rising standard of living,
widening circles of comparison as to what this standard
should be, and a determination not to be left behind in the
struggle'.[12] But one may ask, why 1969? We return to this
question after examining the experience of other countries.

It is difficult to fault the Swedish labour relations system
if industrial peace is the criterion of success. For many
years, strikes almost vanished from the scene. This remarkable achievement was facilitated by the practice of negoti-

12. B. C. Roberts and Sheila Rothwell, 'Recent Trends in Collective
Bargaining in the United Kingdom', *International Labour Review*, December 1972, p. 562.

ating nationwide agreements between the central federations of employers and employees, which established the framework of particularistic bargaining at the industry and local levels. In contrast with Britain, the government refrained from direct intervention in the labour market, notwithstanding the fact that, during the entire period, it was led by the Social Democratic Party.

The Swedish Federation of Labour is committed to wage equalisation through special increases for the lowest paid – the so-called solidaristic wage policy. Although there was a considerable compression of the wage structure, the union intent has been frustrated by wage drift, resulting from individually negotiated wage increases for workers with higher skills on top of increases negotiated collectively by the unions.

Towards the end of the 1960s, some clouds began to appear on the horizon. In 1969 there were a number of unofficial strikes, attributed variously to dissatisfaction on the part of groups 'which considered themselves unfairly treated by the levelling nature of the [centralised] agreements',[13] and to 'grass-roots discontent with an overly centralised institution which leaves insufficient room for individual participation in the decision-making process'.[14] Opposition to the bargaining system also came from a most unexpected source. In 1966 the Confederation of Professional Associations won a 17 per cent increase for its members after the blue-collar workers in the public sector had settled for 5 to 7 per cent. This came after a long strike of teachers, the effects of which are clearly visible from the strike data in Table 17. A similar situation occurred in 1971. Some 50,000 teachers, railroad employees and other civil servants were locked out when their Confederation again demanded salary increases in excess of the blue-collar settlement, to compensate the higher paid employees for the levelling effect of Sweden's high marginal income

13. Gösta Edgren, Karl-Olof Faxen, and Clas-Erik Odhner, *Wage Formation and the Economy*, London, 1973, p. 56.

14. Lloyd Ulman and Robert J. Flanagan, *Wage Restraint*, Berkeley, Calif., 1971. p. 103.

tax rates. When it appeared that unionised army officers might have to be locked out as well, the dispute was settled by legislation.

The fact that all socio-economic groups in Sweden are organised for collective bargaining poses some difficult problems for industrial relations. What began in 1930 as labour-management bargaining for blue-collar workers has become a system of interest group bargaining involving most of the population. No single group can hope any longer to raise claims that will not lead to offsetting claims by other groups. By the end of the 1960s it appeared increasingly that some other mechanism would have to be found to determine the distribution of income among blue-collar and white-collar employees, professionals, civil servants, farmers, entrepreneurs, and retired people. It hardly seems possible for the government to avoid this role. Sweden may be reaching the logical end of traditional collective bargaining. When everyone is prepared to strike, the strike loses its meaning.

Germany has not gone that far. For a decade after the war, the German worker, recovering from the devastation and poverty imposed by defeat in war and subsequent military occupation, was quiescent. Codetermination, a system that accorded trade unions representation on the governing boards of corporations, was a major union demand, designed to prevent any repetition of the business support that had been so important in bringing Hitler to power. Rapid economic growth made it relatively easy to satisfy demands for higher wages.

German collective bargaining is highly centralised. The sixteen industrial unions conclude agreements with associations of employers on a regional basis, and these agreements can be extended by law to all employees in the region if they are signed by employers of a majority of the workers in the regional industry. In many cases it proved easier for unions to gain broad representation rights by organising employers rather than workers. Government-imposed incomes policy proved unnecessary because of the success achieved by collective bargaining in keeping wages in line with productivity. A Council of Economic Experts was established in 1963 to report annually on wage-price developments. It has had some influence on wage norms, but through the logic of its findings rather than compulsion.

The first sign that German industrial relations might be in for some difficulties came in September 1969, when more than a million workers engaged in unofficial strikes for higher pay.[15] The strikes came as a great surprise not only to employers but to the union leadership as well. Steelworkers, miners, shipyard workers, and public service employees were involved, among others. The result was an increase in wages substantially greater than had been expected.

This experience was unsettling to the unions and to the Social Democratic government that had just assumed office. The unions had to answer charges that they were being too co-operative with employers. Their reaction was to raise their bargaining sights in 1970, and as a result, collectively bargained wage rates rose at twice the 1969 rate. Another outbreak of unofficial strikes in 1973 suggested that the events of 1969 were not a transitory surface phenomenon, but represented, rather, a turning-point in worker attitudes similar to what was taking place elsewhere in Europe. The foundations of German collective bargaining were certainly not yet threatened, but the clockwork pattern of the negotiations of earlier years seemed to be at an end.

The development of collective bargaining in France lagged behind that of Northern Europe after the war, as it had done earlier. The idea of fixed-term contracts, with negotiation confined to regular intervals, was slow in getting established. Indeed, it was still true in 1970 that in many industries negotiations for new agreements took place erratically, and that pressure was applied most often at the plant level in the form of flash strikes. The coexistence of competing trade union federations, often divided on strategy, has hindered the development of a more orderly bargaining system.

15. These strikes are not reflected in the data in Table 17.

Nor can French employers claim to have made any real contribution in this respect. Collective bargaining came to a virtual halt from 1960 to 1964 when employers claimed that they were under government pressure to hold wages down.[16] The government exercised its influence mainly through price controls, which were imposed sporadically when inflation threatened. This is a recipe not designed to bring about industrial peace. Efforts to bring about labour-management consensus on appropriate wage-price relationships ran up against lack of trust in government fairness by the unions and employer desire to retain complete freedom of action in determining wages at the plant level.

The stagnation in French industrial relations came to an abrupt end in May and June 1968. A three-week general strike, involving two-thirds of the entire labour force, shook the nation to its core. The settlement came in the form of a tripartite agreement, the *Protocole de Grenelle*, which was a landmark in French industrial relations much as the Matignon Agreement had been thirty years earlier. Minimum wages were raised by 35 per cent, average wages by 10 per cent, and the government undertook to introduce legislation to protect union rights within the enterprise.

The significance of *Grenelle* has been summarised in these terms:

> . . . after Grenelle there was a good deal more collective bargaining in France. The social crisis of May 1968 and trade union insistence both had a good deal to do with it, but there was also a change in the employers' attitude, encouraged by the emergence of new men and a government policy of introducing collective bargaining into the nationalized industries (and even the civil service), which in turn fostered it in the private sector as well.[17]

National agreements were reached on job security and industrial training. The nationalised firms were given

16. Yves Delamotte, 'Recent Collective Bargaining Trends in France', *International Labour Review*, April 1971, p. 356.
17. Yves Delamotte, *op. cit.*, p. 361.

greater freedom to conclude agreements. But old attitudes die hard, and *Grenelle* did not once and for all destroy deep seated antagonisms. The Communist CGT and the CFDT, which was moving rapidly to the left, were reluctant to embrace collective bargaining wholeheartedly. Despite a shift in the attitude of both government and employers towards collective bargaining, prompted at least in part by fears engendered by the events of 1968, it is proving difficult to persuade unions dedicated to the overthrow of capitalism to accept the implications of working within the system. Schemes for profit sharing and worker participation in management were being advanced as a means of furthering reconciliation, but as of 1970 they had not advanced very far. The difficulty is that even if the French unions would like to move in this direction, their members, or more accurately, the great number of non-members who support them at times of crisis, may not let them do so.

We come finally to Italy. During the 1950s unemployment was relatively high and the trade unions were weak. Bargaining took the form primarily of industry-wide agreements in which only minimum wages were set, giving the individual employer a great deal of latitude. There was already a good deal of conflict, but the decade of the 1950s must be seen as a golden age of labour peace compared with what came after. The influence of fascism had not yet been fully eradicated. 'The trade unions took over from fascism the centralised collective agreement structure and continued a national focus in agreements which later created multiple problems for the trade unions and the wage earners. More important was a continuation of the fascist practice of decision-making from the top and discouragement of assumption of responsibility or initiative at intermediate levels or among individuals.'[18]

With the gradual tightening of the labour market some change took place. A so-called 'articulated' bargaining system was introduced, which had as its component parts national agreements on general issues and minimum wages,

18. Daniel Horowitz, *op. cit.*, p. 337.

supplemented by detailed plant agreements on piece rates, job classification schemes, and productivity bonuses. The new practice had its origin in a series of strikes in 1962 in the metalworking industry, including Fiat and Olivetti, and although its spread was slowed by the economic recession of 1963, the precedent had been established.

National agreements in 1965 and 1966 provided Italian workers with only moderate wage increases. The response was a considerable increase in local strikes and demonstrations. Not only wages but an inadequate social welfare system were at issue, and in November 1968 CISL and CIGL co-operated in a nationwide demonstration strike for improved pensions. The real breakthrough came in 1969. The year began with unofficial strikes throughout the country. Local delegates were elected at many factories, reminiscent of the British shop-stewards, an innovation for Italy. The unions were eventually able to re-establish their leadership, and in the fall of 1969 a repetition of the French 1968 events took place in Italy:

> In all, some 4 million industrial workers were involved in the strikes of this hot autumn – not to mention another 1.5 million in agriculture. A total of 520 million working hours were lost, 400 million of them in industry. Picketing was energetic and there were quite a few incidents with the police, management personnel and blacklegs, as well as a few cases of sabotage. The extremist groups often engaged in provocation, which the trade unions tried to counteract or contain, in the main successfully. They relied heavily on mass demonstrations, culminating in an imposing but peaceful march through Rome by 150,000 metalworkers in November 1969.[19]

One of the consequences of this mass strike was enactment into law of the Workers' Charter, which protected local trade union activity and made it more difficult for employers to resist plant level unions. The metalworkers

19. Gino Guigni, 'Recent Trends in Collective Bargaining in Italy', *International Labour Review*, October 1971, p. 317.

won a substantial wage increase, a reduction of the work week, and a limitation of overtime. Plant level bargaining spread during the following years, and the articulated system became firmly established.

Of equal import was the evolution of a new type of direct political action on the part of the trade union federations, acting in concert. This arose largely out of the failure of a series of weak national governments to adopt some badly needed social reforms. The pension strike of 1968 was followed by national and local strikes for improvement in housing and health care, in 1969 and 1970. There was success in getting housing legislation enacted, and a commitment to improve the national health service. The unions continued this technique in demanding better urban transportation and schools, and tax reform. The political parties, including the Communists and the various socialist groups, were not happy at being bypassed, but their incapacity to act and the mood of the working people left them no option but to co-operate with the union initiatives.

A collective bargaining system was not yet firmly established in Italy by 1970. The basic elements were in place: powerful unions apparently prepared to work together on bread-and-butter issues despite conflicting ideologies; acceptance of plant level bargaining by employers; and a strong desire on the part of most political parties to see the unions settle down to a more businesslike approach to economic problems. But the tactics of strike and demonstration have become a way of life for Italian workers, and there are few countries where they are practiced with as much enthusiasm.

There still remains the puzzling matter of the strike climacteric of 1968–1970 that swept through Europe. The initiative appears to have come from the rank and file rather than from union leadership. In France and Italy, where collective bargaining was less firmly established, it came in the form of explosions that many contemporary observers feared might have a revolutionary potential. It led everywhere to a sharp increase in wages and, eventually, in union power.

Widespread social phenomena are exceedingly complex in nature, and the events of 1968–1970 are still too close for anything but preliminary speculation. Among the factors that may have contributed to the outburst are the following:

1. By 1970 a substantial proportion of the labour force was composed of individuals with only dim, if any, recollections of the hardships suffered during the Great Depression and World War II. This is indicated by the data in Table 18. Employees under 35 years of age in 1970 would have been at most only 10 years old at the conclusion of hostilities, while those under 40 years of age would have entered the labour force in 1945 at the earliest. In most of the countries, but particularly in France and Italy, younger people played an important role in the strike movement. The student unrest of the period, which in France preceded the strikes, was undoubtedly transmitted through younger workers.

TABLE 18: Proportion of Labour Force in 1970 less than 35 and 40
Years of Age
(Per cent)

	Less than 35 years	Less than 40 years
France[a]	47	58
Germany[b]	44	56
Sweden[c]	39	48
United Kingdom[d]	40	49

(a) Per cent of total male population 15–65 years of age, January 1, 1972.
(b) Per cent of total labour force, April 1971.
(c) Per cent of economically active population, November 1, 1970.
(d) Per cent of male employees, 1970.

Source: Statistical yearbooks of individual countries.

2. Western Europe experienced a favourable rate of economic growth in the 1960s, and unemployment *circa* 1970 must have been near an irreducible frictional level, except perhaps for Italy. Not only the postwar generation,

but all workers, would not have been greatly concerned with loss of jobs as a consequence of striking.

3. There is no unique relationship between wage and price movements, on the one hand, and industrial disputes on the other, but the former do have great influence on the latter. Large upward movements in consumer prices tend to stimulate dissatisfaction, while rising money wages tend to allay it. The impact of real wages is more subtle, since most people suffer from the money illusion, up to a point. This weakens with time, and eventual perception of what is happening to real income becomes a powerful factor.

Italy had experienced some very sharp price increases early in the 1960s, and Sweden in 1965–1966, but in general the annual rate of price increases was either stable or falling during the five years preceding 1968. However, as Table 19 shows, there was also a tendency for the rate of increase in money wages to fall after 1964 or 1965, and the result was the real wage figures in Table 20. Thus, in France, Italy and Germany, real wages were rising considerably less rapidly during the three years 1965 through 1967 than for the previous four years; in Sweden for two of the three years; and only in Britain, where real wages were rising very slowly in any event, was there any improvement.

TABLE 19: Annual Percentage Increase in Money Wages, 1961–1971

	France	Germany	Italy	Sweden	United Kingdom
1961	7.7	8.6	4.5	8.9	5.5
1962	8.5	10.7	10.7	7.0	3.3
1963	8.6	6.5	14.7	8.7	2.9
1964	6.9	6.9	14.0	6.0	4.9
1965	5.8	7.0	8.5	11.3	5.9
1966	5.9	7.4	3.8	7.6	6.0
1967	6.0	5.3	5.2	9.4	4.3
1968	12.4	4.4	3.6	6.5	8.0
1969	11.3	6.4	7.5	8.1	5.8
1970	10.5	12.6	21.7	13.8	9.6
1971	11.2	13.7	13.5	7.1	11.4

Source: OECD, *Main Economic Indicators*, various issues.

TABLE 20: Annual Percentage Increase in Real Wages, 1961–1971

	France	Germany	Italy	Sweden	United Kingdom
1961	4.4	6.0	2.3	6.2	2.0
1962	3.4	7.6	5.8	2.5	—1.0
1963	3.6	3.4	6.7	5.6	0.8
1964	3.4	4.5	7.6	2.5	1.5
1965	2.5	3.4	3.8	6.0	1.2
1966	3.1	3.8	1.4	1.2	2.0
1967	3.3	3.8	2.0	4.9	1.8
1968	7.5	2.6	2.2	4.4	3.1
1969	4.6	3.7	4.8	5.3	0.0
1970	5.0	8.6	15.8	6.2	3.0
1971	5.4	8.0	8.2	0.0	1.9

Source: OECD, *Main Economic Indicators*, various issues.

Thus, it can be argued that workers had become accustomed to more rapid improvement in their real income than what was being delivered to them in the years immediately preceding 1968.

None of this explains why the challenge to the industrial relations systems of Western Europe came precisely in 1968. However, it does suggest why the strike fever, once it had got started, found such great receptivity among European workers. The trade unions were wakened from their lethargy, and collective bargaining demands soon escalated to new dimensions. The era of double figure wage and price increases had begun.

THE SOCIAL AND ECONOMIC STATUS OF THE WORKER

The status of citizens of Western Europe, and of industrial workers in particular, has undergone a remarkable transformation since 1945. Employment insecurity, penury in old age, slum housing, and inadequate access to health services have been replaced by comprehensive systems of social welfare. There are still gaps, particularly in Italy, but it is fair to say that the level of security and welfare prevailing in 1970 would have been regarded as wildly Utopian a half-century earlier. A major part of the credit for this achievement must go to the trade unions. Directly through the collective bargaining process, and indirectly through their political power, they pressed for and suc-

TABLE 21: Social Security Benefit Expenditures as a Percentage of the Gross National Product[c]

	1950[a]	1955[a]	1960[a]	1963[a]	1966[b]	1970[b]
France	10.9	10.2	12.7	14.6	15.5	15.8
Germany	14.1	13.4	14.9	15.3	16.0	17.2
Italy	7.9	10.2	12.0	12.8	15.9	16.8
Sweden	9.3	10.8	12.1	13.5	15.6	—
United Kingdom	8.9	9.1	10.3	11.2	12.6	—
Japan	3.2	4.8	4.7	5.2	6.0	—
United States	4.0	4.3	6.2	6.2	7.2	—

Sources: (a) International Labour Office, *The Cost of Social Security*, Geneva, 1967, Table 2.
(b) Statistical Office of the European Community, *Basic Statistics of the Community*, 1971, p. 104.
(c) The data for 1966 and 1970 may not be fully comparable with those for the earlier years. Social security as here defined consists of payment for old age pensions, unemployment compensation, family allowances, public health services, and public assistance to the needy.

ceeded in winning a variety of social benefits that are scarcely likely to have come in their absence.

Social indicators are still in their infancy, making it difficult to document this assertion. However, a few sets of available data may serve to make the statement more concrete. The first of these is contained in Table 21, showing the growth of social security payments relative to national product for the postwar years. To put the European figures in better perspective, data for Japan and the United States are included. While there is some variation among the European states, the contrast between the European group and the two large non-European nations is very sharp.

A second set of indicators relates to housing (Table 22). European housing standards have improved dramatically

TABLE 22: Indicators of Housing Standards

		Average number of persons per room	Per cent of dwellings with water piped inside	Per cent of dwellings with flush toilets
France	1954	1.0	58.4	—
	1968	0.9	90.8	51.8
Germany	1954	1.0	79.4	51.9
	1968	0.7	99.0	86.5
Italy	1951	1.1	35.1	40.5
	1961	1.1	62.3	—
Sweden	1945	—	88.5	—
	1970	0.7	97.0	89.6
United Kingdom	1951	0.8	94.5	92.3
	1966	0.6	—	98.2
Japan	1955	3.4	—	—
	1968	1.1	94.9	17.1
United States	1950	0.7	81.6	—
	1970	0.6	97.5	96.0

Source: United Nations, *Statistical Yearbook*, 1972.

T.C.

TABLE 23: Weekly Hours of Work in Manufacturing

	1953	1970
France	44.6 (1954)	44.5
Germany	48.0	43.8
Italy	8.1 (daily)	7.8 (daily)
Sweden	176 (monthly)	151 (monthly)
United Kingdom	47.9	43.6

Source: United Nations, *Statistical Yearbook*, 1972, p. 102.

since the war, particularly with respect to amenities. By 1970, Germany, Sweden and Britain were approaching a level of two rooms per person, with France and Italy lagging behind somewhat.

Working hours have been coming down (Table 23), and the quality of health care, as measured by the availability of physicians, has risen substantially during the postwar years (Table 24).

By 1970, a retired worker in Western Europe could expect to receive a pension equal to 50 to 75 per cent of his final earnings, linked to the consumer price index. Unemployment benefits ran from 30 to 90 per cent of previous earnings, but even where benefits were relatively low, as in France and Italy, family allowances continued and helped balance the family budget. Sickness allowances ranged from 50 to 80 per cent of wages. None of this represents the degree

TABLE 24: Population per Physician

	1953	1970
France	1,100	747
Germany	750	561
Italy	800 (1951)	553 (1969)
Sweden	1,400	734
United Kingdom	—	787 (1971)
Japan	1,000	898
United States	770	645

Source: United Nations, *Statistical Yearbook*, various issues.

of economic security enjoyed by the wealthy, but it does mean an enormous advance over conditions prevailing from 1920 to 1940.

What of the future? Perhaps the outstanding result of labour's rise to power, apart from improvements in material conditions, has been the drive for greater equality in the distribution of income. Lower income groups were dissatisfied with their status in the past, but it is only recently that they have secured sufficient economic and political strength to effectuate their demands. The previously favoured groups have been reluctant to accept a reduction in their relative income shares, and the result is a struggle over the distribution of the national product that is one of the major causes of contemporary inflation. As Erik Lundberg has put it, '. . . income after direct taxes is probably distributed more evenly in Sweden than in most Western countries, yet we seem to be more dissatisfied with the positions attained than others. This dissatisfaction has actually been aggravated over the past decade by the achievements of equalisation policies. The unknown targets seem to move more rapidly ahead than the actual achievements so that the gaps between aims and results tend to increase.'[20]

Generally speaking, the same is true for the rest of Europe. Collective bargaining is moving towards a higher plane and is rapidly becoming the focal point of macro-economic policy. How long striking workers can hold out is becoming irrelevant, particularly in countries where strikes are subsidised by government. Inflation has reduced the importance of the elasticity of product demand as a limiting factor in sectoral bargaining. Trade unions have learned that they can force even unfriendly governments into substantial concessions, making incomes policy difficult to enforce. The end of the 1960s may have ushered in a new phase in the history of European labour relations. The impact of the tumultuous events of 1968–1970 is beginning to be felt.

20. Erik Lundberg, 'Sweden', in Walter Galenson (ed.), *Incomes Policy*, Ithaca, N.Y., 1973, p. 47.

4. Management 1920-1970

Giorgio Pellicelli

ECONOMIC AND SOCIAL CONDITIONS AT THE BEGINNING OF THE 1920s.

Economic and social conditions in the countries of Europe at the beginning of the 1920s varied greatly. Some countries, such as Britain, Germany, France, Sweden, Holland and some areas of other countries both in the West and the East, already had an industrial tradition and had confronted phenomena connected with industrial development. Others, such as Spain, Portugal, some areas of Southern France, Central and Southern Italy, part of Austria and much of Eastern Europe, were still at a retarded stage of industrialisation. It is consequently very difficult to give a complete and exact picture of the economic and social conditions prevailing in the various countries and thus of the conditions in which management confronted the beginning of the 1920s in Europe. The rate of industrialisation and social evolution differed widely from region to region. Some countries had been neutral in the First World War and had therefore remained immune from destruction or been only slightly affected by the economic and social repercussions of the war, and the differing degree of international economic interdependence caused variations in the extent to which each country was vulnerable to economic fluctuations and social change. Moreover this picture was made more complex by factors whose roots lay in the economic and social background of the beginning of the century – in differing traditions, types of culture, institutional structures and productive specialisation.

Nevertheless, without attempting to confine so complex a system within a rigid pattern equally applicable to every European country, it can be said that at the beginning of the 1920s management in Europe found itself faced with a situation which differed considerably not only from that of the turn of the century but also from the immediate pre-war period. The fundamental factors of this change were a new social structure, the lack of economic stability, the increased presence of the State in the regulation of national economy and social security, the decline of international economic interdependence, and, lastly, a new method of organising industrial production.

Among all the conditions which gave a particular character to the management of enterprises at the beginning of the 1920s, the change in social structure and in relations between the classes was perhaps the most general but also the one destined to produce the most profound long-term effects. The effects on management of this type of change were of two different kinds which, however, led to closely related results. They concerned the attribution of a greater social responsibility to management and the gradual rise of a new class of technicians which inserted itself between the two traditional classes of workers on the one hand and employer-owners on the other.

Under the pressure of the new technologies, the old clear-cut distinctions between the classes whose job was to perform the more humble and arduous kinds of work requiring no specialised skill, and the classes of owners and directors, tended to become blurred. Moreover wartime experience had made the workers aware that they could play a determining part in the organisation of work at the simpler levels of production without white-collar tutelage. In fact, in some belligerent countries experiments in worker-management had been tried out, and all countries in their efforts to increase production had made an appeal to patriotism rather than to the traditional authority of management.

Thus the power of heads of concerns emerged from the war weakened at the base which had sustained it: the legitimisation of their power deriving from ownership of capital or from belonging to an élite. On the other hand, between the two classes of workers and owners a new class of technicians and managers was gradually making itself felt. Both workers and entrepreneurs contributed to the rise of this new class, the former with specialised technicians demanded by the new technologies of production, and the latter with men who preferred to give up all or some of the control of capital to new shareholders or financial institutions and themselves assume a managerial role in the enterprise.

Other factors contributing to the new situation lay in the effects of wartime devastation on economic resources and in the crisis which hit the countries of Europe at the beginning of the '20s.

North-eastern France, Belgium and Russia had suffered terrible material damage as a result of the war, but even in countries where factories had not been destroyed the situation was often disastrous. Heavy industry had been geared to wartime production and now faced the urgent problem of conversion to peacetime needs, shipbuilding was in a critical state, and the transport system, especially in Central Europe, was disrupted. In addition, in France and even more in Britain much of the industrial plant was out of date; this caused delays in the changeover from forms of direction and control linked with past methods of production, and it also weighed heavily on costs, making some sectors uncompetitive. Though the new sectors gave some impulse to the national economy, they had not yet, by the early 1920s, reached a point where they could contribute materially towards improving the general economic situation.

To all this was added the serious recession which, after a timid revival in the spring of 1919, hit the economies of Central and East European countries in the second half of 1920 and in 1921. The effects of this situation were felt even in countries which had not taken part in the war. Sweden, for instance, experienced an economic crisis which increased exports could only partly alleviate. In some countries (Italy, Germany and Austria in particular) as a result of the economic and social crisis management came under severe pressure, producing tensions which partly explain the subsequent reversion to conservative regimes.

In the United States, development was going ahead at

an unprecedented rate, and the big enterprises were facing the problems of diversification of production and the consequent organisational decentralisation in order to meet changes in demand. But at the same time in Europe management was chiefly concentrating, except for a few rare cases, on problems of reconstruction, industrial transformation, and supply, in other words on conditions which belonged to a great extent to the methods of production of the beginning of the century. In these conditions management lacked the necessary basis from which to develop new managerial techniques, a defect which was to have far-reaching consequences. The predominance of technical functions of production over other functions of management is to be explained by the fact that the most important problems fell into that category.

Nor were production techniques immune from change. The problem of reconstruction and conversion from wartime to peacetime production has already been mentioned. In addition, management in the post-war years found itself faced with some significant changes in the method of production, which called for a considerable degree of adaptation in entrepreneurial skills and which at the same time laid the foundations for an industrial development which was to have wider effects later on. These changes concerned the need to produce on a large scale, the advent of new technology, the development of some sectors of production and the decline of others, a greater insistence on efficiency and on productive rationalisation, and a new quantitative relationship between a firm's administrative costs and its costs of production.

Pressure of demand for the low-cost consumer goods required in a less affluent society was widespread throughout Europe. Though in some countries the economic crisis and the lack of modern industrial plant confined it within pre-war limits, prospects for the coming years pointed to a considerable development of production. The expansion of demand, together with the availability of new productive techniques, opened up the way to large-scale production in certain sectors which was to have some important effects for management. For it involved adopting new methods of production that often differed radically from those evolved before the war, thus setting on foot a process of productive transformation inspired by ideals of standardisation and rationalisation which for some years dominated the thinking of managers of the larger industrial concerns.

Large-scale production was destined to cause two important changes in the attitude of management towards economic decisions, changes whose effects would be seen in the years to come. Big factories meant large investment of capital and therefore a search for new sources of finance outside the familiar circles which had hitherto governed industry. This opening-up to external sources of finance was particularly pronounced in Germany, where around 1920 the Deutsche Bank had shares in more than two hundred business concerns. Increased investment meant a decline in the percentage of production costs as compared with the costs of administration. While the former as a result of new technologies and economies of scale tended to fall, the latter increased steadily. Thus the *economic* administration gradually began to assume greater importance as compared with the organisation of production in a firm; and in its organisational hierarchy the administrator of its economic and financial affairs gradually took the place of the expert on production.

The effects of these changes on the conduct of an enterprise and its management's response to them naturally varied from country to country in Europe according to their different stages of industrialisation, traditions and culture. The reactions of management also differed according to the size of the enterprise and often took the form of individual initiatives which, being sporadic and restricted in character, only rarely applied to the whole of an economic sector.

Few people realised that Europe was losing its old privileged position. While the new industrial powers, the United States and Japan, were moving towards mass production and the establishment of big consumer markets, management in Europe was still striving to defend the old positions which had constituted its strength: small-scale production, complicated methods of production based on a high use of manpower, protection of national markets, autarky, etc.

In the different ways of reacting to this, Britain was perhaps the most representative of the European countries. Her industrial traditions went back a very long way, and her long-standing position as a major economic world power had made management in British institutions highly sensitive to new problems of administration and more open-minded towards innovations.

In Britain, too, the war had left a profound mark on organisation of production and internal relations in factories, while the demand for nationalisation of industries and for workers' participation in the running of factories had become more vocal and more 'legitimised'. The experience of wartime production had implanted certain principles. The increased powers of shop stewards in factories gave legitimacy to the demand for workers' control of production, and the widely publicised regulations for work conditions established by the Ministry of Munitions during the war had implanted the need for new techniques and a new form of control in factory work. Owners too were conscious of the need for change in internal factory relations. Though many of the proposals were destined not to go beyond declarations of principle, there was support for the need to put an enterprise at the service of the social community, to renounce authoritarian methods of management and give greater consideration to the human aspects of labour rather than regarding it as merely one among the many other factors of production.

THE INHERITANCE OF WEBER, TAYLOR AND FAYOL: 'SCIENTIFIC MANAGEMENT'

The idea of 'scientific management' suddenly came on the scene in Europe in the early 1920s. Its emergence at this time was yet another effect of post-war economic and social conditions; but it also represented the logical evolution of a movement initiated in the years before the war.

Historians of an earlier generation have perhaps attached too much importance to the phenomenon of Taylorism, giving undue weight to its principles and providing an unnecessarily detailed account of its application and impact in the United States and Europe. On two fundamental points, however, time has proved it right. First, at the end of the war the world of production in Europe lacked an ideology on which to reconstruct the systems of authority weakened by the war, and certainly the cult of efficiency created by Taylorism, and the rigid delimitation it proposed between directive and executive functions, were well fitted to achieve that end. Secondly, the potential of human and material resources absorbed by production was constantly increasing, but despite this the world of production had no matrix of principles from which to derive rules for practical action, no doctrine which could elevate it and put it conceptually on a level comparable with the amazing progress of the century's first two decades in physics, biochemistry, and other fields. Looking back now, it is no doubt true to say that Taylorism was widely discussed and written about in Europe at the time, but these new ideas were never applied there on any wide scale; and in the United States, as Taylor himself admitted, the number of workers involved in scientific management experiments did not exceed 50,000. In Europe they were confined to a few big concerns, to the virtual exclusion of the small-scale concerns which were the nerve-centre of European production.

Nevertheless the 'scientific movement' has a decisive importance in the history of management, for it directed interest towards the *method* of production and called public attention to the administration of enterprises, thus laying the foundation both for present-day studies of management and for a series of empirical investigations. After 1930 the situation changed completely when the scientific movement was accused of having neglected 'human needs' and moved to the defensive.

Long before Taylor's ideas gained ground in the United States, the conclusion had been reached in Europe, and especially in Britain, that the organisation of work should be governed by general principles based on scientific analysis, and the main spheres of action of management in this context such as time-studies and analyses of production processes, had been worked out. James Watt Jr., M. R. Boulton, Robert Owen and in particular Charles Babbage in the nineteenth century had anticipated the fundamental lines of these new trends. This is not really surprising when one reflects that in these early attempts management was concerning itself mainly with the organisation of factory work, i.e. with a form of organisation directly linked with production. Production itself implies seeking for the perfect method, and thus it is natural that a pioneer country in industrialisation such as Britain should be among the first to tackle these problems.

The scientific management movement differed from those early attempts at innovation in four particular ways: a) its more solidly based methodology, linked indirectly to the advances in the physical sciences in the second half of the nineteenth century of which Taylor and his followers made use; b) the different dimension of the problems to be solved, due to large-scale production and the need to saturate rapidly expanding markets, a condition which applied especially in the United States; c) the fact that, as has been mentioned earlier, scientific management had come to mean not just a technique of management but also an ideology, the watchword of the young engineers and technicians, to whom it afforded the ethical justification for their new position in the world of production, a position based on the search for maximum efficiency which had become a kind of mission with them; d) above all, the fact that scientific management regarded the enterprise as a system, sought to legitimise the authority of management, and identified the worker's principal motivation with gain. Having established that the fundamental aim of a man working in a factory was to earn more, it followed that this coincided perfectly with the owner's aim of profit, and thus scientific management became the means whereby both these objectives could be simultaneously achieved.

The time therefore seemed propitious for launching the new movement in Europe: large-scale production was on the increase, the industrial reconstruction made necessary by wartime destruction favoured the introduction of new methods of management, the big enterprises aspired to copy the American model, and the new ranks of technicians brought in by the new technologies were also in search of a doctrine. But it must also be emphasised that while Taylorism undoubtedly exercised a profound influence on management in the 1920s and '30s, similar or parallel movements had already developed independently in Europe.

The scientific management movement found an analogous manifestation in Eastern Europe in the 'theory of harmonisation' propounded by Karol Adamiecki, born in 1866 and from 1922 Professor of Industrial Organisation and Management at the Warsaw Polytechnic. Adamiecki was an engineer who began as production manager in a big rolling-mill, where problems of organisation first came to his notice. He made a particular study of planning and control of a productive activity consisting of a large number of complex operations of different duration but all linked together. In this situation the fundamental problem was to 'harmonise' the flow of production, keeping both machines and workers fully occupied. Adamiecki's diagrams were widely reproduced in the engineering manuals of this century's early decades in Europe, and this testifies to the general awareness of the need for systematic control of the means of production.

A further contribution at this stage to the efforts to give management a substance and an ideology came from Walther Rathenau (1867–1922), who was a director of numerous companies in Germany, chairman of the Allgemeine Elektrizitäts-Gesellschaft, and a minister, as well as author of several books, among them *Die neue Wirtschaft* (*The New Economy*) (1918). Rathenau's doctrine anticipated in many ways the results of the gradual separation between ownership of capital and administration of enterprises which was to develop more extensively towards the end of the 1930s. It also had an influence on company legislation in Germany and on the position of enterprises within the structure of power in the Nazi period. One of the most important consequences arising from Rathenau's doctrines, a consequence destined to leave its mark even after the Second World War, was the need to ensure a position of stability and independence for the directors vis-à-vis the shareholders in the structure of an enterprise.

Although their works do not deal directly with management as an economic phenomenon, Max Weber and Emile Durkheim must be numbered among those who have contributed by their doctrines to its development. Their sociological studies based on objective and scientific principles quickly led to the formation of a cultural climate, which, not only in Europe but also in the United States, fostered the conceptual systemisation of the 'theory of organisation'. In particular, Weber's study of the distribution of power inside organisations left a deep mark, as also did his examination of the influence of religion and other cultural forms on economic behaviour. His theory of the relationship between the Calvinist ethic and the development of capitalism still attracts scholars seeking to explain the reasons for the survival of national 'styles' in the conduct of the big multinational enterprises, and for the high rate of economic development to be found in certain geographical areas rather than in others.

The scientific movement, basing itself on Taylorism, aimed at increasing a firm's efficiency by improving the organisation of factory work and productive technology. But at the same time a second movement, more authentically European in origin, was advancing into the field of the administrative organisation of an enterprise as a whole, in other words tackling the organisation of the various functions involved in the direction of an enterprise.

The leading exponent of this movement was Henry Fayol (1841–1925), the European scholar who in the history of modern management perhaps made the most original contributions of the first half of the present century. Fayol developed ideas which have today become consecrated by tradition and practice, such as the universality of management (i.e. its possible application not only in private enterprises but also in all other forms of organisation), unity of command in enterprises, the hierarchies of authority, its distribution, and the machinery for its delegation.

Though Britain was the natural channel for the flow of ideas to Europe from the United States, and though because of her long-standing industrial traditions she still led the field in economic studies and studies of the organisation of production, other countries which before the war had contributed little to the study of management were now coming to the fore. The main theme of such investigations was still 'scientific management', which aroused wide interest everywhere, but the European cultural tradition also soon prompted such experiments to turn in new directions such as applied psychology – a field in which Carrard in Switzerland and Sollier in Belgium were particularly active – and the physiology of work. A lot of ideas emerged which, though lacking in real originality, formed the basis for an inter-disciplinary analysis of the business concern which was to develop in Europe after the Second World War. While France remained linked with the names of Fayol, Chatelier and de Fréminville, the studies of Köttgen, Meyemberg, Hellmich and Hegner in Germany, Gerard and Landauer in Belgium, and Lee and Sheldon in Britain achieved some prominence.

Another proof of European interest in the scientific management movement in the 1920s can be seen in the number of research institutes and conferences on work organisation. In 1920 the Conférence de l'Organisation Française was founded in France, in 1921 the German Institute of Management, in 1925 the Polish Institute of Scientific Management, in 1928 the Austrian Board of Efficiency, and in 1919 the Belgian Association of Standardisation and the International Institute for Rationalisation in Geneva. The first International Management

Congress was held in Prague in 1924, followed by the second in Brussels the year after.

The prestige enjoyed by scientific management in Europe in the early 1920s was not merely a reflection of the results achieved in the United States in the sphere of industrial development; it was also due to the fact that European industrialists had themselves been quick to embrace the doctrine. But in fact, apart from specialised literature and numerous articles in its favour, scientific management affected only a small number of enterprises and did little to alter methods of production in European concerns. Reading the literature of the period, one gets the definite impression that these ideas of management were in almost every case the ideas of the owners or administrators of an enterprise. Another fact to emerge is that the majority of those concerned with management at this time regarded Taylorism as a necessary channel for the diffusion of their ideas, with the result that the scientific movement was widely put forward and discussed in different countries. This may have been tantamount to admitting a lack of originality, or it may have been an implicit attempt to advance Taylorism as the explanation for the United States' supremacy over Europe and so to suggest that the ground lost might be regained by following the same path.

ILLUSIONS COLLAPSE. ECONOMIC STABILITY. THE CRISIS OF 1931–2. ECONOMIC AND SOCIAL STAGNATION

With the passage of a few years many enthusiasms faded out and with them the new ideas advanced at the end of the First World War dissolved. The horizons of management contracted to within much more restricted limits than had seemed attainable only a short time before. The economic difficulties of the working classes and the lesser bourgeoisie, the military occupation of the Ruhr, the General Strike in Britain and strikes in other countries, the stifling of trade union activity, and inflationary crises in Austria, Hungary and Germany caused illusions of a revival of the international economic mechanism to collapse, spread anew the spectre of war, and extinguished at birth many hopes or a greater social dynamism, of which management was to have been a protagonist.

In Britain, where there had been strong hopes of a social reorganisation of management, even the most enthusiastic supporters of shared worker control in management began to have second thoughts. The attempts made by management at the end of the war to win support for the experiment both from public opinion and from the workers soon gave way to the opposite view. The need for wider control of management over production was in fact by then regarded as the essential premise for efficiency, and scientific management's idea of workers' participation in administration was rapidly modified, even though such participation might seem to be purely formal. The idea of profit-sharing and co-partnership was replaced by committees with consultative powers, more information was provided about the firm's finances, and the principle of just and equitable regulation of relations between management and workers was affirmed. But in effect relations with the workers tended towards forms which virtually excluded them from the more important decisions. The 'human relations' movement, which like Taylorism originated in the United States, was also interpreted in the same spirit. According to the prevalent view, 'human relations' should be regarded as a means of communication between management and workers. Another, more explicit, version maintained that 'human relations' constituted an instrument for the psychological manipulation of the worker with a view to integrating him into the enterprise and reducing the strength of the trade union or, at least, to inducing the workers to identify themselves with the concern's objectives.

Between 1924 and 1929 Western Europe seemed to be finding the way towards a new society similar to that of the United States, and management appeared to be moving towards new horizons characterised by the revival of international trade, expansion of consumption, new technologies of production, and a greater participation of the poorer classes in economic power. But the countries of Europe, unable to overcome the barriers of nationalism and weakened by the economic depression and fear of war, proved incapable of re-establishing the economic system they had created and under which they had prospered throughout the half-century before the First World War.

But in spite of this, the inter-war period nevertheless provides the key to the pattern of development of European management after the Second World War. Those years in fact saw the decline of competition, the consolidation of the large-scale concern and of economic agreements between enterprises, the strengthening of the public enterprise and of State control of the economy, the intensification of trade union struggles, and the beginning of various forms of national planning. But above all, the leaders in industry and the trade unions and even the civil service were forced to take account of the new ideas and to learn, at the cost of a fresh catastrophe, the mechanisms of social justice and economics, which in the meantime had become much more complex than before and which now called for decisive methods to tackle them.

In 1925, while industrial production was for the first time approaching the pre-war level, management in Europe was girding itself everywhere to face these new and more complex economic and social conditions. This change of attitude found expression in different guide-lines aimed to meet the new demands on management: a new form of rationalisation, more advanced than the early attempts made under the influence of Taylorism, the extension of rationalisation outside the industrial enterprise, the convergence of a number of disciplines in the study of management problems, greater emphasis on managerial accounting and financial controls, and administration on a grand scale, made necessary by the expanded size of enterprises and by industrial concentration.

For some years past the methods of scientific management had not won universal acceptance as a sure principle for the organisation of work. Many industrialists rejected them as too costly, the trade unions objected to them as inhuman, and the economic crisis, by bringing to the forefront the need for employment and efficiency, strengthened this rejection. But it was management itself that set about revising the old methods to adapt them to a radically altered situation. Management was not merely seeking the best way to organise production and commercial distribution: it was also beginning to raise such problems as the optimal dimensions of an enterprise in face of a developing market, how best to meet competition, and what type and range of goods to put on the market. In other words, the horizons of organisation of work and rationalisation had expanded considerably to include, in addition to the original sector of production, the other numerous functions involved in the running of an enterprise. The administrators' renewed interest in organisation of work and more generally in rationalisation was the natural answer to the increase in costs resulting from large-scale production and from the growing demand for standardised products on the European markets. Production called for heavy investments and it therefore raised big risks of technical obsolescence and of decline in the demand for goods, while at the same time because of competition prices could not be raised. Hence the need to find ways of economising, and the surest form of economy within easy reach of the managers lay in better utilisation of labour, machines, materials, and capital.

In Germany, where development of production had reached a very high rate, rationalisation constituted a dominant aim in management, but there was much criticism about the ill-effects of chain production. This led to a number of studies on monotony in work, psychological fatigue, and the dangers of declining vocational skill. All this caused the attention of sociologists and psychologists to be directed towards the large enterprise. All over Europe studies were also undertaken on financial administration, calculation of costs, the framing of budgets, and methods of accounting in general. The theme of the International Management Congress in 1929 was budgetary control.

In Britain, rationalisation assumed three fundamental characteristics. It was mainly orientated towards concentration of enterprises, it aimed at reduction of excess productive capacity and renewal of plant, and it was in part supported by the State. The Bank of England financed the establishment of the Lancashire Cotton Corporation which grouped together some 200 textile concerns; a group of naval shipyards, representing 90 per cent of production, formed the National Shipbuilders' Security with the aim of reorganising the whole sector; and in 1926, as a result of fusion between Nobel Industries, Brunner & Co., United Alkali, and British Dyestuffs, Imperial Chemical Industries (ICI) was created, accounting for a third of all chemical production in Britain. ICI, which represented the most important industrial combine of the period, was formed with the declared aim of rationalising the use of its four components' resources, reducing costs, coordinating technological research, and improving the level of competitiveness on national and international markets. [1]

It is clearly impossible to find any general trend in management in Europe, given the great differences between the countries. However, in this period a deep divergence begins to emerge between large and small enterprises in terms both of management problems and of dimensions. In the large-scale concerns new problems of administration arose for two different reasons: their varied and complex historical origins, and the many-sided nature of their current management in view of the differentiation of products and markets. Past experience, whether in recent times or in the wartime era or the relatively prosperous period of the early 1920s, could be of no great help in dealing with these two kinds of problems. Unlike the United States in similar circumstances, the Europeans lacked managerial cadres which had been trained over the earlier years; they therefore responded by falling back on entrepreneurial skill and calling on State intervention to regulate the national

1. J. H. Dunning and C. J. Thomas, *British Industry – Change and Development in the Twentieth Century*, London, Hutchinson, 1961, pp. 43–48.

economy and afford protection against international competititon.

The crisis of 1930 confronted management with vast and unprecedented problems. Production declined rapidly, prices toppled, unemployment increased to a varying extent in every country, and the international monetary system was virtually destroyed. The economic crisis also brought an ideological crisis, and the prestige of management, accused of not having foreseen the crisis and being unable to meet it effectively, fell to the lowest levels of the century. Governments were unprepared to solve such complex problems calling for expert knowledge; in most cases they showed their lack of experience in economic and financial affairs, adopting provisional expedients which often proved mistaken. The consequent changes of programme (especially frequent in Britain) were never based on objectives of long-term stability but aimed merely at producing immediate remedies, with the result that management of enterprises became even more confused.

The lesson that European management drew from this experience was almost as complex as the causes and consequences of the crisis itself, but two effects were especially obvious and also had a profound influence on the subsequent decades. First, the crisis showed that the economy of the European countries was highly vulnerable to international economic fluctuations; and it also showed that the extent of dependence on the United States was far greater than the question of war reparations had led people to suppose. Germany realised how serious it was to depend on American financiers for short-term loans, and the countries that based their parity on sterling were compelled to follow Britain in abandoning the gold standard without being able to reach agreement on a common monetary policy. Foreign investments were devalued and credits became difficult to liquidate.

Secondly, under the threat of the depression the only salvation seemed to be linked with action by the State. Economic protection, it was thought, would help enterprises to recover and extricate themselves from the international monetary chaos, and it could probably shelter them from thorny problems in relation to the trade unions and the workers. When France, Germany and almost all the other countries imposed measures for monetary control and restrictions or quotas on imports or raised customs tariffs, management regarded these moves as necessary and desirable for economic revival. In 1932 even Britain, with its new Conservative Government, abandoned its traditional position as a champion of international trade and brought in the Import Duties Act which marked the end of seventy years of free trade on world markets. Though these measures were everywhere applied without much enthusiasm or strictness, they had a negative influence on European management, for they frustrated the aspirations of the past ten years towards broader horizons and spread the idea of the private concern's intrinsic weakness vis-à-vis the State, an idea which was to become more deep-rooted in the next decade.

It would nevertheless be wrong to suggest that management made no progress during this period. In Britain, Urwick, in his *Principles of Direction and Control* (1928), considered the possibility of an *a priori* model for business management. He thought it should be possible to study the principles of organisation as a purely technical problem independently of a firm's aims and of the motives governing its members. These principles – which could be built up on an inductive basis, presupposing also a study of the firm's past and of other firms – would ensure the 'neutrality' of the organisation and would consequently contribute, among other things, towards reducing conflicts within the firm itself.

Other works on management which aroused interest at the time were Urwick's *Management of Tomorrow* (1933), Lee's *Dictionary of Industrial Administration* (1928), and Elbourne's *Fundamentals of Industrial Management* (1934). Meanwhile from the United States came echoes of Elton Mayo's researches on 'human relations'; but in contrast to America, that movement had little influence in Britain and the other European countries, and the new trends were absorbed by European management without giving the impression that it had come into contact with completely new ideas. It seems likely, however, that the Hawthorne experiments won rapid acceptance in Britain since they gave support to ideas already adopted by management there. In other words, as in the case of scientific management, one has the impression that the 'human relations' movement served to help to legitimise the function of management.[2] The importance of such studies was only realised some years later, when Urwick's formulation of inductive principles of management came under discussion. Studies in the social sciences led to a negative conclusion about the validity of rigid principles of management. It was argued that in a system based on a plurality of individual and group behaviours the same action could not in fact give the same results in the same enterprise at a different time, or in a different enterprise. At the same time psychologists warned of the dangerous effects that application of rigid principles of management could have on important elements of the organisational structure such as responsibility, identification with the aims of the firm, loyalty to the firm, and individual initiative.

In Britain, France and Germany studies of the organisation of production were extended to embrace organisation of the structures of an enterprise as a whole, and there were a number of studies on the dualism between 'line and staff' positions and between organisational centralisation and decentralisation, on delegation of authority, and on span of control. In Germany, where the tradition of management studies had temporarily fallen into abeyance owing to the economic and political crisis, various scholars revived their interest in the economic and financial aspects of an enterprise.

One change at this time passed almost unnoticed. But it is to this period that we can date the appearance on the European scene of a new interlocutor in the dialogue between management and authority – the civil service.

2. J. Child, *British Management Thought, A Critical Analysis*, London, Allen and Unwin, 1969, p. 101.

The crisis had shown how ill-prepared many governments were to tackle an increasingly complex financial situation, and this had set in motion an irreversible trend towards the transfer of effective economic power from parliament to the officials of the State, who were the only people capable of dealing with so complex a subject and were, moreover, the only element to give some stability to the governments' policies. These officials were invariably, however, highly conservative in background and education.

A completely negative factor, on the other hand, was the enforced emigration of many leading figures in finance and industry, managers included, who had to flee their countries to escape from political persecution. At a time when the ranks of professional managers were still small, this exodus had profound consequences.

ECONOMIC AND SOCIAL CONDITIONS IN THE 1950s AND 1960s. RECONVERSION TO PEACETIME ECONOMY. THE COMMON MARKET AND THE NEW INTERNATIONAL CLIMATE

As had happened after the First World War, economic life in Europe in 1945 resumed and embarked on reconstruction. The war had destroyed bridges, roads, port installations, and railways and had hit basic industries hard. True, damage to industry was more apparent than real, for many factories, even in Germany, had been kept intact, and the productive potential had in fact increased during the war; but the whole industrial system was dislocated, and total production in Europe fell to less than half the 1938 level. Agriculture had suffered serious damage from intensive exploitation of the land and the suspension of techniques to preserve its fertility, while the machinery of international trade had ceased to function and attempts at revival were still hampered by pre-war protectionism. But the most serious consequences were in human resources. The greatest losses had been among men of working age, while European society had to reabsorb many returning ex-servicemen incapable of working and youths who had had no training except for the fighting services. There was thus a big disproportion between the labour force and those who were not of working age or fit for work.

The years between 1945 and 1950 were dominated by the needs of revival and adaptation to national conditions which, especially in the countries emerging from the war, differed greatly in each country and involved some radical changes. In Britain, part of the economy remained under strict control by the State, with nationalisation extending to the basic industrial sectors as well as finance. Germany, on the other hand, took the opposite course, returning to a market economy with a vigour sustained by the wish to leave behind a period in which everything had been centralised in the State. The big industrial combines were divided up and so too were the three main banks, the Deutsche Bank, the Dresdner Bank and the Commerz Bank, each bank and its branches being forbidden to operate outside an individual *Land*. Meanwhile Italy and France were in the grip of inflation and the black market, and in politics were struggling to reach agreement between the various parties which had emerged at the end of the war – parties of widely differing ideologies, whether Communist, Socialist, or Christian Democrat. Production revived slowly, but the path to normality was tortuous everywhere, even in countries such as Switzerland and Sweden which had not taken part in the war.

The war and State intervention left deep marks on organisational structures everywhere. In addition to nationalisation of the aircraft, electricity and transport industries and the big combines such as Renault in France, the State had made its weight felt in at least two other ways. First, during the war the most important orders had gone to the most efficient concerns, which had consequently enlarged their productive potential, and secondly, control of costs had brought about a certain degree of uniformity in the methods adopted in concerns that supplied the State.

The establishment of the European Economic Community

(EEC) in 1958 and the European Free Trade Association (EFTA) in 1960 marked the beginning of an era of closer relationships in European management. Until then management had developed on roughly parallel lines in the different countries, carried forward by a common movement towards expansion but strongly influenced by local traditions and economic conditions. The great variety of conditions in the countries made it difficult to give an overall picture of the earlier decades, and European management had virtually no supranational code of beliefs. The attraction exercised by the American model, then indisputably in the forefront on the technical plane, the need to deal with individual national situations, and the fact that the international economic contacts of European firms were based mainly on importing and exporting rather than on global strategies of international expansion, all tended to retard the development of a European movement in management. But from 1960 onwards the move towards European economic integration, the disputes which dragged on throughout the 1960s about the managerial gap vis-à-vis the United States, and an ideological crisis of which student unrest was the most obvious manifestation, combined to bring about a decisive change.

The new class of European managers had been trained in technical and economic subjects and came from a much broader social background than their predecessors, who came from a narrow social élite with a classical education. They thus became participants in a movement towards closer European integration which, grafted as it was on to different traditions and economic structures, marked the definite transition towards a new society. Thus the decade of 1960–70 witnessed the beginning of a process of closer integration which in dimensions recalled that experienced in America at the end of the last century, but which in variety of cultural background had no precedent in history.

The period between 1950 and 1970 saw new developments on the part of European management in marketing, in organisational structures, in financial controls, and in personnel management. Various factors combined to stimulate these developments: the formation of a big continental market, the strengthening of oligopolistic positions, the development of multinational enterprises, advances in State planning, new labour problems, and a new role for the smaller concern.

The European market was a long way from being fully integrated at the beginning of the 1960s, and even ten years later not much progress had been made in that direction. But all the same the prospect of a market of 200 million consumers with one of the highest standards of living in the world caused many European enterprises to concentrate on improving their marketing capabilities. In doing this they drew on past experience, both national and international, but the European market as a whole had some quite unique characteristics. The tastes of young people were becoming of greater importance in the consumer market, consumption itself was on the increase, and the national origin of goods tended to matter less. But marketing strategy had to take into account considerable difficulties in two spheres, those of publicity and distribution. When advertising a product it was necessary to present the message in several languages, reckon with the differences in habits, mentality and tastes, and respect the various countries' different laws. Only a very few mass-media covered several European countries simultaneously and they were directed to a narrow circle of people, and even in the national field the most effective means of publicity, TV and radio, were much sought after and so hard to come by.

Retail conditions were even more difficult in Europe. As to distribution, there had always been a great many small retail dealers whose presence contributed to diminish the sector's productivity and increase its costs. On the other hand they were quite important politically, especially in France and Italy, and succeeded in restricting to a minimum the introduction of large-scale retail concerns which would have made things easier and more economical for the wholesalers. A further complication for marketing strategies in Europe was State intervention. Planning was very difficult under an economic regime in which taxation, financial and social burdens, and controlled prices could change within a short space of time.

But the really new problem for European management arose from the variety of goods demanded by a rapidly expanding market. Higher incomes, the drift towards the towns, and the first symptoms of a consumer society resembling that of America had a shattering effect on European management's traditional habit of concentrating its forces on internal productivity rather than on marketing, and on expanding the sales of a particular product rather than on large-scale production and distribution. That habit had grown up in the two preceding decades largely as a result of autarky and the efforts to exploit scarce national resources to the maximum. Management now found itself compelled to adapt its marketing strategies to the changed conditions.

No less important for management were the effects of centralised planning of the economy. At the beginning of the 1960s national economic plans existed in France, Britain, Italy, Sweden, Norway, Holland, Belgium and Austria. Besides contributing to the stability of the national economy, the various experiments in State intervention showed that public action could give a direct stimulus to the development of management, and this helped to narrow the traditional gap between private enterprises and the State. The public enterprises in France, ENI and IRI[3] in Italy, and later on the Industrial Reorganisation Corporation in Britain were all active in introducing new methods of management, while the attempts made in Holland to control wages and incomes, and in Sweden to meet the needs of full employment, development and social welfare, had an effect on management there as well as indirectly influencing other countries.

The only sector to remain partly outside this new trend was that of the public services organisations – municipal

3. ENI = Ente Nazionale Idrocarburi, the National Hydrocarburates Corporation; IRI = Istituto per la Ricostruzione Industriale, the Institute for Industrial Reconstruction (the State holding Corporation).

concerns, hospitals and public transport bodies. Here the technical need to supply services of a certain standard, and the fact that costs were regarded as a burden for the whole community, caused management in the traditional sense to have a purely secondary role.

By the mid-1970s European management was beginning to see its social responsibilities in new terms. The basic conflict was still the same: on the one hand responsibility towards the owners of capital to produce a profit, on the other hand responsibilities towards the workers and the community. In recent years, however, there had been a great change in the attitude of the public towards the enterprise. A smoking chimney no longer meant the existence of a prosperous industrial centre but a source of pollution and therefore a liability in the defence of the ecological balance which the enterprise was transferring to society. The big concern came to be regarded, especially by young people, not so much as a source of national pride but rather as a centre of power in which decisions were taken without the participation of the workers, let alone of the citizens. There was also a new awareness of the need to recall the enterprise to its responsibilities towards consumers in maintaining the quality of its goods and the credibility of its advertising, and towards workers in respect of their physical and mental health and their vocational status.

PORTRAIT OF THE EUROPEAN MANAGER

Style of Management
A study of the past fifty years demonstrates the validity of certain theories advanced by scholars about the relationship between the evolution of management and the evolution of some fundamental variables in economic and social development. The variables which have gradually assumed increasing weight in the evolution of management are social change, the diversification of markets, technological progress, the rising proportion of fixed costs of administra-

tion in relation to costs of production, and the introduction of new management techniques.

That being so, two aspects may contribute further to illustrate the evolution of management in Europe in the last fifty years: the changes in the pattern of authority in an enterprise and the professional training of managers.

The system of authority of management is generally taken to mean two closely complementary things: the way in which authority is exercised within the organisational hierarchy, and the way in which decisions are distributed according to their degree of importance among the various levels of the hierarchy. This means in practice that the system of authority of management is fundamentally based on the way in which the behaviour of subordinates is 'influenced' and on the way in which a balance is achieved between centralisation and decentralisation of decisions by means of delegation of responsibilities.

The past fifty years have witnessed profound changes in Europe in the system of authority of management in enterprises. The transition from 'authoritarian' and 'paternalistic' to 'democratic' and 'participative' management, and from centralisation of decisions to decentralisation, has taken place against a background of different conditions such as the European tradition of the family concern, changes in the social and political scene, the attitude of employers' and workers' organisations, and action by the State. The small-sized enterprise reflects the system of family authority, and this pattern tends to continue for a long time even in an advanced stage of development. Any historical analysis of the systems of authority must therefore take as its starting point the widespread diffusion of small and medium-sized enterprises in Europe and the concentration of the working capital of such enterprises in the hands of family groups.

In the small and medium-sized enterprise authority is exercised by one or more persons who belong to the same family or act as if they belonged to it. When there is some division of duties, it is always accompanied by rigid centralisation of decisions, and the manner of 'influencing' the behaviour of dependants tends to be authoritarian or paternalistic. The independence of the enterprise is strenuously defended: recourse to credit is strictly limited, secrecy about internal operations is maintained, organisational change is resisted, and complete loyalty is expected from dependants. To make the organisational structure still more compact, the enterprise concerns itself solely or predominantly with only one branch of activity – with production, or commercial distribution, or banking, and so on.[4]

This type of small and medium-sized concern was fairly widespread in Europe between the wars and persisted even after 1950, but various factors combined to modify and weaken the traditional system of authority on which it was based. The two World Wars had helped to bring about a change of attitude in the direction of greater social justice and a stronger sense of responsibility towards subordinates. All countries introduced labour laws limiting the arbitrary action of employers. The trade unions' negotiating powers increased, and greater specialisation and the consequent shortage of specialised manpower put the workers in a stronger position vis-à-vis management, a position they exploited by resorting to boycott or rejection of authority. A combination of changes in the economic and social structure together with technological progress contributed further to alter this situation towards the beginning of the 1950s. Thus although the original kind of small and medium-sized concern continued to survive in some sectors, it was gradually yielding place to a new type of enterprise of similar size, highly specialised, innovating, dynamic in both national and international fields, and often highly progressive on the social side, in which the system of authority was completely changed in the direction of 'participation', and in which the gap between top and middle management, and between the latter and the workers, was gradually disappearing. The reason for this evolution in

4. D. Landes, 'French Business and the Businessman: A Social and Cultural Analysis', in Edward M. Earle (ed.), *Modern France: Problems of the Third and Fourth Republic*, Princeton University Press, 1951.

the European small and medium-sized enterprises is to be sought partly in the history of the previous period and partly in the new structure of the consumer-goods markets and the financial markets.

This new type of enterprise, markedly European in character, was under the disadvantage that it could not engage a large staff and was therefore relatively weak on the marketing side and slow to make technological innovations marketable. To compensate for this, however, it could boast an enterprising management not only at the top but at all the other levels; it had kept itself independent of the big enterprises, avoiding any subcontracting links with them; it was often in the top rank in its own sector, and coolly pushed its way into international markets more successfully than many a large concern. These enterprises probably provided the source of European management's most authentic and original representatives.[5]

While the small and medium-sized enterprise in Europe was evolving in a different way from that of similar concerns in the United States (which were more dependent on the big enterprises and were still mainly directed towards the domestic market), the evolution of the big European enterprise and its systems of authority reflected much more closely the course already adopted by such enterprises in the United States. In the European enterprise on the way to becoming a large-scale concern the family type of authoritarian structure first became subject to pressure towards decentralisation when the family group or manager-owner was no longer able to keep abreast of all the administrative problems and had to open the door to outside managers. However, expansion in such enterprises usually involved a vertical structure, with responsibilities divided among specialists on the staff; and this enabled many entrepreneurs to preserve a largely authoritarian and paternalistic system in management at the upper levels of the organisational hierarchies. The introduction of scientific management methods, the spread of 'human relations'

5. C. Gasser, 'The European Manager of Tomorrow', in D. Drucker (ed.), *Preparing Tomorrow's Business Leaders Today*, Prentice-Hall, 1969.

studies, the new labour legislation introduced in several countries, and the evolution of the social structure did not, except in rare cases, bring much change in the pattern of authority; this was largely because first rearmament and then the war and the subsequent reconstruction meant that production continued to be the most important function for many enterprises, and it is a recognised fact that control of production lends itself to an authoritarian and centralised pattern.

When, around 1950, the economic and social scene changed completely, many large-scale European enterprises embarked on organisational decentralisation, abandoning the mainly functional structure for a divisional structure which involved a change in the vertical distribution of authority since it aimed at establishing in each operative division the atmosphere of an individual concern. In the first instance this change was probably more psychological than technical, one of form rather than substance, but in the next ten years it took on greater consistency. By the second half of the 1960s European large-scale enterprises can be said to have assumed a less authoritarian structure as compared with the preceding decades: this applied both to relations between the financially controlling groups and the specialist managers and relations with colleagues lower down in the organisational hierarchy, as well as to relations with the trade unions and the outer world in general. An important factor in bringing about this change was the gradual emergence after the war of a class of managers whose position was based on technological knowledge and information rather than on the fact of belonging to a certain hierarchical level in the organisational structure. Within this new hierarchy, authoritarian, paternalistic or merely manipulative patterns were of little importance and therefore had to give way to more decentralised and more 'democratic' structures.

A factor of some influence in these new trends was undoubtedly the attitude of the public enterprises. With their greater financial possibilities and wider scope in planning, these enterprises quickly moved towards adopting the new forms of organisation and especially in France and Italy distinguished themselves both by making their managements more 'participational' and by acceding to worker's demands for better conditions of work.

Turning to consider enterprises as a whole without distinction of size, if we abandon abstract generalities in our study of the system of authority in European enterprises and instead look at the individual countries we at once find great national differences, due to the differences in tradition and local legislation.

In Britain decentralisation and delegation of authority are perhaps more widespread than elsewhere, but the real national characteristic lies in the coexistence of relations of a 'constitutional' kind between management and trade unions resulting from the tradition of industry-wide bargaining, and relations of a 'neopaternalistic' kind between management and workers at shop floor level.[6]

In Italy and France a centralising trend prevails in the top management, while relations between management and workers reflect the influence of political conditions and the traditional hostility between employers and workers.

In Germany the patterns of authority are the result partly of the structure given by law to the top management and partly of the *Unternehmer*'s (entrepreneur's) traditional way of interpreting the sources of his authority. The top management constitutes by law the *Vorstand*, or governing body, which is the sole organ responsible for administration in the eyes of the law, and which does not include representatives of the shareholders, who form a second, separate, body, the *Aufsichtsrat*. According to Hartmann, these *Unternehmer* claim complete authority over their subordinates by virtue of a superiority which resides in the ownership of capital, in their transcendent power, and in the fact of belonging to a social élite or possessing superior personal capacities.[7] The particular economic and social

6. F. Harbison and C. Myers, *Management in the Industrial World*, New York, McGraw-Hill, 1959, p. 313.

7. H. Hartmann, *Authority and Organisation in German Management*, Princeton, 1951.

conditions existing in Germany since the war may perhaps have delayed any change in this situation, which would seem to be in contrast with industrial development. Although rejection of authority by subordinates has been increasingly evident, and although German management has modified its own attitude, many people nevertheless think it has still retained a strong tinge of paternalism.

In Sweden, too, centralisation of the directive functions is furthered by a law requiring an enterprise of a certain size to have a managing director, but this fact occurred in a historical and social context which by tradition includes the dominating principle of cooperation between the various social forces, and in an environment in which relations between management and trade unions were settled by arbitration and conciliation rather than at the end of wearing disputes, as happened in other countries of Western Europe.[8]

Despite these differences of national situation and tradition, by the end of the 'sixties and after certain common trends began to appear in the systems of authority of the various European enterprises. The centralising tradition of European management, resulting in an unwillingness to delegate responsibility, had arisen from various factors: family ownership of a firm's capital, taxation laws, the precarious future of a firm's development in preceding decades, the lack of qualified managers, and the abiding hostility shown over a long period by both public opinion and the State towards the large-scale enterprise. These considerations now gradually acquired less force in the face of an irresistible trend towards organisational decentralisation.

8. E. F. Heckscher, *An Economic History of Sweden*, Harvard University Press, 1954, pp. 269 ff.

BIBLIOGRAPHY

A large number of publications exist about the evolution of management in Europe, and a list of only the most important among them would be long and, even then, possibly incomplete. The present bibliography is confined to works that deal in greater depth with the subjects treated in the preceding pages.

W. ASHWORTH, *A Short History of the International Economy 1850–1950*, London, Longman, 1960.

S. CARLSON, *Executive Behaviour*, Stockholm, 1951

J. CHILD, *British Management Thought. A Critical Analysis*, London, Allen & Unwin, 1969.

J. H. DUNNING, C. J. THOMAS, *British Industry. Change and Development in the Twentieth Century*, London, Hutchinson, 1961.

H. FAYOL, *Administration Industrielle et Générale – Prévoyance – Organisation – Commandement – Coordination – Contrôle*, Paris, Dunod, 1962.

G. FUA', *Notes on Italian Economic Growth 1861–1964*, Milan, Giuffrè, 1965.

D. GRANICK, *The European Executive*, New York, Doubleday Co., 1964.

S. GROSSET, *Management: European and American Styles*, Belmont, Wadsworth Pub. Co., 1970.

L. F. HABER, *The Chemical Industry 1900–1930. International Growth and Technological Change*, Oxford, Clarendon Press, 1971.

F. HARBISON and C. MYERS, *Management in the Industrial World*, New York, McGraw–Hill, 1959.

H. HARTMANN, *Authority and Organisation in German Management*, Princeton, 1959.

H. HARTMANN, *La Formation des dirigeants d'enterprises. Le rôle des universités et des grandes écoles techniques allemandes*, Paris, OEEC, 1955.

E. F. HECKSCHER, *An Economic History of Sweden*, Boston, Harvard University Press, 1954.

W. JOHNSON, J. WHYMAN and G. WYKES, *A Short Economic and Social History of Twentieth Century Britain*, London, Allen and Unwin, 1967.

A. MADDISON, *Economic Growth in the West. Comparative Experience in Europe and North America*, New York, Norton & Co. Inc., 1964.

T. M. MOSSON, *Management Education in Five European Countries*, London, Business Publications Ltd., 1965.

S. POLLARD, *The Development of the British Economy 1914–1967*, London, E. Arnold Ltd., 1969.

M. M. POSTAN, *An Economic History of Western Europe: 1945–1964*, London, Methuen & Co., 1967.

S. B. PRASAD, *Management in International Perspective*, New York, Appleton-Century-Crofts, 1967.

O. SHELDON, *The Philosophy of Management*, London, Sir Isaac Pitman & Sons Ltd., 1965.

A. SHONFIELD, *Modern Capitalism. The Changing Balance of Public and Private Power*, London, Oxford University Press, 1965.

L. URWICK, *The Golden Book of Management. An Historical Record of the Life and Work of Seventy Pioneers*, London, Newman Neame Ltd., 1963.

C. WILSON, *The History of Unilever. A Study in Economic Growth and Social Change*, London, Cassell & Co., 1954.

ARTICLES

H. DOUGIER, 'From Confusion to Fusion: Assessing Management Education in Europe', in *European Business*, October 1969.

C. GASSER, 'The European Manager of Tomorrow', in D. Drucker (ed.), *Preparing Tomorrow's Business Leaders Today*, Prentice–Hall, 1969.

J. GROVES and E. TROTMAN, 'A New Look at European Marketing', in *European Business*, January 1968.

D. HALL, H. C. L. DE BETTIGNIES and G. AMADO-FISCH-GRUND, 'The European Business Elite', *European Business*, October 1969.

D. LANDES, 'French Business and the Businessman: A Social and Cultural Analysis', in Edward M. Earle (ed.), *Modern France: Problems of the Third and Fourth Republics*, Princeton University Press, 1951.

F. REDLICH, 'Academic Education for Business: Its Development and the Contribution of Ignaz Jastrow (1856–1937). In commemoration of the Hundredth Anniversary of Jastrow's Birth', *Business History Review*, Spring 1957.

Soon shall they arm, unconquered steam, afar
Drag the slow barge, or drive the rapid car;
Or on wide waving wings expanded bear
The flying chariot through the fields of air.
Fair crews triumphant, leaning from above
Shall wave their flutt'ring kerchiefs as they move
Or warrior bands alarm the gaping crowd
And armies shrink beneath the shadowy cloud.

ERASMUS DARWIN — 1791

5. The Sources of Energy 1920–1970

Georges Brondel

INTRODUCTION

From the beginning of time, Man has tried to tame the forces of Nature, and harness them to make life easier for himself. Indeed, human progress is directly related to mankind's ability to exploit different sources of energy.

The discovery of fire, in prehistoric times, marks the beginning of Man's power. Eighteenth-century progress was given a great boost by the steam-engine, running on coal. Electricity was discovered at the beginning of the nineteenth century, while at the end of it came the internal combustion engine, running on petroleum, which has given much greater autonomy to energy. The twentieth century will be especially marked by the use of nuclear energy for peaceful ends, which through the direct conversion of matter into energy, will give almost unlimited power to mankind.

Important developments in history have followed man's skill in using other forms of energy to replace or supplement his own unaided physical strength. The discovery of a practical form of coal-burning steam engine in the eighteenth century and its widespread use for power and transport in the nineteenth is one notable example; others are the discovery of electric power in the early nineteenth century and of the internal combustion engine at its close, both of which have promoted the use of compact, transportable power units. It is to be hoped that the development of nuclear power for peaceful uses in the second half of this century will continue the process of giving more power to man's elbow.

In the fifty years – 1920 to 1970 – covered in this survey, there has been a noticeable increase in the number of ways in which energy can be used in all aspects of economic life, and also in the diversity of sources of energy and means of tapping them.

We shall first examine the way in which the demand for energy has evolved in various areas of consumption in Europe since 1920, and the contribution made by the different sources of energy towards the satisfaction of those needs.

We shall then deal with the origin of the main sources of energy and some problems posed by developing them: coal, oil, natural gas, hydro-electric and nuclear power.

In the following sections, different aspects of the part played by energy in the economic life of European countries will be discussed.

Widespread usage of energy has allowed many countries to attain a high degree of industrialisation, and has led to a noticeably more comfortable standard of living. It will be seen that the gross national product (GNP) is closely linked to the level of consumption of energy.

The development of sources of energy has largely moulded the economic geography of Europe, and we shall show the influence that energy has had on the location of the great industries.

Energy has already benefited from scientific progress, in the area of fossil fuels – coal or oil – and more especially in the field of nuclear energy, where there has been sufficient incentive for massive research to be carried out, bringing to light techniques for the future. Equally, progress has been made in methods of converting raw materials into energy, leading to increased output and important economic savings.

The energy-producing industry has undergone major changes, and its structure has evolved greatly in the past fifty years; the effect of size is preponderant here, and energy-based enterprises have become among the biggest in the world.

Lastly, the energy-producing sector has undergone profound changes, mainly due to innovations resulting from competition between rival sources of power, and the countries involved have had to solve some difficult social problems.

All these changes, and the prominent part which energy

plays in economic life, have led various governments to recognise that energy can contribute to the public good.

Since World War II they have become increasingly conscious of their responsibility to guarantee a stable supply of power. The concept of a policy related to energy is becoming progressively more acceptable in different countries. This will lead to a comparative study of the policies followed in each of them, in a final chapter.

In this way the major role played by energy in fashioning the economic world in which we live should be made clear.

In Europe, the last fifty years have been marked by the passing of an economy based principally on agriculture and cottage industry, and the adoption of the type of industrial economy with high standards of living that we have today. It is thanks to the existence of abundant sources of energy that such an evolution has been able to take place in such a short time.

GROWTH IN DEMAND FOR ENERGY

Since 1920 the demand for energy has grown constantly, in a pattern caused by such factors as demographic development, greater mechanisation, a higher standard of living; as well as by finding new ways of utilising power, mainly in the form of primary energy. This increase in demand has only partially been compensated for by improvements in production methods.

In Western Europe, consumption rose from 310 million metric tons of oil equivalent in 1920 to 1,040 million in 1970.[1] Three stages can be defined in this development:

1. Since the part played by different sources of power varies greatly according to the ways of extracting and using it, a common term of reference must be found to evaluate relative amounts of power. As, by the end of the period we are surveying, oil had become the main source of energy, the other forms of energy have been evaluated in measures equivalent to metric tons of petroleum, on the basis of their calorific content. If this conversion seems arbitrary in view of the different methods of output, one can see that they are proportionally comparable when one uses the results to compare the evolution in consumption during the period. The conversion rates used are:

(1) From 1920 to 1937 there was moderate growth at an average rate of 1·3% per annum, which raised energy consumption to 388 million metric tons. However, this period was marked by serious depression in the years 1929 to 1932, which reduced consumption to a level close to that of 1920.

(2) The period from 1940 to 1950 was one of relative stagnation. After rapid growth promoted by the war effort, production potential was considerably reduced in the aftermath of the war, and took nearly five years to be restored. A serious shortage of reserves underlay the economic slump which preceded the re-establishment of balance between supply and demand for energy at the end of this period.

(3) From 1950 to 1970 a return to continued growth at a very rapid average rate of 4·6% per annum could be seen. There were no longer sufficient local reserves of fuel to satisfy demand, and it was necessary to have recourse to importing greater and greater quantities, especially of oil, to overcome the shortage. During the entire period, supply remained plentiful, and competition between different sources of power allowed consumers to benefit from cheap energy, especially during the 1960s.

ENERGY DISTRIBUTION BETWEEN DIFFERENT CONSUMER GROUPS ACCORDING TO THEIR NEEDS

The demand for the use of energy can be divided into four main categories: industry, transport, household consumption, and a fourth miscellaneous group composed of cottage industry, commerce, agriculture, and uses unconnected with the actual production of power.

The effect that economic growth has had on demand for energy has varied within these categories. The need for energy has depended mainly on the degree of industrialisa-

Petroleum and its products	1·0
Lignite	0·2
Manufactured gas	0·42
Coal	0·7
Natural gas	0·9
Electricity (kilowatt-hour)	0·1

tion reached by each country and, to a certain extent, on climatic conditions.

In *industry* the demand for fuel has not generally increased as rapidly as industrial production. There are two main reasons for this. Firstly, the efficiency of converting fuel into useful energy has increased as a result of modernisation of plant equipment and improved techniques. Secondly, economic savings due to the scale of operations have made themselves felt as much on energy consumption as on other elements contributing to manufacturing costs. A growing amount of this energy has been utilised in the form of electricity which, as a result of being produced in central power stations, has given rise to an appreciable growth in fuel consumption.

Economic growth has also had a direct influence on the demand for energy where *commercial transport* is concerned. The replacement of coal-fuelled locomotives by diesel or electric engines has led to a great improvement in the efficiency of converting fuel on the railways, and consequently a lowering of the costs of rail transport. However, faced with competition from road transport, and to a small extent from air transport, the growth has been relatively minor.

Road transport has been much more rapidly developed, both for professional and private purposes. Its expansion has been brought about by the economic activity and income level in each country. In fact, road transport has been one of the most dynamic factors in the structural evolution undergone through demand for energy. It has changed living conditions enormously and it is no exaggeration to say that it is one of the elements of industrial evolution which has most affected contemporary civilisation.

The demand for energy *in the home* resulted from improved living standards. Such demand depends on economic progress, but it is, as I have already mentioned, also strongly influenced by climatic conditions. At the beginning of the period household consumption consisted mainly of fuel for cooking and individual heating appliances. Following this, energy consumption grew, as people changed over to central appliances for heating water and the home; lighting; and electrical equipment covering most household needs. Recently, air conditioning has been developed in hotter areas. At the same time, people have abandoned primitive forms of fuel, such as wood, and changed, first to coal, then to fuel-oil or diesel, and more recently to natural gas.

Despite their generally higher prices, the demand for secondary forms of energy such as gas and especially electricity has grown, mainly because gas and electricity are more flexible and easier to use than coal or oil-based fuels. In most countries household consumption has grown to a much greater extent than the overall demand for energy.

Growth in demand for energy where the *fourth miscellaneous group* is concerned is the result of a number of heterogeneous factors which are difficult to analyse. At a glance it can be seen that the growth has clearly followed the same pattern of development as in the other groups. All the same, demand for uses not connected with actually producing power, which played a very small part in the need for energy up until 1960, has developed very rapidly since then, with the expansion of the chemical industry.

DIVISION OF CONSUMPTION BETWEEN DIFFERENT TYPES OF ENERGY

The consumer's choice of fuel is based both on the nature of its use, which in certain cases necessitates a specific type of fuel, and also on the relative prices of different types of fuel, and the advantages offered by their use.

The most important of those fuels which cater for specific demands are coal, destined for the manufacture of coke; motor fuels for road or air transport; and products with uses other than producing power (such as lubricants, or base products for the chemical industry). All in all, specific needs represent about a third of the total demand for energy. Electricity constitutes a unique case; to a large extent its consumption meets a specific demand, such as

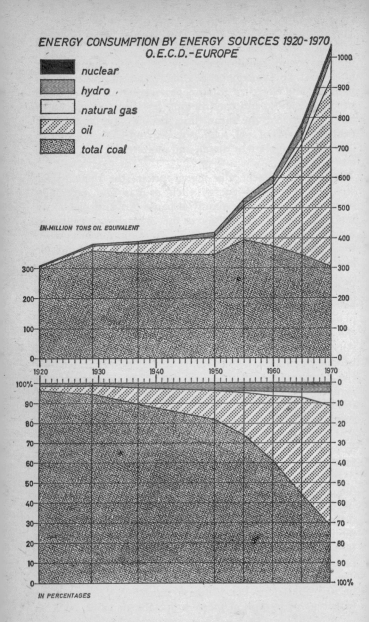

ENERGY CONSUMPTION BY ENERGY SOURCES 1920-1970
O.E.C.D.-EUROPE

nuclear
hydro
natural gas
oil
total coal

IN MILLION TONS OIL EQUIVALENT

IN PERCENTAGES

driving machinery, lighting, electrolysis, etc. but it can be produced from all sources of primary energy.

Where the rest of the market is concerned, in those cases where different types of fuel are interchangeable, choice is determined competitively, and the determining factor is the price asked for an equivalent calorific content. In certain cases, however, when the difference in price of various sources of power is not too great, flexibility and ease of use can become decisive. This fact applies especially to the domestic consumer, who is ready to pay more for a source of energy which is easier to use. Thus the importance of electricity in household demand is explained.

In the 1920s the consumer, whether industrial or domestic, had practically no choice. Coal met more than 95% of all needs, whereas oil, which did not even meet 3% of energy consumed, was used exclusively for road transport, in the form of petrol. Hydro-electric power represented about 1% of total consumption.

Later on, many more different forms of power were available. As early as 1940, it was found that coal no longer covered more than 90% of consumers' needs, as liquid fuel had become popular. But it was not until after the war that oil had its greatest effect upon consumption. The amount of oil being used rose from 14% in 1950 to more than 32% in 1960, reaching 60% in 1970. Natural gas has made similar progress, with a percentage of 0·3% in 1950, 1·8% in 1960, and 6·6% in 1970. Lastly, nuclear power, in spite of the considerable future hope that it offers, only supplied 0·5% of all demand in 1970.

This continually increasing change-over from coal to oil-based fuels has been most important in those countries which have always had to import power, whilst those countries with local coal deposits have tried to maintain an outlet for their product for as long as possible. It is for this reason that in 1965 the proportion of coal meeting the overall demand for energy was still 66% in Great Britain, 62% in Germany, 56% in Belgium, and 46% in France; while it had already fallen to 30% in Holland and Denmark, 14% in Switzerland, and only 12% in Italy.

The rapid change-over from coal to oil from the 1950s onwards is mainly explained by the fact that much lower prices were demanded for the latter. But we shall see that such a transformation has not taken place without causing certain problems, notably from the point of view of the security of supplies. But what is certain is that the European consumer has found it advantageous, continuing to profit from relatively cheap power, while the costs of extracting coal keep on growing all the time.

WAYS OF IMPROVING AND ADAPTING POWER TO CATER FOR SPECIFIC NEEDS

At the same time that a greater number of sources of primary energy contributed to satisfying demand, these were presented to the consumer in more and more elaborate forms, in order to conform more closely to the specific uses required of them.

In the 1920s coal was channelled into three main uses as a result of its characteristics. Coal with a low gas content was used for domestic heating; that with the necessary characteristics for being made into coke was, according to its greater or lesser gas content reserved for gas or coke manufacture; while the intermediate grades of coal were used in industry for steam-power production. Very rapidly, however, consumers demanded products with better defined grades. Where coal for domestic use was concerned, washing and grading led to cleaner products, which were at the same time better adapted to heating equipment. Coal with coke-making characteristics was blended to improve the quality of the coke; and steam coal was crushed and delivered in reliably consistent grades, which meant that more consistent heating conditions could be obtained with it.

Where oil was concerned this process of categorisation was taken even further. Refineries, which in the beginning had carried only simple distillation equipment, became much more sophisticated, with a much greater variety of methods for producing a much wider range of products. From time to time they have even been combined with

TABLE 1: Consumption in Western Europe of primary sources of energy

In original unit

	Solid fuels M.t. of coal equivalent	Petroleum M.t.	Natural gas $10^9 m^3$	Hydro power Gross electricity production Twh	Nuclear energy Gross electricity production Twh
1920	423·0	12·0	—	21	—
1929	513·7	16·0	—	41·6	—
1937	496·8	33·0	—	62·0	—
1950	494·6	60·0	1·4	106·9	—
1955	563·0	113·2	5·5	151·7	—
1960	532·7	196·9	12·5	220·9	2·4
1965	502·6	377·9	20·0	282·6	19·8
1970	434·0	625·8	76·2	320·5	42·8

In millions of tons of equivalent petroleum

	Solid fuels	Petroleum	Natural gas	Hydraulic Energy	Nuclear Energy	TOTAL
1920	296·0	12·0	—	2·4	—	310·4
1929	359·6	16·0	—	4·8	—	380·4
1937	347·8	33·0	—	7·2	—	388·0
1950	346·5	60·0	1·2	12·3	—	420·0
1955	393·9	113·2	4·9	17·4	—	529·4
1960	372·7	196·9	11·2	25·4	0·8	607·0
1965	351·8	377·9	18·0	32·5	2·3	782·5
1970	303·8	625·8	68·6	36·9	4·9	1040·0

In percentage

	Solid fuels	Petroleum	Natural gas	Hydraulic Energy	Nuclear Energy	TOTAL
1920	96·5	2·6	—	0·9	—	100
1929	94·5	4·2	—	1·3	—	100
1937	89·6	8·5	—	1·9	—	100
1950	82·5	14·0	0·3	3·2	—	100
1955	74·4	21·4	0·9	3·3	—	100
1960	61·4	32·5	1·8	4·2	0·1	100
1965	45·0	48·3	2·3	4·1	0·3	100
1970	29·2	60·2	6·6	3·5	0·5	100

TABLE 2: Energy requirements by main sectors of consumption
1950–1970 as percentages of total requirements

in million tons oil equivalent

| | Western Europe | | | | | |
| | 1950 | | 1960 | | 1970 | |
	*tec	%	tec	%	tec	%
End use consumption						
domestic	113·4	27	153·6	25·3	269·4	25·9
transport	67·2	16	94·7	15·6	174·7	16·8
industry	121·8	29	190·0	31·3	294·3	28·3
energy sector	50·4	12	58·9	9·7	83·2	8·0
TOTAL and USE CONSUMPTION	352·8	84	497·2	81·9	821·6	79·0
Conversion losses and non-energy products	67·2	16	109·8	18·1	218·4	21·0
TOTAL ENERGY REQUIREMENTS	420·0	100	607·0	100	1040·0	100

* total energy consumption
N.B. Corresponding figure not available for period 1920–1950

chemical works so that further value can be extracted from products which cannot be sold as fuel on the market.

The enormous development of 'secondary' energy is explained in the same way. 'Secondary energy' is energy presented in a more elaborate and easy-to-use form than 'primary energy'. The steam-engine, which at the beginning of the century provided all the mechanical power in factories, has been replaced by less cumbersome and unwieldy electric machines. Gas or electric cooking has almost universally replaced cooking by solid fuel. In the same way central heating is in the process of being converted to oil or natural gas, leading to the time when electricity will replace them.

In the course of the past fifty years, the economy of the energy industry has thus been completely transformed. From being one industry, which had as its sole aim the extraction of raw materials from the ground, it has gradually become an industry for changing and refining, transporting and marketing these raw materials. As we shall see later, production procedures are being constantly perfected; but even more important than this, all the new conversion and transport techniques have been directed towards the end of getting power of the type required to the place in which the consumer wants it.

Management problems in the industry have, at the same time, become more complicated and specialised. Power producing operations have become more and more sophisticated and function at all stages from production to distribution, in order to ensure the best possible service for the consumer.

These different aspects will successively be studied, but the first question that needs to be answered concerns where the energy consumed in Europe comes from; and how supply has been able to develop at a rate corresponding to the demand.

THE GENERAL ENERGY BALANCE IN EUROPE AND WORLD EXCHANGES

We have just seen the part played by each form of energy in covering overall needs. It remains to examine the way in which the world balance for supplying Europe was established; distinguishing internal production from imports, and to see how Europe compares in this respect with the other great industrial regions of the world.

For as long as coal met essential needs for energy, Europe's balance of exchanges with the exterior remained on a more or less equal basis. But since World War II, with the use of oil becoming so much more intense, international commerce for these products has become appreciably one-sided, to the deficit of Europe. In 1970, imports accounted for 65% of total supplies.

Of all the major industrial regions in the world, Western Europe is the only one, apart from Japan, to be so largely dependent upon external sources for supplies of energy. The USA possess considerable reserves both of coal and hydrocarbons in liquid and gas forms. As a result their overall imports of refined oil products, although they are increasing rapidly, did not exceed 23% of total internal consumption of these products in 1970. The USSR, thanks mainly to the enormous amount of territory it comprises, has sufficient reserves to cover most of its needs. The only factors restricting the USSR from exporting energy are the scattered nature of deposits, and their distance from main consumption areas.

The huge deposits of oil in Latin America, Africa and the Middle East are, on the contrary, not needed locally, and the countries in these areas gain an appreciable source of revenue from the dues paid from exploitation of their resources. Altogether these three regions exported more than one thousand million metric tons in 1970.

Thus, where exchanges of energy products are concerned, oil has taken over the position occupied by coal up until World War I. Moreover, its liquid state makes it much more easily and economically handled and transported.

Within Europe, on the other hand, exchanges of energy have rapidly diminished. Outlets for coal have over the years become centred around production areas as a result of competition from imported products. Where oil is concerned, the tendency has been to build big refineries nearer consumption areas, as transport costs are always higher for the various different refined products than for bulk crude oil.

In the same way, the various European countries which, when coal was still the most important source of energy, were in very different situations according to the size and type of local deposits of energy, are now finding themselves in similar situations, relying on outside resources. Certainly, the existence of local coal deposits is still an advantage, insofar as it means a certain security of supplies, but the high cost of coal constitutes a handicap rather than an advantage in the international competition between great industrial nations.

This change has tended to bring European countries closer together, to work together to obtain supplies of energy. It has also served to unite them so that they can deal together with the great problems of economic development that they are facing.

TABLE 3: The evolution of Western Europe's Energy situation between 1920 and 1970 (*in million tons oil equivalent*)

Source of energy	Year	Production	Inland consumption	Surplus (+) or deficits (−)	Production over inland consumption
Solid fuels	1920	284·0	296·0	− 12·0	0·96
(coal and	1937	358·0	347·8	+ 10·2	1·03
lignite)	1950	364·0	346·5	+ 17·5	1·05
	1970	261·0	303·8	− 42·8	0·86
Oil and	1920	0·1	12·0	− 11·9	0·01
natural	1937	0·6	33·0	− 32·4	0·02
gas	1950	4·0	61·2	− 57·2	0·07
	1970	83·0	694·4	−611·4	0·12
Electricity	1920	2·4	2·4	—	1·00
(Hydro	1937	7·2	7·2	—	1·00
+	1950	12·3	12·3	—	1·00
nuclear)	1970	41·8	41·8	—	1·00
Total	1920	286·5	310·4	− 23·9	0·92
energy	1937	365·8	388·0	− 22·2	0·94
	1950	380·3	420·0	− 39·7	0·91
	1970	385·8	1040·0	−654·2	0·37

TABLE 4: Estimated geographical breakdown of world energy production and consumption in 1970

(*in million tons oil equivalent*)	Production m. tons	%	Inland consumption m. tons	%	Surplus (+) or deficit (−)	Production over inland consumption
Western Europe	386	7·8	1,040	21·3	−654	0·37
North America	1,650	33·5	1,720	35·3	− 70	0·96
Latin America	290	5·9	180	3·7	+110	1·61
Japan	40	0·8	280	5·7	−240	0·14
Eastern countries	1,470	29·8	1,410	28·9	+ 60	1·04
Middle East	700	14·2	70	1·4	+630	10·00
Africa	344	7·0	80	1·7	+264	4·30
Other	50	1·0	100	2·0	− 50	0·50
TOTAL	4,930	100	4,880	100	+ 50	1·01

SOLID FUEL

Coal had formed the basis of the Industrial Revolution. It ensured that those countries with deposits remained industrially supreme until as recently as 1913.

Great Britain was, at this time, the main producer, with 290 million metric tons, and, more important, it was the largest exporter in the world, selling 90 million metric tons abroad. There are four main reasons for British supremacy: the importance of its deposits (180 thousand million metric tons that could be economically exploited), the proximity of many of its large coal deposits to the coast, the importance of its merchant navy, and its advantageous geographical position for shipping.

Germany came second in 1913 with 220 million metric tons (including lignite). Production mainly supplied internal needs, in particular those of the iron and steel industry, which formed the basis of Germany's supremacy on the Continent. Production further increased to reach 425 million metric tons in 1943.

In comparison, other countries had low production levels: France produced 41 million metric tons, Belgium 23 million metric tons, and Holland 2 million metric tons.

Altogether, production in Western Europe rose to 589 million metric tons of coal in 1913, whereas the USA had only reached 517 million metric tons.

LOCATION OF COALFIELDS

The principal British coalfields are in Yorkshire (30% of production); South Wales (20%), the Northumberland and Durham belts (17%), and the lowlands of Scotland (12%).

The continental coalfields are grouped around four huge axes which stretch as follows:
(1) From the north of France to the German border through Borinage, Hainaut, the country around Liege and Aachen;
(2) From Aachen to Kempen in the north of Belgium across Limburg in Holland;

TABLE 5: The evolution of solid fuel production in Western Europe
Coal and Lignite

	Coal (in million tons)	Lignite (in million tons)	Total (in million tons)
1920	391·9	13·1	405·0
1929	508·6	20·0	528·6
1937	490·2	20·9	511·1
1950	452·6	24·8	477·4
1955	489·9	30·0	519·9
1960	456·6	33·7	490·3
1965	434·4	36·3	470·7
1970	333·9	38·4	372·3

Source: OECD – Energy Statistics

(3) In Westphalia, north of the Ruhr;
(4) In northern Lorraine.

There are other more widely scattered belts in the Loire, and to the south of the Massif Central in France, and also in Spain.

EVOLUTION OF COAL PRODUCTION IN EUROPE FROM 1920 TO 1939

Although coalmining necessitates a large manual labour force, and cost prices are high, between 1870 and 1913 production continued to expand in a regular pattern. Thus coal met 95% of the demand for power; and both the metallurgical industry and steam transport were booming.

At the end of the 1914–18 war, normal conditions of economic activity were thrown into chaos. War-torn Europe had to meet enormous needs and to set about rebuilding both itself and its stocks. Devastated and impoverished countries had to resort to borrowing from more fortunate ones, which distributed stocks of raw materials and enjoyed an unimpaired financial capacity. Widespread demand led to price increases. By 1920, European coal production had once again risen to 392 million metric tons. Meanwhile the lending countries were becoming worried about what would happen to their loans, and, when the USA and Britain put a brake on credit at the beginning of 1920, there was a resulting decline in production, and prices dropped harshly. Industrial depression marked the whole of 1921, with unemployment having a serious effect on coal production, which went down by 60 million metric tons. This re-building crisis tended towards inflation; the effects of which lasted until 1924.

Two years later a serious social crisis took place in England. In order to maintain exports, the coal industry vetoed any pay rises, sparking off a huge miners' strike lasting eight months. Throughout the country industrial activity was paralysed, and many workers left the mines. By 1926 coal production in Europe was reduced to 355 million metric tons.

Thanks to financial stabilisation in 1926, matters improved, helped by international expansion – the Locarno treaty was signed in 1925 – and the coal situation started to improve again. 491 million metric tons were produced in 1927. But already, from that year onwards, the American economy was suffering from endemic troubles (excess of credit, over-production, and speculation), and in 1929 the Wall Street crash unleashed a worldwide crisis, plunging the industrial nations of the world into universal economic depression. From 1929 to 1933 the world index of industrial production (excluding the USSR) decreased from 100 to 64. All areas of energy production in Europe were affected by this collapse, in particular coalmining, where production went down from 508 to 401 million metric tons, leading to another massive slump. It was 1933 before an improvement was felt which, with increased coal production and industrial activity, steadily continued until 1940.

THE PERIOD OF EXPANSION FROM 1945 TO 1957

Demand born of post-war expansion had repercussions on power consumption, which rose rapidly. In 1950, coal pro-

TOTAL PRODUCTION OF COAL AND LIGNITE. O.E.C.D. EUROPE 1920-1970

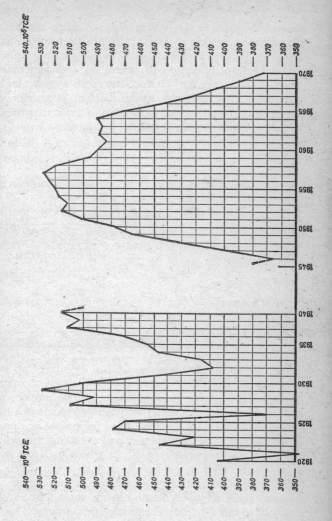

duction returned to the 1936 level, 453 million metric tons. Nevertheless, it soon became apparent that coal producers could not hope to keep pace with rapidly growing demand. They ran into difficulty with recruiting sufficient manual labour, while mining productivity rose slowly, lacking favourable conditions for mechanisation. It was only at the price of important modernisation schemes that the coal industry could regain pre-war production levels; 496 million metric tons in 1957, compared to 509 in 1929, and 492 in 1939.

TABLE 6: Production of coal in the main European countries in 1950, 1960, 1970 (in million tons)

	1950	1960	1970
France	50·8	55·9	37·3
Germany	129·2	148·0	116·9
Belgium	27·3	22·5	11·4
United Kingdom	219·5	197·8	147·2
Others	25·8	32·4	21·1
TOTAL	452·6	456·6	333·9

Coal demand continued to increase regularly up until 1957, but it could only be satisfied by recourse to massive imports. From 45 million metric tons in 1950, imports rose to more than 85 million metric tons in 1957. At this time, coal still met 61% of the total need for power in Europe. It was almost universally used in power stations for making electricity, the sector, above all, in which fuel cost is the determining factor.

Since the reserve production capacity of the international coal market is relatively limited in the short term, import prices have rapidly reached excessive proportions. This has led to competition by the oil industry and paved the way for conversion to this fairly new form of power by many industrial consumers in Europe.

This triggered off a period of great economic opportunity,

with the consolidation of the beneficial effects of the Marshall plan, measures for the liberation of commerce within the framework of the OEEC, such as enlarging of import and export quotas, and facilities for multilateral trade agreements. Thus European countries were driven to pool their resources and rebuild the organisation of coal-mining in an enlarged framework, for two reasons. Firstly, the position of the coal industry needed to be strengthened to avoid a shortage of power, and also it needed to be strengthened to cope with competition from oil that had been foreseen for the future.

In 1958 the European Community for Coal and Steel (ECSC) was instituted between six European countries: Belgium, France, Germany, Italy, Luxembourg and the Netherlands.

THE DECLINE IN COAL PRODUCTION SINCE 1957

It very soon became clear that the coal industry was not going to maintain its dominant position in the power market. Not only did its share in relative value decrease rapidly, but its production rate declined in terms of actual figures. In 1961, production had already decreased to 450 million metric tons, in 1968 it only reached 369 million metric tons.

The interaction of the following factors seems to have led to the slump in coal production. First, a slight economic recession in 1957–58; a favourable year for hydraulic power, which lessened the work of power stations; and two successive mild winters, which cut down on household demands.

But there were also organisational factors which were permanent. Despite the development in mechanisation, coal output improved only very slowly, and cost prices rose. Coal became rapidly unable to compete with oil, which had abundant resources for the world market.

All coalfields were affected by this change, to a greater or lesser degree according to regions and types of coal mined.

The situation was particularly serious in the *Belgian* coalfields. Since the beginning, these deposits were the least competitive in ECSC. To facilitate modernisation, large sums of money were invested. From 1953 to 1958, 141 million dollars were collected; of these, 91 million were found by the Belgian government, and 50 levied on an equal distribution basis, supplied by German and Dutch producers, the most competitive of ECSC. However, the results have not been outstanding, many pits have been closed, and those with very tight profit margins regrouped. In five years production decreased from 19 to 13 million metric tons, and in Borinage, the region most affected, depression was unavoidable.

France, on the other hand, was in a better position to cope with the situation. To begin with, it had pursued a more prudent policy on imports within the framework of the 'Association Technique de l'Importation Charbonnière' (ATIC).[2] Moreover, the government was able to orientate power-based economy more easily and thus ensure the continuance of coalmining thanks to nationalisation of most forms of energy production.

Since the *British* and *German* coal industries were more competitive, they suffered less at the beginning of the crisis. Thanks to concentration of production in the most profitable pits, production levels could be maintained for another decade or so.

In spite of this, all countries were forced to draw upon ever-increasing amounts of aid to cover the losses incurred through mining. This aid, co-ordinated within the framework of the ECSC where mining on the continent was concerned, had been scaled up from $2 to $4 a metric ton, according to the degree of need in a particular coalfield. In 1970 there were, within the ECSC, few coal workings which covered production costs. The situation was better in Great Britain, although here too an irreversible decline set in from 1957 onwards.

THE COMPETITION BETWEEN COAL AND OIL

The advantageous cost of crude oil which characterised the

2. 'Technical Association for Coal Import.'

whole of the period from 1955 to 1970 was not the only factor influencing the rapid changeover from coal to oil.

First of all there is the fact that when crude oil is refined there are a large number of by-products, which are released on to separate markets, with different profit margins; for instance, heavy fuel oil for industry, diesel oil for heating, petrol for road transport, lubricants, etc.

A considerable proportion of crude oil was refined into fuel oil, and from the 1960s onwards it was disposed of commercially as soon as it was refined, at a price always $2 or $3 a metric ton cheaper ($3 to $4 for an equivalent amount of coal) than other products which did not have to compete with other forms of energy for a market.

But the decline of coal in the face of competition from the oil industry is also explained in terms of the structure of the two industries.

The coal industry was handicapped by widespread inertia which limited its ability to adapt supplies of products to meet demand. Since it is an industry where investments are spaced out over long periods, it can respond only very slowly to a rise in demand; for instance, a decade is necessary to start production in a new pit. Being an industry which needs a large body of manual workers, it is difficult for it to adapt to an abrupt drop in demand without serious unemployment, resulting in more men leaving the pits and finding permanent work elsewhere. The marginal costs of production are very high in these conditions, and confronted with fluctuation in demand, the rate of production can only drop.

Oil, on the contrary, can be easily adapted to meet demand. Production potential in the main fields can be increased from 10 to 15% or even more, within six months to a year, giving a good return on investment. When there is a period of high demand, oil takes over new marketing outlets formerly supplied but no longer satisfied by coal. They are retained later on, since consumers' equipment have been adapted accordingly. But still more important is the fact that in nearly every case oil withstands pressure on capital, and as production costs fluctuate very little, short-term cost margins can be very narrow.

However, if one looks at the competition between coal and oil, it is not necessarily true, as has often been claimed, that a systematic policy of monopolisation is being exercised by the major oil companies to cut down on the use of coal. It is rather, that out of two widely differing industries, one can adapt much more readily than the other to an ever-changing market.

LIQUID FUEL

The economy of the nineteenth century and beginning of the twentieth century was built on coal, furnishing the beginnings of industry with the power necessary to drive machines and ensure that for the first time raw materials or manufactured products were transported in bulk. However, since the end of World War II, oil, with a greater calorific power, easier to transport and to use than coal, led the process of mechanisation into new territory. In Europe, consumption of oil in 1970 was 52 times as much as it had been in 1920, rising from 12 to 626 million metric tons. Where did this petroleum come from, and how could its consumption grow to such an extent?

EUROPEAN RESOURCES

Europe was relatively slow to convert to the use of oil, as compared with the USA, mainly because of the scarcity of European resources.

Small fields had been known for a long time; production was started in 1813 at Pechelbronn in Alsace, and in 1875 at Wietze in northern Germany. But in spite of fairly large sedimentary fields, where prospecting was possible, exploration was considered too risky and for a long time attracted very little in the way of investment.

It was not until the 1930s that more active exploration was carried out. At about this time important discoveries were made in Germany, in the plains by the North Sea; then in the 1950s in France, in Aquitaine (Parentis and

Cazaux) and in Sicily (in the Gela-Ragussa region).

Petroleum was also found, but in smaller quantities, in the Parisian basin in France, in the basin of the Middle Rhine in Germany, in the Po valley in Italy, and in Austria. The deposits in these fields were not very great, however, and since 1964–5 their production ceiling of a little more than 20 million metric tons a year has been reached.

The outlook has become more optimistic with two important discoveries of natural gas. The first, a huge deposit at Groningen in the Netherlands, boosted research throughout northern Europe; and the second, on the continental shelf area under the North Sea, is offering continued hope. It is still not possible to estimate the importance of reserves in this area, but it is quite likely that Europe will be able to extract up to 15% of its oil resources from them in the years to come.

Looking back over the period, it was in 1957 that the European contribution of crude oil was at its most important, with a share equivalent to 10% of demand; since then, this amount has decreased, and in 1970 was less than 4%.

IMPORTS OF REFINED PRODUCTS

In the beginning, oil imports to supply the European market were almost exclusively in the form of refined products. Large refineries were built near the deposits, first of all in the USA, then in the Dutch Antilles, where Venezuelan oil was refined, finally at Abadan in the Persian Gulf near the rich Persian oilfields.

Since then, however, a number of economic factors have led to refineries being consumer located rather than resource located. On one hand, refining has become a much more sophisticated and complex process, leading to greater output value from the raw product. Also, and perhaps more important, shipping costs decrease as larger tankers are developed. Thus, it is much cheaper to move crude oil, which can be transported in bulk, than refined products which have to be moved separately in smaller units.

This tendency is accentuated by political factors which

have forced the governing bodies of many consumer countries to develop refining systems in their own countries for security reasons. Since the 1930s France has encouraged the building of an important refining industry. This example has been followed by Germany and Italy, and large refineries have also been built in Great Britain and the Netherlands.

By 1970 Europe had built up a network of refineries capable of meeting all its needs. Exchanges of refined products continued to take place with external countries solely for reasons of quality, or for economic reasons connected with the structure of the industry.

IMPORTS OF CRUDE OIL

In 1920 there were practically no imports of crude oil; by 1938 they had reached 11 million metric tons. Post-war import figures reached the 50 million mark in 1950, to attain 605 million in 1970.

Petroleum deposits are very unequally distributed throughout the world, as Nature seems to have favoured certain privileged regions on the American continent, in the Middle East and Africa.

The *USA* has always been by far the greatest producer of petroleum, followed by the *USSR*, which even overtook it during a short period. In 1970 American and Russian production reached 478 and 355 million metric tons respectively; but almost all of this was consumed locally, leaving in both cases a very small amount of excess fuel for export.

Since the end of the war, growth in production has been most spectacular in the *Middle East*, thanks to a succession of major discoveries. It has been important both from the point of view of the size of reserves brought to light and the amount actually produced from the wells. At the present time this region contains more than 60% of known world reserves; and production, which had only reached 16 million metric tons in 1938, neared 700 million in 1970.

Iran, the oldest oil-producing country in this area, saw its production rise steadily until it reached 32 million tons in 1950. It was stopped completely in March 1951 when the president of Iran decided to expropriate the concessionary company, the Anglo-Iranian Oil Company; and only revived in 1955 after an agreement was finalised between the new government and a consortium of international companies. In 1970 production reached 190 million metric tons.

Saudi Arabia, where the most important reserves lie (about 20% of total world reserves), was only at the prospecting stage before the war. From a negligible amount in 1945, production figures reached 19 million metric tons in 1947 and 176 million metric tons in 1970. *Kuwait* and the other sheikdoms in the Persian Gulf (*Bahrain*, *Qatar*, *Abu-Dhabi*, *Oman* and *Dubai*) have made similarly spectacular progress. Production in these states only began in 1947, yet it reached more than 230 million metric tons in 1970.

Production in *Iraq* is divided between two principal oilfields; the first, near Kirkuk, is 900 kilometres[3] from the sea, and petroleum has to be routed to the Mediterranean by pipe-line. The other, near the port of Basrah, has an outlet into the Persian Gulf. After rising rapidly up until 1960, production has been stabilised at about 75 million metric tons since then, following a dispute between the government and the concessionary companies.

The most recent great oil-producing region to be discovered and developed has been *Africa*. Since 1953 French companies have been investing large sums in *Algeria*; and as a result, around 1958 the production rate started to gain momentum, reaching 48 million metric tons in 1970. Production in *Libya* did not start until 1961, yet already by 1970 a rate of 160 million metric tons had been reached, making this country the sixth largest producer in the world. A similarly brilliant future is forecast for *Nigeria*, where production, although suffering a setback with the Biafran war, has recovered swiftly to reach nearly 53 million metric tons in 1970.

This brief survey shows the extent to which different

3. Approximately 560 miles.

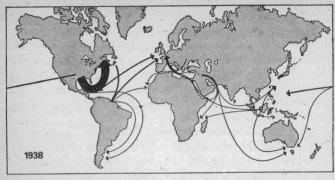

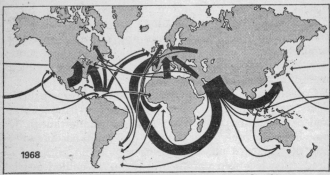

Development of the main flow of oil supplies 1938-1968

regions of production have varied in importance from one
decade to another. The origins of European imports have
similarly changed extensively.

Before World War II, the world oil market was dominated
by the American continent. During the 1950s it was the
turn of the Middle East to take the lead. In 1955 the Middle
East supplied 86% of the petroleum needed in Europe,
compared with 11% coming from the Western hemisphere,
mainly from Venezuela.

From 1960 onwards the new production zones in Africa,
advantageously situated geographically, on account of their
proximity to European areas of consumption, increased

their contribution rapidly, to reach nearly 40% in 1970; while the Middle East went down to 52%.

The other sources of supply play only a limited part, but special mention must be made of those eastern countries which in the 1930s exported appreciable amounts of oil to Europe. The main belts were near the Caspian Sea, and in Rumania. Sales improved towards the 1960s, mainly to Germany, France and Italy, but their proportion of the total never exceeded 5%.

TABLE 7: The origin of crude oil supplies to Europe

Origin	1960		1970	
	Million	%	Million	%
American continent	17·8	10·5	24·0	4·0
Middle East				
Iraq	33·4	19·8	52·9	8·9
Kuwait and Neutral Zone	48·7	28·8	79·5	13·4
Saudi Arabia	24·5	14·5	81·8	13·8
Iran	19·5	11·5	44·2	7·4
Others	7·6	4·5	50·6	8·5
Sub-total	133·7	79·1	309·0	52·0
Africa				
Algeria	8·1	4·8	43·1	7·3
Libya	—	—	150·6	25·4
Others, including Nigeria	1·0	0·6	42·7	7·2
Sub-total	9·1	5·4	236·4	39·9
Eastern countries	6·3	3·7	23·8	4·0
Others	2·1	1·3	0·6	0·1
TOTAL	169·0	100	593·8	100

CONSEQUENCES OF THE GROWING DEPENDENCE ON EXTERNAL SUPPLY SOURCES

Oil and petroleum-based products have accounted in 1970 for a share of about 20% in tonnage, and 10% in value of all imports into Western Europe in the course of the past few years. Furthermore, an analysis of the importance of petroleum in the balance of payments shows that attention should be paid to the movement of capital brought about by oil companies based in Europe. Certain of them possess important external holdings: British Petroleum (BP), Royal Dutch Shell, and to a lesser extent the Compagnie Française des Petroles (CFP), ENI, Petrofina, etc. Much plant machinery is exported, and the profits are brought back into the companies' countries of origin. Besides, the company-owned fleets are assured of an important share in transporting the oil, so that only minor cash expenditure is involved. Only a relatively small sum can be put against petroleum on the debit side of the balance sheet.

Even if the relative cost of imports is not at all exaggerated, it still remains true that Europe has become heavily dependent upon other countries for a product of vital importance to its economy. Political or economic revolution and change is a menacing possibility that overshadows all of Europe's supplies and sources.

Three times in the past the imports from certain sources have been cut off, allowing supplies to become dangerously low. In 1951 the Persian President's decision to nationalise the international companies' holdings in Iran, and in particular the large refinery at Abadan (with a capacity of 40 million metric tons a year), deprived Europe of its main source of oil for more than three years. The closure of the Suez Canal by General Nasser's government in 1956 blocked the route to the Middle East for several months, forcing Europe to turn to other sources, without, however, being able to cover its losses completely. At the time of the Six Days' War in 1967, the Suez Canal was definitively closed, but in the meantime the oil companies had built a fleet of high-capacity tankers, which meant that they were able to maintain supplies by using the longer route round the Cape of Good Hope. Oil rationing was avoided in Europe, but spectacular rises in costs and prices had to be borne by consumers for fairly long periods.

The major European countries have decided upon three main courses of action in order to reduce the risks of too great a dependence on the outside world.

Under the auspices of the Organisation for European Economic Co-operation (OEEC), it was decided that from 1962 all companies should hold in reserve stocks sufficient for a minimum of two months' consumption. At the same time they drew up a procedure for equitable distribution of resources in times of crisis.

Oil companies adopted a policy of using as great a variety of sources as possible, thanks to intense exploration programmes carried out in all those parts of the world in which it was possible that oil could be found.

The major discoveries, at first in Africa then in the North Sea, must be attributed to this policy of diversification and have largely contributed to the greater security of oil supplies.

Finally, a certain number of European countries endeavoured to relate oil exploration and production throughout the world to national interests. British and Dutch companies already held major interests in oil, but other countries were rather slower in this respect. France made a great effort, following a clearly defined oil policy, aimed at obtaining sufficient resources for the country's needs through two French oil companies, one privately owned (CFP) and the other state controlled (ERAP). In Italy the ENI carried out a similar policy, but as it was adopted later than in the other countries, it had only limited results. In the Federal Republic of Germany, the national companies went into partnership with DEMINEX in 1966, for the purpose of exploration and exploitation of foreign resources, with financial backing from the government.

Thus the problems of oil reserves have become progressively more political in character. Consumer countries, as they have become more aware of their responsibilities, have carried out research under the auspices of government policies on power to improve the security of their supplies (see p. 81).

CHANGES IN OIL COSTS

With oil companies working on a world scale, and oil being the object of major international commerce, the price of crude oil and oil-based products has always been set at a standard rate throughout the world.

Before World War II, the main exporting area was the Gulf of Mexico. The prices in European countries were US Gulf prices plus; that is, the prices set on the Gulf of Mexico market, plus transport costs to the area of consumption.

Where products from other sources were concerned, f.o.b. prices were set at a rate to make the c.i.f. prices comparable to those obtained for similar products when they left the Gulf of Mexico.

The major part played by oil from the Persian Gulf during and after the war led to the setting up of a second point of reference. From then on calculations for the f.o.b. prices from the Persian Gulf were based on the f.o.b. prices for the Gulf of Mexico, so that, taking shipping costs into consideration, the prices for products from the two different sources were standardised in a set place, which was at first Great Britain, then New York.

The cost of crude oil from the Middle East became therefore appreciably lower than that from Venezuela (the only crude oil exporter in the Gulf of Mexico). Production revenues, split on a fifty/fifty basis between producer countries and the companies, were considerable. Also, as a result of the great size of Middle East resources, and intense competition between companies, it was not long before Middle East prices broke away from the standard rates set in the Gulf of Mexico. This brought about an important drop in prices for European consumers.

However, producer countries refused to accept a cut in their revenues, and so the practice was started of maintaining official 'posted' prices, at a constant fictitious level, and of giving buyers discounts, paid for out of the companies' profits. The proportion of revenue split between country of production and oil companies has progressively changed from fifty/fifty to seventy/thirty or even less towards the end of the 1960s.

Thus the world petroleum market became increasingly divided into two distinct zones, with only limited exchanges between them. The Western hemisphere was composed of the USA and two major exporting countries, Canada and

Venezuela. The Eastern hemisphere was made up of Europe, with the later addition of Japan, supplied by major oilfields in the Middle East and Africa.

The Western hemisphere has remained a region of high-priced oil, because in order to ensure sufficient continued internal production, the US government has put strict controls on imports to a level of almost 20% of demand.

Europe and Japan, on the other hand, have seen their oil costs fall progressively lower, as a result of the spate of new discoveries in the Middle East and Africa. Thus the benefit of the economic rent has accrued more and more to the consumers.

If the atmosphere of plenty, which has characterised the period from 1955 to 1970, should once again give way to a situation of tension, it is likely that prices would gradually rise until they reached the American level. Thus, where the consumer is concerned, petroleum prices can be very precarious, and there is always the risk that they might contribute to economic or political unrest.

NATURAL GAS

Up until World War II, the gas industry outside the USA could be defined as a network of gasworks supplying big towns and their suburbs with coal gas by means of an intermediary distribution system. In mining areas, and near iron and steel foundries, manufactured gas, a by-product of coke ovens and blast furnaces, completed this network.

Gas had at first been destined primarily for lighting purposes; but at the beginning of this century it was supplanted in this respect by electricity. Since then it has been used mainly for cooking, and in certain cases for water and central heating. It was a costly form of energy, but one that was easy to use, especially in large towns where its usage quickly became widespread.

In the 1950s developments in the oil industry gave the gas industry new sources of supplies. Residual gases from refineries, and certain petroleum products that could easily be converted into gas, were piped to consumers in the place of coal gas.

Moreover, 'butane' and 'propane' gas, sold by the oil companies in a liquid state in bottles or tanks, set up serious competition for companies distributing piped gas.

But the situation in the European gas industry was to be completely upset by the discovery of deposits of natural gas relatively close to main consumer centres.

Natural gas has the advantage of being a clean source of energy; it is adaptable, of a greater calorific power, and less bulky than gas manufactured by traditional methods, or its substitutes.

As the source of supplies were changed, the scale of production was correspondingly increased. Whereas the traditional gas industry kept within the limits of urban development, or in exceptional cases within regional limits, the new gas industry often spread across a country, or even a continent.

On the technical side, the use of steel pipes formed the basis of the development of the first gas-carrying pipe-lines, in the USA, around 1930. These gas-carrying pipe-lines were constructed from pipes with enormous diameters, similar to the pipe-lines used for transporting oil. Thanks to them, and the fact that they were rapidly developed and constructed in Europe, gas was transported for distances upwards of 1,000 kilometres. International agreements allowed international boundaries to be crossed, and the network of gas-carrying pipe-lines is being continually extended throughout Europe.

A second innovation was the discovery that it was possible to liquefy natural gas on an industrial scale, which led to transport of the gas in a liquid state. This was put into operation with the construction of specially adapted methane-carrying ships. From 1965 onwards liquid natural gas has been transported by this means, first from Algeria to France, and later to Great Britain.

Like crude oil, which, with the construction of tankers, had followed the same course of development earlier, natural gas managed to overcome the obstacle presented by the sea, and is becoming continually more important in terms of international trade. In the case of large deposits of natural gas (in the Sahara, Libya, Venezuela, the Middle East, etc.), where formerly, as a result of their geographical situation, the gas was hardly used, or even burnt off because of a lack of local outlets, profitable exploitation can now take place.

Thus natural gas has come to occupy an increasingly important place in the balance sheet for primary energy in Europe. In 1970, out of a total availability of gas estimated to be 240 thousand million cu.m (at 4,200 kcal), natural gas already accounted for 163 thousand million cu.m.

As natural gas deposits have been discovered, countries have rapidly changed over to this new form of energy. A transition period has sometimes been observed, during which the new gas has been 'converted' to half its calorific power (4,200 kcal instead of 8,000 to 9,000 kcal per cu. m) so that it can be substituted without necessitating any immediate changes where the existing manufactured gas consumers are concerned. Meanwhile, the gas companies have instigated huge programmes for converting their customers' appliances so that they can eventually profit from all the benefits that natural gas can offer when distributed in its original state.

NATURAL GAS DEPOSITS IN WESTERN EUROPE

The first important discoveries of natural gas in Europe were made in the 1950s in the Po valley in *Italy*. At the end of the war Enrico Mattei had been appointed by the Italian government to carry out liquidation procedures on an oil-prospecting company which had previously had rather poor results. He noticed, however, that this region had favourable geological structures and decided to resume research. His dogmatic enthusiasm was to lead to exploitation of highly valuable gas deposits, which formed the beginnings of the exceptional development of the gas industry in the area.

From 1950 to 1960 consumption of natural gas in Italy was multiplied by 12·5, and although concentrated in the northern part of the country, its proportion of the total demand for energy went up from 2% to 10%. This natural gas was initially used for heating in industry, and for supplying power stations.

Around the 1960s, however, reserves started to run out and the amount of gas produced for consumption was not able to cope with ever-increasing needs. A policy of priorities was instituted, reserving supplies of natural gas for specially privileged consumers. Sales to manufacturing industry remained almost unchanged, whilst they had to double where chemical industries, such as synthetic fibre manu-facturing, were involved, or those industries such as ceramics and glass-making, which needed high quality energy.

Other discoveries were made later, in Sicily and on the continental shelf of the Adriatic; but to remedy its increas-ing lack of resources, Italy had to resort to importing its gas, mainly from the USSR and Libya.

In 1950, *France*, in its turn, discovered a major natural gas deposit in the south-west, at Lacq. With reserves of 215 thousand million cu.m, this deposit, put into operation from 1957 onwards, has met up to 4% of the country's needs in energy. This gas has been transported into three areas of high consumption, namely Nantes, Lyons and Paris, and has served mainly to supply household needs. But it has also been welcomed by industry on account of its favourable propensities for satisfying a need for high grade energy. As a result of this, an additional, bigger network was added to these three pipe-lines, including a pipe-line which carries Algerian gas from Le Havre to the Paris area, and a system supplying Dutch gas to the north and east of the country. Thus France has built an increasingly complex supply network, fed by both national reserves and imports.

The most important discoveries for Europe were to be those made in 1960 in the *Netherlands*, when a considerable deposit, even by international standards, came to light in the province of Groningen at Slochteren. Gas reserves found in this region alone were in excess of two thousand million cu.m, that is, nearly two-thirds of total European reserves in 1970.

The consumption of natural gas has rapidly increased to 30% of the country's total energy consumption, leaving considerable amounts for export. Delivery contracts have been drawn up with Germany, Belgium, France and, for lesser amounts, with Italy. In this way all the highly industrialised regions in northern Europe have been able to benefit from a plentiful, good quality source of energy; and the economic geography of the entire region has been profoundly changed.

There have been no outstanding discoveries in *Germany*, but numerous deposits of average importance have been found. The result of this has been that natural gas has met an appreciable proportion of the country's demand for power. Between 1962 and 1963 reserves rose from 48 thousand million to 136 thousand million cu.m. Some of the deposits are to be found in Bavaria and in the Rhine valley, but more than nine-tenths of the reserves lie in the north-west of the country.

Together with a certain number of imports, natural gas met 7% of the country's needs for energy in 1970.

Among the major European countries, *Great Britain* has been the last to enter the natural gas era. But it is adding considerably to its reserves following discoveries offshore in the North Sea. In 1970, when it was decided to direct natural gas supplies throughout the country, a programme was set up to convert all consumers' appliances. It is estimated that from 1975 to 1980 production will be able to meet more than 15% of the country's energy consumption. On the continental shelf adjacent to *Norway* there are still more major deposits waiting to be exploited.

Some natural gas resources have been found in other countries, such as in *Austria*, but in much smaller amounts, and, unless there are some as yet unforeseen discoveries, this form of energy will only be able to play a minimal part in supplying the country's needs for energy.

SUBSTITUTION OF NATURAL GAS FOR OTHER FORMS OF ENERGY

Wherever natural gas has been discovered in large quantities, it has supplanted other forms of energy by fulfilling their traditional functions. Without any doubt it heightened the pressure already brought to bear on the coal industry by competition from oil-based fuels, but it did not fundamentally affect the course of subsequent events. Where petroleum products are concerned, this has occurred on several occasions: light oil products have been supplanted in certain uses for the chemical industry, but this has been compensated for as other uses have been found for them, especially as automotive fuels.

Other forms of energy used for domestic heating have also experienced a slower rate of expansion; and in regions near natural gas deposits, production has even been curtailed slightly. Where natural gas has penetrated into industry, its use has been of a very selective nature, only affecting those sectors in need of high quality energy. As for the loss of outlets for electric power stations, it was in general localised, and only slightly affected the balance sheet for overall supplies.

Thus natural gas appeared to be a source of energy of a complementary nature, particularly well adapted to certain uses, and consequently able to profit from its higher calorific value compared to the other forms of energy with which it was in competition. Far from bringing disorder to the energy market, natural gas has given Europe an unexpected stroke of luck at a time when it was having to have increasing recourse to imports to meet demand. It has also had a favourable influence on the security of supplies and has contributed to keeping price rises within reasonable limits.

ELECTRICITY AND NUCLEAR ENERGY

It is only relatively recently that electricity has appeared on the energy-based economic scene. In fact, the industrial era for electricity only dates from the beginning of the century. Since then it has made spectacular progress, with its rate of development being almost double the average growth rate of energy consumed.

One frequently quoted rule is that consumption doubles every ten years. It must be remembered that this rule is not a law, but a statistical statement, that up until the present has been more or less supported by events, with the speeding up of consumption resulting from new ways of using energy compensating for a slowing down in other areas.

From a level of 44 thousand million kwh in 1920, electricity production in Western Europe has risen to 1,145 thousand million kwh in 1970, a clear twenty-six fold increase.

Electricity is produced either in hydro-electric power stations, using power from flowing water; in power stations burning coal, fuel-oil or gas; or, during the past few years, in nuclear power stations.

Technical progress has been more rapid where the electrical industry is concerned than in any other area. In 50 years power stations have been developed so that:

The capital outlay for building them has been cut to a third or a quarter of what it was initially.
The amount of fuel consumption per kilowatt hour has been cut to a sixth.
Running costs have also been cut to a sixth.

In spite of regular price increases for the fuel used, the cost per kwh produced in coal, oil or gas-fuelled power stations has, in terms of actual value, decreased continually at a rate of 2 to 3% a year. Nuclear power stations, which are being called upon more and more to take over the job of traditional power stations, are similarly capable of being improved and perfected; and this tendency towards a decrease in the cost per kwh should continue for another 20 to 30 years, assuring electricity of a progressively widening range of uses and possibilities.

EXPLOITATION OF HYDRAULIC POWER

At the beginning of the century, in an early phase of the exploitation of hydro-electric resources, dams were built all along mountain rivers, at intervals of 5 to 20 kilometres (according to the drop in height), and equipped with small turbines to capture the driving force of the water. When all the available sites had been used up, integrated programmes for re-planning river systems were set up to increase production capacity by using greater heights, thus creating longer drops, or by constructing larger dams, to improve the strength of the driving force of water. Nowadays, almost all Europe's hydro resources are from dammed sources, and maximum production capacity has almost been reached.

Hydro resources are very unequally distributed between different regions. The main sources are to be found in Scandinavia, where all electricity is made in this way. Then come the areas around the Alps, with France having the greatest amount of hydro-electric power in this group, then Italy, Austria, Switzerland, and Germany having the least. In these countries hydro power has an active role in regulating electricity output, while electricity produced by thermal methods forms the basis of overall production. Other, more limited hydro-electric facilities are to be found in the Pyrenees, serving Spain and France, in the Massif Central in France, and also in the Scottish highlands.

Initially electricity production was resource-located, where it led to the development of industries requiring enormous consumption of power, such as the electro-chemical and electro-metallurgical industries. Later, electricity produced by this method was integrated with existing transport networks, and could be used by consumers farther away.

From 1920 to 1970, hydro-electric power has risen from 21 to 320 thousand million kwh. Its share of the total amount of primary energy consumed has increased from 0·9% to 3·5%, but its contribution to the amount of electricity produced has decreased from 48% to 28%.

CONVENTIONAL THERMAL POWER STATIONS

Unlike hydro-electric plants, thermal power stations are not dependent upon geography or climate. They produce power as and when needed to the limits of their equipment. Another advantage of thermal power stations is that they can be built very close to consumer centres, while hydro power must, of necessity, be resource-located. However, this advantage is outweighed in those cases where low grade coal is used, as it is costly to transport and must be used on the spot.

As consumption has increased, so too have the capacities of thermal power stations. In the 1920s, the biggest systems of alternators could not produce more than 20 to 30,000 kw, whilst certain stations in 1970 reached 600,000 kilowatts. Thus the number of new sites has not noticeably grown during the years, since newer stations have been built on sites formerly occupied by obsolete equipment.

Transport lines between stations have been greatly developed. On one hand the tension carried by the lines has increased from 30,000 to 380,000 volts; on the other hand, the number of lines has multiplied to such an extent that they now form a huge international network. In the 1950s there was a very progressive move, when the countries on the mainland of Europe, following a recommendation by the OECD Council, decided that their stations should be interconnected at 380,000 volts. It was thus possible to reduce amounts that had previously to be held in reserve to cover possible breakdowns in certain stations, and also to make better use of existing equipment. Thus priority has been given to the more economic stations (which are assured of a regular market) to form a basis for supplies, while stations with higher production costs are reserved for peak-period consumption. At the present time, use of the network has almost reached its optimum level.

In the 1960s, first Scandinavia, then Great Britain were connected to the continent by undersea cables. The electricity industry provides one of the best examples of the solidarity developed between European countries to exploit their energy resources. This closer and closer integration of the electrical economy of European countries, which took place at first within the framework of the OECD then under the more binding but more generalised influence of the European Community, has come about mainly as a result of technical and economic development.

Nuclear energy provides another example of this integration of European effort, which allows advantage of modern techniques to be taken more rapidly.

NUCLEAR POWER STATIONS

Nuclear energy marks an important turning-point in the development of energy-based economy. Without this discovery, industrialised countries would have been rapidly forced to take the retrograde step of preoccupying themselves with attempts to increase the output of fossil fuels. Certainly, coal exists in very large quantities in most parts of the world: 2,500 thousand million metric tons, that is, enough to last nearly 1,000 years at the present rate of consumption; however, conditions for extracting it are getting more and more onerous and difficult. Already in Europe it is probable that the remaining important resources in Great Britain and Germany will soon cease to be economically exploitable. As for hydrocarbons, whether oil or gas, such resources are much more limited; established and estimated reserves (600 thousand million metric tons, according to optimistic forecasts) can cover a good few years' consumption, but the production ceiling will be reached long before that, certainly (as far as we can tell at present) by the end of the century, and will decrease gradually from then on.

Happily, nuclear energy is there to assure us of a successor to power coming from fossil sources. Uranium and thorium deposits, the base matter for nuclear energy, are plentiful. Taking into account the much fuller usage that can be made of them when advanced reactors are in operation, the amount of power that man will be able to extract from known reserves will be very much greater than power drawn from the reserves of coal, oil and natural gas put together. Moreover, it is almost certain that before these reserves are exhausted, other processes, based on nuclear energy, especially power from fusion – the hydrogen bomb under control – will have been made operational and will be industrially exploitable.

The progress made in the nuclear field during the last twenty-odd years has been spectacular. Great Britain has played an avant-garde role in it; on 17 October 1956, the first nuclear power station in the world was opened at Calder Hall, and up until 1970 Britain on its own has produced as much nuclear kwh as all the other countries put together.

In France, too, thanks to the impetus given by the Commissariat for atomic energy, rapid progress has been made in putting this new source of energy into operation. Since 1959 a high-capacity station has been in operation at Marcoule; since then, eight other stations have been put into service, such as Chinon and Saint-Laurent-des-Eaux, which produced almost 4% of the country's electricity in 1970.

In 1970 nuclear power stations with a capacity of 55 million MWe were already at the planning stage in the USA. In Western Europe progress has been slower, since production of industrial materials and equipment is not so highly developed as in the United States. Even so, by 1 January 1970 almost 8,500 MWe were already in service and much more was planned.

So far, several types of stations have been experimented with. The reactor of natural uranium, with graphite as moderator and carbonic gas as coolant, has been developed mainly in Great Britain and France; it uses a cheap fuel in natural uranium, but necessitates high capital outlay, almost double that necessary for a traditional power station. The United States, with its vast establishments for refining and enriching uranium, has, right from the beginning, preferred to use a reactor with enriched uranium as fuel, and water as moderator and coolant. Fuel is more expensive but stations are more compact and a lower capital outlay

TABLE 8: Main nuclear power stations in service on 1 January 1970 – in Western Europe*

Germany		Great Britain	
Gundremmingen	250	Calder Hall (4 units)	219
Lingen	250	Chapelcross (4 units)	228
Obrigheim	280	Berkeley (2 units)	334·4
Belgium		Bradwell (2 units)	374·1
Chooz (Sena)	266	Hunterston (2 units)	360
Spain		Hinkley Point (2 units)	664·1
Zorita	160	Trawsfynydd (2 units)	884·8
France		Dungeness-A (2 units)	576·6
Marcoule (2 units)	80	Sizewell (2 units)	652·5
Chinon (EDF 1, 2, 3)	760	Oldbury (2 units)	633·5
St Laurent-des-Eaux	500	Dounreay DFR	13·5
		Winfrith SCHWR	100
Italy		*Holland*	
Latina	210	Dodewaard	54
Garigliano	169	*Switzerland*	
Trino	252	Berznau – 1	364

* Gross capacity in megawatts of electricity (MWe.)

is necessary. European countries as well seem to be adopting the second type nowadays.

The other type, called 'advanced generators', so far only account for 1% of existing reactors. This type aims to reach higher temperatures so that there is greater output from conversion of heat to electricity. The first stations of this type are so far only at the experimental stage, but they should be more widespread by the 1980s.

But all these reactors, whether in operation or of the advanced type, consume sufficiently large amounts of uranium to cause anxiety about a power shortage. Such fears will only be allayed when it becomes possible to build 'breeders' which produce more fissile matter than they consume. Periodic treatment of the fuel will be all that is necessary to eliminate anything produced by fission which slows down reaction, but the operation will also produce a quantity of radio-active plutonium 239, greater than that initially put into the reactor. Research is being carried out in this field, but only at the laboratory stage, or in small experimental stations.

Besides its use for making electricity, nuclear energy has been adopted for maritime transport. It allows ships to spend almost unlimited periods at sea, as well as giving them freedom from dependence on fuel; and there is no smoke. Several military ships, both submarine and surface vessels, are equipped with it.

Finally, a new possibility has been found for it: desalination of sea-water; which will bring hopes of irrigation to many desert and arid regions in the world.

Even if nuclear energy has so far only made a small contribution to the satisfaction of the demand for power; the fact that it has been discovered, and that a means of using it successfully will someday be found, have justified the time and money being spent on it, as opposed to conventional sources of power.

Firstly, it would be out of place to lay too much stress upon the importance of fossil fuel reserves in the future; and the known deposits can be mined without any fears about a long-term power shortage. In the second place, following the dwindling reserves law, the continuous increase in costs, which applies to the extraction of all natural resources, does not apply where nuclear energy is concerned, for it is almost certain that costs will continue to go down with developments in technology.

With the discovery of nuclear energy and its future potential, we have been given hope that we will be able to carry on the path to industrial civilisation, up which we have been toiling since the beginning of the nineteenth century. Without nuclear energy it would have been most shortsighted to use up the planet's natural resources as quickly as we have done up until the present. They would have to have been used much more economically; but that would have been (as we shall see) at the cost of economic expansion and of improved living conditions.

POWER: THE SOURCE OF ECONOMIC DEVELOPMENT

The quantity of utilisable energy in a country is one of the essential bases upon which its natural prosperity is founded. This is a necessary condition, but not one that is sufficient in itself. Many underdeveloped countries, although well favoured as far as energy-giving natural resources are concerned, have been unable to utilise them to stimulate economic growth.

A look back into the past at the development process of industrialised countries brings to light a close connection between the output level of the gross national product (GNP) and energy consumption; and the quantities of power used per person reflect quite closely the level of economic development that has been reached. In the classification for 1970, the majority of Western European countries are at the top of the list, surpassed only by the USA.

TABLE 9: Energy Consumption per capita

	Average	In tep per person	
North America	7·6	USA	7·7
		Canada	6·9
Western Europe	3·4	Great Britain	4·1
		Belgium	4·2
		Germany	3·8
		France	2·9
		Italy	2·0
Africa	0·4		
Japan	2·6		

The same connection is to be seen for each country, in particular when the growth of energy is compared with that of the gross national product.

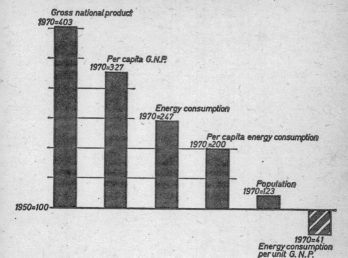

ENERGY CONSUMPTION, GROSS NATIONAL PRODUCT AND POPULATION
CHANGE 1950-1970 O.E.C.D. EUROPE

Gross national product
1970=403

Per capita G.N.P.
1970=327

Energy consumption
1970=247

Per capita energy consumption
1970=200

Population
1970=123

1950=100

1970=41
Energy consumption
per unit G. N. P.

In a recent study,[4] M. Frémont Felix analysed this
connection in detail, for more than a hundred countries,
and ended by classifying different countries according to
their level of economic development. In the initial phase
of development, the rates of annual expansion, as much
from the rise in the GNP as from energy consumption, can
be very rapid, and are easily in excess of 10% a year. When
countries have attained a certain level of development, the
rate of growth tends to reach a ceiling of about 5 or 6% a
year. From that point onwards, that is, when all the
country's economic forces are already in operation, and
saturation point has been reached, the expansion rate is
much slower.

In the course of the past 50 years, the majority of
European countries have moved from the first to the second

4. Frémont Felix, *World market of tomorrow* (Harper and Row, 1972).

TABLE 10: Total energy consumption, population and gross national product – Western Europe – 1950–1970

	Energy Consumption million toe.	Population millions	GNP milliard $	GNP per Capita $	INDICES 1950=100 Energy Consumption	Population	GNP	GNP per Capita	Consumption of energy per capita toe.	per $ 000 GNP toe.
1950	420	300	193	643	100	100	100	100	1·4	2·2
1955	529	315	257	816	126	105	133	127	1·7	2·1
1960	607	330	331	1003	145	110	171	156	1·8	1·8
1965	801	351	523	1490	191	117	271	232	2·3	1·5
1970	1037	370	778	2103	247	123	403	327	2·8	1·3

phase, but none has really reached the last phase of relative decline.

ENERGY THE COMMODITY — ENERGY THE UTILITY

A further analysis of energy-based economy serves to establish a distinction between the growth of energy consumption and the uses to which it is put.

Some of the power is used to produce new products, e.g. elaborating and crafting metals, manufacturing chemical products, improving transport, mechanising agriculture, etc.; thus the production and distribution circuits which form the basis of a healthily expanding economy are stimulated. Some power, on the contrary, is used *directly* to benefit people in their everyday life, and to increase general standards of comfort, whether with heating, lighting, household aids and equipment, travel, relaxation, etc.

M. Louis Armand, in a study of energy-based economy,[5] classified the first category as 'utility' and the second as 'commodity'.

In the first case, energy causes the rise in a country's living standard, whilst in the second it serves to measure this standard, of which it is one of the direct causes.

During the past, energy consumed for 'utility' in industry in European countries has increased noticeably less swiftly than industrial production itself, thanks to better ways and means of utilising power.

On the other hand, energy consumed for 'commodity' purposes has increased very rapidly in conjunction with the amount of ready cash held per person. From the moment when basic needs are satisfied (food and clothing, for example) people have a tendency to put aside larger and larger sums of money to contribute to their comfort, such as for heating of water or rooms, as well as for labour-saving household equipment. During the last few years Europeans have become very sensitive about comfort, although they have a long way to go before they reach

5. *Quelques aspects du problème européen de l'énergie* (OEEC publication, 1955).

the consumption level enjoyed by the inhabitants of the USA.

The rise in consumption of petrol, which is a factor of both utility and commodity, has been, in the same way, considerably greater than average, as a result of very fast development in the car industry in Western Europe. In 1970 the number of cars in Western Europe reached almost three-quarters of that of the United States. If we confine ourselves to the post-war period, the number of cars has more than quadrupled in thirty years. The fact that cars have become more powerful (another element of comfort) has offset improved performance where use of fuel is concerned, and consumption of petrol has risen on average by 10% a year.

Similarly, in the case of electricity, which contributes to both utility and personal comfort, the second element appears predominant. Because of this, growth in demand has followed a largely autonomous tendency, only moderately affected by the rate of progress of economic activity.

ECONOMIC INFLUENCE OF THE PRICE OF ENERGY[6]

There is no doubt that the price of energy exercises an influence over the economy as a whole, but it is difficult, nevertheless, to evaluate it with precision without being able to compare economies having identical structures with energy as the only differentiating factor.

The total sum obtained from the various operations concerned with either producing or converting energy, plus net imports (with slight variations according to country) represents from 7% to 8% of the gross national product in Europe. Although not negligible, this figure remains low, and the importance of energy is drawn more from the fact that it is used so widely than from its intrinsic value.

This figure does, however, mask some profound differences according to consumption areas. The proportional amount of expenditure on energy, as opposed to other

6. *L'influence economique du prix de l'energie* (Study of the Commission of the European Economic Community, 1966).

costs incurred in production, allows these areas to be split into three broad categories:

Sectors where the percentage exceeds 10%. This group includes transport (15 to 20%); electro-chemical and electro-metallurgical industries; iron and steel; glass-making and ceramics; and certain chemical industries.
Sectors which have a percentage of between 5 and 10%. They include conversion of metals, synthetic fibre and paper manufacture.
Sectors which have a percentage of less than 5%: the mechanical and electrical industries, the chemical industry, textile and dietetic industries, etc.

Where offshoots of industry are concerned, for the most part, expenditure on energy only constitutes a small part of overall production costs, and the price of energy can only have a moderate influence on industrial competition.

On the other hand, where some sectors of heavy industry are concerned, the part played by energy can become important, even preponderant from the point of view of international competition.

During the period between the two wars, and immediately after World War II, the price of energy was perceptibly higher in Europe than in the United States. In the 1950s, for example, the production price of coal was from 12 to 15 dollars a metric ton in Europe, whilst in the USA it was not more than 4 to 5 dollars a metric ton. Besides, in America oil and natural gas were available locally and did not carry the transport costs which had to be borne by European countries. This was certainly a handicap to industrial development in Europe and, at least partially, a reason for the lack of competition offered to the world market by European industrial production.

Since the beginning of the 1960s, the gap has progressively changed and widened, mainly due to massive imports of cheap petroleum from the Middle East and Africa. Thus local deposits of energy-giving resources are no longer (as

TABLE II: The share of energy in the production value of various sectors of the economy in Western Europe (% of production value)

Mineral products (excl. metals)	9·3 to 15·7%
Iron and Steel	10·0 to 20·0%
Non-ferrous metals	2·3 to 10·3%
Chemical industry	7·1 to 13·8%
Rubber and asbestos	3·2 to 5·6%
Wooden products	1·5 to 2·9%
Paper and board	5·4 to 8·8%
Textile	2·5 to 3·7%
Clothing	0·7 to 1·1%
Mechanical and electrical equipment	1·5 to 3·0%
Railway and aeronautical equipment	1·2 to 2·9%
Shipbuilding, car industry	1·7 to 3·1%
Agriculture, forestry, fishing	1·8 to 3·6%
Foodstuffs	1·9 to 3·0%
Drink industry	1·0 to 3·8%
Building	1·0 to 3·9%
Trade	2·6 to 4·7%
Services	1·4 to 2·8%

was formerly the case) a condition of economic development; if a country wishes to ensure protection of its own sources of supply by applying quantitative restrictions, customs duties, or consumer taxes, this can even constitute an obstacle to industrial development. The world economic picture has already been profoundly changed by this, and it will continue to be further changed in the future, as not all the repercussions of these changes have as yet been felt.

ENERGY AS A LOCALISATION FACTOR IN INDUSTRIAL OPERATIONS

The history of economic development in Europe can only be explained in terms of the availability and mobility of its energy-giving resources.

It was long before the technical revolution in the nineteenth century that the first industrial regions were born; Flanders, Germany, Lombardy, England, and Wales. In general their origins were based upon the utilisation of local raw materials. All forms of manufacturing (textiles, metal work, etc.) were dependent upon two forms of energy – water for mechanical power, and wood for producing heat; both forms existed practically universally and therefore there were no arbitrary limits imposed on location of industry at this point.

With the introduction of the steam-engine and a coke-based iron and steel industry, coal became an all-important factor, which meant the beginning of a long period of recession for those regions without the necessary deposits. New industrial complexes were built in mining areas, and 'black' countries became the poles of attraction for all the great industries – iron and steel, the mechanical and chemical industries, as well as a large number of associated industries attracted by the existence of easily interchangeable skilled labour. It was thus that the great European industrial centres, consisting of Yorkshire, Northumberland, Wales and the Scottish Lowlands in Great Britain, the Ruhr in Germany, northern and central France, Kempen in Belgium, and Limburg in the Netherlands, were born.

Other regions had to turn to other, secondary industries, usually founded on local traditions, but their economic development has been of necessity rather slower. Labour too has tended to shift away from regions impoverished by the industrial decline to the newer great industrial centres, where there have been concentrated numbers of foreign workers, such as Italians in Belgium, and Poles or mid-Europeans in the north and east of France.

Following a similar process, the existence of hydro-electric resources has initiated the development of several large industrial centres. Major electro-metallurgical industries were established in the Alps, in Switzerland, France and Italy. The most important electric stations have been built in these regions because of the large market they supply. The most advanced hydro-electric industry is still in Switzerland, due to the experience that it has accumulated over the years.

The discovery of natural gas deposits in the 1950s modified the structure and location of certain industries. When deposits were first tapped in the Po valley, industrialisation in northern Italy was given a sufficient boost for the country to be able to make up for a lag of several years behind regions in northern Europe. Likewise, the Lacq region and the south-west became the new industrial centres of France, while an industrial boom has already hit the Netherlands following the discovery of deposits at Slochteren.

But it is principally a preference for oil-based products, because of their ability to meet such a wide variety of needs, that has changed the factors determining location of industry. Once necessary energy has been imported, it is first refined near large ports, with the result that the surrounding areas have been earmarked as privileged zones for the growth of consumer industries.

Since the 1960s, many major iron and steel complexes have been abandoning the great European coal belts to move nearer to the coast, for instance to Bremen in Germany, Rotterdam in the Netherlands, Ghent in Belgium, Dunkirk and Fos in France. Genoa is becoming one of the most important smelting centres in Europe, although Italy used to import nearly all its steel.

These coastal locations led to a lowering of costs of transfer and the internal freight charges incurred in the transport of foreign ore, or of coal for making coke, thus adding to savings on fuel costs resulting from the proximity of the refineries. Numerous coastal refineries are, in turn, associated with chemical complexes, which use by-products from the refineries as their raw materials.

All these new industries necessitate a large capital investment, but need less labour, and therefore major shifts in population are avoided. The comparative decline of coal in favour of oil has not (as happened previously, when the switchover to coal took place) led to a recession in those coal-producing regions, which had time to broaden their activities. The problem of retraining miners to take up other occupations has arisen, but apart from rare exceptions (such as Borinage in Belgium and Lorraine in France) it has been faced under satisfactory social conditions, in that pit closures have been sufficiently staggered to allow for all necessary reorganisation to take place between each closure (see p. 67).

Thus a new selection of industries is progressively coming into operation, influenced by regional differences. Industries relying on primary sources of energy are built near large ports when possible, while other industries tend to be established more in regions with plenty of skilled labour, or close to a flourishing market.

Although it used to be true that highly industrialised regions enjoyed a much better standard of living than poorer agricultural areas, it is no longer the case. There is a tendency towards a better distribution of industrial concerns throughout the whole of Europe, leading to an overall levelling up in living conditions. Most governments, too, are encouraging decentralisation of industry in their appropriate regional policies.

Thus energy has lost its tendency towards polarisation and its influence in determining a fixed location for industries. Henceforth, geographical variability is the rule for new industrial concerns, and it is power which comes to meet the demand wherever those new concerns are put into operation.

ENERGY AND TECHNOLOGICAL PROGRESS

The most important stages in Mankind's progress have been marked by the use of new methods to exploit sources of power which have been in existence in a latent condition in the ground or under the sea. The discovery of fire was Man's first great conquest. The practice of harnessing animals to provide labour in the middle ages, which reduced the amount of manual labour required, made the abolition of serfdom possible. The eighteenth and nineteenth centuries saw the first exploitation of basic sources of natural energy for general use, such as water and windmills. The nineteenth-century Industrial Revolution was instigated by the steam-engine, for it was only through exploiting coalmines that it could be developed.

IMPROVEMENT OF TECHNIQUES FOR PRODUCING POWER

At the beginning of the century, all coal was obtained by pick and shovel, thus a large labour force was necessary. It was not until after World War I that technology had made sufficient progress for mechanical tools to be used for mining. In European mines the amount of coal produced per man-shift rose from a few hundred kilogrammes at the beginning of the century to an average of three metric tons around 1970. In the USA, where geological conditions are more favourable, output reaches 15 metric tons on average, and can go as high as 25 to 30 tons in open pits. Technological progress also benefits the miners, for as mining equipment is perfected they are being freed from their most onerous jobs.

Right from the beginning, oil has called for much more involved techniques; and at the same time needed far fewer men to work the rigs. Exploratory techniques are based on scientific methods of prospecting, and completely mechanised drilling processes allow for the sinking of deeper and deeper wells. Similarly, where refining is concerned, thanks to the progress of chemistry and metallurgy, procedures can be infinitely varied so that consumers can receive power in the form that suits them best.

But indubitably it is in the realm of nuclear energy that technological progress has been most spectacular, and that the most is expected, where future advances are concerned. Thanks to the discovery of nuclear power, Man will be able to take another step forward in his conquest of natural forces. For ages past Man's greatest ambition has been to convert matter into energy. His ambition has already been realised insofar as operations have now reached industrial dimensions and they will soon become universal.

With the coming of nuclear energy, Man is on the threshold of a new era, which will give him the ability to exercise his power over Nature to its greatest extent, and to improve his own living standards.

IMPROVEMENT IN UTILISATION TECHNIQUES

Much progress has also been made where the utilisation of energy is concerned, and this has led to a considerable increase in output.[7]

It is possible to estimate that from 1920 to 1970 the utilisable output from energy for all uses has more than tripled. Thus utilisable energy – that is, energy actually available for use – has practically multiplied by 10 in 50 years.

One can imagine the huge number of generating stations or the degree of atmospheric pollution there would have been if it had been necessary to consume three times as much energy to cover the same amount and diversity of uses. It is certain that with this extra constraint expansion would have taken place much more slowly, to the detriment of improved living conditions.

This improvement in utilisable output has been made possible as a result of perfecting existing techniques, but also as a result of introducing and using new ones.

At the beginning of the century, when wood or coal

7. Claude M. Summers, 'The Conversion of Energy', *Scientific American* (September 1971).

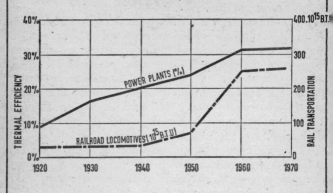

EFFICIENCY OF FUEL-BURNING POWER PLANTS AND RAILROAD LOCOMOTIVES

Source: Scientific American sept. 1971

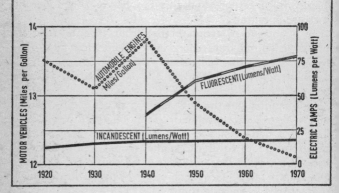

EFFICIENCY OF ELECTRIC LAMPS AND AUTOMOBILE ENGINES

was burnt in open fires, less than 20% of the heat produced was transmitted in the form of radiation, the rest was lost up the chimney. In a modern household, using central heating, more than 75% of the energy is utilised. At the present time the average amount utilised is in the order of 50 to 55%. Without doubt energy consumption for home heating, far from decreasing, has gone up considerably, but then so has the level of comfort.

The same thing has happened where conversion of heat into electricity is concerned. From 5% at the beginning of the century, the average output from conversion has risen to 33% in 1970, while in the most up-to-date power stations it can exceed 40%. This increase was obtained initially by replacing steam-piston engines with steam-driven turbines, then by raising the temperature of the steam and improving the design of the turbines. Over and above this, a proportion of the residual energy is often used in further heating operations, for instance in large industrial complexes or urban centres.

Appreciable progress has also been made where transport is concerned. On the railways conventional steam-engines have been replaced by electric or diesel locomotives. The average output from conversion has risen from 10% to about 35% in 1970.

For motor vehicles the improvement is less marked, as the principle of the internal combustion engine has remained unchanged. Even so, in the USA the number of miles per gallon has increased by 10%, although cars are bigger, more powerful and more comfortable than they were 50 years ago.

Even more spectacular progress has been made with lighting. In an incandescent lamp, nearly 95% of energy irradiated is in the infra-red zone, and only 5% in the zone of visible radiation; this level is almost five times better than what was obtained at the beginning of the century. However, in fluorescent lamps, which went into industrial operation in the 1940s, about 20% of electricity is converted into light.

These are, of course, only stages in a continual process.

Will it go on in the same way in the future? Some people. have their doubts and are worried about exhausting deposits of raw materials; using up too much space; or air and water pollution. But could anyone, 50 years ago, given the state of technology at that time, have foreseen the spectacular progress made since then? Energy gives us an excellent example of that continual process of improvement in traditional methods and innovations which constitute real progress in our industrial civilisation.

In some cases brutal changes resulting from technical innovations have taken place; and it must be admitted that some difficulties in adapting have been experienced, mainly where people and social conditions are concerned.

SOCIAL PROBLEMS IN ENERGY-PRODUCING INDUSTRIES

The technological evolution which has just been described has deeply affected the structure of the energy industry and has manifested itself in important changes in types of jobs and the volume of labour. From an industry necessitating an intensive labour force, such as coal-mining, there was a changeover in the 1950s, and even more so after 1960, towards an industry – oil – which depended to a much greater extent on capital investment (capital intensive) and on a smaller labour force. Nuclear industry, to an even greater extent than oil, will lessen the need for labour, but will necessitate a small, very highly skilled work force. We can see this evolution already beginning to take place.

Such a change-over is very favourable from society's point of view, as it has allowed the most arduous jobs to be replaced by more sophisticated work, which is consequently better paid. However, it has posed some difficult problems where adapting to new conditions is concerned, mainly within the coal industry which has experienced a marked decline in production and where in certain cases occupational rehabilitation has been necessary.

SOCIAL TROUBLES IN COALMINING IN THE INTERIM
PERIOD BETWEEN THE TWO WARS

A labour force with very specialised skills is needed in the
coalpits; and these skills can only be developed after a slow
and difficult 'apprenticeship'. Moreover, mining is an
arduous and even dangerous occupation, demanding a
degree of moral fibre and strength of character beyond
what is normally associated with manual work. The mine-
worker, who is proud of his occupation, has the reputation
of being a desperate fighter when he is defending his
interests, and labour battles in the pits have always been
fiercer than anywhere else.

The most typical example is that of the miners' strike in
1926 in Great Britain, which rapidly assumed a revolutionary character and swelled to national proportions. This
strike lasted for more than eight months and brought un-
believable misery to mining areas, at a time when welfare
funds did not exist. All union movements afterwards took
this strike as an example of the workers' struggle to ensure
guaranteed employment. It remained engraved on people's
memories for a long time, and no doubt was still at the back
of people's minds 25 years later, when there was a big
labour shortage in the pits in Great Britain and it was
proposed that foreign labour should be recruited. The
unions violently opposed the plan, on the grounds that this
would lead to dismissals among the local labour force.

The major economic crisis from 1929 to 1933 had similarly
unfortunate repercussions in mining areas. Cuts that were
unavoidable due to the prolonged slump in the coal market –
it is difficult to find room at the pithead for more than a
fortnight's output – were harshly resented. All mining
areas experienced great hardship, and the impression that
work in the pits was dangerous, arduous and insecure was
perpetuated, leading to an increasingly marked distaste
among young people for mining as a career.

INDUSTRIAL DIVERSIFICATION IN TRADITIONAL COAL-MINING AREAS AFTER WORLD WAR II

Geological conditions in European mines were especially bad and output was generally rather poor. After World War II an initial attempt at adopting mining methods put into operation in the USA did not prove fruitful, but new techniques specially adapted to European conditions, together with a concentration of production in the most profitable areas, led to increased overall output. In 20 years it has almost doubled. Under the dual effort of reduction in production and improved productivity, the labour force in the European mines has gradually decreased from 1·2 million workers underground in 1950 to less than 500,000 in 1970.

Such a large reduction in labour over 20 years has obviously raised some difficult problems, but the effects have differed according to the various different regions.

TABLE 12: Men employed underground

(*in thousands*)

	1929	1937	1950	1960	1970
Great Britain	—	618	539	482	228
Germany	317	239	302	264	124
France	203	152	175	125	63
Belgium	106	100	112	72	25
Netherlands	25	20	27	28	7
Saar	45	32	40	33	14

In *Great Britain* the decline was gradual and continuous. Redundancy problems were almost entirely solved by miners retiring or leaving the pits voluntarily. In certain industrial areas there was even a slight shortage of skilled labour.

In *Germany*, in particular the Ruhr, the region was already highly industrialised and miners who were made redundant quickly found other occupations. In fact, the real problem was one of ensuring sufficient labour recruitment.

The situation was different in *Belgium* and *France*, where there were often no other industries in mining areas and where re-placement of miners into new occupations turned out to be particularly difficult. Intervention at government level had to take place in order to ensure a gradual phasing out of pit-closures, so that excessive numbers of workers were not made redundant at the same time. The Borinage region suffered badly and has still not entirely recovered, although new industries that have moved into the area are starting to give it new life. The miners in the north of France and from the Pas-de-Calais underwent the change-over later, and the authorities had learnt enough from former experience to relieve some of the hardship felt by the miners there. However, the transition was not so well handled in other less important French coalfields, which had to close as a result of low output. In the coalfields in the Loire, and also around Alès and in the Gard in the south, the government had no choice but to grant big subsidies to allow continued workings, in spite of very high production costs.

At this time the High Authority of the ECSC adopted a rehabilitation programme, mainly in the form of giving monetary compensation to workers made redundant.

In the majority of cases the change-over was carried out so that the least possible hardship was caused to the men affected, thanks to intervention by public authorities, including the ECSC. The unions too played an active part in helping to set up replacement infrastructures in those regions affected by the drop in coal production. We have here perhaps one of the first examples of effective collaboration between public authorities, producers and unions, to resolve a particularly difficult social problem.

CHANGES IN THE STRUCTURE OF THE ENERGY INDUSTRY

The existence of large sums of capital is indispensable for the development of energy resources, and it is often foreign capital which is the first to be invested in such operations.

As early as the nineteenth century, English, Belgian and French money was pouring into investments in German coalfields. It was not until later, when a local consumer industry was developed, notably iron and steel, that the Germans took over control.

There are even more typical cases of foreign investment in the oil industry, where American companies have rapidly spread their activities throughout the world, and in particular to European consumer markets.

A second characteristic of these industries is the necessity of their being vertically integrated. The world market for energy in its raw state is very restricted. European consumers realised this in the 1950s when they were on the lookout for coal; supplies were not often available on the world market, and those there were were very expensive. Where oil is concerned, the international companies supply more than 90% of the resources for all of Europe.

A third characteristic, and one which results from the second, is the huge size of the operations. In the *Fortune en 1970* review's classification, four of the ten top industrial companies produced energy. It is the same with the classification of every major European country. As a result, the energy industry is finding itself in a situation where there are a few companies selling to a vast market, which conforms closely to what is prescribed by economic theory.

Various governments, to ensure that consumers are protected, have been induced to exert increasingly close control over the operations of these organisations. In certain cases, the industry has been placed wholly under state control. Where organisations have retained private ownership management has been regulated through various legislative procedures.

STATE CONTROL IN THE COAL INDUSTRY BETWEEN
THE TWO WARS

Very early on, many governments established legislative
procedures to regulate the activities of coal organisations.

In *Great Britain* the ̀Coal Mines Act was passed on 1
August 1930. The law instituted a Commission for the reorganisation of coalmining, comprised of five officials
nominated by the Board of Trade, who had the job of
bringing about amalgamations between various companies
and organisations when it was judged to be for the national
good. It hoped to effect these amalgamations through
persuasion, but if necessary the Commission was empowered
to use constraint.

Another job of the Commission was to regulate production
and prices. The latter depended on the institution of a two-
level system: a national production plan for the country
as a whole, and a regional plan for each coalfield. The
Coal Mines Act, initially put into operation for a two-year
period and extended for five years, was confirmed by a
new clause in 1938. The policy concerning amalgamations
was enforced with the intention of reducing more than a
thousand companies still in existence to about sixty.

In *Germany*, the Third Reich controlled private industry
through the 'Economic Grouping of the Mining Industry',
affiliated to the Chamber of National Economy of the
Reich, itself controlled by the 'Reichwirtschaft Minis-
terium'.

In *France*, a law passed on 18 August 1936 has authorised
the government to subsidise mines working at a loss, it also
allowed for national production plans and controlled coal
prices.

NATIONALISATION OF COAL IN GREAT BRITAIN
AND FRANCE

The tendency towards increasingly narrow state-approved
restrictions reached its ultimate conclusion just after the
war. In Great Britain, as a result of the Coal Industry
Nationalisation Act of 12 July 1946, the state took control

of all British mines, and in France an act was passed on 17 May 1946, nationalising coal and transferring all privately-owned collieries into the hands of the state.

Nationalisation was carried out in a similar manner in both countries. Both governments set up systems of public organisation of an industrial and commercial nature, endowed with a civil character and with financial autonomy. They thus escaped from budgetary control over the administration of public funds; they could not otherwise have been allowed to run at a loss.

Administrative councils and Director-Generals, in England as in France, are nominated by the Ministry, but the way in which they act differs. In France the state exercises total control over all aspects of the organisation, whilst in Great Britain the designated authorities have complete freedom of action.

In *Belgium* the position of a Coal Director was created in 1962. This official had control over all coal production in the country, but coal companies retained private ownership. The Director fixes production programmes, sale prices, makes the decisions concerning pit-closures, and administers aid given to the organisation.

In *Germany* the financial situation in the mines during the post-war period was much more hopeful than in any other European country. But around 1967 to 1968, following a period of severe competition, the state had to take complete control of coalmining in order to avoid an acceleration in pit-closures. Instead of resorting to nationalisation, it took administrative responsibility and covered organisations running at a loss. Shareholders, mainly belonging to iron and steel companies, in return for transfer of their holdings to the state, received monetary compensation, but retained the value of their share capital.

By different means, practically the same result has thus been obtained in each of the countries. That is, a complete transfer to state control of the administration of coalmines, with reserve funds ready to meet any unexpected emergencies in the industry.

STATE CONTROL OVER THE OIL INDUSTRY

The oil industry, unlike coal, is of an essentially international nature; and because of this, it is impossible to bring all its various operations and ramifications under central control. However, there have been numerous cases of certain countries intervening to regulate the activities of the oil companies within their boundaries.

In the course of recent history, these interventions have usually taken place for the following reasons:

To avoid monopolies or other similar dangers to competition.

To ensure a satisfactory balance between different branches of operations.

To protect a national industry, whether coal or oil, from harsh competition from the big international oil companies.

An example of restrictive legislation is that of the French law passed on 30 March 1928. At the end of World War I the supporters and opponents of a state monopoly in oil were bitterly opposed. As a result, after some time, a compromise was accepted, establishing a system of delegated monopoly for oil. Private enterprise continued to operate, but it had to work within the restrictions imposed by government licences authorising it to release oil products on to the national market for consumption. These licences were granted to refiners for a period of ten years, and to importers for a three-year period. They limited the quantities of authorised output, but the licensed amount of supply was greater than demand, to maintain competition between the companies.

Italy has a similar control system, but it has never been enforced so widely nor so stringently as in France. However, it does allow for state intervention if and when it becomes necessary.

Germany, before World War I, kept a strict control over oil operations, mainly in order to uphold military strength in the country. After the war, the system was dismantled and replaced by much less restrictive regulations. In 1965 the government continued itself to offer aid to exploration.

The oil industry in other countries was left to contend as best it could with outside competition where finding a market was concerned. It is true that in two of them, *Great Britain* and the *Netherlands*, national companies, BP and Royal Dutch Shell, became sufficiently powerful to stabilise competition.

Thus it can be seen that the structure of the European oil industry results from both the marketing laws and from countries seeking, to a greater or lesser extent, to protect their own interests. The European oil industry is composed of three types of organisation: the big privately-owned international companies; the groups run by mixed funds; and state-controlled organisations. Their importance and their roles have changed considerably over the years.

The big privately-owned international companies are mainly of Anglo-Saxon origin. All have an integrated structure and operate throughout the world. Classed in order of importance, they are Standard Oil (New Jersey) (Esso),* Royal Dutch Shell, Texaco, Socony Mobil, Standard Oil (California), and Gulf Oil. A greater concentration has been avoided, thanks to anti-trust legislative intervention by the USA. Besides these groups, generally called the 'majors', there are other less important ones, which nonetheless have an active competitive role: Marathon, Sinclair, Continental, Occidental, etc.

Two groups based on a mixed economy, British Petroleum (BP) and Compagnie Française des Petroles (CFP), belong on the list of 'majors', the first in fourth position, the second in eighth position. They control vast crude oil reserves, as they were created to exploit deposits which originally were held by the British and French governments. They constitute an important asset for Europe, in that they reduce balance of payment costs in these two countries. They are also important factors where the security of supplies is concerned.

State-controlled organisations are a more recent innovation.

* now 'EXXON'

The Ente Nazionale Idrocarburi (ENI) in Italy and l'Etablissement de Recherches et d'Activités Petrolières (ERAP) in France are the most typical. Both exploit deposits discovered as a result of exploration programmes mounted by both countries to gain new oil resources. These organisations are not run on such an exclusive profit-making basis as private enterprises, and have established a new relationship with countries where oil is produced, accepting the latters' participation in exploiting the deposits before they are forced to do so.

Thus, from a market that was initially controlled by a few large international companies, European countries have arrived at a very different situation. The consumer has greatly benefited from this evolution, obtaining, thanks to lively competition between these different oil organisations, very good prices for oil-based products. Enrico Mattei, who disappeared tragically in 1963, is considered by many to be the symbol of this policy which, in the 1950s, was beginning to worry the powerful oil companies.[8]

By direct or indirect means, the state has had an overwhelming influence on the structure of the oil industry as it exists in Europe today. Without this influence, we should indubitably be much nearer to a quasi-monopoly, as has been experienced in several major areas concerned with the production of raw materials, where markets are organised on a world scale, fixing both production levels and prices.

STATE CONTROL WHERE GAS AND ELECTRICITY ARE CONCERNED

Gas and electricity have always been recognised as performing a public service. Whether operating under a system of concessions, or whether they are nationalised, in all cases they are under the control of public authorities.

Before World War II, the most widespread system was one of private management, where administrative principles were determined by specifications imposed by public authorities.

After the war gas and electricity were both nationalised

8. Cf. P. H. Frankel's work *Mattei Oil and Power Policies.*

in Great Britain and France, and in 1962 electricity was nationalised in Italy.

These nationalisation laws, as in the case of coal, rest on the assumption that assets of essential interest to the nation must be taken out of the hands of private enterprise and be managed on a non-profit-making basis. Moreover, it must be added that concentration of these activities in one organisation allows much more rational exploitation and lowers cost prices to the consumer's benefit.

In other countries, gas and electricity have remained under private ownership, but with strict administrative control from the state. In fact, regional or civil authorities often hold the balance of power in these companies.

THE CONCEPT OF AN ENERGY POLICY

Energy is playing a sufficiently important part in peoples' lives that it is placing governments under an obligation to define an energy policy; that is, firstly to determine firm objectives and then to put means of attaining them into operation.

The various countries' main aims have been to ensure that there are constant, safe supplies of energy and that the best possible economic conditions are maintained; meanwhile bearing in mind that certain harsh choices can have quite unacceptable social repercussions.

From the outline of this statement it might follow that various European national policies should be analysed in detail. However, we shall try, rather, to sort out the main developments in ideology insofar as they are reflected in the actions of different international organisations, such as the Organisation for European Economic Co-operation (OEEC) (which became the Organisation for European Co-operation and Development (OECD) in 1962) and the European communities.

THE INTERIM PERIOD BETWEEN THE WARS

Up until World War II those countries lacking natural resources dealt with problems of energy supply by having recourse to the international market. Although this was not the perfect solution, it did at least provide some sort of an answer.

Certain countries were in a privileged position in that they had abundant supplies of coal, and it is for this reason that countries with extensive coalfields such as Great Britain, Germany, Belgium and France were more highly industrialised than their neighbours.

The problem for these countries was to rationalise exploitation of their resources in order to avoid waste, and to ensure long-term supplies. Thus state control over coal production was very strict. The authorities recommended special programmes to ensure that mines were not overworked, which would have had the result of lowering cost prices. Apart from which, such over-working would have had an adverse effect on the efficient workings of the mines.

The coal authorities had a dual function, in that apart from controlling production, they had the job of looking after the miners' safety. At the beginning of the century there had been a series of catastrophes, with a high toll of victims in the mines. Explosions of fire-damp, cave-ins in the pits, and flooding were just a few of the many hazards faced by pit workers at the coal face. To limit the risks as far as possible, high safety standards were imposed by state authorities. Obviously this meant that the cost price of coal had to increase; but thanks to the careful watch kept by public authorities since the 1920s, mining has become a much less dangerous occupation. The proportion of fatal accidents has been sufficiently reduced to make mining only a little more dangerous than many other industrial occupations.

But, even as early as this, coal was no longer the only form of energy demanding attention from the state. Oil seemed to be the 'energy of the future', and governments were concerned as to how to procure and increase supplies. In a famous and forward-looking speech, Winston Churchill, at that time First Lord of the Admiralty, declared on 17 July 1913 in the House of Commons that an important aspect of long-term British policy was the necessity of gaining ownership of at least a certain portion of the crude oil reserves needed by the country, or at any rate to gain control of their sources. As a result, the British government created the Anglo-Persian Oil Company to exploit deposits in Iran. This company, which later became British Petroleum, was at its inception largely state-controlled, and it was the British government which dictated most of its actions.

In the same way the French government inaugurated a similar company, called the Compagnie Française des Petroles (CFP), in which it held a third of the capital. The CFP was set up to exploit the resources in Iraq which had been ceded to France after the war. Moreover, by a law made on 30 March 1928, a charter for the French oil industry was drawn up, in which special measures were introduced on one hand to ensure priority to oil produced by the CFP, and on the other hand, to ensure government protection for French refineries, which meant that rapid development was able to take place in this field.

There had, as yet, been no attempt to establish a joint policy for coal and oil, because at this time there were few hints of the harsh competition between the two forms of energy that was to come in later years.

THE POST-WAR PERIOD

The situation changed rapidly after World War II. With the slump in coal production, the market for oil increased throughout the world. Only the USA and USSR were able to produce internally sufficient amounts of energy, from a sufficient number of different sources, to satisfy all their needs. Europe soon had to rely on imports for its essential supplies of oil.

From the beginning of the 1950s Europe ran the risk of a serious energy shortage. Coal supplies were not sufficient to meet rapidly growing needs imposed by the reconstruction effort after the war. The OEEC was entrusted with the task of putting the Marshall plan into operation, and it set about dealing with this problem by creating a limited Ministerial Committee, which had the job of persuading the countries which belonged to it to adopt appropriate measures. Two reports were brought out:

Coal Production. Short-term programmes of Western Europe.
Coal production and supplies for Western Europe in 1952.

These reports emphasised the necessity for action on the part of those countries producing energy. Coal production in Europe was boosted from 440,000 metric tons in 1950 to more than 500,000 metric tons in 1953.

However, it was rapidly becoming apparent throughout Europe that internal coal deposits would no longer be sufficient. The OEEC, following a suggestion made by M. Louis Armand in one of his reports on energy,[9] set up boards of experts to examine the ways in which Europe could continue to obtain sufficient supplies of energy.

Three new reports were brought out between 1956 and 1966.

The Hartley report, on ways in which Europe could meet rising demand for energy, published in 1956, recognised that it was essential to increase energy imports, but it stressed the urgency with which members had to increase production of primary energy, especially of coal, from consideration both of economy and of security. In particular he declared:

'We wish to emphasise that coal will be the mainstay of the energy economy in Western Europe for many years. An increased output of coal will depend on long-term investment, on the development of improved mining methods, on miners' pay and terms of employment being adequate, and on giving coal the outlook of a modernised stable industry which will attract able young men to join it.'

The Robinson report, published four years later, *Towards a New Energy Pattern in Europe*, followed a very different line and recognised that it was vain to hope for an increase in coal production. Conditions had changed considerably

9. *Quelques aspects du problème européen de l'énergie* (OEEC, 1955).

on the energy market. The market for fuel which, in the years immediately after the war was favourable for suppliers, had switched abruptly, and became biassed towards buyers. Shipping charges went down, which meant that fuels could be imported more cheaply; with the result that they threatened national products with increasingly serious competition. The conclusions of the report are concerned with this change:

'In view of the increased diversification of potential energy resources, we do not think that serious difficulties of finding supplies abroad are likely to arise. We do not feel grave fears regarding the probable capacity of most of the economically strong countries of Europe to pay for the imports of energy that seem necessary . . .' (Conclusion 4)

'When formulating a long-term energy-policy, the paramount consideration should, in our view, be a plentiful supply of low-cost energy with a freedom of choice to the consumer . . .' (Conclusion 5)

'We recognise the importance of continuity and regularity of energy supplies. But we do not regard the long-term protection or artificial encouragement of indigenous supplies of energy as the most satisfactory method of obtaining such security . . .' (Conclusion 6)

'The future market for hard coal will depend primarily on the possibility of producing coal at a price that will make its use fully competitive with that of alternative forms of energy . . .' (Conclusion 13)

The report of the Energy Committee, Energy Policy – Problems and Objectives, published in 1966, confirms this policy of liberal direction. In its conclusion it declares in particular:

'While the energy industries will continue to be responsible for the provision of supplies, governments must take the necessary initiative to establish an adequate framework for their operations and in particular to maintain competition and lower prices within all phases of the energy sector; prudently allocate support for research, help industries and workers to adjust to change, protect the public health and eliminate damage to other resource values . . .'

Most European countries followed these objectives to a greater or lesser extent in their energy policies. Competition meant that supplies could be rapidly increased, and up until 1970 imported energy was appreciably cheaper than what was produced internally. Imports, as we have seen, supplied 65% of the overall demand in 1970.

RECENT DEVELOPMENTS

The first signs of a possible change have, however, been apparent since 1967/8. Oil-producing countries have formed an organisation of oil-exporting countries (OPEC). It has been realised that not only is oil tremendously important to those countries in which it is consumed; but that they are to a certain extent dependent upon it; so exporting countries are looking for a larger cut from oil revenues in order to develop their own economies. This will not have a serious effect immediately, but already, by the end of 1970, it meant an appreciable increase (nearly 50%) in dues paid them by the oil companies.

Consumer countries realise that this change is coming. The more that countries depend upon oil supplies, the greater the consequences when supplies are stopped. Thus, various measures have been adopted to ensure adequate reserves, such as increasing stocks, and using as widespread a range of supplies as possible. It is becoming more and more apparent that it is imperative to have an energy policy in order to safeguard the security of supplies.

Great Britain has made an enormous effort to develop nuclear power and to explore all the deposits it controls on the continental shelf under the North Sea. In a White Paper produced in 1966, the government stressed that it was in the country's interests to shift the emphasis, where energy supplies were concerned, from coal and oil alone, to nuclear power and natural gas, as well as the other two.

The Commission for European Communities (EEC) addressed a memorandum[10] to the Council in December 1968, stressing the need for an active energy policy aimed at reinforcing the security of supplies. And with that intention the Commission advocated the following:

(1) Grants to help coalmines resist production shortages.
(2) More nuclear power stations and the definition of a policy concerning supplies of nuclear fuel; in particular, allowing the creation of a station for developing uranium.
(3) The establishment of a watch policy over imports of crude oil, as well as of refined products.
(4) Larger grants within the framework of 'Community projects' to organisations within the EEC undertaking programmes of oil prospection, which might be of interest in securing supplies.

The countries in the EEC agreed to these suggestions in principle, and from 1969 have worked to bring this policy into effect, introducing the appropriate legislative procedures where necessary.

After a long period when European countries had to rely almost exclusively upon the vagaries of the international market for their supplies, it is becoming apparent that energy-producing industries can no longer be expected to deal with problems on their own, and European governments are becoming increasingly aware of their heavy responsibilities.

Imports have become so important that an energy policy must be a part of an overall concept of international economic relations. In particular it must take into account the changing relations between industrialised and developing countries, as well as relations between industrialised countries. With the development of international cooperation to further economic growth in developing countries (such as financial aid; stabilisation of the market for raw materials and technical assistance), it is to be hoped that purchases of energy are to be envisaged in broader

10. *Première orientation pour une politique énergique communautaire* (Publication of the European Community, December 1968).

terms as part of a huge exchange scheme, concluded for the mutual benefit of both parties.

Thus it would appear that the times have changed. Where once problems concerning energy would have to be resolved by the producers and buyers in the particular field affected from a national angle, energy policies are now seen to be closely related to general economic policies in most countries and are thus taking on world-wide importance.

ENERGY AND THE PROTECTION OF THE ENVIRONMENT

Distributed as it is over all inhabitable land, energy has become, over the years, a major pollution factor; and all countries are being constrained to find solutions to this problem.

We have been aware of air pollution from smoke for a long time, but it was generally accepted as a necessary evil, for the horrifying effects it could have on the human organism were not appreciated, nor was there any known way of avoiding it. It was considered the unavoidable counterpart of industrial civilisation, which outweighing the bad effects, procured improved living conditions for the majority of people, leading to better states of health and well-being. At that time people were totally unaware that the smuts, dust and sulphur-dioxide from factory chimneys or even from open fires were often responsible for the thick winter fogs engulfing big cities – like the London smog – or for chronic lung complaints suffered by people living in certain industrial areas.

The construction of high chimneys for industrial use, by dispersing the effects of pollution, then the replacement of coal by diesel oil for household heating, helped the situation considerably just after the war, but this improvement did not last long. With a rapid increase in consumption – it has almost tripled during the last twenty years – the sources of pollution have multiplied, and the pollutant itself has often become more insidious. In Paris, for example, the roofing of houses, which is mainly of zinc, deteriorated rapidly as a result of sulphurous smuts from chimneys. The surfaces of stone walls were eroded, resulting in cracks that could be dangerous; and historical monuments, untouched for centuries, were badly damaged. Constant medical surveillance has led to the discovery of sources of public danger in major industrial regions. In areas experiencing climatic inversion it has been possible to establish an increased mortality rate among the elderly whenever this phenomenon occurs.

As a result of its great density of population, Europe was one of the first regions to take stock of the risks of atmospheric pollution, and from 1955 to 1960 public authorities imposed levels of quality for fuel. The amount of sulphur in gas oil for heating has been limited in all major complexes. Strict regulations have been imposed on major industrial works, requiring them to build higher chimneys and to use less sulphurous fuels.

As at the beginning there had been no control over the situation, the effects of these regulations could be seen at once. The quantity of sulphur in the atmosphere in large cities was greatly reduced. In Paris, for example, the level in 1970 was half what it had been ten years before. New factories have been grouped away from cities in large modern industrial complexes, emitting very little in the way of visible smoke.

Certainly, a lot more has to be done to make the air we breathe healthy again, but since Europe started to deal with the problem earlier than either the USA or Japan, there is less tendency to dramatise the problem here.

Even if the problem of smoke has been greatly improved, there still remains the problem of pollution from exhaust fumes from cars. Carbon-monoxide, nitric oxides, unburnt petrol waste and the leads it contains are highly toxic, and if inhaled in a concentrated form can become dangerous. In narrow streets of large cities the atmosphere has often become unbreatheable. Even the main traffic routes, although open to the countryside, do not escape from this risk. Very strict levels will have to be introduced; and on a long-term basis the petrol-fuelled internal combustion engine will have to be replaced with something that is less of a pollutant.

Water, too, runs the risk of pollution. Biological pollution has always been known, even if the effects could not be measured. Greater and greater amounts of chemical pollutants are now posing serious problems. But the increasing numbers of large thermal power stations are leading to an even more dangerous risk of 'thermal pollution', that is, the raising of the water temperature which could lead to the extinction of all river life.

Protection of the environment has become a major preoccupation in all important industrial countries. Not all the dangers from pollution are as yet known in sufficient detail for measures reducing them to be introduced. Existing procedures for cleaning the atmosphere and water have to be perfected, and new techniques will have to be found. It will be very costly for the consumer, but it is the price that he will have to pay for the technological progress from which he benefits.

The progress that has been made is undeniable, but it is not sufficient. The struggle against pollution has become important for all civilised countries. It will have to remain so in the future.

CONCLUSION

The past fifty years covered briefly in this survey have been characterised mainly by a continual acceleration where energy is concerned, brought about by Man's ever-growing mastery over natural forces.

The main points in this change have been the following:

(1) Demand for energy has increased continually, and at a rate directly linked to economic expansion.

(2) From 1957/8 Europe found itself in a new situation. Shortage was abruptly succeeded by abundant supplies. Repletion followed a bigger opening of the world market, and the vast oil resources available on it.

(3) From 1968 to 1970 there was renewed anxiety concerning adequate supplies, especially of oil. It is possible that this will continue at least until 1980.

(4) Since the 1950s, and even more so since the 1960s, a process of relative decline has developed in the coal industry, since it has been faced with new forms of cheaper energy such as oil and natural gas. In terms of absolute value, coal consumption is only decreasing slowly, thanks to measures giving government support to the mining industry, but the proportion of overall demand for energy met by coal has fallen from 95% in 1920 to only 25% in 1970.

(5) In the years 1955–60 the oil industry grew in a spectacular fashion, thanks to the low cost of petroleum. Reserves in the Middle East and Africa are plentiful; and the protectionist policy adopted by the USA, up until then the main consumer of oil-based products, meant that there was a temporary excess of oil on the market, free for worldwide (and especially European) consumption. With greater supplies came, of course, greater competition between companies selling oil.

(6) Up until the 1960s, the USA were almost the only consumers of natural gas. However, from the 1960s onwards, deposits have been discovered in large quantities in Europe and on the continental shelf under the North Sea, thus contributing further to energy supplies.

(7) Nuclear energy had a very hopeful but perhaps rather premature start at the beginning of the 1950s. After some years of uncertainty, however, it had, especially in Great Britain, reached a state by the end of the 1960s where it could compete realistically with traditional forms of energy for fuelling electric power stations.

(8) If reports of consumption have varied according to the different forms of primary energy used, it is because for each of them the end products go through very different processes. In 1970, coal for coke manufacture represented a good half of the total amount produced, while in 1920 only 15% was converted into coke. If petroleum derivatives are used as examples, the consumption rate in 1970 was 3·5

times the 1938 level for motor gasoline, 10 times for gas oil,
25 times for fuel oil, and 40 times for liquid gas.

(9) The importance of imports is being increasingly felt
(60% in 1970 against 20% in 1950), and European countries
are being forced to realise the risks involved in being dependent on them. As a result, research is being carried out
within the framework of an all-embracing energy policy, to
develop local resources and find means of safeguarding
supplies.

Europe, during the past fifty years, has thus not only been
able to face up to the growth of energy which is indispensable to its economy, and to satisfy consumers' needs; it has
also been able to reduce costs, giving a new impetus to its
economic expansion.

Future prospects for fossil energy, such as coal and oil,
seem less encouraging, for obviously it will not be possible
to avoid fatal price increases for industries which have to
extract dwindling reserves from the ground. But thanks to
nuclear energy, which is just starting to enter a phase of
industrial development, one may be able to look forward
to the future with confidence, safe from fears that one day
all energy supplies will have been exhausted.

It would be a pity if one became too concerned with the
purely quantitative facts and statistics, as it would mean
neglecting the humane aspects of the part that energy is
playing in the development of our industrial civilisation.
Also, in conclusion, it is no doubt a good thing to remember
this thought, from the French philosopher Bergson, who
put the whole problem of energy in its right place in the
scheme of things:[11]

'Man will only succeed in raising himself above the earth
when he finds a tool powerful enough to give him
sufficient support. Machines, whether driven by petroleum, coal, water or wind power, have given our organism

11. Quoted by Jean Majorelle in *L'économie de l'énergie* (course
taught at the Institute of Political Studies at the University of Paris,
1966–7). The quotation from Erasmus Darwin in the introduction is
also taken from this work.

such a vast extension, and such formidable power, so out of proportion to its size and to its strength, that surely none of this had been foreseen when the blueprints for our species were drawn up. In this immoderately swollen body, the soul remains as it always was, too small now to fill it, too weak to direct it. We need new reserves of potential energy – this time moral ones. The enlarged body is waiting for an enlarged soul. The machine requires a mysticism: it will only find its true direction, it will only be able to give service in proportion to its size when humanity, as yet still bowed towards the earth beneath its weight, manages to use it to stand upright and look towards the stars.'

BIBLIOGRAPHY

BLANCHET, *Dix ans d'application du Traité de la CECA à l'industrie charbonnière* (Centre international d'études et de recherches Européennes, Cours 1964, Editions Heule (Belgique)).

D. BLONDEL-SPINELLI, *L'énergie dans l'Europe des Six* (Editions Cujas, Paris, 1966).

COMMONWEALTH ECONOMIC COMMITTEE, *Sources of Energy* (London, 1966).

J. COUTURE and J. WALCH, 'L'industrie charbonnière en Europe occidentale', *Revue de l'industrie minérale* (August 1961).

G. DE CARMOY, *Le dossier européen de l'énergie – Les marchés, les industries, les politiques* (Collection INSEAD Management, 1971).

FRÉMONT FELIX, *World markets of tomorrow – a documented rebuttal to the theories of exponential growth* (Harper and Row, 1972).

P. GARDENT, 'Quelques aspects de la coordination de l'énergie, *Revue française de l'Energie* (November 1959).

R. GENDARME, 'La politique énergique européenne', *Revue économique* (July 1962).

N. B. GUYOL, *The world electric power industry* (University of California Press, Berkeley and Los Angeles, 1969).

MARC IPPOLITO, *Contribution à l'étude du problème énergique communautaire* (Librairie générale de Droit et de Jurisprudence, Paris, 1969).

Y. MAINGUY, *L'économie de l'énergie* (Collection Henri Hierche, Dunod, Paris, 1967).

J. MAJORELLE, *L'économie de l'énergie* (Université de Paris, Institut, d'Etudes politiques, 1966/7).

STATISTICS

SOCIÉTE DES NATIONS, *Annuaire statistique international de 1927 à 1941* (Geneva, 1928).

UNITED NATIONS, *Statistical papers – world energy supplies in selected years 1929–1950* (New York, September 1952).

OECD, *Statistiques de base de 1956 à 1970 – Statistiques de l'Energie* (Paris, 1972).

PUBLICATIONS OF THE OECD (FORMERLY OEEC)

Coal production and supplies for Western Europe in 1952 and 1953
(Second report of the Ministerial Coal Production Group, January
1953).

Quelques aspects du problème européen de l'énergie (Report prepared
for the OEEC by M. Louis Armand, June 1955).

L'Europe face à ses besoins croissants en énergie (Report prepared by
a group of experts, May/June 1956).

L'Energie en Europe – nouvelles perspectives (Consultative Commission
on Energy report, November 1960).

*Impact of natural gas on the consumption of energy in the OECD European
member countries* (OECD Publications, No. 25951, 1969).

6. The Social Relations of Science and Technology 1914-1939

Roy and Kay MacLeod

INTRODUCTION

Since the Second World War, the world has become accustomed to the arguments for investing public and private resources in scientific research and scientific education. Quite apart from military uses, science and technology, if widely used, are assumed capable of providing East and West with material prosperity, rational instruction, and an ordered world view. Most developing countries, until recently, have sought to share a fundamental view of science and technology – involving an acceptance of the values of scientific knowledge and its practical benefits for national economic developments. Since the late 1960s, however, the premise that science and technology are value-neutral, objectively beneficial activities, has come into question. The merits of industrial rationalisation, administrative centralisation and theories of competitive economic behaviour in relation to government policy, derived from hard won nineteenth-century beliefs in the efficacy of 'scientific method', are now widely disputed. The apparent misuse of environmental resources on a global scale has drawn attention to the possibility that wrong decisions can be arrived at scientifically, and to the responsibility of the scientific community to be candid and outspoken in the public debates which such issues involve.

Many of these questions, particularly as they affect international trade, the diffusion of skills, the deployment of technically qualified labour, and the uses of 'scientific management', have been discussed elsewhere in this volume and the next. Similarly, many of the substantive economic issues arising from the uses of science and technology have their origins in the Industrial Revolution, and have been discussed in volume 3, chapters 3 and 5 of the Fontana series. Many other issues germane to the present *Krise der Wissenschaft* belong more properly to a different essay, while still others, notably the set of epistemological questions concerning the possible effects of economic conditions upon the structure of scientific knowledge, require a different approach altogether.

The present essay has as its very limited object the task of describing a set of central themes which, with varying emphasis, have recurred in the social and economic history of science and technology within the last fifty years. This task is further limited by the fact that primary research has yet to be done on many historical questions concerning the relationship between economic development and the direction of scientific research, the role of research in innovation, the influence of government policy in application to industrial, medical, agricultural and social needs and the impact of science on war. If this is true of Britain, it is even more true of other countries of Western Europe, where flourishing scholarly interest in the history of industrialisation stands in sharp contrast to the overwhelming neglect of scientists and science in the social and economic history of this century. At present, an essay in this field which focuses on Britain exclusively, is distinctly incomplete.

Whatever its limitations, it may, however, pose questions which future historians might try to answer. In this context, the period chosen for this essay has a double importance. First, it is a period within which the historian can recognise – in the rise of European 'R and D efforts', the organisation of government research, the support of university science, and the repeated self-definition of professional interests – certain features of our contemporary institutional landscape. The germ of ideas – some current, some no longer fashionable – about possible connections between scientific investment and economic growth, about the role of government towards increasing and improving the stock of scientific manpower, and about the virtues of government intervention in high-technology industry, can be traced to this formative period. Second, it is within the period 1914–39 that scientists became recognised as, and saw themselves to be, economic creatures, and as such, no less vulnerable to military or commercial competition or economic fluctuation than other sections of society, set apart from the maelstrom only by the exceptional and self-regulated status accorded to custodians of scientific knowledge. These two themes form the subject of this chapter. Drawing upon a literature that is more frequently interpreted than analysed, these pages will chart, impressionistically, and in very broad outline, those aspects of public confidence, professional insecurity, government initiative and social responsibility which formed the social context of science in what our post-war generation know as the 'Aspirin Age'.

SCIENCE, TECHNOLOGY AND WAR

Between 1914 and 1918, the relationship between government, science and industry in Britain, as in most other European countries, was profoundly altered. In every country the war forced governments to assume direct responsibility for the direction of scientific research, for stimulating the supply of scientific manpower and for encouraging the application of scientific research to industry. That such a revolution was necessary had long been advocated by scientific lobbies in Britain, France and Germany which, since the 1870s, had unceasingly urged governments and manufacturing industry to extend their patronage of research and encourage its application. By the turn of the century the force of these arguments was, in Britain,[1] dramatised by evidence of the loss of critical science-based industries (particularly chemical dyes and optical instruments)[2] to Germany, and by growing

1. In Britain, one of the most important lobbies was the British Science Guild, formed in 1905 by Norman (later Sir Norman) Lockyer, editor of *Nature* (1869–1920). It functioned as a scientific 'ginger-group' for the promotion of scientific research and education until it was absorbed into the British Association in 1936.

2. On the loss of the chemical and optical industries to Germany, see, respectively, Lutz Haber, *The Chemical Industry, 1900–1930* (OUP, 1971), and Roy and Kay MacLeod, 'War and economic development: government and the optical industry in Britain,' in J. Winter (ed.), *War and Economic Development* (Cambridge, 1975), pp. 165–203.

appreciation of the competitive power of America and Japan. The key to technological, commercial and, ultimately, military supremacy, it was emphasised, came in the effective liaison between academic research and industrial development.

These arguments, frequently overdrawn for effect, masked important strengths and ignored certain weaknesses in the arrangements of all European powers. However, between 1895 and 1914, 'reformers' enjoyed a definite vogue in Britain and France, as fears of German efficiency increased. In Britain, for example, the National Physical Laboratory – a direct imitation of its German predecessor, the *Physikalische-technische Reichanstalt* in Charlottenburg – opened in 1900, with the intention of promoting the application of research to industry.[3] With the creation of the Development Commission in 1911 and the Medical Research Committee in 1913, the British government began to assume fresh responsibilities towards the promotion of agricultural and medical research. By 1910, through its Treasury Grant to the Universities, begun in 1889, Britain was spending annually almost £200,000[4] of public money on higher education, and about half of this sum was going towards provision for science and engineering. In France, a substantial scientific research fund – the Caisse Nationale des Recherches Scientifiques – was created in 1901. This, too, was designed to support fundamental research, especially with a view to industrial applications.[5]

These varied attempts on the part of both Britain and France to recover economic initiative through the support of science were, however, lacklustre in comparison with the example set by Germany. Indeed, the relative indifference shown by British manufacturers towards the use of research, and the education of managers, was, on the evidence of

3. On the early history of the NPL, see Richard Glazebrook, *Early Days at the N.P.L.* (London, 1933).
4. See H. Perkin, *Key Profession: A History of the Association of Scientific Workers*, (London, 1969), p. 33.
5. R. Gilpin, *France in the Age of the Scientific State* (Princeton, 1968), p. 154.

contemporaries, notorious.[6] In Germany, by contrast, it appeared that increased efforts were being made to improve the relations between science and industry, a process encouraged by officials and managers alike. Between 1900 and 1914, several industrial foundations, such as the Göttinger Vereinigung zür Förderung, were created with the help of the Prussian government. Even more important was the creation, in 1911, of the Kaiser Wilhelm Gesellschaft, with contributions of £750,000 from government and industry to support independent scientists in particular domains of physical and chemical research. The economic impact of such investments was not, in most cases, immediately apparent; yet, this 'endowment' of research was undertaken on a significant scale, as a token of faith in the eventual benefits to be derived in terms of industrial growth and national prestige.

From at least the 1880s, the British educational system, relatively insensitive to many economic changes, had begun to respond to pressure for greater numbers of scientific and technical graduates. Not in every case, however, did the 'career prospects' of these graduates match their own expectations.

By 1914, in Germany, the United States and, to a degree, in France, the scientific graduate could look forward to a career which might employ his knowledge of science. In Britain this was much less true. By 1914, there was a paradoxical contrast between the image of the scientist as the gifted, independent amateur of popular imagination, and the poverty of his prospects in the market place. With the exception of a few senior industrial posts, scientific salaries compared poorly with those of other 'professional'

6. The prevailing impression of the anti-scientific prejudices of British industry has been fixed by the pronouncements of such contemporary critics as the British Science Guild, and largely unchallenged by historians. Recently, however, it has been argued that this impression may have been misleading, since research was being undertaken by a number of firms before the war, and that its extent may have been deliberately obscured in the interests of trade secrecy. See Michael Sanderson, 'Research and the Firm in British Industry, 1919–1939,' *Science Studies*, 2 (April 1972), pp. 107–52.

men such as lawyers or doctors.[7]

Between 1902 and 1914, the 'pool' of scientific graduates in Britain, produced largely by the new, provincial university colleges such as Leeds, Manchester, Birmingham, Sheffield and Liverpool, had swollen from 2,000 to 8,000.[8] Four options were open to the young graduate – the universities, government service, private industry or school teaching. However, the first three options were very limited, and the majority of scientists, by default, chose school teaching. There were, for example, about 300[9] teaching posts for scientists in British universities in 1902, a further 250 places in government laboratories, and perhaps 180–230 posts in British industry. This was in stark contrast with Germany, where the chemical industries alone employed over 1,500 scientists.[10] Opportunities for research in Britain were rare. In 1914, apart from the highly competitive scholarships available from the '1851 Exhibition', there were only 214 full-time postgraduate research awards open to graduates anywhere in the kingdom;[11] moreover, since there was a 'long waiting list' for such awards, they were rarely accessible to recent graduates. Given the preoccupation of the majority of university teachers with the prior demands of teaching, it was not surprising that research in the universities seemed to be 'a hobby', and most universities apparently incapable of generating much original research, or of applying that knowledge to economic development.[12]

7. In 1914, for example, the salary of a university lecturer varied between about £150 and £250. See W. Makiowiez, *Morning Post* (4 June 1914). This compared badly with the salaries available to other professional men: a barrister, for example, enjoyed an average salary of £478; a dentist, £368; and a Treasury Principal, £855. See Guy Routh, *Occupation and Pay in Great Britain, 1906–1960* (Cambridge, 1965), pp. 64, 66.

8. R. M. Pike, *The Growth of Scientific Institutions and the Employment of Natural Science Graduates in Britain, 1900–1960* (unpublished MSc thesis, University of London, 1961), pp. 2–3; p. 36.   9. *Ibid.*, p. 35.

10. D. S. L. Cardwell, *The Organisation of Science in Britain* (London, 1972), pp. 207–9.

11. PRO, DSIR 17/1, Research Paper D.

12. F. Soddy, *Science and Life* (London, 1920), p. 63.

Thanks, in part, to the zealous claims made for scientific education between 1880–1910, the scientific graduate perceived his economic poverty more sharply than his predecessors. In Britain, the formation of the Junior Staff Association in 1909 was symptomatic of a growing militancy among younger scientists.[13] This phenomenon of rising economic expectations and mounting professional frustration was not confined to Britain. Both in England and France, as Sidney and Beatrice Webb noted, 'the teachers in the schools and the professors in the colleges began to assert their right to manage the institutions as they alone know.'[14] Finally, in 1914, the relative insecurity of younger scientists impelled the journal *Science Progress* to urge the formation of a 'National Union of Scientific Workers.'[15]

This evident frustration among scientists must be seen, to an extent, in the context of widespread industrial and political turmoil in the period 1910–14.[16] When war came, social and economic relationships were radically altered, and within this alteration came decisive changes in the role of the man of science, and in the public image of science. In Britain, the scientist became a national hero – somewhere lower than the fighting soldier, perhaps, but vastly higher than the politician. Technical expertise and rational judgement offered solutions, not excuses. As the *Cambridge Magazine* commented in 1916:

the word 'science' was on everyone's lips and does yeoman's service in almost every newspaper . . . Its very name seems to have suddenly discovered a talismanic power which is somewhat perplexing to those who find their paths menaced by the glare of limelight.[17]

Moreover, between 1915 and 1918, the exigencies of war made the setting of national goals a necessary task. This task

13. See H. Perkin, *op. cit.*, (note 4).

14. Sidney and Beatrice Webb, *The History of Trade Unionism* (London, 1920), p. 654.

15. *Science Progress*, IX (July 1914), pp. 353–4.

16. See George Dangerfield, *The Strange Death of Liberal England* (London, 1935, 1961).

17. *Cambridge Magazine*, 6 (4 November 1916), p. 76.

required, and embraced, policies for scientific research, education and industry.

That such sweeping developments would actually occur within thirty-six months, after so many years of discussion, could not have been foreseen on the eve of the war, when it seemed that all psychological and technical advantages lay with Germany. It was, after all, the essential moment for Germany to demonstrate her scientific superiority. For the first year of the war, she dictated the pattern of warfare. On the Western Front, as H. G. Wells remarked, Germany produced 'novelty after novelty', and 'each novelty . . . more or less saved their men and unexpectedly destroyed ours'. Britain, on the other hand, could produce nothing to match – 'except in the field of recruiting posters.' As Wells went on to describe, Britain lacked aeroplanes capable of destroying Zeppelins; she could not compete with Germany in the techniques of trench construction; the shortage of high explosives was 'notorious'; and there was no antidote to the enemy's submarine. Most significant, Britain still had

> to make efficient use of poison gas and of armoured protection in advances against machine guns in trench warfare. And so throughout almost the entire range of our belligerent activities we are to this day being conservative, imitative and amateurish, when victory can fall only to the most vigorous employment of the best scientific knowledge.[18]

Crises on the battlefield were matched by difficulties on the Home Front, where from the outset of war, imports of critical materials – chemical dyes, drugs, optical and chemical glass, and optical munitions, all normally supplied from Germany – immediately ceased. Until mid-1915, as younger scientists were casually directed to the trenches,[19] scientific societies vainly attempted to interest government in the usefulness of scientists as advisers and innovators in the products of war material. It was not until July 1915 that, with the formation of the Ministry of Munitions under

18. H. G. Wells, *The Times*, 11 June 1915.
19. See R. W. Reid, *Tongues of Conscience: War and the Scientist's Dilemma* (London, 1969), p. 39.

Lloyd George, systematic attempts were made to apply scientific expertise to the solution of the specific problems of submarine, aerial and trench warfare.

In July 1915, the British government set up a Munitions Invention Department (MID) and a Board of Invention and Research (BIR),[20] to service the army and navy, respectively. These organisations drew their membership from among the most distinguished scientists of the day, and deployed enormous intellectual resources to the tasks of submarine detection and high energy explosives, and the uses of new materials and explosives. Similar steps were taken in France, where the Minister of Public Instruction and Fine Arts, M. Paul Painlevé, urged his government to 'follow the example of the National Convention' and 'call on the services of scientists and engineers as well as those of the makers of armaments and blacksmiths'. He recommended the formation of a Central Department of Inventions,

> to direct the endeavours of the inventors to certain fixed ends and to coordinate their researches; to sift from the mass of proposals those which are likely to be useful and to help move them towards practical realisation.[21]

The *Direction des Inventions*, formed in December 1915, brought together in France, scientists of 'conspicuous distinction' to direct research on behalf of all the services.[22] Laboratories and workshops were placed at their disposal. From these developments emerged fresh experience with new machinery for centralisation and co-ordination – items which would later feature prominently on the agenda of

20. On the work of the BIR, see Roy MacLeod and Kay Andrews, 'Scientific Advice for the War at Sea: The Board of Invention and Research,' *Journal of Contemporary History*, VI (1971), pp. 3–40.

21. PRO, Min/Mun 5/43: 263. 8/14. Munitions Inventions Department: Coordination with the French *Direction des Inventions*.

22. The central organisation of science for military purposes had occurred earlier in France – during the Napoleonic era and, again, during the Franco-Prussian war. See M. Crosland, 'Science and the Franco-Prussian War,' *Social Studies of Science*, VI (1976), 185–214. Little of this experience remained, however, to guide the French government in 1914, which had to relearn techniques of directing research to immediate military goals.

T.C.   L

peacetime policy-making.

Within the European scientific community, the war had other consequences. The cherished ethos of value-free, objective scholarship, knowing no national boundaries, withered in the blasts of the first year of war. Propaganda exhorted the application of intellectual skills to military endeavour, and particularly in France and Germany, scientists fell prey to war fever. The opposing sides flocked to war work. Among the most ardent German chauvinists was the chemist Wilhelm Ostwald, at whose laboratories many British chemists had studied before the war, but who contributed to the infamous 'Academics Declaration' of 1915.[23] Perhaps the best known German scientist to emerge from the war was Fritz Haber, who held responsibility for the organisation of gas warfare. More important in an economic and scientific sense, however, was Haber's pre-war work on the 'fixation' of atmospheric nitrogen, which enabled Germany to survive for a considerable time the British blockade of nitrates. Without the ability to synthesise ammonia, the German explosives and fertiliser industries would have been paralysed by 1916.[24]

In Britain and France, praise for German scholarship and *Kultur* ended abruptly with the beginning of war. Scientific communications were disrupted, and international cooperation between the Allies and the Central Powers came to a standstill. Among the Allies, however, there grew procedures for the sharing of technical information which became of lasting importance. In both Britain and France (and later, in America) rapid strides were made in the application of physics, chemistry, physiology and mathematics to problems of aerodynamics, offensive armaments, high explosives, gas defence and range-finding. Medical science, especially in the fields of bacteriology, parisitology and nutrition, was directly stimulated by military and

23. On the propagandist activities of German academics, see Fritz Ringer, *The Decline of the German Mandarins* (Cambridge, 1969), pp. 180–99; Harry Paul, *The Sorcerer's Apprentice: The French Scientist's Image of German Science, 1840–1919* (University of Florida, 1972), pp. 29–53.

24. See Reid, *op. cit.* (note 19), pp. 36–7; 40–2; 45–6.

civilian necessities. In France, Marie Curie devoted herself
to the organisation of a radiological service, which by the
end of the war had treated over a million soldiers with
techniques developed, but not applied, before 1914.[25]

Given the direct bearing of chemical knowledge on the
manufacture and use of munitions, the rank and file of
chemists came into particular prominence. In Britain, and
later in America, they were directed to the Chemical
Warfare service, the government arsenals, or to the munitions industries. Such was the demand for their skills that
'men flocked back from abroad; schools were depleted of
their teachers, and many who were on the point of abandoning chemistry found at last the opportunity (of employment) which had been denied them.'[26] By the end of the
war, nearly 2,000 of the 3,000-odd members of the Institute
of Chemistry in Britain had taken some part in war service.[27]
At the same time, though fewer in number, physicists were
drafted to the engineering and aeronautical departments of
the National Physical Laboratory, the Royal Aircraft
Establishment, Farnborough, and to laboratories under the
supervision of the Admiralty and the War Office. Among
the most striking scientific achievements in this sphere was
the development of sound-ranging techniques from the
acoustics research of W. H. Bragg and Ernest Rutherford.
Everywhere in Britain, university laboratories became
'small factories' for the testing, preparation and development of materials. As H. A. L. Fisher, later responsible for
the Education Act of 1918, observed, 'the Professor, the
Lecturer, the Research Assistant and the Research Student'
had

> suddenly become powerful assets to the nation. Whatever
> university you may choose to visit you will find it to be
> the scene of delicate and recondite investigations, result-
> ing here in a more deadly explosive, there in a stronger
> army boot.[28]

25. *Ibid.*, pp. 41–5.   26. *Proc. Inst. Chem.*, 1918 (Pt. 1), p. 33.
27. *Proc. Inst. Chem.*, 1919 (Pt. I), p. 3.
28. Preface to *The British Universities and the War: A Record and its
Meaning* (London, 1917).

Evidently the universities were no longer 'ivory towers', but were deeply implicated in the military and economic embattlement of Europe.

With the mobilisation of science, came a slow extension of 'scientific method' into government administration. In July 1915, with the formation of the Advisory Council for Scientific and Industrial Research, a government White Paper announced:

> There is a strong consensus of opinion among persons engaged both in science and in industry, that a special need exists at the present time for new machinery and for additional State assistance in order to promote and organise scientific research with a view especially to its application to trade and industry. It is well known that many of our industries have, since the outbreak of war, suffered through our inability to produce at home certain articles and materials required in trade processes, the manufacture of which has become localised abroad and particularly in Germany because science has there been more thoroughly and effectively applied to the solution of scientific problems bearing on trade and industry and to the elaboration of economical and improved processes of manufacture.[29]

The major significance of Britain's first attempts at the central direction of science lay not in the creation of *ad hoc* advisory bodies to deal with specific problems created by the war, but in its willingness to consider policies of economic intervention and planning as necessary for 'winning the peace'. As the White Paper went on:

> It appears incontrovertible that if we are to advance or even maintain our industrial position, we must as a nation, aim at such a development of scientific and industrial research as will place us in a position to expand and strengthen our industries and to compete successfully with the most highly organised of our rivals . . .

For the next fifty years, the Department of Scientific and Industrial Research (DSIR) applied itself to these policies.

29. *Scheme for the Organisation and Development of Scientific and Industrial Research* (Cd. 8005), I, 1914–16, p. 351.

Eventually, its work was complemented by the activities of the Medical, and Agricultural Research Councils and (after 1965) was continued by the Science and Social Science Research Councils; but throughout the period 1918–39, the DSIR assumed the leadership of government science in Britain, and greatly influenced work done in the British universities.[30] From its organisational model developed variations which found their way into the machinery of government in Australia, South Africa, India, Ceylon and Canada.

From the outset, the DSIR adopted three, interdependent priorities: 1) the promotion of fundamental research through a programme of awards to students and university researchers; 2) the definition of national objectives in certain fields of applied research, closely linked to economic and social goals; and 3) the promotion of co-operative industrial research through the formation of Research Associations.

Although the creation of the DSIR had been precipitated by the war, the Advisory Council were, from the first, anxious to emphasise their concern with fundamental as well as applied research. To encourage the supply of 'competent researchers' was a vital element in the Department's strategy, but since most eligible scientists were absorbed in war work, it was not until 1919–20 that the first awards to researchers were made on a significant scale. In that year, 159 grants were made, at a cost of about £50,000. The support of university scientists through research grants and studentships did not, however, entirely appease those critics of government policy who saw science as woefully absent from systematic secondary education and from the higher echelons of management and the civil service. In May 1916, Sir Ray Lankester, a noted zoologist and a leading advocate of scientific education, organised a

30. On the history and organisation of the DSIR, see Sir Harry Melville, *The Department of Scientific and Industrial Research* (London, 1962); for the history of the MRC, see Sir A. Landsborough Thomson, *Half a Century of Medical Research*, vol. 1, *Origins and Policy of the M.R.C.* (HMSO, 1973).

public meeting on the 'Neglect of Science'. This meeting, chaired by Lord Rayleigh, and attended by scores of leading British scientists and educators, provoked a flurry of comment in the national press, much of it condemning, *inter alia* the dangerous ignorance of civil servants who had permitted the export of glycerine to Germany for months after the outbreak of war. The proposed solution lay in the radical restructuring of secondary education, and in the introduction of technical experts and advisers on many levels of government.

In 1916, the Asquith government, in terms broadly sympathetic to these arguments, appointed a committee under Professor J. J. Thomson, director of the Cavendish Laboratory, to examine

the position occupied by natural science in the educational system of Great Britain . . . and to advise what measures are needed to promote its study, regard being had to the requirements of a liberal education, to the advancement of pure science, and to the interests of the trades, industries and professions which particularly depend upon applied science.[31]

Eighteen months later the Thomson Committee reported, urging that science be recognised as an essential subject in the entrance examinations of the public schools and in the examinations for the School Certificate.

Like many other proposals undertaken with a view to post-war 'reconstruction',[32] the Thomson Committee's recommendations, and other educational recommendations arising from the 'Neglect of Science' campaign, were to fall foul of legislative obstacles and economic retrenchment. However, better luck attended the Government, and the DSIR, in the achievement of its second major objective – the formation of national priorities for government research. Between 1916 and 1920, acting through several new 'Research Boards', the DSIR encouraged the economic and

31. *Report of the Committee appointed to inquire into the position of natural science in the educational system of Great Britain* (Cd. 9011), ix, 1918, p. 471.
32. On the Government's policies for reconstruction, see Paul Johnson, *Land Fit for Heroes* (Chicago, 1968).

industrial exploitation of knowledge in several well-defined sectors. The creation of the Fuel Research Board, for example, derived from fears that coal – the source of Britain's industrial power – would be overtaken after the war by oil, with serious consequences for the economy. The Board set itself the task, first, of surveying the country's coal reserves, and, second, of reviewing their usefulness for industrial purposes with a view to producing economically useful by-products, including smokeless fuels.

In a different sphere, the Industrial Fatigue Research Board worked on problems arising directly from operational conditions in munitions factories, and on strategies for works management that could be applied to civilian industries generally. The Food Research Board, which owed its origins to the German submarine blockade, began by studying the physiology of organic and synthetic foodstuffs, and the chemistry of food preservatives. The Forest Products Research Board owed its conception to the world shortage of softwood building timber, and the consequent wholesale felling of British woodlands. By 1920, Britain was importing £20 million worth of timber annually. While the new Forestry Commission began to replant British trees, the Forest Products Research Board undertook to study the most economic ways of cultivating and processing timber at home and in the Empire. Other Research Boards were directed towards more immediate returns. The Building Research Board, for example, was directly related to the supposed 'housing boom' which was to have been a major plank in the reconstruction programme. Its function was to advise on the most economic uses of building materials. The Radio Research Board, reflecting wartime developments in communications, was intended to stimulate wireless research for consumer needs.

The third objective of the DSIR – the encouragement of scientific research in industry – was also on a secure footing by the end of the war. Meeting the demands of total war had required dramatic changes in the procurement and use of resources, the supply of machinery, the setting of wage levels and the enforcement of price controls. For the science-based industries, closely involved in the production of munitions, this relationship was made more complex by unprecedented government attempts to stimulate technological innovation by regulating supply and demand, production and distribution. This was done directly, through industrial rationalisation and product specialisation, accompanied by the mobilisation and deployment of scientific and technical assistance to specific industrial priorities.

In no industry did this combination of financial and technical assistance have more dramatic results than in the optical glass and instruments industry. At the beginning of the war, 60% of Britain's supply of optical glass – essential for the manufacture of binoculars, field glasses, telescopes, surveying instruments and range-finders – was imported from Germany. Thanks to financial and technical assistance from the Board of Trade Optical Munitions and Glassware Department (OMGD), the glass firm of Chance Brothers were able to increase their annual optical glass output from 12,000 lbs in 1914 to about 200,000 lbs by the end of the war. At the same time, Chance was able to diversify and market 72 types of optical glasses, many of which were previously made only in Germany. With this new capital investment, and the introduction of new machinery and skilled labour, the optical instrument firms increased their output by a factor of twenty. By the end of the war, there was every reason to anticipate a prosperous future for an industry which had effectively overcome its structural, financial and technical deficiencies during the war.[33]

In addition, there was a vigorous commitment to scientific research among glass manufacturers, symbolised in the formation of a Society of Glass Technology, established to promote continuous dialogue between manufacturers and scientists. Most significant, the DSIR had promoted the formation of two university departments for the training of optical designers, and had established three Research Associations for the glass, scientific instruments and photographic industries.

The Government's third objective was intended to be

33. See MacLeod, *op. cit.* (note 2).

met by these several Research Associations, which were founded in the belief that technical problems beyond the capacity of an individual firm could be tackled successfully (both scientifically and commercially) on a co-operative basis, with funds provided jointly by government and industry. In August 1916, £1,000,000 of public money was set aside for this scheme, and the DSIR was given its supervision. Each Research Association was financed on a pound for pound basis, but the presumption was that within a few years each would be self-sufficient. By 1918, there were eight Research Associations, operating at an annual cost of £198,000.

This example of government participation was by no means the most drastic form of government intervention in industry, nor did it involve government resources as conspicuously as did the take-over of private chemical interests to form British Dyes Ltd. The critical state of the dyestuffs industry demanded 'something more than a loan or a grant-in-aid'.[34] The Government began with an investment of £1,700,000 in the spring of 1915; by November 1918, following a merger with Levinstein Ltd it became the British Dyestuffs Corporation, with a share capital of £10 million. Through this combine, 75% of synthetic dye manufacture in Britain was brought under unified financial control. For the next seven years, until the creation of Imperial Chemical Industries Ltd, the Government played a key financial role in ensuring the survival of the industry. Indeed, under pressure of war, the Government had assisted many essential industries; but it was in the science-based industries, with their appreciable uncertainties and high development costs, that government participation became a continuing feature, long after the immediate pressures of war had ended.

Within the scientific community, the Government's policy towards science-based industry bred a new confidence. In 1917, Professor J. J. Dobbie, President of the Institute of Chemistry, caught the optimistic mood of his fellow chemists when he described the 'enormous impetus' the war had

34. Haber, *op. cit.* (note 2), pp. 234–5.

given the chemical industries. There was every expectation that industries, conceived in the conditions of war, 'would not be allowed to perish when peace comes.' On the contrary, the expansion of industry would mean 'a greatly increased demand for chemists'.[35] Presumably, a similar demand for physicists would eventually follow.

There were other reasons for optimism among scientists. The war had upset traditional relationships between managers and men; it had confirmed and extended the power of the trade unions, bringing a measure of worker-participation in industry, and giving wide publicity to ideas of social reconstruction, based in part on an 'alliance' between workers 'by hand and by brain' widely proclaimed by the emerging Labour Party. For many professional scientists, these developments were, to say the least, provocative. As many had found, the war had not only put a value on their labour; it had also forced them out of their previous professional isolation. The institutional barriers which had frustrated collective action before the war gave way to the experience of working together on centrally-directed tactical projects. This in turn promoted a sense of professional identity among scientists based often in government departments, universities and in the qualifying institutions. In 1917, Beatrice Webb called attention to the growing importance of the 'professional association'.[36] Between 1917 and 1920, new associations were formed in the universities (the Association of University Teachers), the civil service (the Institution of Professional Civil Servants), the chemical industry (the British Association of Chemists), and among physicists (the Institute of Physics). Some members of these associations joined a small group of militant scientists who founded in 1917 a National Union of Scientific Workers (NUSW) to advance the economic interests of scientists and to represent their opinions on

35. Presidential Address to the Institute of Chemistry, *Proc. Inst. Chem.*, 1917 (Pt. II), p. 21.

36. Special Supplement on Professional Associations, *The New Statesman*, IX (Pt. I) (2 April 1917), pp. 2–24; Pt. II (28 April 1917), pp. 26–40.

national scientific and political issues.

The war had vividly demonstrated the power of *organised* scientific invention for material destruction. Reviewing, in 1919, the role of Minerva in the service of Mars, Lord Moulton, Cambridge mathematician, Liberal MP, and director of wartime munitions work, reflected that

> but for the stupendous advances that Science had made in times within . . . memory . . . no catastrophe at once so wide-spreading and so deep reaching could have happened. In scale and intensity alike, this War represents the results of the totality of scientific progress.[37]

In these circumstances, it was not difficult to be sceptical of the 'totality of scientific progress'. A new range of barbarous inventions symbolised this progress, and it was by no means clear whether post-war European civilisation was better for their appearance. If any lesson could be learned, however, it was that State intervention, and the organisation of scientific endeavour, had joined forces to remarkable effect. The pursuit of science, as a social enterprise, emerged from the war strengthened by the experience. It was true that, as Sir Charles Parsons put it, the work of scientists had been 'directed more to the application of known principles, trade knowledge and properties of matter . . . than to the making of new . . . discoveries',[38] but this temporary pause in scientific discovery (if such there was) witnessed the invention of machinery to promote scientific education and research in peacetime. In Britain, an elaborate structure of governmental and industrial coordination had been devised, and the DSIR was given almost unanimous support. With this structure, and this coordination, came also the association of scientists in collective economic and, later, political action on an unprecedented scale. Mediated by the State, research bearing upon national and corporate economic interests became a hallmark of scientific activity in Britain and Western Europe. In the process, the scientist lost his amateur status and

---

37. Lord Moulton, *Science and War* (Rede Lecture, Cambridge, 1919).
38. Sir Charles Parsons, *Presidential Address to the British Association*, 1919, reprinted in *Chemical News* (19 September 1919), p. 141.

entered a world in which professional goals, the pursuit of knowledge and the demands of economic interest were to fitfully co-exist.

SCIENTISTS, GOVERNMENT AND TECHNOLOGICAL DEVELOPMENT, 1920-1929

After the brief euphoria of armistice, the immediate postwar years saw enormous displacements in economic, social and political beliefs in Britain and on the Continent. The landscape of world politics in the early 1920s was altered, dramatically, by the socialist revolution in Russia, the emergence of the USA as a major power, and the overthrow of the monarchy in Germany. At the same time, France was crippled by the physical devastation of war, while in Britain, the decline of international markets and the shift in world trade, plunged the country into a deflationary spiral of depressed wages and unemployment. By mid-1921, as hyper-inflation raged in Europe, and industrial recession savaged social policies in Britain, the brave hopes of reconstruction faded.

While each country in Europe faced special economic and political problems, there were certain common factors which affected public attitudes towards science, its professional character and organisation, and its political importance. First, there was a continuing concern, shared by laymen and scientists alike, with the paradox of 'scientific progress'. For some scientists, this was complicated by the question, raised by the war, of their personal responsibility for the effects of science in the postwar world. The different responses to that question within the scientific community reflected conflicting views of science and whether it should remain chiefly a vocation of autonomous intellectuals, or become chiefly a tool of government and industry. Second, while research in certain sectors of private industry flourished, government support of research was curtailed by policies of economic retrenchment which blighted the prospects of scientists, whether in government service or in the universities. As the Depression overtook Europe in 1929, these tensions, between the public and professional expectations of science, became acute.

Public Science and Personal Responsibility

In Britain, the effects of retrenchment were particularly severe, partly because post-war optimism had set expectations so high. At the end of the war there were an estimated 13,000 scientists in Britain. In the words of an early member of the National Union of Scientific Workers, they were facing a new world:

> The League of Nations is arriving, woman is arriving, the scientist is arriving. But the workers of science in a new land, without landmarks, will be for some time faced with conditions altogether more complex and dynamic than those which confronted their predecessors.[39]

The war had destroyed both the notional neutrality of science, and the idea that the scientist was an unequivocally benevolent agent of social well-being. Instead, science seemed to many to be both 'Destroyer and Healer in One,'[40] and led Robert Blatchford to reflect that 'Putting the power of modern science into the hands of man was like giving an urchin an axe. What will he do with it? Will he chop firewood for his mother or axe down father's cherry tree?'[41]

For the most part, the public audience welcomed the 'marvels and mysteries' of science with enthusiasm. In the midst of excitement generated by quantum physics, cosmic rays, and the 'new biology', J. W. N. Sullivan celebrated the 'spirit of adventure, the sense of boundless and glorious possibilities' of 'our romantic and daring men of science'.[42] The newspapers responded eagerly to this wave of interest,

39. *Cambridge Review*, XXXIX (14 February 1918), pp. 263–4.
40. William Archer, *Daily News* (7 October 1918).
41. R. Blatchford, *As I lay a-thinking* (London, 1924), p. 206. Blatchford himself was optimistic that science offered 'a welfare and happiness beyond the dreams of most idealistic builders of utopias.'
42. J. W. N. Sullivan, *Aspects of Science* (London, 1923), p. 147.

titillating their audiences with details of advances in medicine, and terrifying them with stories of new and secret 'death-rays'. On balance, however, people were not interested in abstruse discoveries:

> they liked a man who invented amusing or useful things rather than one who merely expanded the corpus of heavy knowledge . . . The sort of scientific invention . . . that made the most popular reading was a wireless receiver that could be fitted inside a hat.[43]

Most of all, the public appreciated those technical miracles which had brought electricity, entertainment and new materials into their lives.[44]

In the 1920s, Europe moved from the age of steam to an age of electricity. Germany and America led the way, and by 1924, 67% and 73% of their industrial power, respectively, came from electricity.[45] The post-war years saw the rationalisation of power supply and the massive expansion of the electrical supply industries in Europe and America. In Britain, the creation of the Central Electricity Generating Board in 1926 finally reduced the 592 generating stations in operation into 144 base-load stations linked, six years later in a National Grid. At the same time, voltages, which had previously varied even from street to street, were standardised. The results were dramatic. In 1920 there were 730,000 electrical consumers; by 1939, there were almost 9 million; moreover the average price per unit had halved. As domestic consumption increased, so did the demand for electrical appliances, which were supplied in Europe by research-intensive firms such as GEC and Siemens in Britain, and Phillips in Holland.

43. R. Graves and A. Hodge, *The Long Weekend* (New York, 1963), p. 92.

44. On the growth and impact of the electrical, radio, synthetic fabrics and motor vehicles industries, see David S. Landes, *The Unbound Prometheus: Technological Change and Industrial Development in Western Europe from 1750 to the Present* (Cambridge, 1970), pp. 419–85; A. Plummer, *New British Industries in the Twentieth Century* (London, 1937); Derek H. Aldcroft, *The Inter-war Economy: Britain, 1919–1939* (London, 1970), pp. 177–202.

45. Aldcroft, *ibid.*, p. 191.

Another technical development which transformed the lives of almost every citizen, irrespective of income bracket, was radio. In Britain, the number of radio licences increased after the establishment of the first wireless station – '2LO' – from 36,000 in 1924 to 217,000 in 1928. By 1930, the wireless industry in Britain was reputed to have an annual turnover of £30 million. Like radio, synthetic fibres, particularly rayon, found a popular market. As skirts rose during the war, and public taste and tolerance changed, so did the demand for rayon for stockings and underwear. Firms such as Courtaulds established an early lead during the war, and between 1920 and 1929 British manufacture of rayon increased from 6 million pounds to 52.7 million pounds. While most people could afford radio and silk stockings, the motor car was still a symbol of relative affluence in the 1920s. British producers lagged behind their American competitors. Nevertheless, with the rationalisation of motor manufacturers and increasing public demand, the number of motor vehicles in Britain grew from 160,000 in 1918 to over a million by 1926.

Among a growing audience, however, the pleasure to be had from new technology was qualified by concern about the future consequences of scientific research. Antipositivist movements in France, and Weimar Germany, and a rash of predictive literature[46] in Britain, were, in different ways, hallmarks of this uncertainty. In Britain, some scientists argued that the future would find an accommodation between knowledge and wisdom. Others predicted that scientific discovery had brought not a more refined moral sense, but rather a greater arrogance which would lead not to the victory of Daedalus, but to the destruction of Icarus.[47] The future of chemical warfare was a particular case in point. The twenties saw a proliferation of arguments for and against the use of gas as a 'humane'

46. The Routledge series, *Today and Tomorrow*, which began in 1921 and published over 100 titles, is one illustration of this phenomenon.
47. See J. B. S. Haldane, *Daedalus* (London, 1924) and Bertrand Russell, *Icarus* (London, 1924).

instrument of war.[48] In Holland, the Dutch Chemical Society questioned the perversion of chemical research for military purposes,[49] and in Britain, Professor Frederick Soddy, a leading socialist, and Nobel prizewinner in Chemistry, protested in 1920 against the attempts of the War Office to involve the universities in chemical weapons research.

For a very few scientists, in Britain, and on the Continent, the situation required a positive choice. He could either return to his vocation, shutting the laboratory door firmly behind him, or he could come forward to play an active role as any other man of knowledge might do. But if he did the first, he could not escape the consequences of denying the second. In Germany, during the 1920s, academics were deeply divided on the desirability of preserving a Weberian traditionalism, or supporting university reforms which would involve the academic community intimately in the life of the nation.[50] In France, a symposium on *L'Avenir de la France* in 1921 drew an appeal to French scientists to abandon the *tour d'ivoire* and, in particular, to extend the benefits of scientific research to industry. In Britain, Sir Richard Gregory, successor to Sir Norman Lockyer as editor of the influential journal *Nature* (1920–39), preached the necessity of political participation, urging that the proven rationality of the scientist gave him a particular responsibility to bring 'reason' to politics. He urged scientists to work as 'political insiders' in Parliament, or as 'scientific outsiders' in pressure groups, and associations, advising and commenting on issues where scientific knowledge was instrumental.[51]

48. See, for example, J. B. S. Haldane, *Callinicus: A Defence of Chemical Warfare* (London, 1925).

49. Arie Rip and Egbert Boeker, 'Scientists and Social Responsibility in the Netherlands,' *Social Studies of Science*, 5 (1975), p. 459.

50. Ringer, *op. cit.* (note 23), pp. 352–434.

51. In 1921, Gregory reminded the British Association that 'unsatisfactory social conditions were not a necessary consequence of the advance of science but of the incapacity to use it rightly.' Address to the Corresponding Societies of the British Association, September 1921, p. 488.

In the event, Gregory's appeal was ignored by most British scientists who preferred the traditional neutrality of the scientific institutions. They were content, as J. W. N. Sullivan complained bitterly 'to sit in the circle and help beat the tomtoms', leaving political matters 'in the hands of the witchdoctors'.[52] But among a small minority, searching arguments about the social conduct of science, amplified by doubts about the uses to which their knowledge was being put, and given force by the economic plight in which many young scientists found themselves, contributed to their association in Britain with political groups such as the Guild Socialists, the Labour Party and even the embryonic Communist Party. The economic and political pressures upon scientists underlined Julien Benda's argument that it was pointless to deplore the 'corruption' of the 'clerk' in the modern world; the 'real evil' was not the 'great betrayal' of the clerk in his passion for politics, but 'the impossibility of leading the life of the clerk in the world today'.[53] In Britain, political action among scientists was motivated, not only by 'a desire for much higher remuneration . . . decent status and social standing', but by a social and political vision 'of the possibilities in science, whether pure or applied, of manpower and organisation'.[54] In response to such a vision, left-wing 'scientific outsiders' demanded for scientists not only a share in the profits of research, but a voice in the internal management of research and the direction of research in the national interest.

This conflict between professional ideals and economic realities was sharpened by the failure of the post-war world to bring that material prosperity which had been anticipated during the war. The relative success of the communications, electricity and transport industries, which were based on scientific discoveries pre-dating the war, and which were strengthened by an industrial structure developed during the war, stood in stark contrast with the poor performance

52. Sullivan, *op. cit.* (note 42), pp. 102–4.
53. Julien Benda, *The Great Betrayal* (London, 1928), pp. 127–8.
54. *Cambridge Magazine* (16 February 1918), pp. 445–6.

of other industries. Research investment in the dyestuffs industry in Britain, for example, proved an immediate victim of the recession. British Dyes, after spending £250,000 on improving their laboratories in 1919, went into a 'swift decline which impaired the quality of work, destroyed the continuity of the research programme, and lowered the morale of the staff'.[55] At Levenstein's, the chemical laboratory staff was reduced from 80 to 30 between 1920 and 1923, while during the same years, the Institute of Chemistry recorded an increase in the number of unemployed chemists from 0.7% of its membership to 5.3%.[56] Although industry had largely recovered from the recession by 1924, the chemical industry throughout the 1920s failed to absorb the output of university chemists attracted into the profession during and after the war. By 1928, the British dyestuffs industry as a whole was employing only two thirds of the technical and research staff it had employed in 1920.[57]

Moreover, discontinuities in the supply and demand of professionals became commonplace. Thus, at a time when the British market was overstocked with chemists, there was a conspicuous shortage of chemical engineers, oil engineers, metallurgists and applied chemists.[58] This situation was not unique to Britain. Evidence collected by the International Labour Office in 1924 revealed that 'engineers and chemists complain of unemployment in Austria, Finland, Great Britain, Hungary, the Netherlands, Poland, Russia,

---

55. Haber, *op. cit.* (note 2), pp. 355–6.

56. *Proc. Inst. Chem.*, 1923 (Pt. I), p. 29. One unemployed chemist warned his more fortunate colleagues against complacency: 'Can you look into the future', he asked, 'without seeking the grim spectre of unemployment obstructing your view, a ghostly figure that is a stern reality . . . at the present moment?' 'A Safe Job,' *British Association of Chemists Bulletin* (July 1922), p. 10.

57. In 1920 the industry employed 714 full time technical and research staff; in 1928 the industry employed only 483. Plummer, *op. cit.* (note 44), p. 266.

58. See M. Sanderson, *The Universities and British Industry* (London, 1972), pp. 289–91.

Spain and Sweden'.[59] In France, where Henri Le Chatelier complained bitterly of the 'ludicrous indifference' and the 'encyclopedic ignorance' of industrialists towards science,[60] only 50% of all chemists leaving French technical colleges each year could find employment in research.[61] The situation was worse in Germany where hyper-inflation devastated the professional classes:

> Professorial salaries, in terms of their purchasing power lagged far behind their pre-war levels, institute budgets still further behind, and savings, whether personal wealth or institutional endowment, were wiped out.[62]

This situation caused C. F. G. Masterman to warn that throughout Europe, the class which 'makes ideas and diffuses knowledge' was 'perishing of hunger and cold'.[63] As events would show, the political response of academic scientists to promises of national economic improvement, whether achieved by national socialism or by other means, was to be, at best, problematic.

The direction of research and the organisation of scientists

In the years immediately after the war, the relative success of the science-based industries, often in contrast to the debilitation of traditional industries, led governments in European countries to explore alternative ways of invigorating industry through the applications of research. There were two models – one provided by the USA – where science was applied to the service of *laissez-faire* capitalism: and another provided by the USSR – where science was applied to the task of socialist reconstruction. Both models

59. ILO (1924), series L: *Engineers and Chemists: Status and Employment in Industry*, p. 35.

60. Henry Guerlac, 'Science and French National Strength,' in E. M. Earle, *Modern France* (Princeton, 1951), p. 98.

61. ILO, *op. cit.* (note 59).

62. Paul Forman, 'The Financial Support and Political Alignment of Physicists in Weimar Germany,' *Minerva*, XII (January 1974), p. 39.

63. C. F. G. Masterman, *England After the War* (London, 1922), pp. 66–7.

involved the creation of new organisational machinery.

In the USA, as in Britain, the 1920s opened on an era of optimism in scientific affairs. Powerful groups of American scientists sought to carry a sense of 'national science', generated by the war, into peacetime, to identify science with the social and political values of democracy, to popularise scientific developments through new scientific journals, and to urge the case for a national programme of scientific research.[64] Their campaign was assisted by the sympathetic support of Herbert Hoover, who, as Secretary of State for Commerce, called for 'a marriage of science and individualism'. Certainly, the message was popular and the *New York Times* proclaimed industrial research to be 'A Scientific Santa'.[65] Between 1920 and 1928, the number of industrial research laboratories in America increased from 300 to 1,000.[66] Moreover, these laboratories did not confine themselves to routine technical problems of industrial development. Du Pont and Standard Oil, for example, soon became engaged in fundamental research on polymerisation, while Westinghouse applied itself to discharge phenomena in gases. Bell laboratories and GEC even produced two Nobel prizewinners – Davisson and Langmuir. By 1926, industries in America were reputed to be spending about $200 million on applied research and development, and engaging over 30,000 scientists.[67]

The influence of 'scientific management,' pioneered by Frederick Taylor and implemented, *par excellence*, by Henry Ford, was felt not only in the United States. The concept of 'American efficiency' was to have as profound an impact on socialist experiments in the USSR as it would later have on capitalist imitators in Europe. According to N. S. Borodin, writing in 1916, there was

> only one road for Russia to follow, and that is the road
> that the United States has pursued. We must try

64. See Ronald C. Tobey, *The American Ideology of National Science, 1919–1930* (Pittsburg, 1971).

65. Robert Kargon, *The Maturing of American Science* (Washington, DC, 1974), p. 11.

66. *Ibid.*, p. 14.

67. *Ibid.*, p. 17.

America's experiment, and, at the same time, try to bring over her enormous capital, and her mighty technical means.[68]

Lenin himself was keenly aware of the need for 'more and more engineers, agronomists, technicians, scientific experts of every kind'. The programme popularly attributed to him asserted that communism equalled 'socialism plus electrification'. Between 1924 and the start of the First Five Year Plan in 1928, Soviet expenditure on science and technology increased by a factor of four.[69] Soviet youth were systematically conscripted into science and technology, and harnessed to a massive programme of industrialisation. Between 1917 and 1923, university students, concentrated in the new universities and *technicums*, increased from 100,000 to 217,000, while over 90 specialist research institutes were created to pioneer the manufacture of chemicals, pharmaceuticals, fertilisers, artificial fibres, tyres, rubber and plastics. Often, these industrial enterprises were supervised by American technicians and engineers.[70]

By contrast with the Soviet Union, government policies towards scientific research in Western Europe were relatively haphazard. There were, however, a few specific attempts to strengthen the organisation of science. In France, the war had wrought terrific damage to the educated elite from which scientists were mainly drawn. For example, over 80% of the class of 1914 of the École Normale Supérieure, and 90% of the class of 1914 of the École Polytechnique, died during the war.[71] As Robert Gilpin has written, 'There can be no doubt that this carnage set French science back by at least a generation.'[72] In 1920,

68. N. A. Borodin in *Russian Review* (New York, 1916), p. 75, quoted in W. H. G. Armytage, *The Rise of the Technocrats: A Social History of Engineering* (London, 1965), p. 219.

69. Robert S. Lewis, 'Some Aspects of the Research and Development Effort of the Soviet Union, 1924–35,' *Science Studies*, 2 (1972), p. 155.

70. Armytage, *op. cit.* (note 68), pp. 219–37.

71. J. G. Crowther, *The Social Function of Science* (London, 1941), p. 542.

72. R. Gilpin, *op. cit.* (note 5), p. 155.

attempts were made to restructure the organisation of research in the creation of an *Office Nationale des Recherches Scientifiques, Industrielles et Inventions*, the function of which was 'to provoke, co-ordinate and encourage' all types of research – particularly that which might have potential industrial importance.[73] A similar trend became evident in Holland, where pressure for improved scientific organisation came from the Dutch chemical community.[74] The organisational model most widely favoured was the Mellon Institute in Pittsburgh. In 1920, C. J. Van Nieuwenburg proposed the formation of a research institute on similar lines, but one which, financed by government, would also rent laboratory space to industries, and perform contract research. In 1923, a committee of scientists was set up to examine the idea, but it was not until 1927 that the proposal for a State-financed research institute received formal approval. It was another five years before the Dutch 'Organisation for Applied Research' (the 'TNO') came into existence.

In Germany, the collapse of the monarchy, the loss of overseas assets, and military failure, reinforced the national importance of scientific industries as symbols of prestige and future prosperity. Immediately after the war, in the conviction that research would be increasingly vital to German self-sufficiency, but in the knowledge that government would not be capable of its support, German industrialists, buoyant with war profits, invested heavily in new research organisations. Between 1918 and 1922, several foundations for the promotion of research were established, among the most important of which was the *Notgemeinschaft für deutschen Wissenschaft*. Founded in 1921, this was a self-governing union composed of institutions of research and higher education which distributed research funds and subsidised scientific publications. Funds were provided jointly by industry and government. The same year, the first foundation for the support of physical research, the Helmholtz-Gesellschaft, was created. Its function was

73. *Ibid.*
74. Rip and Boeker, *op. cit.* (note 49), pp. 459–60.

to support the physical institutes at German-Hochschulen by providing funds for research purposes. To be counted as physical laboratories are not merely those which pursue scientific problems, but also those which are intended to serve such fields of applied physics as materials science, metallurgy, etc.[75]

By March 1922, subscriptions to the Helmholtz-Gesellschaft from firms such as I. G. Farben totalled 72 million marks. These foundations, although themselves weakened by inflation, provided vital support for German scientists during the bleak years between 1921 and 1923.

In Britain, government intervention in some science-based industries continued. For industries producing commodities such as optical glass, scientific instruments, chemical dyes or magnetos, the productive capacity generated by the war had outstripped demand, and produced a characteristic neo-classical problem of over-supply, fuelled by falling prices, declining profits and resulting in reduced investment in research and development. By 1920, British industries, especially some newer science-based firms, not only faced diminished markets, but renewed German and American competition. In 1921, the Government, through the 'Safeguarding of Industries Act', imposed export duties on key commodities which, in 1925, were increased to 50%. But this did not succeed in stimulating investment in British technology. Although there was a considerable increase in the research capacity of individual firms in the electricity, communications and food industries,[76] the Government's co-operative research scheme made little progress. The twenty-three different Research Associations created by 1924 – an uneven mixture of success and miscalculation – not only failed to achieve independence from government aid, but often failed to win active co-operation from industry. Small firms needed help but feared to share what few 'commercial secrets' they possessed. Large

75. See Paul Forman, *The Helmholtz-Gesellschaft: Support of Academic Physical Research by German Industry after the First World War* (in press), pp. 2–3.

76. See Sanderson, *op. cit.* (note 6).

firms, with their own R & D efforts, saw little point in sharing knowledge with their competitors. The Research Associations themselves could not always boast of their research records. The Scientific Instruments Research Association, for example, soon established a reputation for pioneering work; the Glass Research Association, weakened by administrative incompetence, collapsed from lack of industrial support after only five years. From the graduate's point of view, the prospects of the Research Association were also disappointing. By 1925, they were employing only 144 research scientists.

In the early 1920s Britain extended the machinery for sponsoring fundamental research in medicine and agriculture. The 'Haldane principle', enshrined in the Report of the Committee on the Machinery of Government,[77] which had laid down that the pursuit of research should remain independent of the exigencies of departmental policy, had led in 1921 to the creation of a Medical Research Council (MRC) from the Medical Research Committee. From 1921, the MRC would become responsible for supporting the greater part of medical research in the United Kingdom. Like the DSIR, many of its first research priorities reflected problems raised by the war. For its first decade, in addition to its original concern with tuberculosis, the Council concentrated on such questions as the control of epidemic viral diseases, including influenza, the relationship between 'vitamins' and nutritional deficiencies, and the improvement of radiology. With a quinquennial budget, fixed in 1920, providing between £125,000 and £130,000 annually, the MRC was able to withstand government cutbacks in expenditure rather better than the DSIR.[78]

Apart from the formation of the MRC, however, the administrative emphasis lay in co-ordinating existing provision for research rather than in introducing new machinery. In 1920, the DSIR assumed responsibility for the

77. *Report of the Committee on the Machinery of Government* (Cd. 9230), xii, 1918.

78. Landsborough Thomson, *op. cit.* (note 30), p. 193.

NPL and the Geological Museum. The same year, steps were taken to co-ordinate civil and military scientific research through the creation of Co-ordinating Boards for physical, chemical and engineering research. The principle of co-ordination extended to medical and agricultural research. The importance of agricultural research had been emphasised by the possibilities offered by the newly acquired German territories – such as East Africa – as a source of revenue and raw materials. Lord Milner, then Colonial Secretary, was convinced that these acquired territories could be successfuly exploited, using the applications of scientific research. Between 1920 and 1929 an Inter-Departmental Committee on the co-ordination of agricultural research in the colonies attempted to further this end. In 1931, however, on the advice of the Committee of Civil Research, new and more vigorous machinery – in the form of the Agricultural Research Council (ARC) – was created. For the next thirty years, the administrative structure of science would remain virtually unaltered.

Following the recession of 1921–2, the DSIR and the universities were forced to curtail their research activities. Under instruction from the Geddes Committee on public expenditure, the DSIR was obliged to reduce its budget from £556,868 to £330,287.[79] At the same time, the government grant to the universities was reduced by £300,000. By restricting the growth of the NPL, and by superceding a new chemical research station, the DSIR maintained its commitment to the individual researcher, and continued with its fuel and food programmes. But it was not until 1925 that the economy permitted these cuts to be restored, and the DSIR and the universities to embark on modest schemes of expansion.

The frustration of research by economic recession had an immediate impact on the prospects of scientific workers in government laboratories, research stations, and universities. The British experience, better documented than most, is probably typical of the situation confronting scientists in Western Europe. Between 1920 and 1929, owing to low

79. Calculated from *Annual Reports* of the DSIR, 1920–1 to 1922–3.

ceilings imposed by government and academic establishments, their 'scientific population' remained static. For the 1,200-odd scientists in the British civil service, this stagnation was aggravated by disparities in pay and grading between themselves and administrative civil servants. Following the growth and diversification of the professional civil service during the war, many 'temporary' grades had been admitted to the research establishments. These scientists, unlike administrative civil servants who enjoyed a relatively attractive career structure, remained ungraded.[80] Moreover, formal government enquiries into their prospects denied their claims for parity with, and independence from, the administrative grades. Apart from the limited application of one grading system, developed for NPL scientists, to other laboratories, most government scientists remained ungraded until the mid-1930s. One measure of the frustration of scientists in Britain can be seen in the support gained by the Institution of Professional Civil Servants which by 1930 had a membership of over 6,000.[81]

This trend towards militant professional association was no less important in the universities. Employment prospects for university faculty (including by the mid-1920s, 1,000 natural scientists), were also demoralising. Between 1914 and 1924, with the influx of demobilised students, the population of British universities increased by 56% to about 42,000.[82] Such an increase would have imposed strains on the capacity of a growing economy. As it was, it coincided with recession. The result was five years of what the University Grants Committee (UGC) called 'acute

80. The medley of grades comprising the structures of the professional and technical classes of the civil service, according to F. A. A. Menzler, resembled 'an accumulation of outbuildings about an historic edifice. Those outbuildings do not conform to the period or style of the main structure, nor are they themselves of one period or style.' F. A. A. Menzler, 'The Expert in the Civil Service,' in W. A. Robson (ed.), *The British Civil Servant* (London, 1937), p. 172.

81. *State Service*, 9 (October 1929), p. 155.

82. University Grants Committee, *Returns from Universities and University Colleges, 1919–20 to 1923–24*, p. 6.

anxiety'.[83] Teaching conditions suffered accordingly. As Soddy observed, science classes were 'packed with men, crammed three to a bench in laboratories which even before . . . were in many cases a disgrace to the nation'.[84] Expenditure cuts hit the young university teacher particularly hard and the low level of university salaries in the early 1920s contributed to the conception of scientific life as a 'vocation' or calling in which men worked for pleasure, not for material reward. As the UGC commented:

> The principal motive which leads men and women to adopt university teaching as a career is obviously not a desire for great material prosperity . . . They cannot hope to make a fortune or to secure such incomes as fall to the leaders of other learned professions and are relatively common in business.[85]

Although salaries improved in the course of the decade,[86] the universities remained perplexed by the conflicting demands made upon them. As Hyman Levy described it, they were

> torn on the one hand by the insistent demand of educationalists for the extension of their functions for the further pursuit of research, for the preservation of the liberal spirit in education, for the development of the vocational side, and for the provision of training facilities for teachers – and on the other, by the equally clamorous demands of national and local Geddes committees for retrenchment.[87]

By 1924, with the political triumph of the Labour Party, it was hoped that, despite economic uncertainties, provision for meeting these demands would improve. Since 1918, the Labour Party had shown an explicit interest in the promotion of scientific research. In its earliest manifestoes it

83. University Grants Committee, *Returns from Universities and University Colleges, 1923–24 to 1928–29*, p. 3.

84. *Scientific Worker* (Supplement to May 1920), p. 17.

85. University Grants Committee, *op. cit.* (note 82), p. 15.

86. On the role of the AUT in winning improvements for university scientists, see Perkin, *op. cit.* (note 13), pp. 72–9.

87. *Scientific Worker* (July 1922), pp. 20–1.

pledged itself to the advancement of science,[88] and in 1921, deplored the fact that this advancement had previously given profits 'solely to capitalists'. Once in office, Labour promised that 'the pursuit of knowledge' would no longer 'depend on individual philanthropy or capitalist greed'.[89] Most important, Ramsay MacDonald, Labour's first Prime Minister, was understood to be sympathetic to scientific research, and as an old friend of Sir Richard Gregory, seemed to bring a personal commitment to its promotion.

In practice, however, Labour (in office during 1924 and, again, in 1929) proved a disappointment. First, while in principle Labour governments accepted the Fabian idea of extending 'scientific method' in government, they did little to promote scientific research itself. In 1924, at a conference on *Science and Labour*[90] organised by Sir Richard Gregory, MacDonald confined himself to pledging 'rational' administrative reforms in the machinery of government. 'Until we regard administration and legislation in precisely the same manner as a scientific worker approaches his work in a laboratory,' he argued, 'we shall never be able to get results of a permanent character.' The Labour Government did establish a Parliamentary Science Advisory Committee in 1924, to keep Labour members 'informed on matters of scientific moment', but little notice was taken of the Committee's specific recommendations.[91] By 1930, the Com-

88. In 1918 the Labour Party proclaimed that it stood for 'increased study, for the scientific investigation of each succeeding problem, for the deliberate reorganisation of research, and for a much more rapid dissemination among the whole people of all the science that exists . . .' Arthur Henderson, *The Aims of Labour* (London, 1918), Appendix II, 'Labour and the Social Order,' p. 112.

89. Labour Party, *Memorandum on the DSIR* (1921).

90. Gregory had tried to set up a conference along similar lines in 1921, but 'the disturbed industrial conditions' defeated him. For an account of the conference, see the *British Science Guild Journal* (June 1924), p. 23.

91. For example, the Committee prepared a memorandum urging the creation of new, government-financed industries. Although this recommendation was accepted by the National Executive of the Labour Party,

mittee was disbanded. MacDonald even missed an opportunity to create a scientific advisory body at Cabinet level, and it fell to Stanley Baldwin to carry out the experiment.

Indeed, it was the Conservatives, guided in particular by Arthur Balfour, Lord President of the Council for the second time between 1925 and 1929,[92] who were able to commit more resources to science. Their parliamentary success coincided with an upturn in the economy which, in turn, permitted some relief to the DSIR and the universities. With the goodwill of Winston Churchill, then Chancellor of the Exchequer, the DSIR embarked on plans for new research stations for fishery and forest products, a new national chemical laboratory, and the extension of X-ray and other facilities at the National Physical Laboratory. Between 1924–5 and 1929–30, the budget of the DSIR was increased from £405,755 to £561,400 to take account of these programmes.[93] Moreover, expansion was accompanied by a measure of administrative innovation. Building upon the concept of a 'Research Department' which MacDonald had seen as an advisory committee of economists, Baldwin was persuaded to create a Committee of Civil Research (CCR) directly answerable to the Cabinet. Between 1925 and its disappearance in 1930, the CCR investigated a range of problems of concern at home and in the Empire on such topics as the eradication of the tsetse fly and the locust in East Africa, the state of the iron and steel trade in Britain, and the co-ordination of government research.[94]

Reviewing government policies towards research during the 1920s, it is apparent, therefore, that, although there

it was not taken up by the Parliamentary Labour Party. Hyman Levy, *Modern Science* (London, 1939), pp. 96–7.

92. For Balfour's role in promoting scientific research during the 1920s, and for an account of his fundamental interest in science, see R. J. Strutt, *Lord Balfour in his Relation to Science* (Cambridge, 1930).

93. Figures calculated from the *Annual Reports* of the DSIR.

94. See Roy MacLeod and Kay Andrews, 'The Committee of Civil Research: Scientific Advice for Economic Development,' *Minerva*, 7 (1969), pp. 680–705.

had been some slow growth in terms of its budget, the early promise of the DSIR, at least, had been frustrated, in part by economic events and in part by political failure. Co-ordination had proved no substitute for political commitment. Moreover, while research in private industry showed definite signs of vitality,[95] there had been no attempt on the part of government to extend the co-operative research scheme, or to take further initiatives in the promotion of new industries. Such conservatism, together with the impact of recession on the universities and certain sectors of industry, had a marked effect on the mood of scientific graduates. The spirit of solidarity created during the war, which had been manifest among members of the National Union of Scientific Workers (NUSW) in a new awareness of the social and political effects of science, had largely disappeared as scientists retreated to the professional security offered by the Institutes of Chemistry and Physics, the Institutions of Engineering and the professional associations within the universities and the civil service. By 1929, the political ideals of the NUSW had been submerged into the professional aspirations of the Association of Scientific Workers.

Finally, anxiety about the future, symbolised by a fresh profusion of predictive literature, towards the end of the decade, revealed disquiet with the outcome of science and technology. The 'machine age' had many critics, among them the Bishop of Ripon who called, in 1927, for a 'moratorium' on research.[96] There were, of course, more positive forecasts. In 1928, H. G. Wells, reverting to a favourite theme, laid down a blueprint for the future which allotted a key role to scientific 'samurai', who would

95. It was estimated, for example, that the number of patents taken out by British industry doubled during the 1920s, and the number of laboratory technicians increased from 5,000 to 11,000. (Sanderson, *op. cit.*, note 6, p. 119.) By the end of the decade, the FBI estimated that about 422 firms were spending £1,736,000 annually on research and development. FBI, *Industry and Research*, 1943, p. 6.

96. On the proposed moratorium on research, see Carroll Purcell, 'A Savage Struck by Lightning: The Idea of a Research Moratorium, 1927–1937,' *Lux et Scientia*, *10* (October–December 1974), pp. 146–61.

bring about a 'transition from speculative adventure to organised foresight in the common interest'.[97] But as Charles Beard argued in *Whither Mankind?* (1928) and *Toward Civilisation* (1930), the balance between scientific 'progress' and technological dislocation was difficult to strike and could not be decided without some recognition of social and economic priorities. In the determination of these it was clear that science and technology were too important to be left in the untutored hands of scientists.

THE SOCIAL CONTEXT OF SCIENCE, 1929–1939

The world-wide depression between 1929 and 1934 ushered in a decade of violent economic and political change which played havoc with public, professional and political attitudes towards science. First, in every European country, scientists were thrown out of work in great numbers. Second, the practice of science itself came under attack as mechanisation, overproduction and the prospect of a 'technological war' became associated, in the popular idiom, with the unthinking advance of knowledge. Third, massive evidence of misery brought to light during and after the Depression by economists and social scientists in Britain, brought anger and scepticism which, fed by the failure of conservative economics, attracted young intellectuals towards more radical political alternatives. Moreover, the traditional and respected neutrality of scientists in political affairs became meaningless as Jewish and liberal scientists were persecuted in Nazi Germany.

In the light of these events, a debate opened in Britain about the scientist's proper role in economic and social reconstruction. Through the propaganda of a new generation of politically committed researchers and science writers, the debate became a popular issue; through disagreements among these protagonists and the 'scientific establishment', it became a political issue. Some scientists argued, in terms reminiscent of the early 1920s, that 'scientific rationality'

97. H. G. Wells, *The Open Conspiracy* (London, 1928), p. 122.

should be applied to politics, and sought to explain the
disbenefits of 'progress' in terms of the abuse of science
by foolish politicians; others stressed that since science was
clearly a function of society, it would inevitably be frustrated within a capitalist system, and it could only be
applied to the advantage of the people generally under a
system of socialist regulation.[98]

By the end of the 1930s, this debate had reached a wide
audience. Indeed, by 1939, science had become part of the
'grammar of politics', and the use of science in the 'national
interest' an accepted principle in the industrialised world.
Both for economic purposes in peacetime, and for military
purposes in wartime, scientific knowledge had become a
political quantity. The expansion of scientific effort in
wartime, the transformation of scientific research from a
marginal to a central place in government policy, and
the elevation of scientists from academic 'outsiders' to
political 'insiders' marked a profound transformation in the
public standing of science. In the troubled peace that
followed 1945 it would be the scientific community's task
first to plan for its security and for its future growth in
numerical strength and research support, and, second, to
define what, in practice, would be the contribution of 'the
Republic of Science' to the future well-being of society.

The Depression and the Community of Science

By 1931, the number of unemployed men in Britain
had soared to almost three million. British scientists,
however, did not suffer that degree of unemployment which
was common among their contemporaries in Europe. By
1933, for example, there were 50,000 unemployed graduates
in Germany; 3,000 out of 16,000 chemists were reputed to be
unemployed or diverted to other fields of employment. In
Holland, graduate output was twice the number in demand.

98. For an analysis of the ideological and tactical differences between
these 'reformist' and 'radical' groups, see P. G. Werskey, 'British
scientists and "outsider politics",' *Science Studies, I* (1971), pp. 67–84.

In France, unemployed students were prominent in the political unrest which threatened civil war in February 1932; in Austria and Romania it seemed to at least one observer that 'dissatisfied and harassed students and graduates out of work' might bring down the regimes.[99] In Britain, isolated statistics showed an element of unemployment amongst graduates in 'technical work',[100] but the main problem for scientists was not so much actual unemployment as the demoralisation caused by uncertain prospects. As J. D. Bernal, the Cambridge crystallographer recalled, when student's grants had expired, they were 'practically bundled off into the first job that came'.[101]

One explanation of the reasonably good prospects of British scientists lay in the fact that many of the country's science-based industries survived the Depression quite well. The rayon industry, for example, was 'scarcely affected'; between 1930 and 1935 the electricity supply industry recorded 'rapid growth', and the cinematograph industry spoke of a 'sensational advance'. Other science-based industries proved equally resilient, particularly the dye-stuffs industry – 'one of the most encouraging features of British trade',[102] and the building industry, which was stimulated by the housing boom of the thirties.

Some commentators, like Hugh Dalton, saw in this success story merely the irony of widespread poverty in an age of scientific miracles: 'Need poverty continue,' he asked, 'in this age . . . which has given us the aeroplane, and the wireless, and all the modern miracles of electricity, and chemistry and mechanics and botany?'[103] Other critics of

99. W. M. Kotschnig, *Unemployment in the Learned Professions* (Oxford, 1937), pp. 119; 122–3; 174–5.

100. In 1934, a survey conducted by Eleanor Rathbone, MP for the Combined Universities, revealed that the highest rate of unemployment (9.9% in a sample of 4,327 graduates) was amongst graduates in 'technical work', *New University* (December 1934), pp. 11–13.

101. *Bernal Papers* (Birkbeck College), Unpublished manuscript, 1934.

102. *Manchester Guardian Commercial Annual Review* (January 1933), p. 16, quoted in Plummer, *op. cit.* (note 44), p. 265. The value of exported British dyestuffs rose from £908,976 in 1930 to £1,071,205 in 1932.

103. Graham Hutton (ed)., *The Burden of Plenty* (London, 1935), p. 38.

T.C.   M

science saw, too, how science contributed to 'our present discontents'. First, there was the disastrous role of technology in creating unemployment. Indeed, the role of automation became both a feature of popular polemic and the subject for intensive research.[104] Thus, in *Love on the Dole*, Walter Greenwood powerfully described the impact on one family of

> newer and more up-to-date machinery whose functions were marvellous, whose capacity was manifold and infinite, that could work ceaselessly, remorselessly, twenty four hours a day, seven days a week, without pause for meals . . .[105]

At the same time, passions were roused at the havoc caused by overproduction at a time of under-consumption. Absurd illustrations of the 'burden of plenty' abounded. In 1934, for example, Julian Huxley reported how 'mountains of coffee' were burnt, and milk dumped into rivers at a time when many families went hungry.[106]

Science came under renewed attack when fears of war again rode through Europe. The technology of gas and germ warfare had been refined, until governments of the 1930s could choose between

> bombs filled with deadly plague bacilli, or with anthrax . . . yellow fever, dysentery, diphtheria, malaria, typhus, plague, cholera . . . [107]

Little wonder in reviewing such a catalogue of pestilence, that science seemed to be 'about the most dangerous thing ever loosed on mankind'. In 1934, it seemed that the nightmare was about to come true when Italy used poison gas in her conquest of Abyssinia.

Moreover, John Strachey maintained, the most lethal aspect of science was the indifference and 'simpleminded-

104. The literature on the social and economic effects of automation is vast. See, for example, Stuart Chase, *Men and Machines* (London, 1929); V. Demand, *This Unemployment: Disaster or Opportunity?* (London, 1931); and Fred. Henderson, *The Economic Consequences of Power Production* (London, 1931).

105. Walter Greenwood, *Love on the Dole* (London, 1933), p. 92.

106. Julian Huxley, *If I were a Dictator* (London, 1934), p. 63.

107. Chase, *op. cit.* (note 104), p. 309.

ness' of scientists themselves.[108] The belief that scientists were resolutely indifferent to the misapplication of their discoveries was reinforced by the headlines of the early 1930s, which conveyed the thrilling advances in atomic physics, crystallography, biochemistry, and biology. Cambridge, in particular, was the focus of these 'golden years' of scientific discovery, where the brilliant work of Rutherford, Bernal and Blackett at the Cavendish laboratory, and Gowland-Hopkins, in bio-chemistry, captured the public imagination.[109] Most scientists, however, failed to appreciate the contrast marked by 'the steel pylons of the National Grid Scheme – heralds of the clean age of electricity, as they march through the squalor of our tumbledown and out of date towns'.[110] Or, as the radical journal *Plebs* put it more brutally, 'Science offers the worker a split atom when what he wants is bread.'[111]

It could also be argued, with equal validity, that not enough was being done to bring about the vital translation of basic research into industrial development. In 1932, for example, Oswald Mosley, formerly a Labour MP, called on 'the new world of science to redress the balance of the old world of industry'. He argued that

No country produces a greater wealth of inventive talent and no country more recklessly squanders that talent; yet no country is so peculiarly dependent in our present position upon the . . . advance of new industries.[112]

Recommendations for a new organisation to promote industrial research were put before a sub-committee of the Economic Advisory Council which was commissioned to study new industrial development. It was suggested that an

108. John Strachey, *The Coming Struggle for Power* (London, 1932), p. 177.

109. See, for example, the description of the excitement of Cambridge science in the early 1930s in C. P. Snow, *The Search* (London, 1934), pp. 87–9.

110. H. V. Morton, *What I Saw in the Slums* (London, 1933), p. 16.

111. *Gregory Papers* (University of Sussex Library), *The Plebs* (October 1933).

112. Oswald Mosley, *The Greater Britain* (London, 1932, and 1934), pp. 168–9.

institution, analogous to the Mellon Institute, should be created to 'draw up programmes of research into the practical application in industry of ideas, inventions or processes at present undeveloped'. This Committee, under the chairmanship of J. H. Thomas were, however, un-impressed. Instead, they argued that liaison between research and industry, in the form of the Research Associa-tions, was adequate. It would be another seventeen years before new machinery in such forms as the British National Research and Development Corporation would find political support, and longer still before the problem of ensuring better management of research and development became a cornerstone of government economic and in-dustrial policy.

Scientists, planning and politics

Between 1932 and 1935, these discussions expanded into wider debate as scientists in Western Europe, in the words of Ritchie Calder, 'invaded politics'. This debate over what Julian Huxley and later J. D. Bernal called 'the social function of science' absorbed scientists in Holland and France as well as in Britain, but it was in Britain that the protagonists were the most vocal, and most articulate. The debate drew its inspiration from three contexts. First, the political and economic debacle of the Depression urgently prompted the search for political alternatives to *laissez-faire* capitalism, and for a new role for science. Early in the 1930s, a wide political consensus had formed around demands for planning, varying in emphasis from pro-posals for economic and industrial rationalisation put forward by Harold Macmillan, MP,[113] to the visions of a technocratic world state posited by H. G. Wells.[114] Second,

113. See, for example, Harold Macmillan, *Reconstruction* (London, 1933), quoted in Arthur Marwick, 'Middle Opinion in the 1930s: Planning, Progress and Political Agreement,' *English Historical Review*, 79 (April 1964), pp. 285–98.
114. H. G. Wells, *The Shape of Things to Come* (London, 1933), p. 381. The idea of a technocratic utopia did not appeal to all. It was, for

the debate was informed by the knowledge of what had been achieved in terms of industrial and economic growth through the planning of science and technology in the Soviet Union. As Julian Huxley wrote on returning from a visit to the USSR in 1932, 'Proper planning is itself the application of scientific method to human affairs . . . It demands for pure science a very large and special position in society.'[115] Nowhere in the world had science been allotted a more 'special' a position than in the USSR where, by 1935, a higher proportion of National Income was being spent on 'R & D' than in the United States or any country of Western Europe.

The debate was intensified by a third factor – the knowledge that certain fields of science were being distorted by political interference in the USSR, while, from 1933 onwards, science in Germany was subordinate to Nazi dogma. In pursuit of national 'purification', Nazi science was redefined in such a way that 'the founders of research in physics, and the discoverers from Newton to the physical pioneers of our own time, were almost exclusively Aryan'.[116] In purging science of its 'Jewish spirit', German science suffered enormously. By the end of the 1930s, 1,800 scientists (including many of Germany's most distinguished scientific men) had been expelled.[117] Whole laboratories and scientific specialities were dismantled. Experimental embryology, according to Joseph Needham, became 'a ruin in the country of its origin'. Moreover, as Germany prepared for war, industrial research was re-tooled towards programmes supporting economic self-sufficiency. The improvisation of synthetic substitutes, particularly of petroleum, rubber, cotton and cellulose, was given industrial priority. *Wissenschaft* was transformed into *Wehrwissenschaft*.

example, powerfully parodied and rejected in Aldous Huxley, *Brave New World* (London, 1932).

115. Julian Huxley, *A Scientist Among the Soviets* (London, 1932), p. 52.

116. The Nazi physicist, Johannes Stark, quoted in J. D. Bernal, *The Social Function of Science* (London, 1939), pp. 215–16.

117. In Britain the Academic Assistance Council was set up in 1933 to aid persecuted European scholars. See Lord Beveridge, *A Defence of Free Learning* (Oxford, 1959).

As one journal described the process:

> Logarithms find their most beautiful application in the science of ballistics . . . Chemistry has as much application in military struggles with poison gas as in the fight for daily bread. Physics problems can best be explained with the aid of a tank.[118]

In Britain, rearmament in response to Germany did not affect many scientists until 1938. Until then, concern focused primarily on the frustration of research. On the one hand, there was an attempt, led by Sir Richard Gregory in the columns of *Nature*, to assert the higher 'morality' of science against its misuse by politicians, and to secure an appropriate place for scientists in advising government decisions. Second, there was an attempt by a small group of younger socialist and Marxist scientists outside the 'scientific establishment', to demonstrate that the benefits of science were inevitably frustrated under capitalism and could only be liberated by fundamental social change. Neither 'group' was either monolithic or exclusive in any formal structural sense. At most, they represented divergent tendencies among a generation of scientists of which the majority, while deeply affected by external social and political events, chose to remain silent.

Between 1932 and 1935 the debate between the two factions crystallised. The discussion was given particular scope by several scientific journalists – particularly Ritchie Calder of the *Daily Herald* and J. G. Crowther of the *Manchester Guardian*. Interest in science was not confined to the newspapers. The BBC, with regular scientific broadcasts, began to play an important role in popularising the central issues. In 1933, for example, the BBC broadcast, and later published, a series of talks on *Science in the Changing World*. Among the contributors were Julian Huxley and Hyman Levy.[119]

118. Quoted in Joseph Needham, *The Nazi Attack on International Science* (London, 1941), p. 34.

119. See also Julian Huxley and Hyman Levy, *Scientific Research and Social Needs* (London, 1934).

It was predictable that Gregory would appeal to the British Association to support the creation of a 'National Science Council' and an Advisory Council of Scientists, to investigate the causes of the world crisis. With the active support of Ritchie Calder,[120] the proposals gained maximum publicity. While assured of the support of 'a number of leading scientists' and (according to Calder) many rank and file engineers, Gregory's proposals were killed by the 'ologist' sections and rejected by the British Association's Committee of Recommendations.[121] However, in 1933, Gregory was instrumental, first, in creating a Parliamentary Scientific Committee, with the support of many professional scientific institutions, and in launching an 'Engineers Study Group' with a membership of eighty, for the study of social questions from a technical standpoint. This group described itself as a representative body of engineers

> dissatisfied with the fact that the community is not enjoying a standard of living and leisure commensurate with the potential advance for which science and technology are responsible. We are meeting to discuss why this paradox arises and how it can be solved.

Such evidence of a 'social conscience' among senior scientists was hardly sufficient for some younger scientists, however, while the 'scientistic' nature of the argument seemed to others merely naïve. The unresponsiveness of the British Association merely confirmed suspicions that the 'prevalent ideology of the scientific caste'[122] was not only resistant to change but hostile to any attempts to involve scientists in political discussions. Between 1932 and 1934, in the context of a 'decided swing to the left' among undergraduates, Cambridge proved a fertile breeding ground for radicalism among younger scientists, organised into two related groups – the Cambridge Scientists Anti-War Group (CASWG), and the rejuvenated Cambridge branch

120. See, for example, the series organised by Ritchie Calder on 'How can science help us?' (*Daily Express*, 15 September 1933).

121. Quoted in W. H. G. Armytage, *Sir Richard Gregory* (London, 1957), pp. 115–16.

122. 'British scientists and the world crisis,' by an anonymous group of scientists in *Labour Monthly* (19 November 1932), pp. 702–9.

of the Association of Scientific Workers (ASCW). The charismatic element in these groups came from the leadership of a few eminent scientists – since well described as a 'Visible College'[123] – J. D. Bernal, P. M. S. Blackett, Hyman Levy, Joseph Needham, J. B. S. Haldane and Lancelot Hogben, each of whom had been profoundly impressed by the visit of the Soviet delegation to the International Congress for the History of Science and Technology, held in London in June 1931.[124] The sustained Marxist analysis deployed by the visiting Russians to describe the role of social and economic forces in scientific and technological development came as a 'trumpet blast'. What became clear to Hyman Levy, for example, was not only

> the social conditioning of science and the vital need for planning, but the impossibility of carrying this through within the framework of a chaotic capitalism. What emerged afterwards was the necessity, nevertheless, of demanding that this impossible task be undertaken in order to educate the great body of scientific men in the reasons for its impossibility.[125]

For the next ten years, Bernal, above all, campaigned ceaselessly for an understanding among men of science and laymen of the social determinants of science. In socialist and Marxist journals, in the context of the international peace movement, in defence of their colleagues in fascist countries, on political platforms, and in their individual writings, the views of this small group gradually permeated the scientific community until it seemed to some that their influence was paramount in British science.[126]

In 1935, with the publication of *The Frustration of Science* this campaign began in earnest. The publication of this

123. P. G. Werskey, *The Visible College: A Study of Radical Scientists in Britain, 1919–1939.* (Unpublished Ph.D. dissertation, Harvard, 1972.)

124. See *Science at the Crossroads* (London, reprinted 1971), with a preface by Joseph Needham and an Introduction by P. G. Werskey.

125. H. Levy, *Modern Science* (London, 1939), p. 97.

126. For one account of the impact of communism on the scientific community see Neal Wood, *Communism and British Intellectuals* (London, 1955), pp. 121–51.

book, in the words of the Introduction (contributed by that veteran activist, Frederick Soddy), was 'an indication of the growing sense of responsibility among individual scientific men'. Its message was that the scientist 'must . . . be directly concerned with the great political struggles of the day'.[127] Looking to Sir John Boyd Orr's findings on the relationship between food, health and income in Britain,[128] the authors described how the benefits of research were wilfully misused or neglected. In the concluding essay, the physicist P. M. S. Blackett argued that the choice seemed to lie between fascism and socialism; for him the only alternative was socialism, which 'would want all the science it can get to produce the greatest possible wealth'.[129]

In Britain, however, scientists were still political outsiders. Indeed, disillusion among scientists with the Labour Party had led to a complete collapse of what machinery existed for liaison between scientists and Labour politicians.[130] In France, the situation was different. In Western Europe, France had suffered most from the Depression. Deflationary policies and political paralysis had delayed her recovery. Between 1933 and 1935 when other European countries were pulling out of the Depression, industrial production in France was still stagnant. Economic failure fed political extremism. In May 1936, a Popular Front of Radical-Socialists, Socialists and Communists under the

127. Sir Daniel Hall, *et al.*, *The Frustration of Science* (London, 1935), p. 130.

128. In his study of *Food, Health and Income* (London, 1936), Sir John Boyd Orr published statistics showing that half the British population were predestined, by lower income levels, to an inadequate diet and inferior health. Nutrition immediately became a controversial political issue.

129. *The Frustration of Science* (note 127), p. 144.

130. In the words of Hyman Levy, one-time Secretary of the Labour Party's Scientific Advisory Committee, its failure

marked the end of one phase of disillusionment of a forward wing of the scientific movement. Thereafter it became important to take stock of the situation, to weigh up what possibilities political pressure offered . . . and to seek for the clarification of the views of scientific workers themselves.

Levy (note 125).

direction of Leon Blum, assumed power.

The formation of the Popular Front Government had immediate consequences for scientific research. Largely through the efforts of the scientists, Jean Perrin, a lifelong socialist and close friend of Blum, and Paul Langevin, the Government took steps to centralise research in a single *Caisse Nationale*, to create a new corps of government scientific workers with a hierarchical structure analogous to that of academic scientists, to revive the laboratories at Bellevue, and to create a post of Under-Secretary of State for Scientific Research. The first scientist to hold this post was Mme Irene Joliot Curie.[131]

Compared with this decisive strategy on the part of the French government, there was little change in British policy towards science during the 1930s. The research budget of the DSIR had again been cut during the Depression, so that those research programmes which had been begun in the late 1920s suffered the harassment of stop-go policies. The universities' budget had also been reduced by £150,000 in the expenditure cuts of 1931. By 1936, however, as J. D. Bernal commented, 'The curtailment and stagnation of research which was a feature of the depression has definitely ceased, and gives way to an expansion which has reached, and in many cases surpassed, the average of postwar years.'[132] First, the DSIR had been compelled in 1933, to extend support to the Research Associations on a permanent basis. From 1934 onwards support was provided in two forms; first, a guaranteed block grant for five years, plus additional grants for selected researches by selected industries. The decision proved a watershed in the history of corporate research. Between 1933 and 1939, industrial contributions to the Research Associations rose from £167,000 to £372,000.[133] Second, industrial research was stimulated by the re-armament programme, begun in 1935, which encouraged the expansion of R & D labs in the communications and aircraft industries. By the end of the

131. Gilpin, *op. cit.* (note 5), pp. 158–9.
132. J. D. Bernal, *Scientific Worker* (March 1936), p. 37.
133. Ian Varcoe, *Organising for Science in Britain* (Oxford, 1974), p. 32.

decade there was a noticeable increase in industrial research capacity.[134] The FBI recorded that the number of scientists had increased from 1,381 in about 400 firms, to 4,382 in about 520 firms. At the same time, the research budget had grown from £1,636,000 to £5,442,000.[135] Third, the budget of the DSIR had also kept pace with the growth of the economy. Between 1932 and 1938 it had increased by about 40% to about £800,000.[136]

Despite these increases, however, there were those who argued that the national research budget in Britain was minimal in relation to that spent by the USA and USSR, and totally inadequate in terms of national needs. Between 1935 and 1938, J. D. Bernal prepared a comprehensive memorandum on the *Finance of Research in Britain* which argued that research suffered from four key weaknesses – it was inadequately supported; it was vulnerable to economic fluctuations; it was unco-ordinated; and it had developed without thought as to the relative social benefits which might accrue from different types of research. He proposed the creation of an Endowment Fund of £50 million, to be managed by a Board composed of representatives of science, government and industry which would provide for a steady increase in scientific research to supply industry with a greater quantity and better quality of research. Such an arrangement would permit 'long-range experiment without fear of interruption . . .' It would secure investment and enable planned industrial development, and, thus, he promised, 'co-ordination . . . and research would pay for its cost many times over.'[137]

While the Parliamentary and Scientific Committee which sponsored Bernal's investigation were convinced by his arguments, the British government were not. In particular,

134. Among the firms to expand their 'R and D' capacity at this time were, for example, EMI, GEC, Metro-Vickers, Standard Telephones, and Pye Radios. M. Postan *et al.*, *The Design and Development of Weapons* (London, 1964), pp. 383–7; 428.

135. Federation of British Industries, *op. cit.* (note 95), p. 7.

136. 'The Finance of Research,' *Scientific Worker* (November–December 1938), p. 127.

137. *Ibid.*, pp. 145–6.

the DSIR rejected Bernal's criticisms, and pointed to the significant improvements in its research budget and in the 'research-mindedness' of industry during the decade. In vain did the Parliamentary and Scientific Committee appeal to the DSIR not to wait until a national emergency forced them to improvise new machinery. Their arguments were rejected, and Bernal himself turned to a more receptive audience outside government.

Between 1937 and 1939 the debate on the 'social function of science' took on a definite shape and substance. Through the Cambridge Scientists Anti-War Group, the Scientists' Group of the Left Book Club, the Peace movement, the Scientists' Advisory Group of the TUC and the Association of Scientific Workers, the views of socialist and Marxist scientists became widely known. Indeed, through the interest displayed in questions of 'social responsibility' by the International Council of Scientific Unions [138] and the League of Nations, and the formation of 'associations of scientific workers' in Australia and the United States, and later in Holland and Canada,[139] the debate assumed an international dimension. Moreover, in Britain, radicals and reformers could congratulate themselves when, in 1938, the British Association agreed to the formation of a new Division devoted to the social and international relations of science. Its formation not only provided a common platform for scientists of different views, but 'strengthened the hope for a better world' through 'the more intelligent use of science'.[140]

Most important in the campaign to educate scientists and laymen of the social functions of science, was the publication of a series of critical Marxist and socialist studies

138. On the work of the Committee on Science and Social Relations set up by ICSU in 1937, see Roy MacLeod, 'The Historical Context of the International Council for Science Policy Studies,' *Archives Internationales de l'Histoire des Sciences* 25 (1975) pp. 314–323.

139. The American Association of Scientific Workers was formed in 1937 and the Australian Association of Scientific Workers in 1939. Both were inspired by ex-members of the British Association of Scientific Workers.

140. J. G. Crowther, *op. cit.* (note 71), pp. 631–2.

between 1937 and 1939.[141] These culminated in Bernal's blueprint for science in a better world – *The Social Function of Science*. As he wrote:

> there is no longer any technical reason why everyone should not have enough to eat. There is no reason why anyone *should* have to do more than three or four hours of disagreeable or monotonous work a day, or why they should be forced by economic pressure, to do even that. War, in a period of potential plenty and ease for all, is sheer folly and cruelty. The greater part of disease in the world today is due directly or indirectly to làck of food and good living conditions. All these are plainly remediable evils and no one can feel that science has been properly applied until they are swept off the face of the earth. But that is only the beginning.[142]

How these changes would come about, Bernal was not clear. He looked forward merely to the 'ending of the struggle . . . [when] mankind will come into its material heritage', and far from needing science less,

> will make even greater demands on it to solve the greater human problems which will have to be faced. To meet this task science itself will change and develop and in so doing will cease to be a special discipline of a selected few and become the common heritage of mankind.[143]

The ideas in *The Social Function of Science* were hardly new, but they provided a powerful Marxist interpretation of the interdependence of scientific and social progress. The book encapsulated Bernal's personal optimism that science, as an agent of social change, held the key to the future. It influenced a generation of scientists and economists, persuading them of the uncomplicated virtues of planning. At the time, however, it was not universally welcomed. The Marxist emphasis of 'Bernalism' not only offended such

141. These included (anon.), *Britain Without Capitalists* (London, 1937), J. B.-S. Haldane, *The Marxist Philosophy and the Sciences* (London, 1938), Hyman Levy, *A Philosophy for a Modern Man* (London, 1938), and *Modern Science* (London, 1939); L. Hogben, *Science for the Citizen* (London, 1938), and, in 1941, J. G. Crowther, *The Social Relations of Science*.

142. Bernal, *op. cit.* (note 133), p. 410.

143. *Ibid.*, p. 415.

liberal scientists as Wells and Gregory,[144] but also produced a 'counter-blast' from those who, like J. R. Baker, A. V. Hill, and Michael Polanyi,[145] asserted the vital importance of maintaining the freedom of science from political manipulation.

The coming of war brought to Europe and America the mass mobilisation of scientists and the co-operation of scientists and industry on a massive scale. From radar to antibiotics, the contribution of 'boffins', culminating in the atomic bomb, gave scientists status and authority in government and society. The post-war period looked to the application of similar strategies for the solution of economic problems, as had been applied so successfully to the solution of military problems. In the planning of these strategies, Bernal's ideas would pass as a rich but problematic legacy to a post-war generation of national science policy planners, and to the international agencies such as UNESCO, FAO, WHO and OECD, in which hopes for the future would be invested.

CONCLUSION

With the end of the Second World War, plans for economic recovery in Western Europe were based to a large extent on plans for scientific and technological development. America, dominant politically, helped spur Europe's revival and expansion by setting an example in technological innovation, and by penetrating European economies with new corporate technologies, many of them based on pre-war or wartime research and development. In 1945, the potential benefits of science and technology, represented by nuclear power, computerisation, synthetic fabrics, electronics, television and plastics, were apparently limitless. The charisma of the scientist and the technologist (the two were easily confused to men of business not looking for cognitive distinctions, but commercial results) held a power-

144. See Armytage, *op. cit.* (note 121), p. 152.
145. See the discussions by A. V. Hill, Michael Polanyi and J. R. Baker in the *New Statesman* in January and February 1940.

ful sway. In so far as business needed science-based technology, in so far as that technology needed fundamental research, and in so far as that research required massive long-term investment of a kind only governments could afford, foundations were laid for a close partnership between government, science and industry within the economic framework of Europe.

The countries of Western Europe reacted differently to these new 'technological frontiers' opening in the 1950s and 1960s. Germany and Italy capitalised on opportunities to rebuild their chemical, electrical and engineering industries; Britain and France invested in computers, aerospace, and (in Britain especially) nuclear power. To serve and manage these efforts, universities were urged to expand, even doubling their production of graduate scientists and engineers; programmes were devised to stimulate university research; and government science budgets were increased in line with expectations of fresh discoveries in agriculture and medicine. To bring order to unco-ordinated efforts, governments were urged to create national and institutional 'science policies', and to define criteria for scientific development, which in turn presupposed prior knowledge of factors which 'push' or 'pull' development at different rates and in different directions. As governments, research councils and university departments entered the 1950s, their assumptions were shaped by pressures from that underground river of attitudes, beliefs and troubled conjectures which had its source in the European experience of the interwar years.

In Britain, it was argued, innovation would be encouraged by intervention (in selected cases, nationalisation); industrial demand for qualified scientists and engineers would be stimulated by 'manpower policies'; and university staff would be safeguarded (and professional insecurity removed) by far-sighted quinquennial planning, uniform salary scales, generous provision for research, and the encouragement of academic-industrial contact. Economic growth would be achieved, to the betterment of the quality of life overall. Politically and militarily, the decade following the Korean War created a favourable climate for these views. Expenditure on military, space and nuclear research and development in the 1950s and early 1960s increased between 15–20% per annum – a far faster growth rate than any European economy enjoyed during the same period. So-called 'Big Science', led by developments in the USA and USSR, spread to Western Europe and conditioned the expectations of scientists, economists and governments in the Third World.

This optimistic vision, foreseen in the 1950s, has not, of course, materialised. In Europe and elsewhere, industrial investment based on shaky extrapolations, government policies based on inadequate understanding of possible contingencies, 'manpower' predictions based on fragile demographic assumptions, educational policies based on facile interpretations of possible relationships between educational investment and economic growth – all provided evidence that simplistic strategies do not work. Moreover, by the early 1970s, it was evident that governmental intervention is not uniformly favourable to economic growth. In Britain perhaps more than elsewhere in Western Europe, priorities for the radical reconstruction of basic industries (particularly iron and steel, shipbuilding and mechanical engineering) had not been well-defined or acted upon. Encouragement given to research and development had in many cases concentrated qualified scientists and engineers in non-productive parts of the industrial structure, while the mystique attaching to sheer size in 'R & D' effort had obscured the decisive importance of management to any successful innovation. Finally, and most ironically, given the hopeful promise of the 1920s, where significant economic growth had followed technological development, its benefits proved quite compatible with the exploitation and misuse of resources and people, not only in Europe and North America, but in the Third World as well.

There was nothing really new in many of these developments. Many involved questions of political and economic principle which, arguably, lay quite outside the scientists' sphere. But there was an increasing tendency to hold the 'scientific community' more accountable, especially in light of its avowed interest in 'efficiency', and in its apparent collusion with vested capitalist and bureaucratic interests. Moreover, it was clear that scientists had gained appreciable status and power. As foreseen in the 1920s, Western Europe witnessed the emergence of a 'scientific estate'. Countries were not being run by scientists, nor were national decisions notably taken on 'scientific' principles. But the growing scale and effort of science and technology throughout the 1950s and 1960s required scientists to play an increasing part in policy-making, partly because of the cost of their activities, but also because of the enormous implications of scientific research for national prestige, defence, education and the economy.

By the late 1960s, there was perceptible scepticism about the 'scientific enterprise' in many quarters. Some scientists, prompted by Michael Polanyi's defence of the 'Republic of Science,' sought greater freedom from the vexatious and uninformed interference of governments in the processes of scientific discovery. Others sought to retreat into a kind of ethically neutral 'isolationism', disclaiming responsibility for the way governments or industries or multinational corporations use or abuse scientific knowledge. Still others – a small but growing minority – argued that science could not be separated from its social uses, and that they, as scientists, had a special duty to develop different, more 'critically aware', styles of teaching and research. The interwar argument that 'planning' (and its corollary, centralisation) held the key to social and material betterment gave way to angry denunciations of 'scientism' and 'instrumental rationality'. Student disaffection, beginning in France and Germany, moving soon to Holland, Britain and the entire industrialised world, converged with growing government concern that the relationship between overall rates of investment in R & D and education and overall rates of economic growth was not simple or necessarily positive. From America came voices condemning the despoliation of the global environment, and the abuse of scientific knowl-

edge in the Vietnam War. By 1970, 'Pandora's Box' became, in popular usage, as familiar a description for science
as the 'Book of Wonders' had been a generation earlier.
Belief in the wisdom of scientific 'samurai', in how to
control the social organisation of knowledge and the distribution of economic benefit was widely suspended.

Against this background of scepticism and uncertainty
the goals of science and technology in Europe are now
undergoing a process of redefinition. As in the 1920s and
1930s, but with far more complex overtones, this process
involves not only graduate scientists who find themselves
part of a large corporate enterprise, with values which
question the autonomy of science as a vocation, but also
industrialists for whom fresh scientific and technological
developments seem at best doubtful avenues to profit-
ability; and governments, for whom the applications of
science and technology involve intricate economic and
political calculations more complex than even the scientific
and technological possibilities would suggest. It may well be
that Europeans in the 1970s will be obliged to form a more
realistic view of the strengths and limitations of science and
technology in adding to economic and social well-being.
After a half-century of discussion about science in its social
context, uncritical 'scientism' is in retreat. We await a new,
critical philosophy to take its place.

BIBLIOGRAPHY

The social context of science in the period covered by this essay has not yet been the subject of sustained treatment, thus the student quickly finds himself having to use primary source material. Most of the sources cited are in English and are concerned with the British experience, but far more awaits the reader of French, German and Dutch archives. Some relevant studies are, however, beginning to find their way into specialised journals and several of these have been cited in the footnotes.

For general surveys of economic and social trends in Britain during the inter-war decades, see A. J. P. Taylor, *English History, 1914–45* (Oxford, 1965); C. L. Mowat, *Britain between the Wars* (London, 1964); Robert Graves and Alan Hodge, *The Long Weekend*, (New York, 1963); J. Montgomery, *The Twenties* (London, 1957); M. Muggeridge, *The Thirties* (London, 1940); G. D. H. Cole, *The Condition of Britain* (London, 1937). For analyses of the Depression and economic recovery, see Derek H. Aldcroft, *The Inter-War Economy, 1919–1939* (London, 1970); and I. W. Richardson, *Economic Recovery in Britain 1932–1939* (London, 1967). For economic and social surveys of Europe, see in particular, David S. Landes, *The Unbound Prometheus: Technological Change and Industrial Development in Western Europe from 1750 to the Present* (Cambridge, 1970); and G. W. Guillebaud, *The Economic Recovery of Europe, 1933–1938*. See also, Gustav Stolper *et al.*, *The German Economy, 1870 to the Present* (London, 1967), and Edward M. Earle, *Modern France* (Princeton, 1951). There is little secondary material on science and technology during the First World War: There is, however, a comprehensive bibliography on the effect of war on economic, scientific and technological developments in J. M. Winter, *War and Economic Development* (Cambridge, 1975). For accounts of the impact of the war on science, see E. B. Poulton, *Science and the Great War* (Oxford, 1915), and Lord Moulton, *Science and the War* (London. 1919); for the role of scientists during the war, see Harry Paul, *The Sorcerer's Apprentice: The French Scientist's Image of German Science* (University of Florida, 1972); and R. W. Reid, *Tongues of Conscience: War and the Scientist's Dilemma* (London, 1969). On the deployment of scientists in anti-submarine warfare, see Roy MacLeod and Kay Andrews, 'Scientific Advice for the War at Sea: The Board of Invention and Research,' *J. Contemp. Hist.*, VI (1971), 3–40.

Research on science and technology between the wars has tended to be fragmentary and relating to specific developments in specific countries. For Britain, see, for example, Ian Varcoe, *Organising for Science in Britain* (Oxford, 1974), which contains chapters on the DSIR in the inter-war years; J. B. Poole and Kay Andrews, *The Government of Science in Britain* (London, 1972), a collection of readings which includes a section on science in the inter-war decades. On Germany, Fritz Ringer, *The Decline of the German Mandarins* (Cambridge, Mass, 1969); and Paul Forman, 'The Financial Support and Political Alignment of Physicists in Weimar Germany,' *Minerva*, XII (January 1974), 40–66, and Forman, *The Helmholtz-Gesellschaft: Support of Academic Physical Research by German Industry after the First World War*. On contemporary France, there is little work available in English, apart from Robert Gilpin, *France in the Age of the Scientific State* (Princeton, 1968); see also the essay by Henry Guerlac, 'Science and French National Strength,' in Edward M. Earle, *Modern France* (Princeton, 1951), 81–108. For an American perspective, see Ronald C. Tobey, *The American Ideology of National Science, 1919–1930* (Pittsburg, 1971). For an impressionistic study of the Soviet Union in the inter-war years, see W. H. G. Armytage, *The Rise of the Technocrats: A Social History of Engineering* (London, 1965). For more recent research, see R. S. Lewis, 'Some Aspects of the Research and Development Efforts of the Soviet Union, 1924–35,' *Science Studies*, 2, (1972), 155–79.

On scientific research in industry between the wars, the following contemporary studies provide a useful overview: A. Plummer, *British Industries in the Twentieth Century*

(London, 1937) and A. M. Low, *Science in Industry* (London, 1939). Specifically on Research and Development, see the FBI study, *Industry and Research* (October 1943); on the growth of R and D in British firms, see Michael Sanderson, 'Research and the Firm in British Industry, 1919–1939,' *Science Studies, 2* (1972), 107–51, while for an account of the relations between British universities and industry, see Michael Sanderson, *The Universities and British Industry* (London, 1972). On specific industries, the following are useful: on the radio industry, W. R. MacLaurin, *Invention and Innovation in the Radio Industry* (New York, 1949); on the chemical industry there is Lutz Haber, *The Chemical Industry* (Oxford, 1971) and W. J. Reader, *Imperial Chemical Industries: A History*, vol. 1, *1870–1926* (Oxford, 1970); on the history of synthetic fabrics, see Donald C. Coleman, *Courtaulds: An Economic and Social History* (Oxford, 1969).

Among studies of the professions during the inter-war years the standard work remains, A. M. Carr-Saunders and P. A. Wilson, *The Professions* (Oxford, 1933) which includes sections on chemists and engineers. On the chemical profession see R. B. Pilcher, *The Profession of Chemistry* (London, 1927). Although there are no general histories of the professionalisation of science during the inter-war years, there are contextual studies of professions which are tangentially relevant. See, for example, Guy Routh, *Occupation and Pay in Great Britain, 1906–1960* (Cambridge, 1965). On the universities, see Harold Perkin, *Key Profession: The History of the Association of University Teachers* (London, 1969); on scientists in the civil service, see F. A. A. Menzler, 'The Expert in the Civil Service,' in W. A. Robson (ed.), *The British Civil Servant* (London, 1937), 165–85; and Eric Hutchinson, 'Government laboratories and the Influence of Organised Scientists,' *Science Studies, 1* (1971), 331–56.

For any study of the social relations of science in the 1930s, the starting point must be J. D. Bernal, *The Social Function of Science* (London, 1939); other works in the canon include Hyman Levy, *Modern Science* (London, 1939); J. G. Crowther, *The Social Function of Science* (London,

1941). See also N. Bukharin *et al.*, *Science at the Crossroads* (1931, reprinted, London, 1971). For the response to the 'planners' see J. R. Baker, *The Scientific Life* (London, 1942), and *Science and the Planned State* (London, 1942); and M. Polanyi, *The Contempt of Freedom* (London, 1940), and *Personal Knowledge* (London, 1958). The debate is set in perspective in P. G. Werskey, 'British Scientists and "Outsider" Politics, 1931–1945,' *Science Studies, I* (1971), 67–84.

The history of the impact of science on the Second World War in Britain is, as yet, unwritten. This is a reflection of the fact that until very recently, access to government documents for the war years was forbidden. There are, however, a few books which provide an introduction to these complex years. For an impressionistic account of the scientific effort in general, see Ronald Clark, *The Rise of the Boffins* (London, 1962); while for a more detailed account of some technical developments such as radar, see M. Postan (*et al.*) *The Design and Development of Weapons* (London, 1964). There are several important biographies – particularly Ronald Clark, *Tizard* (London, 1965), and F. W. F. S. Birkenhead, *The Prof in Two Worlds: Professor L. A. Lindemann, Viscount Cherwell* (London, 1961). For an account of the conflict between Tizard and Cherwell, see C. P. Snow, *Science and Government* (Oxford, 1960). See also, Sir Solly Zuckerman, *Scientists and War* (London, 1966) – a collection of essays which refer, *inter alia* to the progress of atomic research during the war. For a detailed account of the British atomic effort, see M. Gowing, *Britain and Atomic Energy, 1939–45* (London, 1965). Finally, for a contemporary view of what science had achieved during the war, and an optimistic statement of what it might achieve after the war, see The Association of Scientific Workers, *Science and the Nation* (London, 1947).

For contemporary accounts of science and political affairs, see Jean-Jacques Salomon, *Science and Politics* (London, 1973); E. Shils, *The Criteria for Scientific Development* (Cambridge, Mass, 1968); and Christopher Freeman, 'The Goals of R and D in the 1970s,' *Science Studies, I*

(October 1971), 357–406. See also the publications of OECD, particularly *The Research System*, 3 vols. (1972–5), and the several OECD 'Country Reports' which have appeared since the 1960s.

7. The Keynesian Revolution 1920-1970

ECONOMICS IN THE TWENTIETH CENTURY

Robert Campbell

INTRODUCTION

The new science of economics[1] entered the twentieth century as a full-fledged academic discipline. It had acquired schools, orthodox texts, professors and students:

> . . . We leave behind us the world of historical iron-masters and banker-historians, geological divines and scholar tobacconists, with its genial watchword: to know something of everything and everything of something: and through the gateway of the Competitive Examination we go out into the Wasteland of Experts, each knowing so much about so little that he can neither be contradicted nor is worth contradicting.[2]

What the new social science shared with Adam Smith and his fellow founders of classical political economy was a common vision; a way of characterising and interpreting man's economic problems. Adam Smith's 'obvious and simple system of natural liberty,' stripped of its natural law trappings, was simply an assertion of the possibility of a market exchange system. In such a system individual worker-producers joined together to share their specialised products through voluntary trade. In these social acts they were presumably guided only by their self-interest:

> It is not from the benevolence of the butcher, the brewer, or the baker, that we expect our dinner, but

1. The reader of this essay is urged to review Donald Winch's 'Emergence of Economics as a Science 1750–1870' which appeared in Volume 3 of this History.

2. G. M. Young, *Victorian England, Portrait of an Age*, p. 160. Quoted in T. W. Hutchison, *A Review of Economic Doctrines 1870–1929*, p. 31.

from their regard to their own interest. We address ourselves, not to their humanity but to their self-love, and never talk to them of our own necessities but of their advantages. [3]

While this sardonic view of human nature was hardly new in social thought what was new was the view that it could be left unleashed without threatening the aims of society:

From the standpoint of the economic analyst, the chief merit of the classics consists in their dispelling, along with many other gross errors, the naïve idea that economic activity in capitalist society, because it turns on the profit motive, must by virtue of that fact alone necessarily run counter to the interests of consumers; or, to put it differently, that money-making necessarily deflects producing from its social goals. [4]

The classical political economists, from Smith to Marx, had used their system primarily to explore the possibilities of economic growth through capital accumulation. The greatest advantages of 'natural liberty' – read voluntary market-guided choice – lay in the decisions to save and allocate those savings over alternative investment opportunities. The outcome, if society followed the advice of the political economist, was a socially desirable rate of growth in real output per capita. The shorter range analysis of how market price adjustments could guide the allocation of resources among all the various products competing for consumer attention received relatively short shrift in the classics. Smith's two chapters devoted exclusively to the market mechanism were reduced to a single chapter in Ricardo with advice to consult Smith for more detail. While a tedious literature grew out of the Marxist texts on the transformation of values into prices, the subject was

3. Adam Smith, *Wealth of Nations* (New York, Modern Library, 1937) p. 14.
4. J. A. Schumpeter, *Capitalism, Socialism and Democracy* (New York, Harper and Row, 1962) pp. 75, 76.

not of major importance for the central Marxist arguments about the motive forces of capital accumulation – arguments presented in the only part of *Das Kapital* that Marx himself completed and published.

Thus it came about that the 'marginalist revolution' of the 1870's was more than an argument over the appropriate explanation of exchange value in markets, even though the replacement of the labour cost theory by a marginal utility theory took the centre of the stage. Most importantly, it was a revolution about the objectives of the science; a revolution in which the broad vision of market exchange which had served the classical economists as a sanction for their prescriptions on income distribution and economic growth was enlisted in support of statements about the efficiency with which an economy allocated its resources in the short-run: '. . . Given, a certain population, with various needs and powers of production, in possession of certain lands and other sources of material: required, the mode of employing their labour which will maximise the utility of the produce.'[5]

Although the ostensible purpose of this marginalist or neo-classical approach was to provide norms of satisfactory performance, '. . . between realising that hunting for a maximum profit and striving for maximum productive performance are not necessarily incompatible, to proving that the former will necessarily . . . imply the latter, there is a gulf much wider than the classics thought.'[6] Given the elusiveness of the goal, what actually came to occupy most of the new economic scientists' time was the elaboration of an increasingly complex and more formal description of a price system:

For Ricardo the Theory of Value was a means of studying the distribution of total output between wages, rent and profit, each considered as a whole. This is a big question. [Alfred] Marshall turned the meaning of Value into a little question: why does an egg cost more than a cup of

5. W. S. Jevons, *The Theory of Political Economy*, p. 267.
6. Schumpeter, *op. cit.*, p. 76.

tea? It may be a small question but it is a very difficult
and complicated one. It takes a lot of time and a lot of
algebra to work out the theory of it. So it kept all
Marshall's pupils preoccupied for fifty years.[7]

This academic preoccupation which tended to turn
economists inward toward refinements in the formal
structure of the discipline rather than outward toward the
less tractable problems of the economy, took two closely
related but methodologically distinct forms.

In its English birthplace, as classical political economy
evolved into a social science, its form was almost uniquely
shaped by one man – Alfred Marshall. It was because of
Alfred Marshall that the new economics of the latter part of
the nineteenth century became, in England, neo-classical
economics. Marshall refused to reject *in toto* the classical
cost theories of market value, but saw the influence of cost
wielded through supply as but one blade of the scissors
which, along with the other blade of utility and demand,
determined market price. Moreover, Marshall focused his
explanation of price on the events in a single market. This
partial equilibrium or industry approach attempted to
artificially fence off the circumstances affecting the price
of a single product from those more general circumstances
affecting all prices. By subjecting the individual market to
microscopic investigation, certain principles of more
general application could then be discovered and, hopefully,
the fences progressively lowered.

In contrast on the continent Leon Walras, his pupil
Vilfredo Pareto and their followers chose instead to develop
a general equilibrium approach to the explanation of
exchange value. This approach stressed the system-wide
interdependencies of all prices and quantities in a market
exchange economy and sought to generalise directly from
individual behaviour in markets to the pattern of all prices.
The general equilibrium approach asked a greater degree

7. Joan Robinson, *On Re-Reading Marx* (Cambridge, Student Book-
shops, Ltd., 1953), p. 22.

of sophistication, economic and mathematical, of both its practitioners and its students. When it was finally exported to England in the 1930's, it had to struggle against the dominance of the Marshallian intellectual tradition as well as against the lower position in the academic hierarchy occupied by its advocates at the London School of Economics.

In spite of important methodological differences, both the Marshallian or Cambridge neo-classical partial equilibrium economics and the continental or Walrasian general equilibrium economics shared two important common characteristics. They were, first of all, theories of relative not absolute prices. That is, they were theories of the exchange of goods for goods or implicit barter theories in which money, if it appeared at all, appeared only as a unit of account or medium of exchange. Increasing or decreasing the amount of money could only alter the number of money units associated with each exchange, it could not alter the terms of trade or the relative numbers of real goods involved in an exchange. They were, secondly, equilibrium theories in the sense that the relative prices being explained were market-clearing prices. The day-to-day prices and price variations to which profit-maximising or satisfaction-maximising sellers and buyers adjusted and reacted were also prices and price variations being moved toward equilibrium states or mutually consistent patterns. The consistency lay in the fact that the quantities voluntarily demanded in each market would be brought into equality with the quantities voluntarily supplied. The great men in both methodological traditions recognised and grappled with the problems of using such theories in explaining a world in which money was apparently much more than a simple counter and in which markets seemed more often in disequilibrium than in equilibrium. Unfortunately each tradition hardened into an orthodoxy and, as Harry Johnson warns us: 'The essence of an orthodoxy of any kind is to reduce the subtle and sophisticated thoughts of great men to a set of simple principles and straightforward slogans that more mediocre brains can think they understand well enough to live by.'[8] It was against the limitations of this kind of orthodoxy that J. M. Keynes rebelled if, in fact, his work does constitute a genuine theoretical revolution.

ORIGINS OF THE KEYNESIAN REVOLUTION

The particular form taken by the Keynesian revolution was uniquely a product of the man, his experiences, and the Cambridge intellectual tradition in which he was trained and in which he lived at least part of the time. But the fact of the revolution reflected a much less unique set of circumstances – circumstances both of history and of the ideas of economists who confronted history. These circumstances produced other theoretical responses which might well have been classified as revolutionary had Keynes never written his *General Theory of Employment, Interest and Money.*

First, the new economic science, like the classical political economy from which it developed, found itself singularly ill-equipped to deal with economic 'crises' or 'gluts' – those troublesome occasions when collapsing prices and profits, unused capacity, unemployment and hunger all seemed, paradoxically, to coexist. From classical political economy economics had inherited 'Say's Law.' The 'Law,' derived from the properties of market equilibrium in a barter system, argued that an excess supply of all goods – or a general deficiency in the demand for all goods together – was impossible. Since the seller only brought goods to the market because he desired there to exchange them for other goods, his supply of one set of goods constituted the demand for another set. A vintage statement of the Law, one cited as a bad example by Keynes himself in the *General Theory,* is found in J. S. Mill's *Principles of Political Economy:*

8. Harry Johnson, 'The Keynesian Revolution and the Monetarist Counter-Revolution,' *American Economic Review,* LXI, 2 (May, 1971).

What constitutes the means of payment for commodities is simply commodities. Each person's means of paying for the productions of other people consist of those which he himself possesses. All sellers are inevitably and by the meaning of the word, buyers. Could we suddenly double the productive powers of the country, we should double the supply of commodities in every market; but we should, by the same stroke, double the purchasing power. Everybody would bring a double demand as well as supply; everybody would be able to buy twice as much, because everyone would have twice as much to offer in exchange. [9]

But Say's Law created a major problem for the economist; real world 'crises' did exist yet the Law said they were impossible. How could economic theory be reconciled with reality? Even the author of the famous Law was not content.

What is the cause of the general glut of all the markets in the world, what is the reason that in the interior of every state . . . there exists universally a difficulty of finding lucrative employments? And when the cause of this chronic disease is found, by what means is it to be remedied? On these questions depend the tranquillity and happiness of nations. [10]

As economists grappled with the problem a literature began to appear and, eventually, a new label: business cycle theory. A critical distinction in the newly evolving area was that between theories which viewed such disturbances as temporary problems of market adjustment and theories which saw them as more fundamental and persistent characteristics of private market exchange in general. An early and prototypical example of this distinction emerged from the controversy between Malthus and Ricardo in the early part of the nineteenth century. Ricardo consistently argued for the temporary market

9. Book III, Chap. XIV, Section 2, p. 557.
10. J. B. Say, *Letters to Mr. Malthus . . .*, Tr. by J. Richter 1821, Reprinted 1936, p. 2.

adjustment view. Chapter XIX of his *Principles of Political Economy*, 'On Sudden Changes in the Channels of Trade,' clearly presents his views. Malthus, on the contrary, in his *Principles of Political Economy*, sought but never found an equally consistent but more general explanation. He 'was unable to explain clearly (apart from an appeal to the facts of common observation) how and why effective demand could be deficient or excessive . . .'[11] The victory of Ricardo over Malthus, which had been characterised by George Stigler as the victory of good logic over good insight, alienated from the mainstream of economic thought those who were most concerned with this particular gap between theory and reality:

> The great puzzle of Effective Demand with which Malthus had wrestled vanished from economic literature. You will not find it mentioned once in the whole works of Marshall, Edgeworth and Professor Pigou, from whose hands the classical theory has received its most mature embodiment. It could only live on furtively, below the surface, in the underworlds of Karl Marx, Silvio Gesell or Major Douglas.[12]

In this judgement Keynes overlooked a considerable literature on business cycles and was particularly remiss in his neglect of work by continental writers.[13]

But there was a second set of circumstances which proved, ultimately, to be more important than the emergence of business cycle theories. These were the responses of economists to the existence and role of money in the economy. It was primarily through the contributions of monetary theory that the separate threads of price or market exchange theory and business cycle theory were to be woven into more general theories of the economy.

Recognition of the role of money in economic processes was as old as history. Almost as old was a simple version of the quantity theory of money. This view, that changes

11. Keynes, *General Theory*, p. 32.   12. *Ibid.*
13. For a useful survey see T. W. Hutchison, *A Review of Economic Doctrines 1870–1929*, Part III.

in the amount of money available were associated with changes in the price level, was inherited by, and generally accepted by, the classical political economists. As we have seen, it was also patched on to the equilibrium theories of market exchange that the new science of economics developed.

As a theory, in the sense of an attempt at explanation, however, the quantity theory was seriously deficient. While linking together the quantity of money and the price level, it was silent on the precise nature of the linkage and, for that matter, on any logical demonstration of the direction of causation. This deficiency prevented a behaviourally grounded integration of the explanations of money prices or the price level with the theory of relative prices. As the attention of economists turned to this problem, two distinct traditions in monetary theory evolved, both developed from the quantity theory. Like the quantity theory also, these two traditions initially viewed the task of monetary theory as that of explaining the level of money prices.

One tradition located its behaviorable roots in the individual's attitude towards holding money as a store of value or as a highly liquid asset. As economic conditions, the properties of other available assets, and the state of expectations altered, the individual's demand for cash balances could be expected to alter also. Interaction between this demand for money and the available supply of money generated a volume of aggregate money expenditure or aggregate demand for goods. Given the aggregate supply of goods, the level of aggregate demand could be said to fix the price level. While this theory came to be closely associated with Alfred Marshall and the Cambridge tradition in England, its essential elements were known to earlier writers both in England and on the continent. Earlier writers were also aware of what such a theory could contribute to an explanation of 'crisis' or business cycle fluctuations. In the very same chapter in which he wrote the description of Say's Law quoted so disapprovingly by Keynes, J. S. Mill gave quite a 'Keynesian' explanation of what he called a 'commercial crisis'. At the same time his explanation involved most of the elements of a cash balance approach to monetary theory:

> At such times there is really an excess of all commodities above the money demand: in other words, there is an undersupply of money. From the sudden annihilation of a great mass of credit, everyone dislikes to part with ready money, and many are anxious to procure it at any sacrifice. Almost everybody therefore is a seller, and there are scarcely any buyers; so that there may really be, though only while the crisis lasts, an extreme depression of general prices, from what may be indiscriminately called a glut of commodities or a dearth of money.[14]

True to his classical predecessors, however, Mill is quick to point out the temporary or transitional nature of such events. 'It is a great error,' he says, 'to suppose, with Sismondi, that a commercial crisis is the effect of a general excess of production.'[15] Instead he identifies its immediate cause as a contraction of credit and prescribes a 'restoration of confidence' as the remedy.

Meanwhile, on the continent, quite a different tradition was evolving. If the supply of money changes, the argument went, the market or money rate of interest – one of those relative prices linked together in a general market equilibrium system – can be directly affected. If it is affected so that it deviates from the real or 'natural' rate set by the expectation of returns on physical capital, a process of cumulative expansion or contraction in money expenditure can be initiated. In an expansion, for example, which could be triggered by an increase in the supply of money and a fall in the market rate of interest, a rise in expenditure on new capital goods would initiate the process, as entrepreneurs seek to profit from the excess of what they expect to earn over the rate they would have to pay for loans to finance the expenditure. As the boom develops the opti-

14. J. S. Mill, *op. cit*, Book III, Chap XIV, Section 4, p. 561.
15. *Ibid.*

mistic expectations of entrepreneurs are reinforced and the process is accelerated, with upward ratcheting of the prices of first producers' goods then consumers' goods as entrepreneurs in both sectors bid for the scarce resources needed to realise their plans. The cumulative process ends only when the market rate of interest has been driven up to the level of the real rate of return on capital. This condition then becomes the requirement for price level stability. Knut Wicksell was the leading spokesman for this approach to monetary theory and it became the foundation of a Swedish tradition which also had a German language branch (Wicksell had been a student of Böhm-Bawerk and the Austrian School.) This branch was transplanted to England in the early 30's when its most important expositor, F. A. von Hayek, moved to the London School of Economics.

Wicksell started from the position that Say's Law was an unnecessarily severe constraint on thought: 'Any monetary theory of value which wants to deserve the name must, therefore, be able to show how and why the monetary or pecuniary demand for commodities can exceed the supply of commodities under given circumstances, or *vice versa*, can fall short of it.'[16] To Wicksell this difference, as it persisted in a cumulative expansion or contraction of aggregate money expenditure, corresponded to a difference between saving and investment. In Myrdal's summary:

> This proposition should seem obvious to the unsophisticated mind, since decisions to buy and sell a commodity are made by quite different individuals. Similarly, one cannot assume that capital (investment) demand and capital (saving) supply are identically equal; for they, too, originate with non-identical groups of individuals. To treat supply and demand in these cases as being *identically*, rather than *conditionally* equal, would involve a highly unreal and abstract concept of equilibrium.[17]

16. Quoted in Myrdal, *Monetary Equilibrium*, p. 21 (From *Vorlesungen*, p. 181).

17. *Ibid.*, p. 23.

As developed by his followers, Wicksell's ideas on the determination of the level of money prices differed dramatically from the orthodox explanations of relative prices. The traditional theory, which went back to Chapter VII of Book I of Adam Smith's *Wealth of Nations,* held that the appearance of an excess demand or excess supply of a particular commodity would lead to either a rise or fall in its relative price and profit prospects, and that this would signal entrepreneurs to shift resources to or from the production of that particular commodity. In this way, any departure of relative prices from equilibrium or market-clearing values would rapidly generate self-correcting 'feedback' reactions which would correct the disturbance. The cumulative growth or shrinkage in the aggregate monetary demand for *all* commodities were, however, in Wicksell's view, processes in which the balance of 'negative feedback' or self-correcting adjustments permitted a movement away from an equilibrium level of money prices to continue and even accelerate. Only the presence of ultimate constraints, in the form of limitations on credit changes or on the real return on capital assets, could eventually bring a cumulative process to a halt. In Myrdal's phrase, monetary equilibrium was *labile* not stable – there is no 'tendency' toward an equilibrium price *level* to parallel traditional theory's 'tendency' toward equilibrium prices in individual markets.

Both of these theoretical traditions, which attempted to bring monetary considerations into the analysis of markets, were important intellectual preconditions for the Keynesian revolution. But without dramatic changes in the historical reality which theory attempted to explain, the synthesis of market price theory, monetary theory, and business cycle theory which was to become modern macro-economic analysis could have been either long delayed or could have developed in quite a different form. During most of the period of rapid industrialisation taking place before World War I, the course followed by the business cycle was one in which price and profit movements were able to bear the major burden of adjustment. 'The average level of employment was, of course, substantially below full employment,' says Keynes of the period, 'but not so intolerably below it as to provoke revolutionary changes.'[18]

The First World War, even without those harsh economic settlements so eloquently condemned by Keynes in his *Economic Consequences of the Peace*, would have just as surely turned the pre-war trading economy on its head. As the nations struggled to rediscover something like the old patterns of international economic relations, they brought intolerable pressures to bear upon the price adjustment mechanisms that seemed to have at least worked, if not worked well, before the war. Under the gold standard the full burden of adjustment to radically different trading relationships was turned inward onto monetary policy and wage and price level shifts. Given the magnitude of the changes necessary and given the stubborness of institutional resistance to them, the pre-war mechanisms proved unworkable. In the face of forces as strong as the English coal workers' refusal to accept drastic wage cuts, Mill's nineteenth-century 'depression of general prices' was converted into a twentieth-century depression of output and employment. The 'dearth of money' was, in this case, not (at least initially) a result of credit collapse, but a result of deliberately restrictive monetary policy. This was the way, for example, that the Bank of England attempted to protect sterling parity in the foreign exchange market after restoration in 1925. Only by forcing down internal price (and wage) levels could British goods once more be made competitive in world markets. As similar efforts strained the fabric of all the European economies, the economic 'crisis' which economists had been able to characterise as transitory phenomena in the nineteenth century, seemed to have become transferred into a permanent feature of the post-war world. Furthermore, economists could not explain, nor policy makers deal with, the decline. By the 1930's the credit collapse had come: 'we are now in the phase where the risk of carrying assets with borrowed money is so great

18. Keynes, *General Theory*, p. 308.

that there is a competitive struggle to get liquid,' said Keynes in 1931:

> Today the primary problem is to avoid a far-reaching financial crisis. There is now no possibility of reaching a normal level of production in the near future. Our efforts are directed toward the attainment of more limited hopes. Can we prevent an almost complete collapse of the financial structure of modern capitalism? With no financial leadership left in the world and profound intellectual error as to causes and cures prevailing in the responsible seats of power, one begins to wonder and doubt.[19]

KEYNES' ECONOMICS

At the very beginning of his classic biography of Keynes, Harrod asks:

> Will that life-work in due course have to be regarded as a splendid after-glow of a civilisation fast disappearing, or may it perhaps be a link between one phase of British civilisation and the next, stretching across a period of confusion and uncertainty?[20]

While events since those words were written (1951) have cast increasing doubt on Britain's prospects, there is little doubt that Keynes was the product of an earlier and fast-disappearing civilisation. He was also a genius – a member of that exclusive club of the intellect whose members make their mark on any civilisation in which they appear. Bertrand Russell, writing of the Keynes he knew as a student and young man, said:

> Keynes' intellect was the sharpest and clearest that I have ever known. When I argued with him, I felt that I took my life into my hands, and I seldom emerged without feeling something of a fool. I was sometimes inclined to

19. *The World's Economic Crisis and the Way of Escape* (Halley-Stewart Lecture, 1931), p. 71.
20. *Life of Keynes*, p. 3.

feel that so much cleverness must be incompatible with depth but I do not think this feeling was justified. [21]

Again, Lionel Robbins, writing in his journal in 1944 at the other end of Keynes' life span, is even more persuasive:

. . . I often find myself thinking that Keynes must be one of the most remarkable men that have ever lived – the quick logic, the birdlike swoop of intuition, the vivid fancy, the wide vision, above all the incomparable sense of the fitness of words, all combine to make something several degrees beyond the limit of ordinary human achievement. Certainly, in our own age, only the Prime Minister is of comparable stature. He, of course, surpasses him. But the greatness of the Prime Minister is something much easier to understand than the genius of Keynes. For, in the last analysis, the special qualities of the Prime Minister are the traditional qualities of our race raised to the scale of grandeur. Whereas the special qualities of Keynes are something outside all that. He uses the classic style of our life and language, it is true, but it is shot through with something which is not traditional, a unique unearthly quality of which one can only say that it is pure genius. [22]

But the genius developed within a unique sub-culture which was in turn a part of the larger civilisation of which Harrod spoke. The intellectual sub-culture of the universities still aimed, in Keynes' time, at producing that Aristotelian ideal, cultured gentlemen; Bertrand Russell's 'men who combine the aristocratic mentality with love of learning the arts.' [23] Yet the Victorian and Edwardian embodiments of this ancient ideal had their differences. Russell, writing of his own generation, said, 'We believed in ordered progress by means of politics and free discussion.' 'The more self-confident among us may have hoped to be leaders of the multitude, but none of us wished to be

21. Bertrand Russell, *Autobiography*, Vol. 1, p. 97.
22. Quoted in Harrod, *Life of Keynes*, p. 576.
23. *History of Western Philosophy*, p. 194.

divorced from it.' In contrast, Russell argued that the
generation of Keynes 'did not seek to preserve any kinship
with the Philistine.' They aimed rather at a life of retirement among fine shades and nice feelings, and conceived
of the good as consisting in the passionate mutual admira-
tions of a clique of the elite.' While Keynes escaped from
this into the world, Russell held that his escape was never
complete: 'He went about the world carrying with him
everywhere the feeling of the' bishop *in partibus*.' 'True
salvation was elsewhere, among the faithful at Cambridge.'
'When he concerned himself with politics and economics
he left his soul at home.'[24] One can conclude that the sub-
culture to which Keynes belonged was a remarkably
stimulating one, but it had its limitations. Not only did it
screen him from the major continental developments in his
field, but it fostered a patronising attitude toward developments in the other British Universities as well. Moreover,
it left him, for most of his life, only partly an economist.
The attachments formed in the closely knit intellectual
society of Cambridge were prolonged into an almost lifelong association, through the Bloomsbury group, with a
literary and artistic culture that stood apart from and
perhaps competed with his professional economic interests:

> (Keynes') basic view of life was aesthetic rather than
> political. He hated unemployment because it was stupid
> and poverty because it was ugly. He was disgusted by the
> commercialism of modern life. (It is true he enjoyed
> making money for his College and for himself but only
> as long as it did not take up much time.) He indulged in
> an agreeable vision of a world where economics has
> ceased to be important and our grandchildren can begin
> to lead a civilised life.[25]

Keynes was also delayed in coming to economics, not
accepting his first position until after a stint in the India
Office. Even then he returned to the government service

24. Bertrand Russell, *Autobiography*, Vol. I, p. 95.
25. Joan Robinson, 'What Has Become of the Keynesian Revolution?' *Challenge*, Vol. 16, No. 6 (Jan/Feb 1974, p. 10).

(with the Treasury) after only six years at Cambridge. Thus his earliest professional work was very heavily policy-oriented rather than formal or theoretical. A resulting lack of patience with analytic system-builders is clearly revealed in his biographical essay on Alfred Marshall, even though Marshall was the single most important influence on the shape of Keynes' thought. 'He was too little willing to cast his half-baked bread upon the waters, to trust in the efficacy of the co-operation of many minds, and to let the big world draw from him what sustenance it could'; said Keynes of Marshall. He goes on to compare Marshall with his predecessors:

> . . . It was Jevons' willingness to spill his ideas, to flick them at the world, that won him his great personal position and his unrivalled power of stimulating other minds. Every one of Jevons' contributions to economics was in the nature of a pamphlet. Malthus spoilt the *Essay on Population* when, after the first edition, he converted it into a Treatise. Ricardo's greatest works were written as ephemeral pamphlets. Did not Mill, in achieving by his peculiar gifts a successful treatise, do more for pedagogics than for science, and end by sitting like an Old Man of the Sea on the voyaging Sinbads of the next generation? Economists must leave to Adam Smith alone the glory of the Quarto, must pluck the day, fling pamphlets into the wind, write always *sub specis temporis*, and achieve immortality by accident, if at all. [26]

One cannot accuse Keynes of having failed to accept his own advice, for with very few lapses, he kept the wind full of pamphlets. Unfortunately his bread, half-baked or not, found many shoppers but few buyers once he was led, as early as 1924, to abandon the conservative 'Treasury' views on the economy which he had helped to propagate during World War I. Then he had been concerned about avoiding inflation under the pressures of war finance and warned the government about the consequences of large

26. *Essays in Biography* (on Marshall, 1924), pp. 173, 174.

increases in debt-financed expenditure in an economy
operating at close to full capacity. His *Tract on Monetary
Reform* (1923), before its more unorthodox suggestions on
the international monetary order, contains a classic
discussion of the dangers of monetary inflation. After 1924
in pamphlet after pamphlet he attacked the policies of
both the Bank of England and the Federal Reserve System
of the United States and argued instead for public works
and other debt-financed expenditure programmes to
support the unemployed. In 1925 his *Economic Consequences
of Mr. Churchill* predicted the unfortunate results of the
return to the gold standard. Other vintage examples of his
gift for policy polemics were *Can Lloyd George do it?* (1928)
and *The Means to Prosperity* (1933). In these as in his newspaper and journal pieces, he first directed his advice toward
policy makers and the public. Gradually, however, he came
to the view that the real enemy was his profession – which
had erected the barrier of orthodox principles between
him and those he sought to advise. 'It is my fellow economists, not the general public, whom I must first convince,'
he said in the Preface to the *General Theory*, and he calls his
work 'an attempt by an economist to bring to an issue the
deep divergences of opinion between fellow economists
which have for the time being almost destroyed the practical
influence of economic theory . . .'[27] To this task Keynes
brought the polemical gifts of his pamphlets:

> To some he seemed to take a mischievous pleasure –
> perhaps he did – in criticising revered names. In fact this
> was done of set purpose. It was his deliberate reaction to
> the frustrations he had felt, and was still feeling, as the
> result of the persistent tendency to ignore what was novel
> in his contribution. He felt he would get nowhere if he
> did not raise the dust. He must ram in the point that
> what he was saying was inconsistent with certain lines of
> classical thought, and that those who continued to
> argue that he was merely embroidering old themes had
> not understood his meaning.[28]

27. vi.
28. Harrod, *Life of Keynes*, p. 451.

But that was a friendly voice speaking. There were those who recognised not only his originality, his genius, and the acerbity of his arguments, but also those limitations of time, place, and culture to which he was subject. In his *Monetary Equilibrium*, which originally appeared in 1931, Gunnar Myrdal paid his respects both to D. H. Robertson's *Banking Policy and the Price Level* and Keynes' 'new, brilliant, though not always clear, work, *A Treatise on Money*,' which he argued was 'completely permeated by Wicksell's influence.' Myrdal concluded that Keynes' work 'suffers somewhat from the attractive Anglo-Saxon kind of un-necessary originality, which has its roots in certain systematic gaps in the knowledge of the German language on the part of the majority of English economists.'[29] This opinion is borne out, both for the *Treatise* and for the *General Theory* by the recollections of Bertil Ohlin:

> During our talks in Belgium in 1935, Keynes explained some of the content of the forthcoming *General Theory*. When I pointed out that essential ideas resembled those developed by Wicksell, and were generally accepted by Scandinavian economists, Keynes answered: 'I have always had a very high regard for old Wicksell. At one time I tried to read his *Geldzins und Güterpreise* but my knowledge of German had become so rusty, that I got next to nothing out of it.'[30]

Rather than attempt a complete survey of the *General Theory* let us instead permit Keynes himself to tell us what he thought was important in his book. This can be done because early in 1937, he set out both to answer some of his early critics and to clarify his intentions. In 'The General Theory of Employment' he reaffirmed for his own case, the opinions of 1924 (in his Marshall biography):

> I am more attached to the comparatively simple funda-mental ideas which underlie my theory than to the

29. p. 8.

30. 'On the Slow Development of the Total Demand Idea in Econ-omic Theory,' *Journal of Economic Literature*, XII, 3 (September 1974), p. 894.

particular forms in which I have embodied them, and I have no desire that the latter should be crystallised at the present stage of the debate. If the simple basic ideas can become familiar and acceptable, time and experience and the collaboration of a number of minds will discover the best way of expressing them. [31]

What were the 'simple basic ideas' underlined in the 1937 essay? One was a rejection of the assumption of simple rational behaviour in the orthodox (Keynes called it 'classical') economics of markets. This rejection was rooted in the fact of the uncertainty and inadequacy of the information on which the economic players were expected to act:

> The practice of calmness and immobility, of certainty and security, suddenly breaks down. New fears and hopes will, without warning, take charge of human conduct. The forces of disillusion may suddenly impose a new conventional basis of valuation. All those pretty, polite techniques, made for a well-panelled Board Room and a nicely regulated market, are liable to collapse. At all times the vague panic fears and equally vague and un-reasoned hopes are not really lulled, and lie but a little way below the surface. [32]

Keynes accused the classical economic theory of 'being itself one of these pretty polite techniques which tried to deal with the present by abstracting from the fact that we know very little about the future.' The consequences are particularly critical in the treatment of money and interest. 'Partly on reasonable and partly on instinctive grounds,' said Keynes, 'our desire to hold Money as a store of wealth is a barometer of the degree of our distrust of our own calculations and conventions concerning the future . . . The possession of actual money lulls our disquietude; and the premium which we require to make us part with money is the measure of the degree of our disquietude.' [33]

31. *Quarterly Journal of Economics*, LI (February 1937), pp. 211, 212.
32. *Ibid.*, pp. 214, 215.   33. *Ibid.*, p. 216.

As monetary theorist Keynes pulled together elements from both the Cambridge and Wicksellian traditions and then placed them in an economic world that was often unintelligible or unpredictable to those who inhabited it. Like his predecessors, too, he first rejected the simple quantity theory of money:

> . . . The essential nature of the phenomenon has been misdescribed. For what has attracted attention has been the *quantity* of money which has been hoarded; and importance has been attached to this because it has been supposed to have a direct proportionate effect on the price-level through affecting the velocity of circulation . . . [34]

What then was 'the essential nature of the phenomenon'? For Keynes the new fears and hopes that could affect one's demand for money – the propensity to hoard or the state of liquidity preference – affected not the price level but the rate of interest, 'any effect on prices being produced by repercussion as an ultimate consequence of a change in the rate of interest.' But the rate of interest has more immediate repercussions. Once the wealth-holder had been persuaded not to hoard his wealth he had two alternatives to consider. He could make loans, at the current rate of interest, to those who wanted to buy capital assets or he could choose to buy such assets directly himself. As wealth-holders chose, their actions should bring the advantages of the two alternatives together. For Keynes the market adjustment was borne by the prices of capital-assets: 'the prices of capital-assets move until, having regard to their prospective yields and account being taken of all those elements of doubt and uncertainty, interested and disinterested advice, fashion, convention, and what else you will which affect the mind of the investor, they offer an equal advantage to the marginal investor who is wavering between one kind of investment and another.'[35] A cumulative process begins when the present value of capital goods – their prices as adjusted by the actions of wealth-holders – departs from the

34. *Ibid.*   35. *Ibid.*, p. 217.

costs of producing them: '. . . if the level of the rate of interest taken in conjunction with opinions about their prospective yield raise the prices of capital-assets, the volume of current investment (meaning by this the value of the output of newly produced capital-assets) will be increased; while if, on the other hand, these influences reduce the prices of capital-assets, the volume of current investment will be diminished.'[36] As in Myrdal's version of the Wicksellian cumulative process, investment outlays turn out to be much more volatile than would be the case in a more stable 'classical' world in which the rate of capital accumulation is a joint product of the amount saved out of a given (full employment) income and the technical conditions that govern the productivity of capital. In Keynes' world investment 'depends on two sets of judgements about the future, neither of which rests on an adequate or secure foundation – on the propensity to hoard and on opinions of the future yield of capital-assets.'[37]

But a fluctuation in investment is only the initiating cause. How does it affect the demand for output as a whole and, consequently, the scale of output and employment? Keynes' version of a Wicksellian cumulative process utilised the concepts of the propensity to consume and save and the 'multiplier.' In addition to investment expenditure, determined in the manner just described, the other major component of aggregate demand is consumption expenditure. Consumption expenditure was made to depend upon income, via the propensity to consume: '. . . in the main the prevailing psychological law seems to be that when aggregate income increases, consumption-expenditure will also increase but to a somewhat lesser extent.'[38] But income is itself created partly by entrepreneurs producing investment goods and partly by entrepreneurs producing consumer goods. Since the amount consumers will spend depends upon that income, it follows that the amount of consumer goods it will pay entrepreneurs to produce depends on the amount of investment goods they produce. Keynes gives an example in which consumers divide their income

36. *Ibid.*   37. *Ibid.*, p. 218.   38. *Ibid.*, p. 220.

between consumption and saving in the proportions of 9/10 and 1/10. In this case the output of consumer goods must be just nine times as great as the initial level of investment. At any other level of income and consumer goods output, the expectations of entrepreneurs will be either over- or under-realised and the cumulative process will continue. 'The theory can be summed up by saying that, given the psychology of the public, the level of output and employment as a whole depends on the amount of investment.'[39]

The 1937 article was primarily a discussion and interpretation of the theoretical arguments in the *General Theory*. Only a brief statement by Keynes on the relationship between theory and policy in his work can be found in the article. Nevertheless modern 'Keynesian Economics' has attributed a specific set of policies to the *General Theory*. While many statements on economic policy do appear there, they do not differ significantly from the suggestions Keynes had been making for many years – without the support of the theoretical model of the *General Theory*. The statement in the article is worth quoting in full:

> I consider that my suggestions for a cure, which, avowedly, are not worked out completely, are on a different plane from the diagnosis. They are not meant to be definitive; they are subject to all sorts of special assumptions and are necessarily related to the particular conditions of the time. But the main reasons for departing from the traditional theory go much deeper than this. They are of a highly general character and are meant to be definitive.[40]

THE KEYNESIAN REVOLUTION IN ECONOMIC THEORY AND POLICY

The appearance of the *General Theory* led to an immediate discussion and controversy but, in the brief period before World War II, Keynes' arguments were more successful in converting the younger economists than in converting policymakers to his ideas. The era of 'cultured gentlemen'

39. *Ibid.*, p. 221.   40. *Ibid.*, pp. 221, 222.

had ended with Keynes' own generation. 'Here,' said Harrod, 'was a man whom all knowledgeable people had come to regard as a principal support of the realm, a man truly irreplaceable.' 'Yet he was an ordinary private citizen, holding no official position, having no organised support, scarcely knowing to what political party he belonged . . . the authority that he exerted was solely due to his intrinsic qualities.' 'Happy is the land,' concluded Harrod, 'where a wise man can wield power, simply because he is wise, although he has no support from any political group . . .'[41] How suggestive these words are of Keynes' own views on the role of ideas in history:

> The ideas of economists and political philosphers, both when they are right and when they are wrong, are more powerful than is commonly understood. Indeed the world is ruled by little else. Practical men, who believe themselves to be quite exempt from any intellectual influences, are usually the slaves of some defunct economist. Madmen in authority, who hear voices in the air, are distilling their frenzy from some academic scribbler of a few years back.[42]

And how different from the views of a later and more cynical generation:

> . . . Policy-makers tend to become interested in theories only when they know they have made serious mistakes, or have been floundering and everyone knows it, and when a new theory on offer appears to promise a better understanding of the policy problem and a better basis for future policy-making. In between times, the policy-makers tend to take a superior attitude toward theory, and while they use its language, they do so only for the sake of better rationalisation of policy decisions taken for their own reasons.[43]

41. *Life of Keynes*, p. 644.   42. *General Theory*, p. 383.
43. Harry Johnson, 'Monetary Theory and Monetary Policy,' *Euromoney*, Vol. 2, No. 7 (December 1970), p. 16.

As it turned out, the power of events proved to be more important than that of ideas. Joan Robinson recalls the despondency and frustration of the Keynesian inner group as they watched the Nazis prove Lloyd George's point about public works. 'It was a joke in Germany,' she said, 'that Hitler was planning to give employment in straightening the Crooked Lake, painting the Black Forest white and putting down linoleum in the Polish Corridor.' Meanwhile, in England, 'the Treasury view was that his unsound policies would soon bring him down.'[44] In his 1931 Halley-Stewart Lecture Keynes had hoped that, unlike the past, the world would not have to wait for a war to terminate a major depression and that 'we shall be ready to spend on the enterprises of peace what the financial maxims of the past would only allow us to spend on the devastations of war.' These hopes ended in 1939. Keynes, along with most of his inner circle of friends, returned to the service of his country and there he was to remain for the time left to him. The problems of war finance and post-war reconstruction – both of Britain and the Western World – almost fully occupied that time. The development of the ideas of *The General Theory* – both formal and practical – passed to other hands. Keynes' own special contributions lay in an attempt, through the negotiations ending in the Bretton Woods conference, to reconstruct an international financial order. While the International Monetary Fund proposal was the product of many compromises, Keynes still hoped that it could provide the exchange rate stability of the old Gold Standard without the inflexibility which had sacrificed internal economic objectives in the interest of the external balance of payments. These were ideas which could be traced back well beyond the *General Theory* to the *Tract on Monetary Reform* of 1923.

Meanwhile a small group of Keynes' disciples had become established in the executive bureaucracy of the United States Government. Before World War II they had had some small influence on policy by using common-sense

44. Joan Robinson, 'What Has Become of the Keynesian Revolution', p. 7.

arguments more like those of Keynes' pamphlets than those of the *General Theory*. Like their counterparts in Great Britain they had retained or expanded their positions in the governmental administrative hierarchy during the war. During the same time Keynes' ideas continued to spread and develop among academic economists. These two spheres of influence, in England and the USA, were joined with increasing effect in the post-war planning discussions of both countries. In these discussions the theoretical relationships expounded in the *General Theory* were linked to the new measurement techniques of national or social accounting which had been so important in the wartime mobilisation. [45] Together they were used to produce provisional national planning budgets in which post-war levels of spending on consumer goods and capital goods were forecast and compared with estimated productive capacity. Adjustments in the governmental budget could then be planned to bring aggregate demand for output into equality with full employment aggregate supply. The outcome of these discussions was the formal recognition of a central governmental responsibility for ensuring high levels of employment and output. The Employment Act of 1946 in the USA and the later creation of the National Economic Development Council in Great Britain evolved naturally out of the wartime economic discussions and, just as naturally, reinforced an emphasis on fiscal policy – on the deliberate manipulation of taxation and public spending designed to stabilise the economy. Keynesian economics, as Harry Johnson reminds us, had put 'the seal of intellectual approval' on political events which, even before the war, had already demoted central banks and raised treasuries to prominence 'as the most important policy-making branch of government.' [46]

In the universities, Keynes' ideas were adapted and assimilated into simpler textbook presentations like Joan

45. An account of these developments in the USA is to be found in the symposium on 'The Keynesian Revolution and its Pioneers,' *American Economic Review*, LXII, No. 2 (May 1972).

46. *Op. cit.*, p. 17.

Robinson's *Introduction to the Theory of Employment* and Paul Samuelson's *Economics, an Introductory Analysis* (First Edition, 1948), which became the most successful and influential economics textbook ever written. The *General Theory* itself became a classic – one of those books, in Harry Johnson's phrase, whose message everyone thinks he understands too well to need to read it. As the English language universities produced the first post-war generation of Keynesian economists along with the second generation of Keynesian textbooks, National Income Analysis or Macro-Economic Analysis was well on its way to becoming a new economic orthodoxy.

On the continent of Europe the task of economic reconstruction on the western side of what became an 'Iron Curtain' pre-empted, for a time, the discussion of Keynes' ideas. Events such as The Marshall Plan, the development of the European Economic Community, and the use of indicative planning could certainly be interpreted within the framework of the *General Theory*. But this would neglect a long tradition of administrative intervention in economic affairs going back to the Cameralists and Mercantilists of the seventeenth and eighteenth centuries. What was new in post-war economic policy was the willingness of nations to co-operate. Keynesian policies, when they did arrive, seemed much less revolutionary than they had seemed in England or the United States. Finally, in those (principally Scandinavian) countries under the influence of Wicksell and his followers, the essential elements of Keynes' ideas were already in use and had been for some time, both to train economists and to rationalise economic stabilisation policies. Thus the Keynesian Revolution, in both its theoretical and policy forms was almost exclusively a revolution in the English speaking tradition in economics.

After more than a quarter of a century of experience since the war can we form any general conclusions about the nature and significance of the new economics which Keynes proclaimed in his *General Theory of Employment, Interest and Money*? Let us first look at macro-economic policy.

The post-World War II history of macro-economic policy

has been aptly characterised as a parallel rise and fall of
fiscal policy and fall and rise of monetary policy – with the
transition between stages dated in the second half of the
1960's. In the earlier period the collective memory of
economists was still dominated by the great pre-war
depression and the events associated with it. We have
already noted the failures of central bank policy in the
1920's and 1930's. In addition, there was considerable
scepticism about the effectiveness of monetary policy even
if central bankers acted sensibly. Writing in the dark days
of 1931 Keynes warned that even with a low 'pure' rate of
interest risk considerations might still prevent an adequate
level of private expenditure on investment. 'If this proves
to be so, there will be no means of escape from prolonged
and perhaps interminable depression except by direct
State intervention to promote and subsidise new investment.'[47] Added to this memory with its stagnationist
implications was the great expansion in the size of the
public sector during the war and post-war reconstruction
periods. While this was followed by some brief decline,
both the growth of welfare state programmes and the
political and military demands of the Cold War led to a
steady post-war increase in governmental expenditure. In
the 1920's the public sector had accounted for less than 10%
of Gross National Product in most countries. By the seventh
decade of the century it had, in many cases, grown to
exceed one-third of Gross National Product.

In spite of gloomy forecasts by Keynesians in and out of
governments, the transition from war to peace was accomplished relatively easily. Instead of stagnating, investment
demand was bolstered both by pent-up needs accumulated
during the war and by technological innovation arising
from wartime research. With rather large public budgets
for Treasuries to work with and with relatively buoyant
private demand, the task of fiscal policy proved easier than
had been expected. Through the 1960's business cycles
produced relatively minor ripples in the flow of post-war
economic growth in most western countries. Britain was,

47. Halley-Stewart Lecture, *op. cit.*, p. 84.

however, an exception. Faced with severe balance of payments adjustment problems that ran at cross-purposes with the requirements of full employment growth internally, Britain's experience became a forecast of things to come elsewhere. The alternation of fiscal policy between 'go' and 'stop' as internal and external problems competed for the government's attention turned the business cycle into a policy cycle – this year's macro-economic problem became, in considerable measure, a delayed consequence of the policy of two or three years ago. More important was the persistent inflationary pressure on prices and wages that accompanied 'go' policy phases. By plotting historical data on the level of unemployment against the rate of wage or price inflation, a 'Phillips curve'[48] was constructed to picture this problem of fiscal policy. For a time policy makers seriously considered this statistical artifact as a sound basis for policy. There was much discussion of a precise 'trade off' between employment and inflation. But then it was discovered that the curve shifted, both with shifts in the data and in policies based upon it, so that independent guidelines for policy could not be extracted from it. By the late 1960's the same pattern was observed in the United States. With the recognition of an inflationary rather than a deflationary bias over the course of the policy-business cycle, monetary policy was promoted from its former role of handmaiden to fiscal policy and to the Treasury. But the promotion was not uncontested:

One might regard the abasement of central banks in the 1930's as no more than just retribution for their stupidity and gutlessness in allowing the depression and the collapse of the international monetary system; but the continuing legacy of hostility and suspicion, and especially its concentration on the desirability of low nominal interest rates and hostility to high interest rates on the basis of a variety of completely fallacious economic arguments, is a serious obstacle to efficient policy making in an era when

48. Named after A. W. Phillips who published the first discussion of the curve in 1958.

the chronic problem is to restrain an ebullient and inflation-prone economy.[49]

At this point the rise of monetary policy was given valuable assistance by a counter revolution in monetary theory led by Milton Friedman of the University of Chicago. The 'Monetarism' of Friedman moderated the emphasis on the interest rate as the key monetary policy indicator and restored the traditional quantity theory emphasis on the money supply and its rate of growth. While the manipulation of taxes and public sector expenditures to accomplish precise policy objectives has continued, a contest is developing between 'Fixed Rule' monetary policy and 'Incomes Policy' as to which shall play the major role in controlling the inflationary bias in economic growth. Under a 'fixed rule', as proposed by Friedman and his followers, monetary growth is limited to the average rate of growth in potential full-employment output. The rule is supposed to discipline the scope of private bargaining over wages and other incomes to the limits set by a relatively stable price level since a more rapid wage growth would cause unemployment. 'Incomes policy' assumes that institutional circumstances, especially the price- and wage-setting power of large businesses and trade unions, will almost certainly shift the consequences of monetary restraint from wages and prices to employment and output. Rather than accept this political and social price as necessary for disciplining private bargaining, the advocates of incomes policy call for publicly negotiated voluntary restraint by business and labour to keep wage and income growth within the limits set by the rate of growth in productivity.

Both policies share common objectives: real economic growth at close to the full-employment potential rate but with wages and incomes growing no faster in order to preserve price level stability. Both policies also share a common problem: obtaining the democratic political consensus for restraints that particular interest groups may

49. Harry Johnson, *op. cit.*, p. 17.

find to their disadvantage. In the one case the restraint takes the form of a publicly administered limit on the rate of growth of the money supply with private bargainers left to determine prices and wages at their own risk. In the other case the restraint is imposed on the terms which private bargainers can negotiate, with the money supply left relatively free to be determined on the basis of other considerations. Whether either policy will prove adequate to meet the twin problems of politically unacceptable levels of unemployment accompanied by equally unacceptable rates of price inflation remains to be seen.

These developments in macro-economic policy were closely related to developments in macro-economic theory over the same period. How closely related to the economics of Keynes were these theoretical developments? Our earlier discussion of the *General Theory* taken from Keynes' 1937 interpretative essay emphasised the problem of making long-term commitments rationally when information is scarce, imperfect and uncertain:

> The orthodox theory assumes that we have a knowledge of the future of a kind quite different from that which we actually possess. This false rationalisation follows the line of the Benthamite calculus. The hypothesis of a calculable future leads to a wrong interpretation of the principles of behaviour which the need for action compels us to adopt, and to an underestimation of the concealed factors of utter doubt, precariousness, hope and fear. [50]

In the face of such uncertainty, money can appear to be a superior asset to hold compared to long-lived capital assets or claims on such assets. This places money at the forefront of the analysis and reinforces the interpretation of the *General Theory* as a new step in monetary policy. Chapter 17, on the essential properties of interest and money, is probably the best source of support for this view:

> Unemployment develops . . . because people want the moon; – men cannot be employed when the object of

50. 'The General Theory of Employment,' *op. cit.*, p. 222.

desire (*i.e.*, money) is something which cannot be produced and the demand for which cannot be readily choked off. There is no remedy but to persuade the public that green cheese is practically the same thing and to have a green cheese factory (*i.e.*, a central bank) under public control. [51]

As we have seen, the desire to hold money affects the interest rate and, through it, the volume of investment. The changes in investment then initiate a cumulative process of growth or decline in income, output and employment. But the critical relationships at the heart of this process, the liquidity preference (demand for money) schedule and the investment demand schedule, are both heavily influenced by uncertain expectations about the future. For this reason they are subject to frequent shifts. The dynamics of the cumulative rise or fall of aggregate expenditure thus becomes the normal state of affairs and the neat equilibrium models of orthodox economics are nothing but 'pretty, polite techniques.' Macro-economic analysis becomes, by implication, an analysis of disequilibrium situations – quantities demanded are not usually matched up with quantities offered or supplied in major markets.

Keynes never quite carried this argument to the limit where all efforts at rational choice are abandoned and 'animal spirits' take charge. Rather he describes a system of paradox in which 'normal' rational responses to the signals of the market push the system further into disequilibrium. The famous 'paradox of thrift' is an example: individuals, who reduce their expenditure in order to build their savings as a hedge against uncertainty, end by saving less as the cumulative effects of expenditure reduction pull down income and output. This way of looking at the world had been adopted by Keynes as early as 1931 in his Halley-Stewart Lecture. Speaking of the great collapse of the world monetary system, he described it as an 'extreme example of the disharmony of general and particular interest.' Not only were the beggar-my-neighbour policies of nations used for the lesson but the behaviour of businessmen and consumers as well. 'The modern capitalist is a fair weather sailor.' 'As soon as a storm rises he abandons the duties of navigation and even sinks the boats which might carry him to safety by his haste to push his neighbours off and himself in.'[52] It becomes the responsibility of economic policy to prevent the occurrence of the paradox and to make it possible for individuals and nations to live rationally.

In spite of the interpretation given in the 1937 article, careful readers of the *General Theory* were able to find there a number of competing ways of looking at the economic world. One view that was quickly adopted by some of the more theoretically sophisticated early readers, was the 'missing equation' model. Keynes, in criticising orthodox equilibrium economics, argued that the theory never explained but simply assumed that the level of money-income was fixed at a level compatible with the full employment of resources. It follows that, 'in a system in which the level of money-income is capable of fluctuating, the orthodox theory is one equation short of what is required to give a solution.'[53]

Many volunteers stepped forward to offer the missing equation and describe both the 'classical' and Keynesian systems in formal, static terms. Thus was born an interpretation of Keynesian economics quite distinct from that clearly emphasised by Keynes himself in his 1937 article. Instead of viewing the economy as made up of dynamic disequilibrium processes which kept aggregate expenditure, income and employment constantly moving, this other interpretation ended by defining the properties of an equilibrium level of output and employment not limited to the classical full-employment state. This idea of an under-employment equilibrium as a formal solution to a system of equations quickly became the Keynesian economics of the textbooks. The rather untidy and earthy world of 'vague panic fears and equally vague and unreasoned hopes' was replaced by one exhibiting well-behaved relationships that

52. *Op. cit.*, p. 74.
53. 'The General Theory of Employment,' *op. cit.*, p. 222.

generated precisely defined outcomes. This variety of income-expenditure analysis provided an ostensibly scientific support for fiscal policy to close the 'deflationary' or 'inflationary' gap between the equilibrium level of aggregate demand and the full-employment level. For the reader of the *General Theory* and of Keynes' comments on it, however, the more rigorous and formal income-expenditure analysis became, the more like a 'pretty, polite technique' it became. Moreover, the accumulation of experience with fiscal policy supported by this kind of Keynesian economics cast increasing doubt on its practical value in solving the kind of macro-economic problems faced in the 1960's and 1970's. 'The New Economics was favoured by the opportunity to sell Keynesian policies to meet a Keynesian problem; it encountered disaster when it tried to sell reverse Keynesian policies to meet a non-Keynesian problem' (inflation). [54] Would Keynes have found it ironic that a life's work spent in attacking the consequences of one theoretical orthodoxy had succeeded only in replacing it with another? But his hope of 1937 that the collaboration of a number of minds would discover the best way of expressing his simple basic ideas seems finally on the way to realisation. Those ideas may still advance a theoretical revolution and not simply reinforce a new theoretical orthodoxy. The publication, in 1968, of Axel Leijonhufvud's *On Keynesian Economics and the Economics of Keynes* formalised a return to the simple basic ideas of the *General Theory*. Furthermore it dramatised an attempt 'of a number of minds' to construct a new macro-economics based upon those ideas. It is too early to predict the effects of this attempt to revitalise the Keynesian Revolution – either upon the science of economics or upon the course of economic policy and economic history. One very broad generalisation can be made, however: the model of the economy coming out of this attempt is not compatible with Adam Smith's obvious and simple system of natural liberty. The elaborations on the basic idea of voluntary market exchange as a social organiser which

54. Harry Johnson 'The Keynesian Revolution and the Monetarist Counter Revolution,' *American Economic Review* LXI, 2 (May 1971), p. 8.

make up the principles of the social science of economics are all in danger of being seen as nothing but 'pretty, polite techniques.' As North and Thomas have suggested,[55] the institutions that support market exchange grew up in a period when economic conditions made it possible for private calculations of the costs and benefits of voluntary exchange to converge toward estimates of public costs and benefits. In this way, for example, a public consensus for the granting of relatively exclusive rights to the use of property – essential for the functioning of voluntary exchange – developed. Today, the rebirth of interest in Keynes' basic ideas – those having to do with the problems of rational choice in a world of uncertainty with markets in dynamic disequilibrium – becomes one more indication of a crisis in the development of economics as the science of voluntary market exchange systems. Of similar importance is the growing literature on the economics of externalities. This literature shares with the Keynesian aggregate disequilibrium economics a belief that private calculations of costs and benefits are diverging more and more from estimates of social or public costs and benefits. As evidence, the persistence of unemployment and inflation at the aggregate level is joined by the spreading awareness of pollution, congestion and other examples of environmental deterioration. The continued existence of the formal and informal institutions essential to the operation of a market exchange economy depends upon the ability of rational calculating choices by individuals to produce an acceptable social order. If, instead, Keynes' vision of 'the disharmony of general and particular interest' becomes the commonly shared vision then economics and economic policy are indeed on the verge of a far-reaching revolution.

In 1949, upon his retirement as Editor of the *Economic Journal*, Keynes was given a dinner in his honour by the Council of the Royal Economic Society. On that occasion he offered the following toast: 'I give you the toast of the Royal Economic Society, of economics and economists,

55. D. C. North and R. P. Thomas, *The Rise of the Western World*, 1973.

who are the trustees, not of civilisation, but of the possibility of civilisation.'[56] It would be the ultimate irony for Keynes' memory if his life's work did not simply reflect 'the splendid after-glow of a civilisation fast disappearing' but, in fact, helped to undermine the very possibility of that civilisation.

56. Quoted in Harrod, *Life of Keynes*, p. 193

Notes on the Authors

CARLO M. CIPOLLA
is Professor of Economic History at the University of Pavia and at the University of California at Berkeley. Born in 1922 at Pavia, Italy, he graduated from Pavia University, then proceeded to Paris and London where he continued his studies from 1945 to 1948. Since 1949 he has lectured at various European and American Universities on economic history. His publications in English include *Money, Prices and Civilisation* (1956), *The Economic History of World Population* (1962), *Guns and Sails in the Early Phase of European Expansion* (1965), *Clocks and Culture* (1967), *Literacy and Development in the West* (1969) and *Cristofano and the Plague* (1973).

MILOŠ MACURA
is Scientific Advisor at the Economic Institute of Belgrade and Visiting Professor at the University of Louvain. He was Director of Population Division, United Nations (1966-1971), Director of the Federal Statistical Instititute, Belgrade (1963-1966), Director of Demographic Research Centre (1961-1963) and Professor of Demography, University of Belgrade (1958-1966). He is Corresponding Member of the Serbian Academy of Sciences and Arts, and of the Academie des sciences morales et politiques, Honorary Fellow of the Royal Statistical Society, and President Elect of the International Statistical Institute. Among his publications are *Stanovništvo i radna snaga kao faktori privrednog rasta Jugoslavije* (1958), *Demografska statistika* (1960).

ANGUS DEATON
was born in 1945 and studied in Cambridge where he received his M.A. and Ph.D. degrees. He is at present a Research Officer in the Department of Applied Economics at Cambridge and Fellow of Fitzwilliam College. He is author of *Models and Projections of Demand in Post-War*

Britain and of a number of articles on consumer's behaviour in the academic journals.

WALTER GALENSON

was born in 1914 at New York City and studied at Columbia University. He taught at Harvard University and the University of California at Berkeley, and since 1966 has been Professor of Economics at Cornell University. He has lectured at various European universities, including a year at Cambridge as Pitt Professor. His principal publications are *Rival Unionism in the United States* (1940); *Labor in Norway* (1949); *The Danish System of Labor Relations* (1952); *Labor Productivity in Soviet and American Industry* (1955); *The CIO Challenge to the AFL* (1960); *Trade Union Democracy in Western Europe* (1961); *The Quality of Labor* (with F. G. Pyatt) (1964); *A Primer on Employment and Wages* (1966); and *The Chinese Economy under Communism* (with N. R. Chen) (1969). He is the editor of *Comparative Labor Movements* (1952); *Labor and Economic Development* (1959); *Labor in Developing Economies* (1962); and *Incomes Policy: What Can We Learn From Europe?* (1973).

GIORGIO PELLICELLI

was born in 1936 and is Professor of Business Administration at the University of Turin. He has studied in several international institutions, including Harvard Business School, and has specialised in the field of financial management in multinational firms. Among his most recent publications are *Patterns of Organisational Structures in European Multinational Companies* (1973); *Toward Uniform Patterns in International Financial Reporting: The Rocky Road for European-Based Multinational Companies* (1974).

GEORGES BRONDEL

is a civil engineer of French nationality who spent a year at Balliol College, Oxford, specialising in economics.

After having dealt with energy problems at the Paris headquarters of the Organisation for European Economic Co-operation, he became Head of the Energy Division in the Brussels Commission of the European Economic Community. He is now in charge of the Oil and Gas Directorate for this organisation.

ROY MACLEOD

is Reader in History and Social Studies of Science at Sussex University. He studied at Harvard and Cambridge, and has taught at Indiana University (1969), at the Free University of Amsterdam (1973) and at the Ecole des Hautes Etudes en Sciences Sociales, Paris. He is a co-editor of *Social Studies of Science*, and 'co-animateur' of Project PAREX, a European symposium in the history and sociology of science. His published work has been chiefly in the social and economic history of science and medicine; and in the relations of expertise and bureaucracy in modern industrial states.

KAY MACLEOD

is a Senior Library Clerk in the Research Division, House of Commons Library. She studied at the University of Wales and has written her doctorate at Sussex on 'Professionalization, Politics and Trade Unionism' in the period 1918-1940. With J. R. Poole she has edited *The Government of Science in Britain* (London, 1972), and with Roy MacLeod has written several essays, including 'War and Economic Development: Government and the Optical Industry in Britain, 1914-18', in J. Winter (ed), *War and Economic Development* (Cambridge, 1975).

ROBERT CAMPBELL

was born in 1921 and received his Ph.D. degree from the University of California. He is now Professor and Chairman of the Department of Economics at the University of Oregon. Before coming to Oregon he taught at the University of Illinois and, in 1961-2, was a visiting professor at Trinity College, Dublin. He has published articles and contributed to collections in the areas of public finance and education, among them *The Demand for Higher Education in the U.S.*, 1919-1964 (1967 with B. N. Siegel).

Unended Quest: An Intellectual Autobiography

Karl Popper

Internationally hailed as one of the most outstanding philosophers writing at present – on politics, on science, on human knowledge, on society – this unique book is Sir Karl Popper's own account of his life and of the development of his ideas. In fascinating detail he traces the genesis and formulation of his major works: *The Open Society and Its Enemies*, *The Logic of Scientific Discovery*, *The Poverty of Historicism*, *Objective Knowledge*, and *Conjectures and Refutations: The Growth of Scientific Knowledge*.

'. . . a splendid introduction to the man and his ideas.'
Martin Gardner, *The New Leader*

'. . . a remarkable document of intellectual history.'   Lewis S. Feuer

'This autobiography is part discussion on method; part intellectual history of Popper's major ideas; and part a continuing discussion of his ruling preoccupations.'   Tyrrell Burgess, *New Society*

'. . . few broad areas of human thought remain unillumined by Popper's work.'   Bryan Magee

Fontana History of Europe

Praised by academics, teachers and general readers alike, this series aims to provide an account, based on the latest research, that combines narrative and explanation. Each volume has been specifically commissioned from a leading English, American or European scholar, and is complete in itself.

The general editor of the series in J. H. Plumb, lately Professor of Modern History at Cambridge University, and Fellow of Christ's College, Cambridge.